Mikhail
BAKHTIN

Ann Ferguson

Mikhail
BAKHTIN

Katerina Clark

Michael Holquist

The Belknap Press of

■ Harvard University Press ■

Cambridge, Massachusetts, and London, England

Library of Congress Cataloging in Publication Data

Clark, Katerina.
Mikhail Bakhtin.

Bibliography: p.
Includes index.
1. Bakhtin, M. M. (Mikhail Mikhaĭlovich), 1895–1975.
2. Critics—Soviet Union—Biography. I. Holquist,
Michael, 1935. II. Title.
PG2947.B3C58   1984   801′.95′0924 [B]   84-8979

ISBN 0-674-57417-6 (paper)

To Billye Holquist

PREFACE

The history of reputations is a chronicle of greater or lesser discrepancies. There is always a gap between what someone does and what the world perceives that person to have done. Some discrepancies are temporal, such as the belated "discovery" of Vico; others are spatial, such as the low standing of Jack London in the United States versus his high status in the Soviet Union. But few discrepancies are so myriad as the anachronisms and ironies that characterize the career and reputation of Mikhail Mikhailovich Bakhtin (1895–1975).

Bakhtin is emerging as one of the major thinkers of the twentieth century. His writings encompass linguistics, psychoanalysis, theology, social theory, historical poetics, axiology, and philosophy of the person. In addition, he produced more specialized works devoted to Vitalism, Formalism, Dostoevsky, Freud, Goethe, and Rabelais. Yet in the West, where he has already achieved considerable status among anthropologists, folklorists, linguists, and literary critics, the philosophical work on which are based his contributions to these areas is largely unknown. Major discrepancies in the establishment of his reputation are still in process of being overcome.

Up to this point, the most glaring discontinuities in Bakhtin's reputation have been temporal. During the 1920s Bakhtin was a marginal figure on the Russian intellectual scene, employed by no institute or university and known only to a small group of friends and admirers. For the first half of the 1930s he was in political exile in Kazakhstan. For a brief interlude in 1936–1937 Bakhtin held an academic post at a teachers' college in Mordovia, far from Russia's intellectual centers. Afterward he retreated to a small town near Moscow for the worst of the Stalin purges, where he remained during the Second World War. He returned to his job in Mordovia after the war, retaining it until he retired in 1961.

Throughout this time Bakhtin was writing, but little of what he wrote saw publication. By 1929 he had published under his own name only one short article in an obscure provincial newspaper, all his other works having been published under the name of friends. In that year Bakhtin's fortunes seemed to be changing with his book on Dostoevsky scheduled to come out under his own name, but it appeared only after he had been arrested in a purge of Leningrad intellectuals. Through the rest of the Stalin era Bakhtin published only one article, about bookkeeping on collective farms, which was based on his work in exile and appeared in a trade journal. At the end of the 1930s he attempted to reenter the mainstream of intellectual life by writing a dissertation on Rabelais, but years of jockeying passed before it was accepted. Even after Stalin's death Bakhtin was able to publish only one or two articles, and these only in Mordovian sources.

Thus, in the eyes of the world, Bakhtin had to all purposes died in 1929. He was not reborn until the eve of his retirement from academic life, when Soviet literary scholars again took an interest in him. This revival led to the publication in 1963 of the second edition of the Dostoevsky book, thirty-four years after the first. The reappearance of this book, followed in 1965 by Bakhtin's book on Rabelais, brought him into rapid prominence. He was able to move to Moscow, and a sample of his work in exile, partially translated into English as *The Dialogic Imagination,* was published in 1975, the year he died. Four years later another book of his writings came out, translated into English in two volumes as *The Architectonics of Answerability* and *The Aesthetics of Verbal Creation.* This book, made up mostly of pieces from Bakhtin's earliest years, epitomizes the feature of belatedness that haunts his career.

This pattern of discrepancy between date of creation and date of publication, combined with Bakhtin's habit of publishing under different names, explains some of the bewilderment that has characterized attempts to assess his achievement. As in the case of Jack London, Bakhtin has also been evaluated differently in different countries. The circumstances that accompanied his discovery outside his homeland account for many of these differences. For example, translations of the books on Dostoevsky and Rabelais appeared in France in the late 1960s, during the high tide of Structuralism, so that they seemed best understood in the context of Structuralism or semiotics. Bakhtin's prominence in the Anglophone world arose in the wake of his vogue in Paris, which made it difficult to think of him as other than a literary critic in the Formalist tradition or a theorist of carnival and ritual inversions of hierarchy. The gap widens in the Soviet Union, where many see Bakhtin as a religious philosopher in the Orthodox tradition.

While this discrepancy might at first seem to be spatial—Russia versus the West—it is temporal at root. It has largely to do with a translation gap. Bakhtin's early work expresses most clearly the task which occupied him throughout his life, that of turning his dialogism into a full-fledged world view, and yet the pertinent texts are only now being translated. These early works reveal the broad philosophical base on which rests his more regional thinking in linguistics, literary criticism, and social theory.

The difficulties due to the translation gap are compounded by the problem of authorship, the question of whether Bakhtin actually wrote the three books and assorted articles frequently attributed to him but published under friends' names. This textological dilemma is a manifestation of the still greater dilemma of where to place Bakhtin, given the major gaps and conflicts in the available material.

One difficulty is the paucity of reliable data. Everyone in Bakhtin's family or among his early friends has died, except I. I. Kanaev, who refuses to speak to foreigners. In consequence, the main witnesses are people who knew Bakhtin in his declining years or who knew others who knew him. No personal documents as revealing as a diary survive. Only a few letters are extant, mostly from the 1920s. Bakhtin was notorious for not writing letters. Archival material exists also on some of those closest to him, including his brother Nikolai, Kagan, Pumpiansky, and Yudina.

Although many official Soviet documents on Bakhtin are available, including his employment record and medical history, others cannot be located, such as a document indicating when he graduated from the university. Bakhtin himself was cavalier about things like documents and legal requirements. Moreover, not all the official documents can be taken as reliable. Some of them, particularly his work records, were drawn up long after the period covered, by which time Bakhtin himself was vague about the facts. Even those work records made in the year in question do not always reflect the reality of Bakhtin's employment, because friends, in order to improve his lot, sometimes arranged to have him falsely registered as performing a certain job so that he would receive the money or privileges that went with the position. There are also inconsistencies and contradictions among the extant documents, right down to two conflicting versions of his birth date.

Now that most of Bakhtin's surviving texts have been published, many of them in translation, the time has come for an assessment of his total achievement. To this end, we made three research trips to the Soviet Union, where we had access to the Bakhtin archive, library sources, and most of the surviving figures who knew Bakhtin. We also visited England and Scotland, to do research on Mikhail Bakhtin's brother Nikolai, and Budapest, to investigate possible links between Lukacs and Bakhtin. We were thus able to resolve at least some of the inconsistencies and unanswered questions that surround Bakhtin.

This book would not have been possible without the help of many people and organizations. Most of our oral sources are left unnoted. For financial support, we wish to thank the American Philosophical Society, University of Texas Research Institute, Indiana University Office of Research and Graduate Development, and Humanities Research Centre of the Australian National University. We had frequent recourse to the University of Illinois Library Slavic Reference Service, especially to Mary Stuart, who met even our most arcane requests with courtesy and dispatch. Peter Steiner, Stephen Rudy, Clara Strada Janovic, Vittorio Strada, A. Yakimov, and Militsa Colan helped us with the bibliography. For background on Nikolai Bakhtin, we are grateful to R. F. Christian of Saint Andrews University, who showed us letters that Nikolai had received from his family; Francesca Wilson and Stanley Mitchell in London; R. F. Willetts, Roy Pascal, Fanya Pascal, and George Thomson in Birmingham; the keepers of the Nikolai Bakhtin archive at the University Library in Birmingham; and Professor Serge Konovalov of Oxford University. We owe a special debt to Caryl Emerson, who read all our drafts. Our friend and colleague Vadim Liapunov stood by with useful ideas and help with sources. We thank Gary Saul Morson, James Wertsch, and Sidney Monas for advice that proved crucial, and Susan Layton, Robert Edwards, Carol Avins, and Mark von Hagen for help with sources in Russia. We are grateful to Kate North, Gianna Kirtley, Marilyn Nelson, Shannon Jumper, Dawn Thoma, and, especially, Karen Hohne for typing our chaotic drafts. We owe an unusual debt of gratitude to Virginia LaPlante, our editor at Harvard University Press. Finally, we would like to thank the many people in the Soviet Union who gave us so much of everything. The joy of this book has been in the friends it brought us.

Portions of this book have appeared in a different form in Michael Holquist, "The Politics of Representation," in *Allegory and Representation*, ed. Stephen J. Greenblatt (Baltimore: Johns Hopkins University Press, 1981); Michael Holquist, "Answering as Authoring: Bakhtin's Translinguistics," *Critical Inquiry*, December 1983; Michael Holquist, "Bakhtin and Rabelais: Theory as Praxis," *boundary* 2, September 1983; Katerina Clark and Michael Holquist, "Neo-Kantianism in the Thought of M. M. Bakhtin," in *Aspects of Literary Scholarship*, ed. Joseph P. Strelka (forthcoming); Michael Holquist, "Dostoevsky: Ancient as Modern," *Rossia*, no. 5 (1984); Katerina Clark and Michael Holquist, "Bakhtin in the 1920s," *Esprit*, 1984.

Russian names in the text appear in standard anglicized versions. Russian quotations in the text and Russian citations in the notes are transliterated in accordance with the international scholarly system.

CONTENTS

ILLUSTRATIONS

Нет ничего абсолютно мертвого:
у каждого смысла будет свой
праздник возрождения.

Михаил Михайлович Бахтин,
1974

INTRODUCTION

*They do not apprehend how being at variance it agrees
with itself: there is a connection working in both directions, as in the bow and the lyre.*

HERACLITUS

The one who understands . . . becomes himself *a participant in the dialogue.*

BAKHTIN, *"Toward a Methodology
of the Human Sciences"*

Few thinkers have been as fascinated by the plenitude of
differences in the world as was Mikhail Bakhtin. Paradoxically,
Bakhtin's preoccupation with variety, nonrecurrence, and discor-
respondence serves to join into a coherent whole the bewildering
contradictions of his career. Just as the blind pundits who touched
different parts of the elephant's body gave differing definitions of
the animal, so those critics who have come upon one or another of
Bakhtin's activities in isolation have formulated different impressions of his life and thought, some of which appear mutually contradictory.

One reason for these contradictions is that all of Bakhtin's
work stands under the sign of plurality, the mystery of the one and
the many. This is true in the superficial sense that he published
on a daunting range of subjects from metaphysics to kolkhoz
bookkeeping, sometimes under assumed names. Moreover, different works by him speak different ideological languages: some are
in the Neo-Kantian tradition, others use Marxist vocabulary, and
still others employ impeccable Stalinese. At a more fundamental
level, different Bakhtins emerge in the texts themselves. For instance, some of the principles announced in his theoretical works
are flouted in his more particularized studies. Many Bakhtins are
found even among Soviet specialists who have linked his name
with disparate intellectual movements, ranging from the underground Orthodox Church to the pro-Revolutionary avant-garde.

It is difficult to pin down Bakhtin's viewpoint on a number of
crucial issues, including his relationship to religion and the Orthodox Church, his attitude to Russia, the Soviet Union, and the
West, and his commitment to the various movements, groups, and
friends that formed his intellectual milieu. One reason for this dif-

ficulty is the lack of knowledge about Bakhtin, rendering him a kind of intellectual cartoon figure who may be filled with any number of different hues from the palette of already existing ideological colors. The main reason, however, has to do with his own personality and credo.

An account of a man who gave chief importance to being "unfinalized" and "becoming" cannot be conclusive. Bakhtin stressed that the self never coincides with itself, and he never "coincided" with any group or ideological position. He engaged in dialogue with the major movements and thinkers of his time, preferably on paper rather than in person, but he refused to join, dominate, or even follow any movement. The thinkers and intellectual movements made up the force field in which he moved rather than exerting a definitive influence on him or establishing a position with which he identified.

Bakhtin presented himself to the world as elusive, contradictory, and enigmatic. He discriminated between his public activities and his private life of the mind, treasuring the last most. In his public utterances he accommodated to the regime and its rhetoric. He did not think ill of those who compromised, and he assumed for himself whatever guises political expediency dictated. When asked to make corrections to his texts for reasons of censorship, rather than taking offense or showing distress he passed the matter off with a shrug.

However, Bakhtin's texts are far from mere exercises in accommodation. They may be read at many levels, and he was skillful at expressing his own ideas in them. In his writings he was simultaneously an impassioned ideologue for his own outlook and an impassive ventriloquist for politically acceptable locutions. Ostensibly, most of his writings are acts of scholarly erudition and exercises in literary or linguistic theory, but underneath they are personal manifestoes, often with a political or philosophical message. Yet Bakhtin does not really stand in that hallowed tradition of fighters for truth among the Russian intelligentsia, partly because of his singularly phlegmatic and flexible relations with the official world, but mainly because of his fundamental opposition to the notion that there can be a "single truth."

Even in unofficial exchanges Bakhtin was aloof and superficially accommodating. He was diplomatic with interlocutors of all persuasions and gave them the impression that he agreed with their ideas. When asked direct questions about his own beliefs, he was evasive or silent.

Pinpointing a definitive Bakhtin is further complicated by the fact that there were several periods in his development. There was a philosophical period between 1918 and approximately 1924, when Bakhtin was heavily influenced by Neo-Kantianism and Phenomenology and was trying to think through a comprehensive philosophy of his own. Between 1925 and 1929, Bakhtin moved away from metaphysics and entered into a dialogue with current intellectual movements, such as Freudianism, Soviet Marxism, Formalism, linguistics, and even physiology. In the third period, during the 1930s, Bakhtin searched for a historical poetics in the evolution of the novel. Finally, in the 1960s and 1970s he returned to metaphysics from the new perspective of social theory and the philosophy of language.

Thus Bakhtin reveled in a profusion of subjects, ideas, vocabularies, periods, and authorial disguises. It is small wonder that different factions in the West, such as the Neo-Marxists, Structuralists, and semioticians, have coopted so diffuse a Bakhtin as their own. The power of Bakhtin to speak to each of these factions has been purchased at the price of reducing the apparent scope of his work. Many people have appropriated Bakhtin, but few have seen him whole.

Western scholars tend to focus on only a few of the many possible lines of research opened up by Bakhtin's work. Some literary critics regard Bakhtin primarily as the author of the Dostoevsky book who put forward a new theory of authorial point of view known as polyphony. Other literary critics, folklorists, and anthropologists define Bakhtin through his Rabelais book as the theorist of carnival and the breakdown of social hierarchies. Still other literary critics, social theorists, and intellectual historians appropriate Bakhtin for Marxist theory. For them the crucial text is *Marxism and the Philosophy of Language.* And for Anglophone critics Bakhtin emerges in *The Dialogic Imagination* as a theorist of the novel. All these uses of Bakhtin are legitimate, but none is sufficiently heteroglot to include the categories that Bakhtin himself felt were most important to his thought.

Bakhtin did not view himself as primarily a literary theorist. The term that he found closest to what he sought to do was *philosophical anthropology.* The many and varied subjects that he tackled appeared to him as being valuable chiefly for their own sakes. But at the same time he viewed them as media for working out philosophical problems. When his overriding goal throughout his various topics, disguises, and voices is seen as a philosophical quest, the many Bakhtins merge into a more comprehensive figure.

Yet this more comprehensive figure can never devolve into a single, definitive Bakhtin. In fact, to try to establish a hard-edged, finalized *Gestalt,* the "real Bakhtin," a magisterial figure to whom authority may be ascribed, would be to fly in the face of all that he endorsed. Whatever else he may have been, Bakhtin was an opponent of canons, and to claim that any version of him is somehow the correct one would be to straitjacket the philosopher of variety, to "monologize" the singer of "polyphony."

Unfortunately, all too many people have done this. Bakhtin became a cult figure among the Moscow intelligentsia of the 1960s and 1970s, who drew over him a hagiographic curtain. There is irony, as well as ground for caution, in the fact that most people who met Bakhtin during those two decades now describe him in terms reminiscent of those used to describe Lenin and Stalin at the height of their cults. Many testify that meeting Bakhtin changed their lives, that he gave them the impression of perfect understanding, and that he functioned like a magnet to draw out their innermost thoughts. Extravagant claims are also made about Bakhtin's character. Many see his forbearance in the face of Stalinist persecution as a form of saintliness.

The cult of personality surrounding Bakhtin would have been anathema to him. Rather than reacting to it with outrage or consternation, however, he would more likely have smilingly brushed it off. Bakhtin loved practical jokes, rogues, and eccentrics. He delighted in the radical inversions of social and conceptual hierarchies that are characteristic of carnival, and he would doubtless have been amused even by the misreadings of his own works that have resulted in his canonization. In fact, he had a life-long affection for "How Ser Ciapelletto Became Saint Ciapelletto" in *The Decameron,* a story about the canonization of subversive intentions. In this tale an evil merchant, who throughout his life has lied, cheated, and fornicated, falls ill on a visit to a strange town and recognizes that he is about to die. He calls in a holy friar to make his confession. By subtle indirections and masterful manipulations of Catholic dogma, the wicked man convinces the priest that his life was one of unexampled virtue. After the deceiving merchant dies and is buried in hallowed ground, the priest tells everyone about his discovery of a previously unsuspected holy man. Soon pilgrimages are made to the tomb of the merchant-turned-saint, and miracles begin to occur at the site.

This story, which Bakhtin had read to him in his last days when he could no longer read himself, illuminates attributes of Bakhtin the man, such as his unorthodox religiosity and his belief in the power of dialogue, the carnivalization of authority, and the mysteries of authorship. But the story also has a bearing on Bakhtin's posthumous reputation. It serves as a cautionary tale to us as authors, warning us not to assume the role of duped priests to Bakhtin's Ser Ciapelletto. The tale further serves to remind our readers not to take any particular version of Bakhtin, including ours, as canonical. While we hope to avoid the credulity of Boccaccio's priest, we also hope to celebrate the minor miracle that, after all the vicissitudes of repression, lost or ghosted manuscripts, and translation, Bakhtin's work nevertheless survives, and his dialogue with the world continues.

Tibetan Buddhism speaks of a third eye which gives to those who possess it a vision of the secret unity that holds creation together. Bakhtin seems to have had a third ear, one that permitted him to hear differences where others perceived only sameness. This sensation caused him to rethink the ways in which heterogeneity had traditionally been assigned the appearance of unity. In his several attempts to find a single name for variety, such as *heteroglossia* or *polyphony,* he was at pains never completely to stifle the energizing role of the paradox and conflict at the heart of his enterprise. He always sought the minimum degree of homogenization necessary to any conceptual scheme. He strove to preserve the heterogeneity that less scrupulous or patient thinkers often found intolerable, to which they therefore were quick to assign a unifying label. Such patience as Bakhtin's, in the face of a multiplicity that threatens to elude even the most elastic categories, is its own kind of courage. Bakhtin did not fear being overwhelmed by the flux of existence. He was never so afraid of being charged with theoretical inelegance that he felt compelled to a premature systematization. This sensitivity to variety places an extra burden on those of us who seek to find an overarching design in Bakhtin's own work. We must learn to characterize his thought while still heeding his constant mandate to resist finalization.

The greatest problem that Bakhtin poses for readers is not the need to assimilate an exotic new lexicon or to rethink any of the particular categories of knowledge. It is in fact all too easy to deploy such characteristically Bakhtinian terms as *heteroglossia* or *chronotope,* if only as incantations to dignify already existing analytical habits that have not been affected by Bakhtin's thought in any meaningful way. What is difficult about Bakhtin is the demand that his way of thinking makes on our way of thinking, the demand to change the basic categories that most of us use to organize thought itself. In order to know Bakhtin, we must modify the skills that we have developed for coming to know *anything* previous to our encounter with him. Most of us tend to believe that we are thinking best when we think "logically," when we neatly separate a particular subject into its parts, which are presumed both to be knowable in this atomized form and yet to constitute a whole that would not otherwise give itself to cognition as a unified subject. Post-Aristotelian thinking in the West has always honored the ability to break a big topic down into smaller units that are felt to be more tractable to analysis. This urge to pull apart the subject of analysis, whether in metaphysics or in philology, is so powerful that it alone has been granted the honorific adjective *systematic.* In European epistemologies an impulse to atomize topics into easily classifiable and therefore analyzable fragments has become a norm for all other forms of cognition. The greatest advances in various discrete sciences, such as psychology or anthropology, are perceived as occurring only when what had previously been condemned as chaotic or primitive within these disciplines is finally subjected to analytical dismemberment. Freud's demonstration that psychosis can be a form of highly sequential logic, whose pathology consists precisely in its too sequential logic, or Lévi-Strauss's argument that the apparently chaotic thinking of "primitive" peoples is merely the prosecution of physics or astronomy by other means, is greeted not only as a breakthrough in the understanding of social deviance or of exotic forms of social organization but also as a confirmation of the universally systematic and isolating means of human understanding, even among mental patients and aborigines who were not previously thought to use such means.

But perhaps such an isolating strategy is not the universal basis of thought, or even of systematic thought. As Freud and Lévi-Strauss have demonstrated, there are different ways to think systematically. Bakhtin's life and his thought have in common that each in its own way rejects the prejudice of post-seventeenth-century European culture that only the neat formulations of isolated categories are valid or "scientific." In many ways he is close to that mathetical revolutionary Kenneth Burke. One parallel between the two thinkers is their emphasis on what Burke called "perspective by incongruity," the ability to see the identity of a thing not as a lonely isolate from all other categories but as a contrasting variable of all other categories which might, under different conditions, fill the same position in existence. Instead of cutting off all other things in order to see this particular thing, one must triangulate all the other things that might serve in the same position, and the various resulting ratios of appropriateness will show which of them is most suited to relations of this particular position at this particular time.

Bakhtin's emphasis on relation and the resulting importance of the *in praesentia*/*in absentia* distinction parallels the Structuralist models in post-Saussurian linguistics or literary theory. There are nevertheless great differences between the essentially mechanistic or mentalist impulse of Structuralism and the more organic predilection of Bakhtin. He emphasizes performance, history, actuality, and the openness of dialogue, as opposed to the closed dialectic of Structuralism's binary oppositions. Bakhtin makes the enormous leap from dialectical, or partitive, thinking, which is still presumed to be the universal norm, to dialogic or relational thinking.

One of the difficulties posed by Bakhtin is to avoid thinking from within an all-pervasive simultaneity without at the same time falling into the habit of reducing everything to a series of binary oppositions: not a dialectical either/or, but a dialogic both/and. At the heart of Bakhtin's work is a recognition of existence as a ceaseless activity, an enormous energy, which is constantly in the process of being produced by the very forces that it drives. This energy may be conceived as a force field created by the ceaseless struggle between centrifugal forces, which strive to keep things various, separate, apart, different from each other, and centripetal forces, which strive to keep things together, unified, same. Centrifugal forces compel movement, becoming, and history; they long for change and new life. Centripetal forces urge stasis, resist becoming, abhor history, and desire the seamless quiet of death. The Zoroastrian clash between these powers is enacted at many different levels, as in the interplay between electromagnetic, chemical, and thermodynamic forces in the physical cosmos, the human body, and the universe of subatomic particles. But the yin and yang of such forces are at work as well in the world of social relations, between individual persons, economic classes, and whole cultures. Bakhtin's career was a lifelong attempt to understand and specify the various, particular ways in which the great dialogue between these forces manifests itself in other kinds of dialogue.

It is impossible for participants in the struggle between centripetal and centrifugal forces to remain neutral. Some thinkers, such as Aristotle, Descartes, and Hegel, have favored the orderliness of the centripetal forces, as opposed to those thinkers, from Heraclitus to Emmanuel Levinas, who have preferred the powers that inhere in the centrifugal forces. Bakhtin belongs to the second tradition of thinkers, so that when he calls his undertaking an "architectonics," he takes this technical term not only from philosophy, where it means the science of systematizing knowledge, but also from building, where it has to do with actual measurements and ratios of real stones and timber and the endless variety that these may assume in specific constructions.

Although Bakhtin never abandoned the effort to systematize the Manichaean workings of stasis and change, his various probes at ordering them were always marked by suspicion of the generality and the ahistorical prejudice characterizing most philosophical systems. Thus, he devoted himself to specific areas in which the battle could be observed not in a cosmic encounter of abstractions but in skirmishes of everyday life with all of its contingencies, hesitations, and disorder. These areas changed over the years, moving, for example, from the interplay of literary genres to the striational layers of social discourse making up a natural language. This variety masked the dynamic unity in Bakhtin's constant project to capture the ways in which the great duel between centrifugal and centripetal forces affected the specific historical being of particular individuals. Bakhtin's own career is thus a biographical illustration of the principle formulated by Goethe as *Dauer im Wechsel*, "identity in flux," the principle of simultaneity. Simultaneity is the larger category behind several others that loom large in works by Bakhtin, such as polyphony in the Dostoevsky book, social diversity in *Marxism and the Philosophy of Language,* and heteroglossia in *The Dialogic Imagination.*

One indicator of the overriding continuity amid all the change in Bakhtin's long career is what he has to say about the nature of language at various points in time. Bakhtin is important less because of the abstract problems that he addresses than because of the specific means that he adduces for their study. Many other philosophers have taken as their domain the same set of problems. Bakhtin's distinctiveness consists in his invention of a philosophy of language that has immediate application not only to linguistics and stylistics but also to the most urgent concerns of everyday life. It is, in effect, an Existentialist philology. Several other figures have sought to think through the implications of an interpersonal definition of the world's meaning and of personal identity, but Bakhtin alone posited the social dynamics of observable language practice as the specifying force that structures interpersonal relations in the *Zwischenwelt,* or "world in between consciousnesses." His emphasis on language as both a cognitive and a social practice sets him apart.

The key feature of Bakhtin's thought is its attempt to comprehend the complex factors that make dialogue possible. Dialogue is understood not merely in the obvious sense of two people conversing. Such an everyday occurrence provides an opening into the further reaches of dialogic possibility, much as in Saint Augustine or Heidegger a "vulgar" conception of time must be the beginning of any attempt to grasp time's deeper meanings. Dialogue is more comprehensively conceived as the extensive set of conditions that are immediately modeled in any actual exchange between two persons but are not exhausted in such an exchange. Ultimately, dialogue means communication between simultaneous differences.

A question that fuels Bakhtin's whole enterprise, then, is, What makes differences different? Difference is a major preoccupation of modern philosophical thought, Derrida's *différance* being only one of the more recent and notorious instances. The factor that distinguishes Bakhtin in this tradition is his concentration on the possibility of encompassing differences in a simultaneity. He conceives the old problem of identity along the lines not of "the same as" but of "simultaneous with." He is thus led to meditate on the interaction of forces that are conceived by others to be mutually exclusive. How, for example, can the requirement of language for fixed meanings be yoked together with the no less urgent need of language users for meanings that can be various in the countless different contexts created by the flux of everyday life? How can the requirement of societies for stability be reconciled with their need to adapt to new historical conditions? How can a text be the same and yet different in different contexts? How can an individual self be unique and yet also incorporate so much that is shared with others?

Bakhtin's term for the activity that is able to comprehend such disparate energies simultaneously is *utterance.* This is the basic building block in his dialogic conception. An utterance, spoken or written, is always expressed from a point of view, which for Bakhtin is a process rather than a location. Utterance is an activity that enacts differences in values. On an elementary level, for instance, the same words can mean different things depending on the particular intonation with which they are uttered in a specific context: intonation is the sound that value makes.

The way values get shaped into expression, bringing differences into a tensile complex rather than into a static unity, is what Bakhtin understands as the activity of authoring. All of us who make utterances so understood, whether spoken or written, are thus authors. We operate out of a point of view and shape values into forms. How we do so is the means by which we articulate who we are amid the heteroglossia of ideological possibilities open to us at any given moment. Bakhtin treats values not as an abstract axiology but as the practical work of building. By shaping answers in the constant activity of our dialogue with the world, we enact the architectonics of our own responsibility.

These concerns give rise to a philosophy of language that Bakhtin calls "metalinguistics," but which we call "translinguistics" because the term *meta-* has become so banal in the West. The distinguishing feature of this philosophy of language is its dialogic emphasis on articulations between categories whose opposition is the basis of other linguistic theories. Bakhtin devotes so much attention to difference, variety, and alterity because he wishes to find connections that are hidden to eyes less accustomed to such extreme degrees of plurality and otherness. For instance, although Bakhtin does not exclude the systematicity that characterizes post-Saussurean linguistics, he is also concerned with comprehending the manifold complexity of specific utterances in particular situations, which he perceives as having a different but no less ordered systematicity. He emphasizes articulation, in the sense both of enunciation and of two disparate elements coming together, as a process of mediation. He seeks to understand how the repeatable, formal characteristics of language are turned into the no less formal but *un*repeatable meanings of actual utterances. Bakhtin, then, is in the great tradition of Russian linguistic thought which, from Baudouin de Courtenay through Sergey Kartsevsky and Roman Jakobson, has insisted on the priority of semantics. While Bakhtin differs substantially from professional linguists in his way of prosecuting the study of language, he shares with Jakobson, the greatest linguist of his country, the assumption that everything means.

The only label for Bakhtin that is adequate to the broad scope of his activity is the term commonly used for a nonsystematic philosopher: Bakhtin was a "thinker." And insofar as a single topic can be defined as the subject of his thought, he was a philosopher of freedom. In his work on the play of values as they energize and are constrained by social forces, he attempts to think through the conditions of possibility for greater degrees of personal and political liberty. Liberty for him is grounded not in the will of a monologic God, the inevitable course of history, or the desire of men, but rather in the dialogic nature of language and society. Through his translinguistics Bakhtin seeks to give both individual selves and social ensembles their full due. His attempts to bridge the age-old gap between system and performance by finding connections for both in extrapersonal, but not transcendent, social energies has the effect of putting new movement and possibility for exchange into the dichotomy of self and other.

Bakhtin's view of language differs from two other current conceptions of language. The first view, called "Personalist" and associated with Wilhelm Wundt, Karl Vossler, and Benedetto Croce, holds that *"I* own meaning." A close bond exists between the sense that I have of myself as a unique being and the being of my language. This view, with its heavy investment in the personhood of individuals, is deeply implicated in the Western humanist tradition. It is at the opposite pole from another current view of language, called "Deconstructionist," which holds that *no one* owns meaning. The very conception of meaning, to say nothing of persons, invoked in traditional epistemologies begins by illicitly assuming a presence, whose end Nietzsche announced when he let it be known that God had died in history. Bakhtin holds the contrary view that *"we* own meaning," or if we do not own it, we may at least rent meaning. Personalists maintain that the source of meaning is the unique individual. Deconstructionists locate meaning in the structure of the general possibility of difference underlying all particular differences. Bakhtin roots meaning in the social, though the social is conceived in a special way.

Bakhtin contends that meaning comes about not as the lonely product of an intention willed by a sovereign ego. Nor is meaning ultimately impossible to achieve because of the arbitrary play of a mysterious force called "difference." In the first instance, meaning would give itself as an immediate presence, which would subject it to criticism by Deconstructionists. In the second instance, such criticism would be avoided, or at least robbed of its sting, by deferring to it in the order of our own discourse. But the price of such tact would be the perpetual elusiveness of meaning as it fades away in the phantom relay of the signifying chain.

The Personalist view assumes that we can, by speaking, appropriate to our own use the impersonal structure of language, which is "always already there." The breath of our life is the material of words; our voice weds us to language. The second view goes to the opposite extreme: the human voice is conceived merely as another means for registering differences, one that is not necessarily privileged. It is far less powerful, for instance, than writing.

Bakhtin's account of language is both profound and sensible. It avoids both these extremes. He argues that the apparently mutual contradiction between these two extremes obscures other possible ways to conceive language. The opposition between an overconfident monologue at one extreme and an ascetic silence at the other creates a false *tertium non datur,* a mutual contradiction resulting in a dead end. Bakhtin's point is that I *can* mean what I say, but only indirectly, at a second remove, in words that I take and give back to the community according to the protocols it observes. My voice can mean, but only with others—at times in chorus, but at the best of times in dialogue.

Meaning in this view is made as a product, much as a work of folklore is "made" in societies that strictly hold to their traditions. A work of folklore comes into existence only at the moment it is accepted by a particular community.[1] Many versions of a folk song or epic may be put forth, but only one will be capable of resisting the structural amnesia of the group. Its acceptance by the community is the actual, if chronologically secondary, birth of the text that will be the folk song or epic. As a metaphor for how meaning comes about, this process is extremely crude, but it has the virtue of highlighting a central feature of epistemology as Bakhtin understands it: my words come already wrapped in contextual layers sedimented by the many intralanguages and various social patois, the sum of which constitutes "the" language of my cultural system.

These three ideas about language differ in terms of the semantic space that each presupposes: for Personalists space is inner, for Deconstructionists space is elsewhere, and for Bakhtin space is somewhere in between. This "in betweenness" suggests not only meaning's need always to be shared but also the degree to which multiplicity and struggle characterize Bakhtin's heteroglot view of language. At the highest level of abstraction, the contest may be conceived as a Manichaean struggle. On the one side are ranged those forces that serve to unify and centralize meaning, which conduce to a structuredness that is indispensable if a text is to manifest system. On the opposing side stand those tendencies that foster the diversity and randomness needed to keep paths open to the constantly fluctuating contextual world surrounding any utterance. The normative, systemic aspects of language have attracted the attention of most linguists, from New Grammarians to Structuralists, as well as most literary critics. It is this imbalance that Bakhtin seeks to redress by studying the centrifugal forces in language, particularly as they are made specific in the various professional, class, generational, period, and other patois that the necessary but academic fiction of a unitary national language seeks to contain. This stratification, diversity and randomness, which Bakhtin calls by the term *heteroglossia,* is "not only a static invariant in the life of language, but also what ensures it its dynamics . . . Alongside the centripetal forces, the centrifugal forces of language carry on their uninterrupted work; alongside . . . centralization and unification, the uninterrupted processes of decentralization and disunification go forward."[2]

Stated in such general terms, the struggle must appear to be a bloodless clash of abstractions; but such is far from the case. This conflict animates every concrete utterance made by any speaking subject: "the utterance not only answers the requirements of its own language as an individualized embodiment of a speech act, but it answers the requirements of heteroglossia as well; it is in fact an active participant in such speech diversity."[3] This fact determines an utterance's linguistic profile and style to no less a degree than does its inclusion in any normative centralizing system of a unitary language.

The dialogic exchange between a constantly fluctuating reality and the static signs used to model such a reality was described in 1929 by Kartsevsky: "The signifier (sound) and the signified (meaning) slide continually on the 'slope of reality.' Each one 'overflows' the member assigned to it by its partner: the signifier seeks to express itself by means other than by its sign . . . it is thanks to the asymmetric dualism of the structure of its sign that a linguistic system can evolve: the 'adequate' position of the sign is continuously displaced through its adaptation to the exigencies of the concrete situation."[4] Or as Edward Sapir never tired of repeating, "All systems leak."

Instead of the Neo-Platonic gap between *langue*'s dream of order and *parole*'s necessary deviance, Bakhtin proposes a continuum between system and performance, the complementarity of both. The common element connecting both levels is the never-ending contest between canonization and heteroglossia, which is fought out at each level. The process is fairly obvious at the highest levels of generalization, if only because there the struggle has served as philology's traditional subject, which is the victory of one language over another, the supplanting of one normative dialect by another—indeed, the life and death of whole languages. But the contest is present as well in individual utterances, where it is more difficult to perceive, since at the most immediate levels of engagement neither traditional linguistics, which studies language outside its social context, nor ordinary stylistics, which studies texts as individual hermetic wholes, has provided units of study adequate to the struggle's complexities. The concentration of linguistics on such invariant features as grammatical or phonemic markers misses the point, because so much of the battle is waged through the interplay of essentially the same grammatical and sound systems. The attention devoted by stylistics to units such as whole sentences and paragraphs fails to take into account the fact that the contest may be fought out as a duel of two social codes within a single sentence—indeed within a single word. Bakhtin argues that in such local instances as the English comic novel, what is often written off as mere irony actually constitutes a paradigm for all utterance: I can appropriate meaning to my own purposes only by ventriloquizing.

Insofar as this is the case, we are all authors. We bend language to represent—only by representing languages. The $E = mc^2$ of Bakhtin's system is contained in his conviction that "the word is a two-sided act. It is determined equally by whose word it is and for whom it is meant . . . A word is territory *shared* by both addresser and addressee, by the speaker *and* his interlocutor."[5]

This territorial concept of the word requires a politics of representation. How is the territory governed? What legislates the way in which meaning is parceled out in any given utterance? Bakhtin's life and thought were dedicated to answering these questions.

CHAPTER 1

The Corsican Twins
1895-1917

Mikhail Mikhailovich Bakhtin was born in the provincial town of Orel, south of Moscow, on November 16, 1895 (November 4, old style).[1] His father, Mikhail Fedorovich, was of the untitled nobility and traced his ancestry back to the fourteenth century. There were members of the nobility named Bakhtin in Moscow, Orel, and Siberia. Bakhtin's great-grandfather in Orel had given proceeds from the sale of 3,000 serfs to establish in the town a military cadet school, which until 1918 bore the name The Bakhtin Cadet School of Orel. Bakhtin's grandfather had founded a commercial bank, in various branches of which his father worked as manager.[2]

Bakhtin's family was cultivated and liberal, especially his paternal grandmother, to whom the children were very attached. Bakhtin's parents sought to give their children the best possible education, including access to European culture and thought. In most other respects, however, his family was rather conventional. Relations between parents and children were formal, as were Bakhtin's relations with other people throughout his life. This was a curious feature in a man who stressed the value of unconstrained mingling of persons and bodies, and it is yet another indication of his contradictoriness and the split in him between doctrine and performance.

Mikhail had an older brother, Nikolai, born in 1894, and three younger sisters—Ekaterina, later a provincial school teacher; Maria, born in 1898; and Natalya, of whom virtually nothing is known. His sisters and mother were not especially remarkable. Bakhtin was not close to his family during his adult life. His mother complained in the mid-1920s that the family never heard from "Misha" and that they did not even know his address in Leningrad.[3] Contact must have been renewed, however, for when Bakhtin went into exile in 1930, he made his apartment over to his family so that they could move to the city. His father, who had been in ill health for some time, died during the 1930s, and his mother and Natalya died during the blockade of Leningrad in the Second World War. Nothing is known of the fate of the other two sisters.

For Bakhtin the most important member of his family was his brother Nikolai. The relation between these two was the great defining aspect of Bakhtin's childhood and the most formative contact of his life. Nikolai was the most significant "other" whom Mikhail ever encountered. Alterity would later be a basic feature of both their philosophies. Nikolai defined his relation to Mikhail in a poem of 1924, written when he was living in Paris and addressed to "One of those who stayed behind." In it Nikolai described his relations with his brother in terms that Mikhail would later define as appropriate for the "honorable opponent." The poem opens by remarking on "the enmity that has divided us," but ends with the assurance that "the same tremor will touch two different souls / My enemy and brother—and through the enmity and the years, / You [ty] will hear my greeting and understand."[4]

The "enmity" of this poem may refer to the Revolution and Civil War that separated the two after 1918, for Nikolai joined the White Guards and later left Russia permanently with them, while Mikhail remained in the Soviet Union. But the conflict between the two brothers was not merely fated by history. Each brother reveled in dialogue and debate, and Nikolai was the only person whom Mikhail encountered in childhood with an intellect to match his own. Moreover, their natures were in some respects diametrically opposed. Although both brothers were precocious, gifted, eccentric, and passionate about ideas, Nikolai was flamboyant, outgoing, impulsive, ebullient, and moody, while Mikhail was even-tempered, sanguine, reserved, and socially unassuming. Consequently, Mikhail remained somewhat in his brother's shadow throughout his childhood, although Mikhail was also the only one who could draw Nikolai out of his frequent black moods.

More striking than the differences between the brothers is the similarity of concerns that animated and guided their adult lives even after they had separated forever, giving a strange twist to Bakhtin's theoretical concern for the simultaneity of difference.

Nikolai Bakhtin, the "Corsican twin,"
Cambridge, 1935

The steps by which each of the brothers reached many of the same positions were different and came at different points in their development, but an uncanny series of parallels nevertheless dominated their lives. They are a modern-day version of Dumas' Corsican twins. Beginning as classicists, both brothers later turned to the philosophy of language and reached strikingly similar views. Nikolai is thus an important figure in the dialogizing background of Mikhail's own development.

The two brothers started on separate paths during the First World War, when Nikolai suddenly decided to become an uhlan lancer in the czar's forces. He did so on impulse, when someone told him he would look dashing in the uniform's jodphurs, and he did not want to miss out on the adventure of the war itself. After the Revolution he sought refuge at the poet Voloshin's house in Koktebeil in the Crimea, where many writers were likewise sheltering, including Mandelshtam at one point. While there, Nikolai met by chance his old commanding officer, who convinced him he was morally obliged to join the White Guards. Nikolai left Russia with the retreating White Army and then briefly became a sailor in the Mediterranean. While drunk one night in Constantinople, he joined the French Foreign Legion. He served with the Legion in North Africa for three and a half years until he was severely wounded in battle. The doctors barely saved his shattered right arm and hand. After his discharge, he fended off starvation in Paris by contributing to two emigré journals, *The Link* (*Zveno*) and *Numbers* (*Čisla*). Later he continued his classical studies at the Sorbonne and, after 1932, at Cambridge, where he obtained his Ph.D. for a thesis on the origins of the Centaur-Lapithai myth in thirteenth century B.C. Thessaly.

During his years at Cambridge Nikolai was closely associated with people of leftist leanings. For instance, he impressed the philosopher Wittgenstein, who was then in a radical Tolstoyan phase, and the two decided on principle to live in what they regarded as the "working class" area of the town. In Cambridge at that time some of the finest minds among the young faculty and undergraduates were being attracted into the Communist Party. Nikolai was close to two Communists there, George Thomson, the classicist, and Roy Pascal, the Germanist.[5]

After graduating, Nikolai taught in the Classics Department at Southampton University. In 1939 he went to Birmingham University, where Thomson, now a professor there, had secured him a post. Thomson, a romantic, was trying to find an analogue to ancient Greek civilization among the shepherds of the west of Ireland; in County Galway he was looking for Homeric Greeks.[6] During the Second World War Nikolai came to regret his White Guard past, joined the British Communist Party, and talked of returning to Russia. He even admired Stalin. In 1946 he founded the Linguistics Department at Birmingham, where he remained until his death of a heart attack in 1950.

Nikolai's decision to join the White Guards had been fateful, for it meant that the two brothers, who had for so long been close, would never see each other again. Mikhail wrote to his brother at first, then just the mother and sisters wrote, and after 1926, when it became too dangerous to write, all correspondence between them ceased. Nikolai did not find out about Mikhail's Dostoevsky book until 1930 when he discovered it by chance in a Paris bookshop. Not until the Second World War did he learn of his brother's arrest in 1929, and at the time of Nikolai's death in 1950 he still assumed that his brother must have perished during the purges. Mikhail, however, in the early 1970s received a posthumous greeting from his brother in the form of a packet of materials on Nikolai collected by his friends in Birmingham.[7]

Despite the absence of any communication between them since the mid-1920s, the brothers had maintained a remarkable closeness in their interests and ideas. Both had not only been increasingly concerned with language but had attempted to go beyond Saussure in rethinking the very same subjects. Nikolai, like Mikhail, tried to establish what he called a "functional linguistics" that would be broader-based than the conception of language dominating the academic discipline. Nikolai stressed the semantic aspect of language, its place in the new science of signs that encompassed all mental operations. Like Mikhail, Nikolai had a gift for finding commonplace, everyday experiences to illuminate complex philosophical issues. For example, he used the government-issued booklet on highway signs as a text for his lectures on semiology. Nikolai, like Mikhail, believed that language lies at the heart of psychic life ("the oddly firm hold of words in the oldest strata of the psyche") and that "psychoanalysis had much to teach linguistics, but even more to learn [from it]."[8]

Nikolai was markedly less successful than Mikhail, however, in following through his ideas and producing manuscripts. Nikolai's notebooks are crammed with grandiose schemes for rethinking the nature of language. He was clearly an extraordinary thinker. His conversations with Wittgenstein were one of the factors influencing the philosopher's shift from the logical positivism of the *Tractatus* to the more broadly speculative *Philosophical Investigations*.[9] But except for a textbook on modern Greek prepared for use in the Classics Department at Birmingham, Nikolai was never able to finish anything longer than a lecture. He left five massive boxes of notes toward a magnum opus on rethinking the nature of language, using Plato's *Cratylus* as its theoretical center, but they are chaotic and repetitive, indicating an inability to bring his scattered insights into a coherent whole. His lectures on language for a faculty seminar broke off at the point where he was seeking to answer the question, "What is a sentence?" The irony here is that while Nikolai was failing to articulate a philosophy of

language under the most facilitating conditions, including sympathetic colleagues, interested students, and magnificent libraries,
Mikhail was succeeding at the same task under the most adverse
conditions, including exile, scholarly neglect, and life at the edge
of Russian intellectual life far removed from the great libraries.

The seeds for the closeness in the brothers' later work were
no doubt sown in their childhood. The boys had a German governess until Mikhail was nine, when they both entered school. Mikhail was especially fond of the governess, who was intellectually
inclined and read Darwin. She gave the boys a thorough grounding in European culture, with emphasis on the ancients, but it
was all refracted through the medium of German. The brothers
read the *Iliad* and the *Odyssey,* for instance, in German prose
translation. Most of the time they even communicated with their
governess in German. She organized them in dramatic render-
ings, such as acting out scenes from the *Iliad.* The boys continued
to put on dramatic performances long after the governess had
gone, and Mikhail was still involved with theater in Nevel after his
university days.

The boys also continued to read widely on their own. Well
before entering the university, they were intellectually precocious. Nikolai was so thirsty for knowledge that he arose at four or
five to study Kant and Hegel, exciting both the admiration and the
pity of the servants.[10] The brothers tended to argue about whatever they read, and these debates no doubt had a formative influence on their later work and accounted in part for the Corsican
twin phenomenon.

When Mikhail was nine, his father was transferred from Orel
to Vilnius, where the family remained until Mikhail was fifteen.
Vilnius, the capital of Lithuania, was much larger than Orel, num-
bering about 200,000 in population. Although Lithuania had been
under Russian rule since the third partition of Poland in 1795, it
had also been under the control of different countries during the
course of its history. In consequence, Vilnius was a living museum of contrasting cultures and periods. The old town, full of
narrow, winding cobblestone streets, climbed the slopes of a hill
on which stood the ruins of a castle. There were many churches
and buildings in different styles—baroque, Gothic, Renaissance,
and classical. The town abounded in legends and mysteries.[11]

Having just arrived from an unremarkable provincial town,

Bakhtin was captivated by Vilnius and developed a strong interest in history there. He loved the old buildings seen on walks around the town. Even the school that Mikhail and Nikolai attended, the First Vilnius Gymnasium, was housed in an impressive building in the historic Old University. Its walls were very thick, and instead of a staircase, a broad corridor wound gradually upward. Its yard was surrounded by an ancient wall dividing the First Vilnius Gymnasium from the Second, and over both buildings loomed an observatory tower with a frieze showing signs of the zodiac.[12]

What impressed Bakhtin when he reached Vilnius from provincial Russia was not just the variation of architecture but also the colorful mix of languages, classes, and ethnic groups. Lithuania was virtually a Russian colony, governed by Russians, in which Russian was the official language and Russian Orthodoxy the official religion. The majority of the population, however, were either Poles or Lithuanians, who were Roman Catholic by faith and quite hostile to Orthodox Russians. They looked mostly to Catholic Poland for intellectual and cultural leadership. In Vilnius itself there was also a large Jewish population. Most of the Jews were Yiddish-speaking, although the more prosperous and integrated spoke Russian. Vilnius, an intellectual center of European Jewry, had earned the title "the Jerusalem of the North." The Zionist movement developed a strong following in the town, and the work done at the local Hebrew schools contributed to the later rebirth of the biblical language in Israel. Vilnius was also famous for its exegetes of the Talmud.

The Vilnius of Bakhtin's youth was thus a realized example of heteroglossia, the phenomenon that was to become a cornerstone of his theories. Heteroglossia, or the mingling of different language groups, cultures, and classes, was for Bakhtin the ideal condition, guaranteeing a perpetual linguistic and intellectual revolution which guards against the hegemony of any "single language of truth" or "official language" in a given society, against ossification and stagnation in thought. Indeed, in one of his essays of the 1930s, "The Prehistory of Novelistic Discourse," which maintains that the linguistic pluralism of Hellenistic Greece fostered the development of the Greek novel, Bakhtin describes Samosata, the home town of Lucian, in terms that apply equally to Vilnius as he knew it. The local inhabitants of Samosata were Syrians who spoke Aramaic, while the educated elite spoke and wrote in Greek.

But Samosata was ruled by the Romans, who had a legion stationed there, and hence Latin was the official language. And since the town was situated on a trade route, many other languages were heard there as well.[13]

Ironically, Mikhail and Nikolai belonged to the group in Vilnius which, although in the minority, represented the "official language." They went to Russian schools and Russian churches. Moreover, the various cultural and ethnic language groups were largely hostile toward one another at the time, so that there was little of the intermingling which Bakhtin came to admire. At school, both Mikhail and Nikolai were offered a standard, Russocentric curriculum, presented in a formal scholastic atmosphere, except that since Greek was not taught there, the brothers hired themselves a tutor to teach them the subject. By then, however, changes were under way that would lead to a radical reordering of the ethnic and linguistic mix of the town and to a greater intermingling of the different religious and ethnic groups.

In Russian intellectual and cultural history the first two decades of the twentieth century were a time of turbulence—the preamble, as it were, to 1917. One after the other were born political, aesthetic, and religious movements which sought to disestablish the status quo or current vogues and to replace them with something new and different. Most of these movements were also bent on doing away with bourgeois society or morality, and some were bent on dispensing with the church or overthrowing the state as well. This millenarian excitement percolated through to the First Vilnius Gymnasium.

Nikolai and his friends at age eleven or twelve were captivated by the revolutionary fever then abroad. They formed little study circles to discuss Marxist theory and kept secret notebooks into which they copied revolutionary songs. Nikolai recalls "the exciting thing we called the 'political demonstration.' At twelve o'clock we began discreetly to infiltrate into the lavatory—the only place in the school which enjoyed the immunity of extraterritoriality since it was not haunted by the staff. When the lavatory was packed with boys, we sang the Internationale and the Warshavyanka and other revolutionary songs. That was the political demonstration."[14] Before long, however, their revolutionary ardor cooled and the "political demonstrations" ceased. Now it was no longer Marx and Engels they discussed but Nietzsche, Baudelaire, Wagner, and Leonardo da Vinci. They sang no more revolutionary songs but recited to one another Symbolist poetry and their own imitations of it.

Symbolism was the most dominant of the fashionable trends, owing not only to the power of the poetry but also to the fact that, like Romanticism, it was not a literary movement alone. In Russia there were at least two waves of Symbolism. The first, which dominated until around 1904, was to some extent an echo of the French, with its "decadence." The second, which lasted until the early 1920s and was represented chiefly by Vyacheslav Ivanov, Bely, Blok, and Merezhkovsky, was more heavily influenced by German sources and had a more philosophical and religious bent. The German variety had the greater influence on the two brothers during their school days and student years.

Russian Symbolism had arisen to some extent in reaction against the various isms that had dominated Russian thought since the radical "generation of the sixties," such as positivism, materialism, industrialism, and rationalism. Symbolism stressed the aesthetic value of art and rejected the notion that the duty of the artist was to expose social ills. In the first or French wave of Russian Symbolism, this reaction expressed itself in a fin de siècle aestheticism and a delight in shocking the public. The second or German wave did not abandon a penchant for extravagant nonconformism, but it produced a more philosophical response to the nexus of values under challenge. At the center of its aesthetic was an entire epistemology. These Symbolists believed in a kind of cognition that was beyond the scope of mundane positivism. To their mind, there was a higher reality which could not be known by objective means but to which the poet had access, for artistic intuition and imagination would succeed in this task where rationality had failed. These Symbolists frequently adduced Goethe's statement "All that exists is just a symbol" to prove that an art which provided a symbolic representation of reality would lead, as Ivanov put it, "the soul of the spectator *a realibus ad realiora* [from the real to a higher reality]."[15]

Nikolai was attracted to the Nietzschean strain of the Symbolist movement during his gymnasium years. Reading Nietzsche's *Birth of Tragedy* at the age of eleven was a turning point in his life. He was also influenced by Merezhkovsky's *Death of the Gods*. While still in his teens, Nikolai became the leader and genius of a small and exclusive circle of gymnasium friends who were "in a continuous state of intellectual tension, knowing that they had thousands of books to read and an infinity of things to learn, but believing that when they had absorbed the centuries of human thought, they would evolve a line of their own and in turn become creators." Whether Mikhail was also a member of this group is not known, but at least the circle formed part of the intellectual environment in which he grew up. The group's ethos and structure anticipated a group to which he later belonged in Nevel, although the Vilnius group was more extravagantly nonconformist in the Symbolist mode. A former member of the Vilnius group recalled that "occasionally they spent the night feasting and carousing or, hoping to induce visions, in smoking hashish,-but more often they walked until dawn around Vilna, reciting poetry and philosophizing."[16]

Mikhail was always fond of Symbolist literature, particularly the poetry of Blok, Ivanov, and Annensky. Symbolism was for him, however, more than just a matter of aesthetic predilection. The philosophical-religious writings of certain Symbolists were an early influence in his attempts to balance religion with other aspects of life. The preoccupation of the Russian Symbolists with justifying their poetry in terms of a comprehensive "philosophy of culture" also stimulated Bakhtin to work out a "philosophical anthropology" of his own.

By 1919, when Bakhtin wrote his first surviving work, he had outgrown the more romantic and fanciful ideas developed by the later Symbolists. He now put language and language acquisition at the center of his epistemology and rejected both Freud's notion of the unconscious and the Symbolists' privileging of nonverbal and nonrational sources of cognition, such as music, intuition, frenzy, and symbols. Above all, he denied the Symbolists' Neo-Platonist stress on a higher order of reality inaccessible to the common man. Instead, Bakhtin championed present, everyday reality and experience. To the Symbolists' tag of *realia ad realiora* (from reality to a higher reality) he opposed a radicalization of *hic et nunc* (here and now).

Bakhtin acknowledged his debt, however, to Vyacheslav Ivanov, particularly Ivanov's collection of essays *Furrows and Boundaries (Borozdy i meži)*, which appeared in 1916 but included essays published in journals over an eight-year period.

Ivanov's essay "On Dostoevsky," for instance, originally published in 1911, prefigures Bakhtin's theory of the polyphonic novel. The fact that Ivanov at every turn transposed the philosophical problem of knowledge and the nature of religious truth into the cognate problem of communication was pertinent to Bakhtin, since communication and dialogue were at the heart of his epistemology. The Symbolists of Ivanov's generation, as opposed to the earlier generation of decadents, felt the need to temper the doctrine of individualism with some form of collectivity. Ivanov himself elaborated a theory of communication as the basis of both religious and epistemological experience in terms of the "I" becoming aware of another, inner being, a "thou."[17] This I/thou opposition was a favorite topic of many other Russian and Western thinkers at the time, but given Ivanov's relation to ancient Greek and Orthodox thought, his version had a special resonance for Bakhtin.

Although Ivanov's stress on the value of collectivity distinguished him from Nietzsche, in most other respects he was one of the leading Russian Nietzscheans of his day. He was especially interested in Hellenistic religion, Greek tragedy, and the Dionysian-Apollonian model. His lectures on "The Hellenic Religion of the Suffering God," published in 1906, had a great influence on thought at that time. Although Bakhtin later declared himself an opponent of Nietzsche, it is probable that he, like his brother, passed through an early Nietzschean phase. Indeed, despite Bakhtin's disavowal of the German philosopher, there are hints of Nietzsche in his work.

When Mikhail was fifteen, his father was transferred to Odessa. All the family moved there with him except for Nikolai, who remained behind in Vilnius for two years to finish at the gymnasium before rejoining his family. Mikhail in the meantime completed his own schooling in Odessa.

Odessa was a very special place. Like Vilnius, it had a distinctively Jewish flavor. But whereas Vilnius had looked westward to Polish culture, this bustling city was the main link between czarist Russia and southern Europe. Palm trees, a huge harbor, and a massive opera house gave the city a likeness to Marseilles. It had not only its sailors' taverns and dens of thieves but a rich cultural life as well. This was the city where the violinist Jascha Heifetz began. The city was at this time nurturing the writers and other intellectuals who would pour out of the city to make their mark in the northern capitals during the 1920s, when Jewish intellectuals enjoyed a social mobility undreamed of under the czars. The humorists Ilf and Petrov were born here, as was Petrov's brother, Valentin Kataev, a leading Soviet writer. Babel not only grew up in the city but made it the center of his tales of Benya Krik, the great Jewish gangster.

Odessa, then, like Vilnius, was an appropriate setting for a chapter in the life of a man who was to become the philosopher of heteroglossia and carnival. The same sense of fun and irreverence that gave birth to Babel's Rabelaisian gangster or to the tricks and deceptions of Ostap Bender, the picaro created by Ilf and Petrov, left its mark on Bakhtin.

There was also a serious side to his life in Odessa. A German tutor to one of the merchant families there found Bakhtin remarkable not only for the brilliance of his mind but also for his wide reading at so young an age. This tutor introduced Bakhtin to the work of Martin Buber. Soon after arriving in Odessa, Bakhtin also read Kierkegaard, to whom he was so attracted that he tried to learn Danish in order to read him in the original. But finding his time limited, Bakhtin had to abandon this project and content himself with a German translation. Thus, even before reaching the university, Bakhtin was formidably well read, particularly in the area of speculative theology. The only cloud hanging over his years in Odessa was the onset of osteomyelitis when he was sixteen. This illness, which was extremely painful, would plague him for the rest of his life.

In 1913 Mikhail entered the local university, in the same year that Nikolai entered the Classics Department at Petersburg University. Mikhail studied at Odessa University for only a year and then transferred to Petersburg University, which was to be renamed Petrograd University in World War I when the town changed its name. Following in his brother's footsteps, Mikhail enrolled in the Classics Department of the Historico-Philological Faculty. At one point the brothers lived together as students at 77 Nikolaevsky Street (now Marat Street). Nearby was a riding academy where Nikolai the aristocrat practiced. At another time Nikolai rented a room in the home of a sister of the Symbolist painter Vrubel, where Mikhail may have lived as well.

This was an exciting time in the intellectual life of Petersburg. Young people were challenging the ideas and modes of their elders, and new movements were being formed. Many believed that they were either on the threshold of a new age or on the edge of a major upheaval. Symbolism was turning more attention to questions of national identity and social involvement. But Symbolism was in its turn being challenged by new literary and artistic movements, such as Acmeism and Futurism. Acmeism, whose leading exponents were Mandelshtam, Akhmatova, and Gumilev, opposed the notion that poets should seek a "beautiful beyond" and by working with highly specific images strove instead for "beautiful clarity." Futurism, whose leading exponents included Mayakovsky and Khlebnikov, was an iconoclastic movement whose manifesto was called "A Slap in the Face of Public Taste." The Futurists were known for formal experimentation that reached an extreme in "trans-sense" poetry and subjectless art, for provocativeness, and for opposing Symbolism's traditional imagery by concentrating on images drawn from the city and the technological age.

Of the two movements, Futurism was the more significant in terms of Bakhtin's intellectual stance. He rubbed shoulders with Futurists at many points in his career, and although he was an opponent of this most avant-garde of contemporary movements, his thought shows evidence of its contiguity. The Futurists, their scorn for "the academy" notwithstanding, had connections with the Historical-Philological Faculty at Petersburg University. During Bakhtin's student period, for instance, Mayakovsky frequently visited the campus.

The Futurists' closest allies at the faculty were the Formalists, the group that was to function as the "honorable other" for Bakhtin in his debates of the 1920s on the nature of literature and language. Most of the leading Formalists from Petrograd, such as Tynyanov, Eikhenbaum, Shklovsky, Polivanov, and Yakubinsky, were either studying or teaching at the university while Bakhtin was there. Formalism had come into existence more or less on the eve of Bakhtin's arrival at the university, at an avant-garde cabaret in December 1913 when Shklovsky read a paper arguing that Futurist poetry, by calling attention to the sounds of words, had emancipated words from their traditional significance and made it possible to perceive them afresh. The function of art in general should be to force such new perceptions of the word and the world. In 1914 Shklovsky published this paper under the title

Resurrection of the Word. His work excited the Futurists, whom he joined, and also some graduate students in linguistics. They decided to form a circle called OPOYaZ, or Society for the Study of Poetic Language. The group, joined by scholars of philology, evolved into the full-fledged critical movement known as Russian Formalism, with branches in Moscow and Petrograd.

During his university years, Bakhtin had less to do with either the Formalists or any other literary, artistic, or political group than he did with radical theological circles. He was especially attracted to the Petersburg Religious-Philosophical Society, which existed from 1907 to 1917. Bakhtin's religious views may be gathered from the fact that in 1916 he was sponsored for membership in this society by Anton Kartashev, who a year later, as Minister of Confessions in the Provisional Government, was the first person in Russian history to cut through the ancient bond between state and church in favor of tolerance and belief, thus liberating the Jews and non-Orthodox Christians from religious persecution.

During the first two decades of the twentieth century there was a marked religious revival among the Russian intelligentsia, but the spirit of this revival was in accord with the general revolutionary spirit abroad in the land. Symptomatically, the Petersburg Religious-Philosophical Society was by no means what its name might suggest, a refuge for obscurantism and conservatism in an age of radicalism. It was rather a venue for focusing intelligentsia debate, albeit primarily on religious questions and the role of the church in Russia. As one member put it, the group's debates were open to "all who are adrift in modern society," and at one point it was even decided to admit atheists.[18] The society attracted many who sought an alternative to contemporary czarist society, including mystical anarchists and people close to revolutionary terrorists. During 1908 and 1909 several Social Democrats joined the controversies raging within the Religious-Philosophical Society and even participated in its meetings.

Members of the Petersburg Religious-Philosophical Society and of the many lesser societies spawned by the religious revival generally took a radical position in one or another of three areas of debate: organized religion or the Orthodox Church, politics, and personal or family morality. For many people, concern for the growth of a new religious consciousness in Russia was inextricably involved with the desire to found a new social order, a more communalistic society. Some took their models for this new society from the early Christian communities, others from French Utopian socialism or Russian populism, but still others preached what amounted to a Communist theocracy.[19]

The outbreak of World War I in 1914 caused a crisis within intelligentsia religious groups as they sought to define where they stood on the issue of patriotism versus internationalism or pacificism. This controversy was raging at the very point when Bakhtin entered the Petersburg Religious-Philosophical Society in 1916. His position on the issue of Russophilism or Slavophilism, on the one hand, versus cosmopolitanism or internationalism, on the other, remains a mystery. He was influenced in other respects by leading figures on both sides of the controversy, including A. A. Meier, a spokesman for internationalism, and Father Pavel Florensky, a spokesman for Slavophilism.[20] The fact that Bakhtin did not volunteer for the army, as Nikolai did, is not evidence of his position, for with his chronic osteomyelitis he would have been rejected for military service anyway. Although Bakhtin was a great student and lover of the Russian tradition, he also had a broad, pan-European perspective.

The period that Bakhtin spent at Petrograd University, from 1914 to 1918, coincided almost exactly with the First World War and the two revolutions of 1917. These were years of turmoil and chaos, a fact that inevitably affected life at the university. There were dwindling numbers in the classroom and an increasing laxness about course requirements.[21] The university's loose requirements gave Bakhtin a great deal of choice in what he studied. He nevertheless found in his own Classics Department "the closest thing to a teacher I ever had—if there was such a one (other than Nikolai, whose influence was greater)." Faddei F. Zelinsky, who had been Professor of Classical Philology at the university for over thirty years, was a scholar with an international reputation but also a colorful and eccentric lecturer who influenced the lives of many students. The Symbolist poet Blok cited him as one of his best teachers.[22]

Zelinsky's ideas left their mark both on Bakhtin's writing and on his thought. Much of Bakhtin's later material on comic types in Latin literature came from papers he had written on Ovid and Catullus under Zelinsky's supervision. Zelinsky's idea that the basic forms of all types of literature were already present in antiquity was reflected in Bakhtin's subsequent view of literary evolution. Zelinsky talked of the triumph of prose over poetry, which Bakhtin later described as the novelization of culture. For Zelinsky, as for Bakhtin, dialogue was the literary expression of philosophical freedom, making things present as the reader saw the argument go back and forth before his very eyes. Zelinsky's distinction between the official culture of a society and its more vital unofficial culture also loomed large in Bakhtin. Both men believed in the potential of the folk for undermining the heaviness and dogmatism of the high culture. Both also believed that there should not be an absolute cut-off between the world of god and that of human desires, between the divine and the human, the high and the low. And finally, Zelinsky stressed the revivifying role of humor in the satyr play, which was a favorite example of Bakhtin's. Zelinsky, however, was essentially a phenomenon of the Nietzschean phase in Russian intellectual life, and was closely identified with such Symbolists as Ivanov.[23] Bakhtin developed beyond his early mentor in assimilating sophisticated linguistic and social theory, so that his reformulations of his mentor's ideas have resonance today while his mentor's formulations seem dated.

Because of Zelinsky's identification with Symbolism, he did not capture the imagination of those contemporaries of Bakhtin's who identified with the literary and critical avant-garde, which was bent on superseding Symbolism. Shklovsky, for instance, found Zelinsky learned but arrogant, a Nietzschean who "believed in a superfunctionary who, having finished high school with a classical education, could consider himself above ordinary morality."[24] But Zelinsky had a profound influence on the students of Bakhtin's generation who were not followers of the avant-garde. He was an important ideologue for so-called Hellenism, a movement to which many of Bakhtin's friends and his brother belonged at one time or another, as Bakhtin possibly did himself.

According to the tenets of this movement, the age of Hellenism in Greece, ushered in by the conquests of Alexander the Great, had possessed an ideal ethos for the modern day. During the Hellenistic era when the power of the old city-states was in decline, the Greek empire itself expanded to encompass many other lands, ethnic groups, and cultures of the Orient. Greek society became less authoritarian and developed a strong interest in the individual and in ethical questions. This was a restless age of constant upheavals. Because the old lines separating nations, classes, families, races, and even sexes had faded, a new social cosmos had to be created. Values were in a state of flux; nothing seemed to be certain, and everything was subject to reevaluation. The interest in the outside world was also growing. The Greeks became less nationalistic and elitist. Other ethnic groups were no longer looked upon as barbarians. The Greeks showed a greater tolerance for otherness and were prepared not only to sample the local wares wherever they went but even to assimilate the religions of conquered peoples into their own. At the same time, the Greeks became less interested in military conquest and more concerned with humanity. As W. S. Ferguson expressed it, "the political theory of the Greeks leaped at one bound from the reality of the *polis* to the vision of the 'universe of men,' the *oecumene*."[25]

Zelinsky proselytized for the central role of classical studies in general education, insisting that classical culture should "not be a norm, but a living force in our culture."[26] In his zeal for closing the time gap, he even posited the idea that much could be learned about ancient Greece through modern Greek folklore. This idea was taken further by Zelinsky's "favorite pupil," Bakhtin's brother, who carried his teacher's ideas with him to Birmingham, where he soon had all undergraduates in the Classics Department learning modern Greek in order that Greek might have a living oral expression.

Hellenism thus provided another solution to the old quest of the intelligentsia for true community, a quest that in the nineteenth century had brought forth such panaceas as the village commune or "mir" and the populist movement. In Hellenism, however, the educated intelligentsia did not propose a retrogressive solution, such as reducing their high level of education to that of the folk, nor did they propose a purely local solution. On the contrary, their panacea endorsed high culture and a spirit of free inquiry. They envisaged a sort of perpetual intellectual revolution conducted with the highest degree of ethical responsibility and consciousness.

The Hellenists also were generally God-seeking or Orthodox intellectuals. They saw the Hellenistic tradition as a part of the pedigree of the Russian religious tradition, which followed the Byzantine or Greek Orthodox Church rather than the Roman

Catholic. Yet Hellenism was conceived as being neither narrow nor dogmatic but ecumenical and tolerant in spirit, something that could be achieved in a "renewed" Russian Orthodox Church or even in an altogether new religious association. This new association would be founded in Russia but international in scope.[27] It was above all this ecumenical internationalist spirit of Hellenism that attracted the young Petersburg intellectuals to the movement.

According to the Hellenists, the spirit of inquiry had reasserted itself periodically in history, primarily in opposition to the spirit of dogmatism or authoritarian oppression which the Hellenists deplored. Twice in European history this "Hellenistic" spirit had so prevailed over its antagonist as to dominate an entire epoch and, in so doing, to create a cultural renaissance. These two periods were variously identified as the Hellenistic revival in Rome followed by the Renaissance, or as the Italian Renaissance followed by the German Renaissance.[28] Many Hellenists, including Zelinsky himself, who were fond of grafting Hellenism onto the old Moscow-as-third-Rome theory, predicted a "third Renaissance" in Russia.

Thus, Hellenism was in many respects only a particular expression of the millennial fervor abroad among the Russian intelligentsia on the eve of the 1917 Revolution. It preached intellectual revolution, the abolition of dogmatic authoritarian regimes, and internationalism, combined idiosyncratically with the need of a classical education as a springboard to achieve all these values and the importance of some religious if not actually Orthodox component. Being a Greek scholar seemed to Nikolai at the time, as to his friends, "like participating in a dangerous and exciting conspiracy against the very basis of modern society in the name of the Greek ideal."[29]

How closely Mikhail became involved in the Third Renaissance movement is not known, though most of its ideals informed his writings. But Nikolai was a leading member of a society organized by Zelinsky called the Union of the Third Renaissance, which consisted of a dozen or so young philosophers, poets, and Greek scholars. At the final meeting of the union, held in 1917 on the eve of the October Revolution, with gunfire already heard in the streets below, Zelinsky quoted Tiutchev's lines, "Blessed are those who have visited this world at its fatal moments." Then

Nikolai gave an address comparing the culture of Petersburg Russia with not the Hellenistic period but the earlier Mycenaean civilization. He argued that both civilizations were merely local expressions of greater civilizations—Russia's of European civilization and Mycenae's of Cretan culture. Those Mycenaeans who hid out in the mountains thereby "escaped the charms of Crete and kept their Hellenic spirit pure from Minoan alloy." When their chance came, "they descended from their mountains and, insensitive to the charms of a foreign civilization, swept away the Mycenaean world and the Cretanized elite who had created it and plunged the peninsula into destructive confusion, out of which the true Greece was to arise—but only after long centuries of the Dark Age." By analogy, the moment had now come when Russia, which had long lived under the sway of a westernized elite and the "Petersburg civilization" which they had created, was to be thrown into confusion and darkness by an uprising of workers, peasants, and the poor, to whom the Petersburg civilization was incomprehensible and alien and who were "asserting the rights of the Scythian soul which *we* have betrayed." Nikolai challenged the audience to "examine your allegiances and see which is stronger. Shall we stay here . . . waiting for the new world to arise (and remember we shall have long to wait)? Or shall we make sail for our spiritual home, to Crete (for our Crete is still powerful and our Knossos still stands)?" The unanimous verdict of the group was that they should go to Crete. Two months later, when Nikolai was leaving Petrograd by train to wend his way southward in the guise of a demobilized soldier, he noted that the entire population seemed to be abandoning the city and moving south to Moscow, the original capital, and he concluded with a flourish, "The Petersburg period . . . was now finally closed."

Nikolai was, as usual, being more grandiose than correct. Petersburg culture was still very much alive and would continue to make itself felt. His own departure did mark the end of an era for Mikhail, however, the era when he had been in his brother's shadow, and it signaled Mikhail's emergence into adult intellectual life.

CHAPTER 2

Nevel and Vitebsk
1918-1924

The Russian intelligentsia's reaction to the Bolshevik Revolution was predictably complex. Some intellectuals greeted it with horror, others with exultation. There were those who believed the Revolution merely licensed the philistines to defile and plunder the treasures of Russian culture. Others saw it as the realization of eschatological prophecies. Still others saw it as a cleansing force which had dislodged the czarist regime and made room for new attitudes, tastes, mores, art, literature, and even cities.

In general, the response to the Revolution ran along generational lines. The old intellectual establishment was largely alienated by the Revolution. Especially alienated were religious thinkers, or authors influenced by religion, like Vyacheslav Ivanov. By 1923 most such figures had left Russia or been expelled. But the exodus was not confined to the religious or to the right wing. Even Maxim Gorky left Russia in 1921, not to return until the end of the decade.

The young, by contrast, welcomed the Revolution. These supporters included not just the political left wing but also the cultural avant-garde interested in formal experimentation in literature and art. Among the avant-garde there was an atmosphere of euphoria, millennial enthusiasm, and self-sacrifice. The Futurist poet Mayakovsky, for example, slept on the floor of the Moscow Central Telegraph so as to be able to make propaganda posters out of events as they came hot off the ticker tape.

The young had good reason to hail the Revolution. In the cultural sphere they were its principal beneficiaries. The aloofness or outright migration of their elders afforded the young a greater upward mobility and a chance for earlier recognition in their field. Writers were propelled into prominence at such a

tender age that some of today's leading figures in the Writers'
Union were already well-known in the 1920s. The Futurists were
no longer antiestablishment figures but moved to the top of the
cultural hierarchy, holding posts in the Ministry of Culture and directing art institutes.

The post-Revolutionary period saw an unprecedented expansion in higher education and cultural institutions. The number of
tertiary institutions, for instance, had by late 1920 expanded from
97 in 1913 to 151. A decree of 1918 abolished all educational requirements for faculty; all that was now needed for appointment
was a vote from the faculty board. This expansion, together with
the vacancies caused by dismissals of the politically suspect,
meant that aspiring scholars were often able to get jobs without
having to go through the normal route of the postgraduate degree
and the apprenticeship to a senior academic. So it was that the
Formalists' disciple Kaverin, having just graduated from the university, was able at the age of twenty-two to conduct seminars on
modern literature at the newly accredited Institute for the History
of the Arts in Petrograd, where most of his mentors, themselves
only slightly older, were ensconced in senior positions.[1]

Intellectuals from the outlying areas also benefited from the
Revolution. New universities were set up in the provinces in an
effort to redress the imbalance of privilege held by Moscow and
Petrograd. Conversely, it became easier for provincials to make a
successful career in Moscow or Petrograd. One final category to
benefit were the Jews, who had been kept out of mainstream Russian cultural life unless they were baptized and middle class, like
Boris Pasternak. During the 1920s, many Jews, such as Babel and
most of the Formalists, became prominent in Soviet literary life.

The cost of this greater mobility was upheaval, turmoil, and
chaos. No sooner had the Revolution been won and the Soviet
Union withdrawn from World War I than the country was
plunged into Civil War and assailed by foreign interventionists.
This was a time of great hardship and danger. The most basic
supplies, such as food and fuel, were in short supply, and there
was much looting and general lawlessness.

The two main cities, Moscow and Petrograd, were among the
hardest hit. During the terrible winter of 1918 Petrograd was
buried under snow drifts. It had no trams and no street lights.
People sat in fur coats in their frozen apartments. Instead of bread
they ate rotten dried fish and biscuits made of potato peels. The

following winter was no better. Those living in houses dependent on central heating froze to death. The water mains burst and drain pipes froze. People had to relieve themselves in the streets. Those who were lucky enough to have a pot-bellied stove burned everything in sight—first the furniture, then the books, and finally the floorboards. Many died of hunger or succumbed to cholera or typhoid.[2]

Strangely, the intellectuals were better off than many others. Gorky played a role in this by establishing a kind of Red Cross relief organization for intellectuals, called the Committee for Improving the Living Conditions of Scholars, which gave to those considered worthy an "academic ration" of extra goods. Gorky also helped found places of refuge for writers and scholars in hostels and sanatoria, where residents were supplied with firewood, food, and clothing. These refuges by no means sheltered only party or fellow-traveler writers, for in those years of confusion even dissenters, such as V. Khodasevich and Vyacheslav Ivanov, spent periods in them.

Intellectuals in general were not weighed down by the material discomfort. On the contrary, they experienced a mood of "desperate gaiety." It was a time of great intellectual excitement, and to compensate for the scarcity of paper which made publication difficult, intellectuals conducted much of their business orally. Oral performance is particularly loved by Russians. They met in groups, debated publicly, and gave readings. In the kitchen of the most famous writers' hostel, the House of Arts in Petrograd, writers of all orientations gathered and debated long into the night. Public debates were organized between people of opposing persuasions. For instance, in the Polytechnic Museum in Moscow, Vyacheslav Ivanov undertook a public debate against Lunacharsky, the Commissar of Enlightenment, on the existence of God, a popular topic in those years.[3]

Apart from the material hardships of the times, intellectuals were often in danger of arrest because of politically dubious connections. In consequence, large numbers of them fled Moscow and Petrograd to the provinces, where supplies were better and dangers fewer—rather as the Zhivago family go to the Urals in Pasternak's novel. But many intellectuals could not stay long in their places of refuge. As the Civil War encroached or friends and family called, they moved elsewhere. For literary figures, the Civil War was a period of repeated uprootings.[4]

Out of this restless, caravan existence came brief interludes in one provincial town after another, when fine minds were suddenly gathered together by chance. Their coming together sparked brilliant if short-lived intellectual exchanges, attended perhaps by the founding of a society or a journal. One such place was Kiev, where in 1919, as Victor Shklovsky asserts in his memoirs with typical hyperbole, "the bourgeoisie and the intelligentsia of Russia were wintering."[5] Another provincial pocket of brilliance was the poet Voloshin's house in Koktebeil, the Crimea, where Nikolai stayed for a while. Yet another was Vitebsk, where a group of avant-garde artists, such as Chagall and Malevich, took part in a brief cultural renaissance. A less well-known pocket existed in Nevel, to which Bakhtin moved in the spring of 1918 after graduation to escape the hunger and cold of Petrograd, followed shortly by his family.

The Revolution, which coincided more or less with Bakhtin's entry into adult life, did not propel him into early establishment as a writer and scholar, as it did many other young provincials. He did not enjoy the "academic ration" or find a place for himself in one of the institutions of higher learning where he could teach or publish. For Bakhtin, the post-Revolutionary decade was one long struggle, both to earn a livelihood and to broadcast his word. This struggle came about in part because he was unaggressive and impractical, but mainly because he was, as the Soviets say, "out of step with his age" (*nesozvučen èpoxe*). He was out of step not merely with the dominant Marxist thinking of the period but with the avant-garde nonconformism as well. He preached not a structural revolution but complexity and innerness.

The Revolution nevertheless had a major impact on his intellectual development. The hardship and dislocation coming in the wake of the Revolution, together with Nikolai's consequent departure from Russia, took Bakhtin out of the life he would otherwise have led. For two years in Nevel he taught in what was effectively a gymnasium and served as head of the presidium of the school board.[6] He also became involved with a philosophical circle which, in terms of stimulation and attachments, filled the gap left by his brother's departure. Out of the discussions in this group Bakhtin formulated the concepts and concerns that were to dominate his thinking for the rest of his life.

Nevel was not an auspicious place for an intellectual center. It was a small town about 300 miles south of Petrograd by rail. Its population in 1923 was a mere 13,000, and the area was mostly agricultural, though the town could boast four sawmills, a leather factory, and some ceramics cooperatives.[7] It was a pleasant spot, with surrounding woods and a large lake. Because of its situation in western Russia, the town had a checkered political history. It had belonged to Lithuania, Poland, and, since 1772, Russia. By the time of the Revolution, owing to the czarist imposition of the Pale, the town was essentially Jewish.

In this unlikely place in 1918 a number of intellectuals happened to come together to form a group. Although several members of the group led a peripatetic life in those chaotic times, from their meetings emerged a sense of commitment to each other and a belief that they were doing something important. The members had in common a passion for philosophy and for debating ideas. They met for so-called philosophical nights at which the participants discussed either a major work of philosophy "from the ancient Greeks to Kant and Hegel," a contemporary work, or a work by a religious thinker such as Saint Augustine, Vladimir Soloviev, or Vyacheslav Ivanov. It was a golden time of "strong tea and talk until morning." Spirits were high, the participants were young, most of them were eccentric, and the debates, which became fierce at times, were "magnificent." Indeed, these were more than mere "philosophical nights." In those naive and heady post-Revolutionary years the participants believed they would someday make a philosophical breakthrough and found the "Nevel school of philosophy."[8]

The Nevel circle included a wide range of interests and professional occupations. It was made up of two groups of old friends, as well as some new individuals from the area, such as a certain Kolyubakin who was a local medical bacteriologist. One group of friends comprised Vladimir Zinovievich Rugevich, Valentin Nikolaevich Voloshinov, and Boris Mikhailovich Zubakin, who had attended the gymnasium together, probably in Petersburg. Rugevich, an engineer of Polish extraction, had invited the other two, together with Voloshinov's mother, to take refuge from the exigencies of Petrograd on his family's estate Otradnoe in Izocha, a town just north of Nevel. At this time Rugevich met his future wife, Anna Sergeevna Reibisova, a granddaughter of Rubinstein. Anna Sergeevna, a medical doctor in Nevel, who had a strong interest in art, also became a member of the Nevel circle.

Voloshinov, who had been born in Petersburg in 1895 or

1896, studied briefly at the Law Faculty of Petrograd University before moving in 1916 or 1917 to Izocha, where he taught in a local school. As was typical of members of the circle, Voloshinov had other interests besides philosophy, such as the history of music, in which field he later published. He was unable to pursue study of his chosen instrument, the piano, because of a withered arm, the result of tuberculosis, but he was an amateur composer whose work was influenced by some disciples of Scriabin. Voloshinov also wrote mediocre poetry and regarded himself as a "poet of the heart."[9]

Voloshinov was one of the least colorful members of the circle. By contrast, his best friend in the group, Zubakin, was its most unabashedly nonconformist and ebullient member. Born in Petersburg in 1894, Zubakin was a mystic who later became one of Russia's few surviving masons. He was also an adventurer, who came closest of all the members of the Nevel circle to being a "carnival" personality. Zubakin was famous for his daring pranks. He loved word play and incantation, and had an endless store of party tricks. At one party, for instance, he had fifteen people give him single words; then he made up a sad poem using these words in the order in which they had been given, and afterward he made up a comic poem, reversing the order of the words.

The second group of friends in the Nevel circle comprised Bakhtin, Lev Vasilievich Pumpiansky, and Maria Veniaminovna Yudina. Bakhtin had met Pumpiansky at the university, and Pumpiansky, who had been doing his military service in Nevel sporadically since 1915 or 1916, was the one who originally suggested that Bakhtin come to Nevel. Pumpiansky was a restless but inspiring figure, always surrounded by disciples. Born in Vilnius of a French mother, with French as his first language, he was always oriented toward western Europe. Though three years older than Nikolai, he almost certainly knew him at the gymnasium in Vilnius.[10] Pumpiansky, who was wild in his youth, left home at seventeen and thereafter supported himself by giving private lessons. He was obliged to leave Petersburg University in 1912 without graduating but continued studying there off and on until 1919.

Pumpiansky's closest disciple in Nevel was the future concert pianist Yudina. Yudina, born in 1899, was a native of Nevel, where her father, a Jewish doctor and long-time reformer, had become head of the local Soviet after the Revolution. A student at the conservatory in Petrograd, Yudina responded enthusiastically to the February Revolution and threw herself into first-aid work, assisting the local militia, and learning how to run a playground for children. In 1918 she interrupted her studies and returned to Nevel to tend her dying mother. There she taught kindergarten and music by day and, at night, exhausted herself in the discussions with Bakhtin's group. Yudina and Bakhtin, who were very close, took long walks around the lake together and engaged in philosophical discussions. They had in common not only a love of philosophy but also an immersion from childhood in German culture.

Of all the Nevel circle, however, the person closest to Bakhtin was Matvei Isaevich Kagan. Born in 1889, Kagan did most to fill the intellectual and personal gap left by the departure of Nikolai. With his slightly greater age, and with a doctorate in philosophy from Germany to his name as well as a number of publications in German, Kagan acted as a sort of mentor to the group. He had been born in Pskov province, but his family had lived in Nevel since he was two. He had had the usual upbringing of a poor Jew in Russia, which meant that he had spoken no Russian at all in early childhood. The first Russian words he understood were, "I'll

The Bakhtin circle in Nevel, 1919.
From left: Bakhtin, Pumpiansky, Rugevich, Gutman (?), and Kagan.

kill [you]" and "Passed by the censor."[11] As was common among intellectual Jews at that time, Kagan joined the Social Democrat Party while still at school and in his youth underwent several arrests and exiles. While in Smolensk to work for the party, according to his later claim, he successfully hid Stalin from the law. Although as a Jew Kagan had been unable to attend the local gymnasium in Nevel, he matriculated externally by Petersburg University exams in 1909. He then went to Germany to study philosophy, mathematics, the natural sciences, and economics. At the beginning of World War I he was arrested as an enemy alien and then released two months later, but he was not allowed to leave Germany until the signing of the Brest–Litovsk Treaty in 1918.

Back in Nevel, Kagan worked in the local historical museum, taught school, and organized courses designed to raise the cultural level of the local Jewish youth. He also made frequent visits to Moscow and Petrograd to lecture and participate in debates, as was typical of the Nevel group, which was by no means cut off from the intellectual life of the capital. Like most members of the group, Kagan had broad-ranging interests and was gifted at many things, his principal field being mathematics. While at Nevel, however, he wrote mostly on philosophy. Some minor pieces were published in the local press, and two more substantial works were later published in scholarly journals.[12]

Such, then, were the major personalities that gathered in Nevel after the Revolution. This group dominated the intellectual and cultural life of the town. For instance, a local symphony concert was opened with a lecture by Kagan, and an evening of literary readings was opened with a lecture by Bakhtin. Bakhtin likewise gave the keynote address for commemoration of Chekhov's death, and he and Pumpiansky spoke while Yudina performed for an evening dedicated to Leonardo da Vinci. Bakhtin and Pumpiansky together produced an open-air production of Sophocles' *Oedipus at Colonus*, using a cast of over 500 pupils from local schools, for which Yudina helped organize the music. Bakhtin gave public lectures on such lofty topics as "The Meaning of Life." Sleepy Nevel responded to this barrage with gusto.[13]

Bakhtin and his friends were not the only intellectuals in town. There were also young Marxists, principally Josif Naumovich Gurvich, head of the town's Education Department, and a certain Gutman. There was no enmity between the two groups. As was typical of those early post-Revolutionary years, the representatives of opposing points of view liked to engage in friendly dialogue. Bakhtin and his friends were not hostile to the Revolution or to socialism. Gurvich and Gutman attended several study circles run by Bakhtin's group, and the two groups treated the town to joint debates on controversial issues. Bakhtin, Pumpiansky, and either Kagan or Zubakin ususally formed one team. Among the topics debated in this way were love, art, and culture.[14]

As in the capital cities, in Nevel religion was a popular topic for public debate. Bakhtin took part in at least four debates on this topic. One heavy session on November 27, 1918, attracted an audience of 600, quite a crowd for so small a town. At 6 P.M., two hours before it began, the audience had already filled not only the hall but also the adjacent rooms, the corridor, and the stairs. The debate was opened by Pumpiansky, who acknowledged himself to be an Orthodox Christian and yet praised the Communists, declaring himself to be a mere onlooker (*v storonke*) in their work. He nevertheless spoke in such learned terms that most of the audience could not understand him. Bakhtin, who also acknowledged the value of socialism, erred further in the matter of obscurity, and when he reproached the Revolution for "not worrying about the dead," it was unclear whether he was referring to the bloodshed or the past. The debate appears not to have been conducted in an atmosphere of acrimony, however. Indeed, Pumpiansky and Bakhtin vigorously applauded the final Marxist speaker. And so enthusiastic was the crowd that they stayed until 2 A.M., when the debate was declared officially closed.[15]

Gurvich was an enabling figure for the Nevel group, helping them to find a platform for their ideas. Thanks to him, in August 1919 they founded the Nevel Learned Association. At the opening, Pumpiansky was inspired to declare that in no other corner of the earth than the Soviet Union could art and learning flourish in freedom.[16] Well might Pumpiansky have felt expansive, for in this association Bakhtin was able to run a study group on Kant's *Critique of Pure Reason*, which at that time was viewed as a central "idealist" and therefore anti-Marxist text.

The Nevel group felt a sense of mission to enlighten the masses. In the immediate post-Revolutionary years Russian intellectuals became concerned with the need to share their cultural privilege with the less fortunate and to lessen the gap between the educated classes and the masses, in the same self-sacrificing spirit as the populists of the 1860s and 1870s who had "gone to the people," though this time there was a less overt sense of political mission. In 1919, on Gurvich's initiative, the Nevel Symphony Orchestra traveled to a local village to give a concert in its People's House. Most of the audience in the unheated hall had never experienced classical music before. Later that year, Bakhtin lectured on art at the opening of a similarly conceived village concert.[17]

Under the general rubric of bringing enlightenment to the masses, members of the Nevel group also gave free lectures to local audiences. Pumpiansky gave eighty lectures on European culture sponsored by the Education Department. Under the same auspices Bakhtin gave one lecture series on literature and the arts and another series on the Russian language. He gave two lecture series for the Artists' Trade Union, on theatrical production and the history of literature. He offered a lecture series on literature for young people. In addition, Bakhtin was involved in organizing technical courses for the Metal Workers' Union.[18] Probably the motive for all these lecture series was not solely altruism or proselytizing zeal but also a desire to earn extra money in hard times.

In 1919 Gurvich decided to publish a cultural periodical, *The Day of Art* (*Den' iskusstva*). The first and only issue is imbued with millennial pathos, which gives a sense of the ethos in the town. The feverish tone of the contributions typifies the excitement and expectation of the period following the Bolshevik victory. The most utopian possibilities are ascribed to art, and the most ambitious aims are assigned to it. In his "Greetings to Free Art," Gurvich describes writers, artists, and musicians as the "heralds of freedom" who will "transform the world" now that "the bonds of slavery" have been broken. Art is on the side of oppressed peoples and will confound "academic conservatism."

Contributions by other members of the Nevel group expressed a similar faith in the emergence of a finer world. In one article Kagan reflected the communalist and internationalist spirit abroad in the land when he appealed for art to involve itself more closely with life and not to serve the interests of any one faction or ethnic group. In another article, Kagan offered proposals for improving the appearance of Nevel, including the suggestion that artists decorate the walls of the houses.[19] This proposal, which more or less reflected what the avant-garde had already been doing in Vitebsk, represents one of many clues in the journal to the existence of close links between the intellectual life of the two towns. Culturally Nevel was in many respects an outpost of the larger and more flamboyant center of Vitebsk. Gurvich, who was himself an artist, exhibited in Vitebsk in the same year that he published the journal.

The Bakhtin circle was increasingly drawn to Vitebsk, to which several of its members moved. Pumpiansky moved there first in late 1919. He founded a Neo-Kantian seminar at the conservatory, which he ran until 1920, so that in effect the Nevel group now had two bases, the second in Vitebsk. At this time various members of the Nevel group, including Pumpiansky, Kagan, and Bakhtin, also began to give public lectures in Vitebsk.[20]

Bakhtin followed Pumpiansky to Vitebsk in 1920. He probably made the move not only because of the richer cultural life there but also because of the better supply of food. The group in Nevel was beginning to break up anyway, and it ceased functioning in 1921. In that year Kagan left for Orel to teach philosophy at one of the newly founded provincial universities, Zubakin went to Smolensk to join the local branch of the Moscow Archaeological Institute, and Yudina returned to Petrograd to resume her studies at the conservatory. The rest of the group, now increasingly centered upon Bakhtin, continued functioning in Vitebsk, as new members were added and old members made visits.

Vitebsk, about 70 miles south of Nevel on the same rail line, was a much less provincial town. It had a river port and direct rail connections with Petrograd, Moscow, and Brest. Before the war it had been largely a merchant town, whose population of over 90,000 was about half Jewish; there were over sixty synagogues and Jewish teaching establishments as compared with only thirty churches. The rest of the inhabitants were Russians, Poles, and Lithuanians. In 1924 the district was officially incorporated into Belorussia.

Vitebsk had been a popular resort in pre-Revolutionary days. People came from Moscow and Petersburg to the several mineral spas in the surrounding countryside. The town itself was not, however, prepossessing. Except for a small area near the center, it comprised largely wooden houses and unpaved streets—a landscape immortalized in paintings by Marc Chagall, the town's most famous son.[21]

In the first few years after the Revolution the town was suddenly propelled out of its relative obscurity to become a cultural phenomenon. The so-called Vitebsk renaissance was one of the longest-lived of those small pockets of brilliance that sprang up in the provinces as intellectuals fled the dire conditions in Moscow and Petrograd, although Vitebsk itself was at the time no Shangri-la, since the Civil War front passed close to the town, and it saw many troop movements, bandit raids, and shortages. Since Vitebsk was closer to Petrograd than was Kiev or the Crimea and had direct rail links with the capital, it became a refuge not just for individuals but for entire institutions. The local government funded the activities of the refugee intellectuals, and Vitebsk acquired a rich and cosmopolitan cultural life. Before the Revolution it had been anything but a musical center, but now it boasted a conservatory, five music schools, and a symphony orchestra which in its first season gave 22 concerts and over the next two and a half years gave 240 concerts. Nikolai Malko, a conductor of the Mariinsky Theater for ballet and opera in Petrograd, moved to Vitebsk, as did a professor from the Petrograd Conservatory. Well-known theatrical troupes and artists from Moscow and Petrograd came frequently to perform, prominent scholars and writers visited, and the town founded several new theaters of its own, including an experimental theater.[22]

But what really made Vitebsk in those years was the town's invasion by young avant-garde artists, most of them self-proclaimed champions of "left art." The proponents of left art welcomed the Revolution as an iconoclastic force that would sweep away the corrupt old society. They believed in eradicating the bourgeois order and infusing the world with a revolutionary spirit. However, they also believed that a revolution in consciousness, for which their art would provide the main stimulus, was a precondition for the political and social revolutions taking place. They rejected old-style art as representative of complacency and stagnation, and they stood for a new art of the world of technology and urban life. This art was to be brightly colored, challenging, and in general nonrepresentational. They also wanted to break down the barriers between art and life, as by removing the walls of the theater or taking art out of the stuffy concert halls and museums where it usually resided as an appurtenance of the bourgeoisie.[23]

The invasion of Vitebsk by the new order had begun when Chagall returned from Europe to his home town in 1918, fired with a vision of a new kind of art school for Vitebsk, which would serve the local community and teach the underprivileged but would also operate in the vanguard of the art world. To this end he entered into negotiations with the Commissar of Enlightenment, Lunacharsky, and was appointed Commissar for Art in Vitebsk. Chagall was himself not a proponent of left art. Neither was he infatuated with the modern technological age or enthusiastic about the political revolution then in progress. However, he shared with the left artists an eagerness to transform the world and to take art out into the streets.

Chagall organized a local art museum, primarily to house his own work and left art. He also founded the Vitebsk Art Academy, which attracted as teachers such well-known artists as Mstislav Dobuzhinsky, Ivan Puni, El Lissitzky, Casimir Malevich, Vera Ermolaeva, and Falk. It opened in January 1919, the same year that the Bauhaus opened in Weimar. Thus the Vitebsk experiment was an expression as much of the pan-European avant-garde movement as of the post-Revolutionary euphoria. Vitebsk was no Weimar; it was a drab and sleepy provincial town plunged into the chaos of the Civil War. Yet from this remote outpost artists sought to dazzle and transform the world.

The academy enrolled 600 students. The white facade of the mansion in which it was housed was covered with paintings, mostly by Chagall. The initial philosophy of the school, as outlined by Chagall, was to give the children of the poor an opportunity to learn art, and to turn them "from the most readily 'accessible' path, the path of routine," to "the revolutionary path of art, the path of quest." Chagall called on the townspeople to support this work by paying the students to paint their walls and roofs.[24] Much to the consternation of the townspeople, these surfaces were usually painted with flying Jews, green horses, and other hallmarks of Chagall's work, or with even more avant-garde designs.

The faculty of the academy were far from being of one mind about art. There was much disagreement, particularly between Chagall and Malevich, who was more radical both politically and artistically. After a power struggle, Chagall left Vitebsk in late 1919 for Moscow.[25]

Malevich stayed on, a fervent proselytizer for his new kind of art, known as Suprematism. In early 1920 he founded a group called UNOVIS, the Affirmers of the New Art. The movement, although short-lived, was influential in Russia. Suprematism was meant to be a step beyond Cubism, which was then attracting avant-garde artists in the West. Suprematist paintings, though nonrepresentational, used geometric shapes, such as circles, squares, and crosses, in stark colors to represent what Malevich called "the only true reality of the nonobjective world."[26] The most extreme version of Suprematism is a series of paintings done by Malevich about this time in which he superimposed a white square on another square of a slightly different shade of white.

Chagall's replacement by Malevich meant that the town's artistic activities became even more outré. When the film director Eisenstein came across Vitebsk unexpectedly in 1920 during his Civil War peregrinations on a troop train, he was struck by what he saw: "It was a strange, provincial town, like many in the western region . . . caked in soot and dreary. But this town was particularly strange. Here the brick on the main streets was white-washed. And all over this white background were splashed green circles, orange squares and blue rectangles . . . From these walls there resounded the words 'The squares are our palettes.' "[27]

During 1920 and 1921 many avant-garde spectacles were performed in Vitebsk, most of them with Suprematist stage designs. One of these was the Futurist opera *Victory over the Sun* (1913), which is almost totally abstract. The text is composed of alogical and nonsensical phrases, while the music is atonal, using an out-of-tune piano and a chorus singing off key. Another striking avant-garde spectacle was a ballet produced by Nina Kogan which was conceived as "an abstract dance without plot or narrative line." The sets were intended to "kineticize" the standard shapes found in Suprematist works. They moved and changed their forms constantly—sometimes representing a star, sometimes a circle, and in the finale a square.[28]

Thus Bakhtin moved to Vitebsk at the time when left art most dominated the town's cultural life. With his love of overturning received canons, Bakhtin might have been expected to be attracted by this movement which sought to take art out into the streets and challenge old forms, and he liked Chagall personally. But he did not like left art, largely because of its pro-Soviet stance. He preferred Symbolism, the very movement that the new avant-garde believed they had superseded.

While in Vitebsk, Bakhtin and Pumpiansky led a lively discussion group at the conservatory.[29] But their most treasured intellectual activity took place without auspices, in the discussions of the old Nevel circle, which now met in Vitebsk. Its membership varied according to who was in town. Voloshinov moved to Vitebsk in 1921, Yudina visited periodically to give concerts, and Kagan came a few times, as did Zubakin.

The circle also acquired new members in Vitebsk. One of the most important was Ivan Ivanovich Sollertinsky. Born in Vitebsk in 1902, Sollertinsky had moved to Petersburg in 1906. In 1919, after he graduated from the gymnasium, his family moved back to Vitebsk. Sollertinsky worked in the Cultural Section of the Provincial Education Department.[30] A mere youth, he entered Bakhtin's circle as a disciple of Pumpiansky, but he had such a commanding intellect that he soon became a leader in his own right.

The second important member added to Bakhtin's group in Vitebsk was Pavel Nikolaevich Medvedev, who had been born in Petersburg in 1891 and had graduated from the Law Faculty of Petrograd University before volunteering for the Russian army in World War I. In 1917, after the Revolution, Medvedev came to Vitebsk as rector of the Proletarian University. He also taught in the Pedagogical Institute and in military schools. Before long, he became a leader in the local cultural establishment through his appointment as head of the Section for Theater and Extramural Education of the local Commissariat for Enlightenment. Both the Proletarian University and the Section for Extramural Education were primarily concerned with the cause of enlightening the ignorant masses and increasing literacy.[31] Thus, much of Medvedev's early career was devoted to serving the Revolution's idealistic aims in the cultural sphere. He was the editor of *Art* (*Iskusstvo*), the town's cultural journal and mouthpiece for all the different factions, including the Bolsheviks. Both Medvedev and Voloshinov, but not Bakhtin, contributed reviews, scholarly articles, and, in Voloshinov's case, poetry to this journal.

Medvedev performed for the Bakhtin group in Vitebsk more or less the same function that Gurvich had performed for it in Nevel. His association afforded the members of the group official sponsorship for many of their activities, and he assisted their efforts to obtain work and speaking engagements. He helped Bakhtin rustle up an impressive list of jobs, at least on paper. Bakhtin's main employment was as a teacher in the Vitebsk Higher Institute of Education. He lectured to the conservatory, to a literary circle that he ran at the Regional Communist Party School, to the Party Club, to the Political Department of the Fifth Vitebsk Infantry Division, to the Propaganda Center, to the Union of Communications Workers, and to the Union of Soviet Workers. He worked as a bookkeeper and economic consultant at the Vitebsk Statistical Bureau, presumably using skills he had learned through his father's bank. He participated with Medvedev and Voloshinov in a literary studio organized by the Trade Union of Workers in the Arts. The studio taught courses on aesthetics, the theory of creativity, Western and Russian literature, the history of the arts, and journalism. And Bakhtin was persuaded by the Provincial Women's Department to join a commission to organize public lectures and discussions on women's issues as part of the post-Revolutionary effort at women's liberation.[32] These manifold affiliations show how well implicated in the institutional life of the Soviet regime Bakhtin was in these early years, even if largely under Medvedev's patronage. In Bakhtin's classes for party groups he continued the dialogue with the Marxist position which he had begun in the Nevel debates.

Bakhtin participated in debates and lectures for the general public, as in Nevel. For instance, he took part in a series of "trials" of literary characters, modeled on trials staged in Petrograd at the time, which were organized in the city theater. At these trials Bakhtin always took the role of the defender, and his skills as an orator were such that he won all but one of the trials for the "defendants," who included Khlestakov from Gogol's *Inspector General* and Katerina Maslova from Tolstoy's *Resurrection.*[33]

In addition, Bakhtin gave lectures at the public library, always to a packed auditorium. He showed extraordinary ability at communicating with people from all walks of life and educational levels, captivating their imaginations on the most complex questions of literature and philosophy. He rarely used notes and sometimes interlaced his remarks with dramatic renditions of his favorite poems.

After one of Bakhtin's lectures on Pushkin, ten or twelve people who had heard both it and his performance at the literary trials decided to form a circle for the study of Russian literature, which they asked Bakhtin to lead. For a year they met at his lodgings, which were on the first floor of a low wooden house owned by a doctor. Among those who attended were Rakhil Moiseevna Mirkina and her older sister Miriam. The room where they met was sparsely furnished, but on the wall hung an inscription written by Voloshinov: "Here lived a poet and a philosopher / In bitter wintry days / And many accursed questions / Did they decide then."[34] Voloshinov considered himself to be the "poet" and Bakhtin to be the "philosopher."

When lecturing to this small study circle, Bakhtin always behaved as if he were addressing an entire auditorium. He told the students that if a figure is authoritative, there is no need to know his private life. Bakhtin never made personal remarks to his students, nor did he attempt to get to know them. He apparently did not even realize that the Mirkinas were sisters.

Yet Vitebsk was important in Bakhtin's personal life, for it was there that he met his future wife, Elena Aleksandrovna Okolovich. Elena Aleksandrovna had been born in 1900 in nearby Beshenkovich, where her father was a provincial official (*gubernskij sekretar'*). Her parents had not wanted her to pursue her studies beyond the gymnasium, so she left home and went to work in the Vitebsk Public Library in order to further her self-development. She rented a room in the same house as Bakhtin, and there they met.

Bakhtin's meeting with Elena Aleksandrovna was timely, for in Vitebsk his health had deteriorated further, and he needed a great deal of help. The osteomyelitis had spread to his left shin, thigh, and hip joint and to his right hand. He was permanently handicapped. Indeed, the reason that Voloshinov moved from Nevel to Vitebsk in 1921 was in order to look after Bakhtin, and thus he met his own wife, Nina Arkadievna Alekseevskaya, the landlady's daughter. In the same year Bakhtin was stricken with typhoid, and one of its complications, an inflammation of the bone marrow in his right leg, necessitated an operation. Elena Aleksandrovna nursed him through this illness and operation.[35] Later that year they were married.

As a result of the operation on his right leg, Bakhtin was subject to periodic inflammation of the hip joint, which flared up several times a year, giving him acute pain and high temperatures and obliging him to spend as much as a month or two in bed. The fever was so high that his wife had to change his bedshirt several times a night. The pain was so great that he conducted his classes while lying on a couch.

This condition made Bakhtin especially dependent on his

Bakhtin with his wife, Elena Aleksandrovna,
in Vitebsk, 1923

wife, but they were very close in other ways as well. He was extremely impractical and she was his anchor in reality. He was like a child without his wife. He refused to talk on the telephone and rarely answered letters. Besides performing all those services for him, Elena Aleksandrovna ruled their finances with an iron hand. Her most important function was to attend to all the needs of a man who was very set in his habits, enabling him to think and write. Bakhtin's requirements were simple: quiet, endless cups of strong tea, cigarettes of a particular brand, and meals at fixed times.

Soon after Bakhtin's arrival in Vitebsk, the cultural renaissance began to decline. In part, this was because government funding for local activities began to dry up. In 1921, the orchestra was closed and *Art* ceased publication. The decline intensified in 1922 when Malevich, after losing a power struggle in the art academy, left with most of his followers, although Ermolaeva, a leading member of UNOVIS who directed the Vitebsk Art Academy, remained until 1923.[36]

Neither this decline nor Bakhtin's illness appears to have had much effect on his productivity. Indeed, he welcomed the rest enforced by his illness as a chance to do more reading and writing. The time in Vitebsk was an extremely productive period, not only in his writing but in his teaching and public speaking as well. His characteristic work habits were formed during this period and remained unchanged all his life. Rising very early, he would read and think until evening at a table on which were several of the student copybooks called *tetradi*. He wrote out whole works in pencil on the coarse paper, in a handwriting very difficult to decipher, all the while consuming gallons of tea and smoking pack after pack of cigarettes. He continued working on many of the same issues and even the same works that had preoccupied him in Nevel, and thus the years from 1918 to 1924 constitute a single period in the development of his thinking.

References in journals and newspapers of the time, plus his own correspondence, make it possible to reconstruct the projects on which Bakhtin was working. For example, in a letter to Kagan of February 1921, Bakhtin mentions that he is laboring on a book devoted to "Patterns of Verbal Creativity." The Vitebsk newspaper in March reported that Bakhtin was working on a book devoted to moral philosophy. In a letter of January 1922 to Kagan Bakhtin notes that he has been working on an essay about "the subject in moral life and the subject in the law," which is to serve as an introduction to a major work on moral philosophy. Seven months later, in August 1922, the Petrograd journal *The Life of Art* stated that Bakhtin had finished both a book on Dostoevsky and a monograph called *The Aesthetics of Verbal Creativity*.[37]

Between 1918 and 1924 Bakhtin thus worked on at least six texts: "Art and Answerability," a short article that appeared in September 1919 in the Nevel journal *The Day of Art*; a book on Dostoevsky which is doubtless a version of the Dostoevsky book published in 1929; a monograph *The Aesthetics of Verbal Creativity*, of which "The Problem of Content, Material, and Form in Verbal Artistic Creation" (1924) probably represents a portion; a text on moral philosophy; another text on different ways in which authors relate to the characters they create; and still another text on ethics and the law. The titles and projects mentioned during these years, while devoted to the apparently incompatible topics of aesthetics, on the one hand, and moral philosophy, on the other, are all different attempts to come at the same set of problems. All but one of them, the Dostoevsky book, are not only different treatments of the same project but different versions of the same work. These texts are very likely parts of a larger enterprise, for which the most descriptive collective title is *The Architectonics of Answerability (Arxitektonika otvetstvennosti)*.

Some notebooks from these years have survived, although they carry no dates or titles. The different colors of the notebooks and the variations in handwriting, as well as the subject matter, suggest two different sets of notebooks. One series, which deals with the ethical nature of deeds in everyday life, may well be a portion of the book on moral philosophy referred to in *Art* in 1921, which itself is probably a version of the text on "the subject in ethics and the subject in the law" whose completion was announced in *The Life of Art* in August 1922. This set of notebooks is probably the earlier of the two, since it is more highly colored by the characteristic topics and terms of the Marburg school of Neo-Kantianism, whose leading exponents were Hermann Cohen, Paul Natorp, and Ernst Cassirer, and in this period Bakhtin was working his way out of Neo-Kantianism toward a position more uniquely his own. The text contained in the later and considerably longer set of notebooks, which was published in 1979 under the title "Author and Protagonist in Aesthetic Activity," is devoted to a meditation on what it means to author something.[38]

Despite the different weighting of topics in these two sets of notebooks, it is highly probable that they do not constitute two completely different works but are attempts to write the same book. For example, although the emphases differ, the general topics in both sets are the same. Both are concerned with the nature of the self as defined by the pattern of its responses to the world. The earlier notebooks also seem to be from a much more ambitious work in four parts. One of the parts, an introductory essay, concerns the deed as the subject's answer to the world; another part deals with theoretical questions of authorship. In the third part Bakhtin intended to cover ethics in political life, and the fourth section was meant to treat the relation between ethics and religion, but either he did not actually finish these sections or what he wrote has been lost.

Although Bakhtin was thus able to accomplish major work in Nevel and Vitebsk, neither of these provincial towns could offer him a position with scholarly rank, an opportunity to publish his works, or even a good library. Also the many different jobs that he obtained brought him little income, and he needed more money now that his father was in ill health and the whole family depended on Bakhtin. For these reasons he endeavored throughout his stay in Vitebsk to find an academic job, preferably in Moscow or Petrograd. He tried to use the Kagan connection to get a job in Orel or Moscow and the Zubakin connection to get a job in Smolensk. He also tried to get a job at a publishing house in Petrograd, called World Literature, which was famous in the 1920s for providing work, mostly in translation, for intellectuals who could not find it elsewhere. But all was to no avail. At one point Kagan actually organized a job for Bakhtin in Orel, but when Bakhtin's illness prevented him from traveling there immediately, it fell through.[39]

Bakhtin's reasons for wanting to leave Vitebsk were not merely professional and financial. He was also fired by a dream, shared by others in the Nevel group, of finding a place where its now scattered members might regroup and continue their "magnificent philosophical nights of strong tea and talk until morning" on a more regular basis.[40] Although the group no longer met in Nevel, and after 1921 none of its major members were left there, both the old members and those recruited after Bakhtin's departure still regarded themselves as the "Nevel school" of philosophy. They were still trying to work through many of the same ideas that had engaged them earlier, even using much the same philosophical vocabulary. In consequence, Bakhtin's development during his residence in the two towns constituted a single philosophical phase.

However, the only philosophical work and in fact the only work of any kind that Bakhtin was able to publish during this period was "Art and Answerability." This short essay, which was his first piece ever published, opens by opposing two different conceptions of what constitutes a unity. The first kind of unity is mechanical: the parts making up such a whole are joined by an articulation that is entirely exterior. Such parts are like monads, connected to each other, but each part sufficient unto itself and foreign to all other parts. The second kind of unity is one in which the parts are not mechanically but conceptually joined, as in the unifying thought processes of an individual: each of the parts interacts with and is sensitive to all the other parts. For instance, the components of an automobile are unified into a single machine by mechanical techniques that are in accord with the laws of physics. But a painting's disparate parts are brought into a unity only through an act of perception, governed by the laws of consciousness and social convention.

The space and time of art constitute a world quite different from the space and time of actual experience. There is a cutoff between the two, according to Bakhtin: "When a man is in art, he is not in life, and vice versa." Echoing Cohen's basic principle, Bakhtin observes that nothing is given in the nature of art and nothing is given in the nature of human personality that in itself can assure a meaningful bond between the two. The connection between them is not something that is given but something that must be worked at, shaped, conceptualized. Unity is created by the architectonic activity of the mind. The connection between art and life is made only where a perceiving human being makes it. It is established only when I take on myself a distinctive answerability: "For as much as I have experienced and understood in art, I must answer with my life, so that what I have experienced and understood in art does not remain without effect in life."[41] This aesthetics of personal answerability leads to a sweeping rejection of the more traditional ways of conceiving the connection between art and life.

Art and experience are absolutely different kinds of activity, but they have one thing in common. Each activity—either creating form or giving life—seeks to simplify its task by ignoring the complicating existence of the other. Each side of the opposition strives to rid itself of the burden of the other: "For it is easier to create without answering to life, and it is easier to live without taking into account art. Art and life are not one, but they may become a unity in me, in the unity constituted by the answerability I take on myself to make them come together in my life."[42]

"Art and Answerability" is important insofar as it reveals Bakhtin's thought at a crucial point in its genesis. The unusual density of the piece results from Bakhtin's attempt to compress into six paragraphs some of the major theses of the larger philosophical work, *The Architectonics of Answerability*, which was then occupying him and in which he was endeavoring to fuse the three great subjects of Western metaphysics—epistomology, ethics, and aesthetics—into a single theory of the deed. Bakhtin approached this undertaking by attempting to answer the question, How does the experience and activity of art relate to other kinds of activity and experience? He was not alone in this general area of concern, for many others in the Soviet Union during these years were also actively seeking to understand the place of art in life. This question was at the heart of the differences between Formalist and sociological critics as well as between Futurist and Symbolist poets. All of these controversies occurred within the larger tradition, dating from czarist times, that literature as an institution had a unique importance in Russia. The Revolution gave a new immediacy to these debates, all of which played a role in giving direction to the ambitions of the youthful Bakhtin. Influences closer to home were also important for him, such as the passionate insistence of his teacher Zelinsky that not only art but scholarship—thought about art—must never become remote from the needs of everyday life. Nevertheless the specific turn of Bakhtin's writings at this stage was provided not by any of these native influences but rather by his immersion in Marburg Neo-Kantianism.

Between the 1870s and 1920s Neo-Kantianism was the dominant school of philosophy in Germany, at a time when Germany was considered by most Russians to be the home of philosophy. Chairs of philosophy at the leading universities not only in Germany but in Russia as well were held by Neo-Kantians of one kind or another. They were particularly well entrenched at Petersburg University during the years when Bakhtin studied there.[43] Neo-Kantianism was a widespread phenomenon that contained under its umbrella several philosophies that were highly varied in their concerns. Kant was the starting point for them all, but the aspects of Kant's work on which each Neo-Kantian philosophy chose to focus, the language it used, and the answers it provided were different.

The one feature of Kant's thought that in one way or another they all had to confront was the master's formulation of the mind's relation to the world, which was at the heart of his whole system.

Kant regarded his solution to this problem as a Copernican revolution in philosophy because it overcame the limitations of all other systems by answering the claims both of mind and of the world. Attempts before Kant to describe how the two interact erred on one side of the relationship or the other. Leibniz intellectualized appearances and diminished the role of the world outside mind. Locke went too far in the other direction and sensualized concepts, the mind being a mere receptor of information provided by sensations from the world. Kant's breakthrough was to insist on the necessary interaction—the dialogue—between the two. He argued that thought is a synthesis of two sources of knowledge, sensibility and understanding. Sensibility is roughly what empiricists, such as Locke or Hume, assumed to be the sole basis of knowledge, the realm of sensation. And understanding is roughly what rationalists, such as Leibniz, assumed to be the sole basis of knowledge, the realm of concepts. But the ability to make judgments, which is what Kant understood by thinking, requires that both forms of knowledge be brought together in a simultaneity, a "transcendental synthesis." There are apriori concepts inside the mind independent of any specific experience, such as causality, which it uses to organize sensations from the world outside the mind. The world, the realm of the thing-in-itself, really exists, but so does the mind, the realm of concepts. Thought is the give and take between the two.

Those who came after Kant interpreted this synthesis in various ways. Among the Neo-Kantians, Cohen stood out for his radical revision of the mind/world relation as Kant had defined it. Cohen once again upset the balance between the two by proclaiming a militant idealism in which the realm of concepts, logic, is all and the external, material world is nothing. For this reason, Cohen was singled out for special attack by Lenin.[44] After the Revolution the general Soviet term of abuse, "idealist," took on a particularly odious meaning in connection with the Marburg school. Bakhtin's involvement with Cohen was thus one aspect of his career that made him suspect in the eyes of the authorities.

Cohen was perhaps less a Neo-Kantian than an anti-Kantian insofar as he abhorred the dualism in Kant's account of how internal thought relates to external experience. Cohen had a remarkably precise mind: his philosophy is a marvel of system. He sought to unify all the operations of consciousness. And his method for doing so was to throw out the Kantian thing-in-itself in order to declare that there is only mind, the realm of concepts which is only logical. He argued that the subject of thought, no matter how it is conceived, is still a subject that is thought. And insofar as this is so, it is a reasoned subject formed by the categories of logical thinking.

This struggle to overcome the thing-in-itself gave rise to Cohen's basic principle that "The world is not given, but conceived (*Die Welt ist nicht gegeben, aber aufgegeben*)," which became the rallying cry of the Marburg school. In its Russian version (*Mir ne dan, a zadan*) this principle also became the rallying cry of the Bakhtin circle, so much so that it was used as a parodic tag for identifying them in Konstantin Vaginov's satiric roman à clef *The Satyr's Song*. With this formula Cohen sought to deny categorically that the world is given to us as a prefabricated subject for thought. The process of consciousness consists rather in our coming upon an unknown X and then, by applying the formal categories of thought in a series of syntheses, turning X into a subject of understanding. X is not the thing-in-itself but merely the limit of conceptualization. The process of assimilating it is therefore always approximate and never finished. This aspect of Cohen's thought proved attractive to Bakhtin, who always emphasized activity versus completedness and for whom "unfinished" was a positive term, as opposed to the negative connotations of "completed," or "finished off." But he felt that Cohen had gone to an untenable extreme in the lessons he drew from the world as created by mind. In Cohen's attack on the thing-in-itself, which he pursued through an analysis of the mathematical basis of the modern natural sciences, he went so far as to make claims that the more pragmatic Bakhtin could not accept, such as "Matter is only a hypothesis." Cohen wanted to take Kant out of the world of everyday life, whereas Bakhtin wanted to claim him for a fuller understanding of lived experience. Bakhtin uses Kantian ideas about time and space but differs from Kant "in taking them not as 'transcendental' but as the forms of the most immediate reality."[45]

At the earliest stage of Bakhtin's development, when he was still in the first flush of enthusiasm for the Marburg philosophy, he also differed with Cohen's overwhelming emphasis on unity. As seen in "Art and Answerability," Bakhtin is closer to Kant than to the Neo-Kantians insofar as Bakhtin accepts the master's distinction between mind and world. In fact, if Kant's synthesis of mind and world is thought of as a balance, Cohen is to the "right" of Kant in the sense of tipping the balance in favor of mind, while Bakhtin is "left" of Kant by virtue of claiming an even greater role for the immediacy of the world. Cohen's lust for unity with its attendant rationalism was not what drew Bakhtin to the sage of Marburg. It was rather his emphasis on process, the "ungivenness" of experience, with the openness and energy—the loopholes—that such a view promised, which attracted Bakhtin.

Bakhtin found especially sympathetic the work of Cohen's last years, when that great exegete of Kant had become, in his own militantly intellectual way, a seeker after God. A line of ethical concern descended directly from Kant through Cohen to Bakhtin's dialogism. All three thinkers were obsessed with the need to overcome the split between faith and knowledge, a gap dramatically announced in Pascal's appeal to the "God of Abraham, God of Isaac, God of Jacob—not the God of the philosophers and the scholars." Pascal solved the problem of how to deal with the philosopher's God by abandoning him and giving himself completely to faith. For Kant and Cohen, there could be no absolute translation from a concern for the "God of the philosophers" to the immediate presence of the God who said to Moses, "Here am I."[46] Kant sought to find a basis for God's existence in a philosophy that he hoped would prove more powerful than the arguments provided by theology.

Cohen, like Kant, struggled to overcome the gap between reason and belief, metaphysics and theology, the God of the philosophers and the God of Abraham. In the last years of his life he left the university in Marburg, with whose name his work had become synonymous, and moved to Berlin to work in the Academy of Judaic Studies. This move reflected his growing conviction that he must bring together the two major concerns of his life: systematic philosophy and activism for Jewish causes in Germany. He spent the years from 1912 to his death in 1918 on what was to be the great summing-up statement of his career as both a German and a Jewish thinker, *The Religion of Reason out of Sources in Judaism*, which was an attempt to blend classical metaphysics with Hebraic tradition. His painful struggle between the defense of God as an intellectual concept and the unspoken desire for a direct experience of God had an impact on Bakhtin. The very violence with which Cohen insisted that God is a disembodied idea suggested how hard it was for him to resist the appeal of immediacy in the God of Abraham. Cohen sought to forge a unity between Western metaphysics, culminating in Kant, and the Jewish line of thought going back to the Torah. His attempts to unify Kantian dualism merged with arguments for the necessity of a monotheistic God, as when he wrote, "What is characteristic of [Kant's] theology is the non-personal . . . the truly spiritual principle—the sublimation of God into an idea . . . And nothing less than this is the deepest basis of the Jewish idea of God."[47]

Cohen's was a heroic attempt to domesticate the God of the Old Testament so that he might be assimilated into a tradition that is essentially humanist but in which God is nevertheless conceived as a "completely other" (ganz Andere). Cohen maintained that God's uniqueness rather than his mere oneness was the essential point of Jewish monotheism. At the same time Cohen made God the guarantor of human individuality. Monotheism's "center of gravity lies in the relation between God and the individual."[48] In short, the center of gravity is in the give and take between one unique entity, God, and another unique entity, the individual.

The great split between mind and world that preoccupied Kant was in Cohen treated as a split between man and God. Cohen, like his master, felt the separation deeply precisely because he desired so urgently to overcome it. Cohen devoted much thought to the possible forms of unity, and the term he finally proposed as the bond between man and God was "Holiness." He interpreted Leviticus 19:2, "Ye shall be holy: for I the eternal God am holy," to say, "Holiness . . . means for a man a task, whereas for God it designates being." Cohen argued that the holy spirit is simply the "connecting link," God is merely a "correlation."[49] Cohen is similar to Bakhtin in his emphasis on a split between two different levels of reality and the consequent task of finding terms that can mediate between them.

At the beginning of Bakhtin's career, it had become obvious that neither Kant nor his followers in the Marburg school had succeeded in resolving the tension between God as an idea and God as an experience. They had all gone too far in the direction of intellectualization. Bakhtin continued this ongoing attempt to bring philosophy somehow into congruence with theology. If he were to be placed on a spectrum between the extremes of Kant and Pascal, Bakhtin would fall somewhere closer to Pascal. But much of his early work, especially his lectures, concerned itself not with theology as such but with a philosophy of religion, an attempt to understand and describe a world in which prayer makes sense. Bakhtin's suspicion of bloodless ideas and his corresponding predilection for the densely particular expressed themselves not in an occult, in-turning, individual knowledge of the God of Abraham. Bakhtin sought God not in what John of the Cross called "the flight of the alone to the alone" but in the exact opposite, the space between men that can be bridged by the word, by utterance. Instead of seeking God's place in stasis and silence, Bakhtin sought it in energy and communication. In seeking a connection between God and men, Bakhtin concentrated on the forces enabling connections, in society and in language, between men.

CHAPTER 3

The Architectonics of Answerability

A distinctive feature of Bakhtin's career as a thinker is that he never ceased pursuing differing answers to the same set of questions. The various ways in which he actually posed the problem of relations between self and other, or the problem of how the appearance of sameness emerges from the reality of difference, exhibited a great variety over the years. But the questions themselves remained constant, giving to Bakhtin's life the structure of a quest or project. In the years from 1918 to 1924 this agenda of topics took shape in a series of texts none of which appears to be complete. These texts do not constitute fragments of different works. Rather they represent different attempts to write the same book, to which Bakhtin never assigned a title but which is here called *The Architectonics of Answerability*.[1]

This work is patently philosophical but fits uneasily within the available genres of philosophic discourse. It is a treatise on ethics in the world of everyday experience, a kind of pragmatic axiology. Ethical activity is conceived as a deed *(postupok)*. The emphasis is not on what the action results in, the end product of action, but rather on the ethical deed in its making, as an act in the process of creating or authoring an event that can be called a deed, whether the deed be a physical action, a thought, an utterance, or a written text—the last two being viewed as coextensive. Bakhtin arrives at this process by meditating on the form of authorial activity that is most paradigmatic, namely the creation of literary texts. In order to study the means by which relations between self and other are crafted, he examines the ways in which literary authors mold their relation to characters and the relation of those characters to each other in the fiction of a unified art work.

The Architectonics and Bakhtin's final summing-up essays of the 1970s philosophically bracket all the intervening work devoted to more local and specific topics. This does not mean that Bakhtin failed to change over the years or that *The Architectonics* can be used as a canonical guide for measuring the correctness of conflicting interpretations of later works. Such a claim would deny historicity to one of the most powerful proponents of becoming. *The Architectonics* is rather an agenda of topics so basal and complex that not even a lifetime would suffice to think them through.

The terms "architectonics" and "answerability" best encompass the principal subject of the work, namely the answerability we have for our unique place in existence and the means by which we relate that uniqueness to the rest of the world which is other to it. Bakhtin assumes that each of us is "without an alibi in existence." We must ourselves be responsible, or answerable, for ourselves. Each of us occupies a unique time and place in life, an existence that is conceived not as a passive state but as an activity, an event. I calibrate the time and place of my own position, which is always shifting, in the existence of other human beings and of the natural world by means of the values that I articulate in deeds. Ethics is not abstract principles but the pattern of the actual deeds I perform in the event that is my life. My self is that which through such performance answers other selves and the world from the unique place and time I occupy in existence.

The Architectonics looms large in Bakhtin's later work because of its emphasis on action, movement, energy, and *performance*. Life as event presumes selves that are performers. To be successful, the relation between me and the other must be shaped into a coherent performance, and thus the architectonic activity of authorship, which is the building of a text, parallels the activity of human existence, which is the building of a self. And if the activity of being is generated by the constant slippage between self and other, then communication—the never convergent but always reciprocal interdependence of the two—is of paramount concern. It is a central issue not only in the kind of language studied by linguists and philologists but also in the discourses required for a dialogue between all selves and all others. Utterance occurs not only in words or texts but also in thoughts and deeds. So comprehensive a concept of authorship needs a science more copious than a mere poetics or even an aesthetics. And so generous a notion of utterance requires a science transcending a mere linguistics. Bakhtin's urgent sense of these needs is what drove him to devote his life to dialogism.

Bakhtin conceives of otherness as the ground of all existence and of dialogue as the primal structure of any particular existence, representing a constant exchange between what is already and what is not yet. The register and shaper of these transformations is human consciousness, which modulates the constant exchange between "I" activities and all that is "not-I-in-me." The self/other distinction is thus the primary opposition on which all other differences are based: the highest structural principle of the actual world of deeds is the concrete architectonic and epistemological opposition between I and the other.

The self/other dichotomy in Bakhtin does not, as in Romantic philosophy, emphasize the self alone, a radical subjectivity always in danger of shading off into solipsistic extremes. For the same reason the self, as conceived by Bakhtin, is not a presence wherein is lodged the ultimate privilege of the real, the source of sovereign intention and guarantor of unified meaning. The Bakhtinian self is never whole, since it can exist only dialogically. It is not a substance or essence in its own right but exists only in a tensile relationship with all that is other and, most important, with other selves.

Bakhtin's ideas about language parallel ideas held by German thinkers of the Romantic period such as Wilhelm von Humboldt. But Bakhtin is utterly opposed to the Romantic longing for wholeness, that homesickness which produced the German vision of an ancient Greek *Gemeinschaft* from which all subsequent history has been a falling away, a second exile from Eden into a world of fatally split consciousness in the self and alienation in society. Dialogism, by contrast, celebrates alterity: it is a merry science, a *fröliche Wissenschaft* of the other. As the world needs my alterity to give it meaning, I need the authority of others to define, or author, my self. The other is in the deepest sense my friend, because it is only from the other that I can get my self. The unusual term *drugost'* for alterity draws attention to the pervasiveness of the other through its *-ost'* ending, a grammatical marker indicating abstraction, like *-ness* in English. The word also hints at the relationship between the words for "friend" (*drug*) and "other" (*drugoj*), where *-oj* is the standard adjectival marker added to the root *drug*. This shading suggests the positive values of the other in Bakhtin's thinking. The fact that we can never achieve full presence, a unitary identity complete in itself, either in immediate experience of ourselves or in the logical rigors of dialectical thought, is not to be lamented.

Bakhtin's I/other contrast is mirrored in the natural world, which explains his intense interest in biology. Scientists who study microscopic forms of life use a simple criterion to make the sometimes difficult decision as to whether one of the tiny forms is dead matter or living tissue. If the form has the capacity to react to a stimulus, such as light, it is alive. If it does not change in the presence of altered circumstances, it is construed as not having life. In other words, at this primitive level, the capacity to react to, or interact with, the environment is the test of life, much as when a person fails to respond to any stimuli, that person is said to show no "signs of life" and is pronounced dead. The protozoan could not long survive without the nourishment provided by its environment; it needs what lies outside the oozy borders of its integral shape to ensure continuation of the internal, reactive capacity that is defined as its life. Responding to the environment, being able to answer it, is life itself. Whatever engenders a particular response of the organism in a specific situation—if only the lowly hydra's shrinking from light—is the center of its life. This is what at a higher level of complexity, in human beings, is called the self. Conceived in this way, self is less a metaphysical abstract than the basic fact of life. Self also has no meaning "in itself," for without the environment to engage and test its capacity to respond, it would have no living existence.

Primitive organisms have life insofar as they have what Bakhtin calls "addressivity," but they can answer their environment only in a highly programed manner. They must expand toward or contract from a light source, and every hydra, no matter which one, will react in the same way. The correlation between the brute given of primitive life and the possibility of a created self, in an unpredictable, stylized response, is here at its lowest.

But in organisms that are more complex, such as humans, where the body is a vast universe of variegated cells, the situation becomes quite different. The human body is a social organization of teeming histological communities, each of which is in turn composed of individual cells, all interacting with each other in a constantly interrelating community of "languages," a heteroglossia of electrochemical impulses and hormonal "dialects" and enzymatic "patois." In the same way that all of these subsystems interreact with each other, the integrated system they all constitute in their entirety socially interacts with other persons. Not only are situations in the human social environment more varied than those encountered by protozoa, but even when a situation repeats itself among humans, we cannot know absolutely how each of us will respond. Each of us has a capacity to be unique, which makes all human beings, as a species, unique.

The difference between the way in which John Smith, say, reacts to even so homogenizing a situation as a firing squad, as opposed to the way David Jones answers the same set of circumstances, is a variation in the way individual human beings respond to their environment. The distinctiveness of each response is the specific form of that person's answerability. There is no way for a living organism to avoid answerability, since the very quality that defines whether or not one is alive is the ability to react to the environment, which is a constant responding, or answering, and the total chain of these responses makes up an individual life. This is what Bakhtin means in saying that there is "no alibi for being." How we respond is how we take responsibility for our selves. The self, when conceived as the particular response of a total organism to its specific environment—from the level of brain answering simple stimuli as reflex to the level of mind answering other selves in social exchange—is by definition never complete in itself. Just as the lowly protozoa need the solution in which they swim to nourish themselves, so, at a higher level, selves need a stimulation from the alterity of the social world to sustain their responsibility.

This view is both Neo-Kantian and Darwinian. The Kantian assumption of a gap between mind and world is understood by Bakhtin as a necessary interdependence between the two, making all discussion of a transcendental ego superfluous or at least inadequate. Such an interdependence is Darwinian in the specific sense that the one cannot exist without modification by the other, and thus the privilege of making decisions resides exclusively in neither.

In Bakhtin, the difference between humans and other forms of life is a form of authorship, since the means by which a specific ratio of self-to-other responsibility is achieved in any given action—a deed being understood as an answer—comes about as the result of efforts by the self to shape a meaning out of the encounter between them. What the self is answerable to is the social environment; what the self is answerable for is the authorship of its responses. Self creates itself in crafting an architectonic relation between the unique locus of life activity which the individual human organism constitutes and the constantly changing natural and cultural environment which surrounds it. This is the meaning of Bakhtin's dictum that the self is an act of grace, a gift of the other.

Bakhtin describes this self-appropriation from the other in a short narrative, a kind of "just-so story." The fable is constructed around a number of metaphor clusters involving bookkeeping, sex, and biology, but the most important cluster involves the mechanics of sight. Because of the assumed split between mind and world, a major problem for mind is how to "see" the world, how to translate a world whose conditions cannot in themselves be known into another set of conditions which will represent that world in a way that can be perceived, if only at a second remove. We must constantly find markers that we can see in our minds for things that otherwise would be unknowable, or conceptually invisible to consciousness. Understanding is simultaneous with perception: to know something is to be able to see it. This is close to the old assumption in metaphysics that "to perceive is to be," but Bakhtin's treatment of this *topos* is anything but abstractly philosophical.

Bakhtin begins with an everyday, garden-variety fact so simple that it is often forgotten or overlooked: if, as everyone would admit, no two bodies can occupy the same space at the same time, then my place in existence is unique if only because while I occupy it, no one else can. While I am here, you must be there; I may be with you in this moment, but the situation will look different from the unique places you and I occupy in it. We are both together, yet apart. We may physically change places. But between the moment you occupy the position I was in and I occupy the position you were in, time will have elapsed, if only the fraction of a second. And since the previous situation cannot be repeated, we never see, or know, the same things.

You shape the structure of the setting and our place in it from the unique place you occupy in it, as I do from mine. Only a self, conceived not as a transcendental essence but merely as the locus of apperception, can "see" our configuration. Since it is not transcendental, the self is guided in its architectonic activity by restraints that physical space imposes on the biological mechanisms of sight. Some of the restraints are contingent, such as the amount of available light at any given moment; others are absolute.

The first of these absolute restraints, which might be called the law of placement, is that what I see is governed by the place from which I see it. This law is expressed in physics as Einsteinian relativity at one level and as Heisenberg's uncertainty principle at another.

Bakhtin, in arguing that the particular place from which something is perceived determines the meaning of what is observed, was attempting to do for conscious mind what Einstein was seeking to do for the physical universe when he too, at almost the same time, emphasized the determining role played by the locus from which phenomena are observed. Einstein's first paper of 1905 asserts that every statement about the "objective" time of an event is in reality a statement about the simultaneous occurrence of two events, the event in question and, say, the superposition of the hands of a clock on the numbers painted on a dial. Thus when Einstein says, "the train arrives here at seven," this really means that the passage of the little hand on his watch to the place marked seven and the arrival of the train are simultaneous events.

Einstein admits that this statement contains an undefined concept—one that he, like Bakhtin, was to spend the rest of his life trying to understand—the concept of simultaneity. Simultaneity, as Einstein defines it, normally does not arise as a question, because in everyday life there is so deceptively close a fit between the events on the faces of our watches and the events in the world. Although we are comparing an event that has already occurred with an event that is still occurring on our watches, we are able, as a rule, to ignore this ineluctable posteriority, which we process as simultaneity, because light travels so fast and the distances are so small that such a delay is irrelevant.

When distances increase, however, the delay becomes obvious and unavoidable: if we wish to time events on the moon with clocks that are located on earth, the delay is significant. This raises the essential question of how we can conceive events as being simultaneous on the earth and, say, the moon, that is, how different spaces can have the same time. This problem led Einstein to invent "thought experiments" involving people in elevators, on ocean liners, and on moving trains, which showed that there is no such thing as a fixed interval of time independent of the system to which it refers. There is thus no actual simultaneity: there are only systems of reference by which two different events can be brought into a conceptual unity. In his own work, Einstein developed the Lorentz transformations as such a system of reference.

For Bakhtin, the system of reference that created the effect of simultaneity was to be found in the mechanics of self/other transformations, specifically the law of placement. You can see things behind my back, such as a painting or passing clouds, that are closed to my vision, while I can see things that your placement denies to your vision, such as a different painting on the other wall or other clouds moving behind your head. This difference determines that although we are in the same event, that event is different for us both.

Otherness, then, is not just a metaphysical a priori, since noncoincidence is a constitutive feature of human perception. There is also a structural gap in human vision, a blind spot that is dictated by the law of placement. But since the place each of us occupies is unique, both the things I cannot see and the things I can see are distinctive to, and in important ways help to constitute, myself.

According to a hoary definition, a pessimist is one who says, "We have only come halfway," whereas the optimist says in the same situation, "We have only halfway to go." Analogously, many moderns decry the very same conditions that Bakhtin celebrates. Bakhtin speaks of alterity, which is a condition friendly to man, rather than alienation, which is the same structural situation but has been perceived from Marx to Sartre as hostile: the hell from which there is no way out is not only "the others," but the condition of otherness that they merely specify in given situations. Bakhtin does not ignore the fact that sight is always partial, incomplete. Indeed, his whole concept of otherness depends on recognition of the blindness to "all that" which enables us to see "this."

In Bakhtin's phenomenology of the senses, what is most important is what I can see, not what is denied my vision by the law of placement. From the unique place I occupy in existence there are things only I can see; the distinctive slice of the world that only I perceive is a "surplus of seeing," where excess is defined relative to the lack all others have of that world shaped exclusively by me. This fundamental building block in the construction of the self is something that all people share as a condition but that in specific persons is unique as an experience. What results is a paradox that says we all share uniqueness.

Bakhtin emphasizes the plenitude rather than the paucity of vision, although the two conditions are as simultaneous and inseparable as they are ineluctable. He does so in order that his term for such plenitude, "surplus of seeing," will not be misconstrued as solipsism: surplus is after all a relative term having no meaning without reference to others.[2]

Bakhtin examines the law of placement's implications for the physical sense of sight in order to use visual categories as a means for discussing the elusive concept of the self. Being conscious generally means being conscious of something. Bakhtin argues that to be conscious means to see something. And just as the problem of cognizing things is solved by finding terms that let us see the world, so the problem of cognizing the self is solved by learning how to visualize myself.

The self Bakhtin works with has certain parallels with Kant's "I think," the point to which experience relates for its meaning. This is the self that Kant defined as an "I" which is "in *itself* completely empty." The parallel suggests that the self, conceived as nothing in itself, poses radical problems for its perception by that part of the self/other relation constituted by self. As Bakhtin says, "We least of all are able to apprehend the . . . whole of our personality."[3]

Whether in a rigorous, phenomenological attempt to achieve an eidetic intimation of myself or in the most banal daydream, it is precisely "I myself that I cannot see." An author's attempt to visualize a character parallels my attempt to make sense of this world, in effect to make a coherent story of my role in it. The self is "the main character who is on a different plane from all the other characters I imagine."[4]

Bakhtin moves from the noncoincidence between mind and world to the noncoincidence between the way I and the other deploy categories for organizing the world, the picture I have from my unique place in existence versus the picture you have of it from your unique place. This series of noncoincidences is extended to its limit in the noncoincidence that exists between my self and all forms that are available for the expression of self, not only to others but to me myself, namely time, space, and the values that give time and space specific colors in any particular encounter. This radical noncoincidence of self with the markers for self is the basis not only for the peculiarities of the pronoun *I* among other formal elements of any natural language but also for the inability of all aspects of language to merge with the subject.

The specific manner in which the inadequacy of any system other than the self to model the self makes itself known is as an endless nay-saying by self to all definitions of it. When I develop consciousness of myself, it is not as a growing awareness of something but rather as a "consciousness of the fact that I, in my most fundamental aspect of myself, still am not."[5] I live in an "absolute future."

The importance of an architectonics lies precisely in its ability to give temporal and spatial placement, to give definition, to myriad alterities, an operation that simultaneously defines me. The particular way in which Bakhtin deploys time and space reveals his debt to the Kantian tradition of categories. And so does the critical role played in his thought by Cohen's distinction between what is given and what the mind conceives. All these terms characterize the activity of achieving a self, an activity I can never complete. So the self must be thought of as a project.

The word Bakhtin uses for "project" (*zadanie*) is another turn on the basic distinction between "given" (*dan*) and "conceived" (*zadan*), which helps to define the nature of consciousness as the necessity constantly to create, to author, to posit (*zadat'*) a self. In temporal terms this means that I answer the present by projecting a future. My self then performs itself as a denial of any category's power fully to comprehend it. The influence of Dostoevsky is apparent here, especially the underground man's insistence on his right to negate any definition with which society might label him: he chooses to spit even in the crystal palace. That other philosopher of freedom, Sartre, similarly argues that when the world says of me, "He is a waiter," I must hold back, I must insist I have not become a waiter, for I am still in the process of becoming me.

But if my deepest self, my I-for-myself, is in essence opposed to all categories, the question arises as to where I am to get the categories for fixing the self itself. The answer is: from other selves. I cannot see the self that is my own, so I must try to perceive it in others' eyes. This process of conceptually seeing myself by refracting the world through values of the other begins very early, when children first begin to see themselves through the eyes of their mother, and it continues all their lives.

Consciousness knows the world by visualizing it but can see it, as it were, only through the optic of the self or that of the other. Each of these instruments refracts what is perceived in quite different ways, much as do the right and left eyes in the physiology of vision. In my attempts to make sense out of what confronts me, I shape the world in values that are refracted from one or the other lens.

This pattern is another way in which the I / other duality replicates the pattern increasingly found at other levels of the biology that controls perception. The duality of bifocal vision has been long known, but it now appears that hearing is a dichotic process as well, in which each ear hears differently.[6] The right ear, which is controlled by the left hemisphere in another example of simultaneity, displays a better aptitude for precise recognition of those sounds that are peculiar to human speech. The left ear, controlled by the right hemisphere, is more efficient in discriminating among all sounds other than speech sounds. The brain processes audible signals in two different ways. Two sounds that are physically similar, such as the one made by puffing our cheeks and rapidly exhaling when we blow out a candle and the prevocalic *wh* in words like *when*, are treated in two quite different ways in auditory perception. The right hemisphere handles the purely functional act of blowing out the candle, and the left handles the abstract, semiotic quality of the speech sound. These differences in how the two ears hear nevertheless work together in the consciousness of an individual perceiver to give the appearance of a simultaneous unity, much as do other dualities mandated by the dichotomous working of the bicameral brain. Bakhtin, who was influenced by that great physiologist of the brain A. A. Ukhtomsky, suggests that constant mediation between the role of self and that of other is the mechanism by which we conceptualize and, to a degree, control at the level of mind dualities which are present in biology at the level of mere brain.

Self and other are the two poles of all perceptual possibilities. Their inseparability creates a dyadic mandate that gives direction to Bakhtin's obsessive word play, especially with the Russian prefix *so-*, indicating simultaneity in its aspect of sharing, which is roughly equivalent in English usage to *co-*, as in *co-author*. But *The Architectonics* includes many other examples of straining Russian to meet Bakhtin's particular philosophical needs. It is an extremely dense text; opponents of jargon might even say that the text is clotted. This is due not only to the difficulty of the subject but to the constant experimenting with new usages. Russian, like Greek or German and unlike English, is characterized by the vast number of words that, by adding prefixes or suffixes, can be generated from a relatively small stock of verbal roots. At the time of writing, Bakhtin was fresh from his philological studies in Greek and Latin. This circumstance, combined with his immersion in a tradition of German philosophy which in Hegel's words was "to teach philosophy to speak German," resulted in a pyrotechnic display of neologisms that are peculiar to Bakhtin's early period.

For instance, consciousness is described as joined to existence outside itself through deeds, so Bakhtin describes man's being as *postuplenie*, which means "entering" or "joining," as in entering the army, but which also suggests *postupit'*, "to act," and *postupok*, "deed." A further overtone of *postuplenie* is "receipt," as in bookkeeping, which constitutes Bakhtin's reminder that people enter existence through the deeds that they tot up over their lifetime and for which, like entries in an accounts ledger, they are answerable. Consciousness is always *postupajuščee soznanie*, an "entering/acting consciousness," or even *so-znanie*, "knowing with," another of Bakhtin's frequent word plays with this prefix. The way people are joined to life is described as *priobščën*, which means "associated with" but is also the past passive participle of "to administer a sacrament," meaning that people join the work of life, giving it the wine and wafer of meaning.

This dualistic way of conceiving the bond between consciousness and the world is the source of other dyads which further specify the mind/world relationship. Bakhtin agrees with Kant and differs from Cohen in assuming that the world of things is a "givenness" (*dannost'*) and therefore before consciousness and present to me as a "that-ness" (*ètost'*) or "what's-on-hand" (*naličnost'*), a term that lies somewhere between Heidegger's "facticity" and *Vorhandenheit*. *Naličie* (that is, *en face, na lice*) is what's-on-hand before it has been processed by an act of human consciousness, when what is merely given is transformed into what is conceived or set as an aspect of the "project" (*zadanie*) of acting/entering.

The world as *dannost'* presents me with necessity, "things I must do" (*dolženstvovanie*); the realm of *zadannost'* is one in which these obligations are turned into a "condition of answerability" (*otvetstvennost'*), "things I should do." This transformation of the given world into a world I set myself turns the relationship between my body and other objects around me (rocks, trees, other bodies) into a temporal relationship, one that otherwise is merely spatial (so long as it is purely physical). The merely physical world is an "axiological desert" (*cennostnaja pustota*). The acting out of human projects turns the desert of space into a garden of time. The world as *naličnost'* is, from the point of view of a perceiving consciousness, always already there. It is *uže-stavšee bytie*, a term that suggests "already-having-become-being" but contains overtones as well of an "already-paid-up-existence" or "already-having-begun-being" (where initiative is no longer possible). The undertone of accountancy in Bakhtin's language suggests a possible connection between his thinking and his work in exile as a bookkeeper for the local party chief in Kustanai, besides the fact he was the son of a banker. *Dannost'* is *uže bytie*, "already being"; *zadannost'*, the world transformed by human acts, informed by values, is *ešče-bytie*, "yet-to-be-being" (a formulation close to Ernst Bloch's *das Noch-nicht-sein*). Consciousness is never completely coincidental with the world; its activity fundamentally transforms what is there already. It is "active/initiatory" (*postupajuščee soznanie*), and thus its time is the "absolute future" (*absolutnoe buduščee*). It must always be ahead of any present, since the responsibility to transform what is given makes any present a past; what is on hand is already there.

The world in essence is without meaning. People in essence are nothing but creators and consumers of meaning. The world and people interact in a mutuality of passive need for and active giving of value; their unity is an "intercontradiction" (*vzajmoprotivorečie*), which is not to be read as a mutual contradiction, where the two sides cancel each other out in a bad infinity of irresolution: "In the unitary (*edinoe*) and unique (*edinstvennoe*) event of existence (*sobytie bytija*) it is impossible to be neutral."[7] But far from being an unhappy, fated condition, the need to act out values in deeds is my "architectonic privilege" to "stand out" (*isxodja sebja*, "standing out," *ex-stasen*) from the world of givenness, to find the world outside myself in my act of providing the world with time and space categories that spring from the deed of evaluating it.

To shape the world through the meaning of the values that my deeds articulate is not a necessity but a responsibility, since I am free to avoid making values that are my *own*. It is impossible to be a conscious human being and live a value-neutral life. But I can simply accept the values of my particular time and place, which is an avoidance of activity that has the effect of making my life a subfunction of a self-imposed "axiological reflex" (*cennostnyj refleks*, similar to Heidegger's *das Man*). Thus, my inability to withhold meaning constitutes a responsibility: I am answerable in the sense that I am free to heed or ignore the world's call for a response. But the world's inability to mean is true necessity; "already-being is to be in need . . . to be merely on hand (*naličie*) . . . means to be feminine before the pure expressive activity of the I."[8] The world is not only a passive woman before the virile activity of the mind (*mud-*, the root of *mudrost'*, "wisdom," is related to the word for "testes")—although a mind can also be that of a woman—as it goes out into the world, penetrating and infusing it with significance.

The sexual metaphor for the manner in which world and mind relate (world needs to be entered from "outside," *izvne*, by mind), is only one of several that Bakhtin employs to the same purpose. The world is also a "defenseless child" (*xrupkij rebënok*), requiring the parental love of human consciousness (the maternal-caring metaphor is widespread in Bakhtin's works). In addition, the world requires the gift of meaning which it is mind's to give, and this analogy with free grace is one of Bakhtin's appropriations from traditional Christian *Heilsgeschichte*.

Human consciousness enters the world through deeds in the form of acts that define values, or through "outgoing words" (*isxodjaščie slova*) that no less effectively express the shape of values (Bakhtin's word for this, chosen probably because it is closer to the sense of *Ausdruck* in German, is *iz-obraž-enie*, "imagining-out values").

Having established the cut-off between mind and world, Bakhtin is confronted with the problem of finding a way to mediate between the two, as is anyone who accepts the categories of Kant's first critique. The term Bakhtin proposes for this bridging function is "answerability" (close to Heidegger's *Sorge*, a response to the "call" or *Ruf* of Being), where the responding aspect of the word, the *otvet* of *otvetstvennost'*, is given its fullest weight. Responsibility is conceived as the action of responding to the world's need, and is accomplished through the activity of the self's responding to its own need for an other. The armature of this whole philosophy is the phenomenological account it provides of the relations between self and all else that is other from the point of view of such a self.

There are no isolated acts in consciousness. Every thought is connected to other thoughts and, what is more, to the thoughts of others. Thus the world has "being" (*bytie*), but consciousness is always co-consciousness (the normal Russian word for consciousness in its aspect of awareness is *soznanie*, "co-knowing"). Being is therefore the activity of "being with" (*sobytie bytija*), in which the first term, "deed," itself can be broken down into "co-being," so that an alternative rendering of the two-word term is the "co-being of being." This emphasis on simultaneity and sharing characterizes all Bakhtin's work. His suspicion of capitalism, like Dostoevsky's, was grounded in his perception of an all-pervasive alienation in the West, the isolation of its persons, and its emphasis on unconnected ego. His commitment to a kind of socialism was motivated by the necessity of sharing not only our material possessions but our very selves.

But if mind, language, and society all operate as one great pulsating simultaneity, the question arises as to what keeps them from indiscriminately flowing into each other. What, in other words, is the mechanism that ensures the uniqueness and integrity of all these interacting forces by keeping them apart? What is the ground of difference in our consciousness? Here is where the separating power of the distinction between self and other makes itself felt.

Bakhtin's basic categories for organizing the world, like Kant's, are still time and space. A first step in my making the self/other distinction is to gain a sense of the constant inadequacy of even the most basic categories that I use for shaping the other—such as time, space, and the values that give them a particular color in specific situation—to shape a perception of my self. This basic difference serves to distinguish two different ways of perceiving space, two different kinds of time, and two different sets of values. In each case, the difference is in the gap between a time, space, and evaluation that are appropriate to me and a time, space, and evaluation that are appropriate to others.

The way in which I create myself is by means of a quest: I go out to the other in order to come back with a self. I "live into" an other's consciousness; I see the world through that other's eyes. But I must never completely meld with that version of things, for the more successfully I do so, the more I will fall prey to the limitations of the other's horizon. A complete fusion (a dialectical *Aufhebung*), even were it possible, would preclude the difference required by dialogue. When I have investigated the other's consciousness as completely as I can, I will be inside his horizon, and what he cannot see, I shall be unable to see. Thus, a necessary second step for me is to return to my own horizon, where I can perceive the other not only in the form of what he himself is seeing as he looks out, not only from his eyes, but also from my own eyes. I see him both as a subject and as an object.

The classical example is how I perceive an other's suffering. I see her pain but do not feel it, or at least not in the same way that she experiences her own pain. But I can conceptually enter her cognitive space and perceive through her eyes that the world's appearance is colored in all its aspects by the sensation of suffering. When the sufferer sees the trees surrounding us, she perceives suffering trees, as it were; when she sees other persons, she perceives them too through the optic of her pain. The world is homogeneous in her perception of it. And by going out to this suffering other, I can know all this; through her eyes I can see the world as an extension of her suffering.

But when I return to the time and space of my own unique place in existence, in addition to the knowledge I have gained of the sufferer's world, I can add to the catalogue of things she sees the things that she is unable to see from her situation and that can be perceived only from mine, such as the grimace on her face or the rictus of her limbs. More, I see all this in the context of the same trees she perceived through her pain. But those trees have quite a different aspect from my place. I render the other complete by the additions I make to her from my position of being both inside and outside her, a position Bakhtin calles "transgredience" or "extralocality" (*vnenaxodimost'*). From the storehouse of my "surplus of seeing" I am able to provide those features that are denied the sufferer herself, since she cannot herself be transgredient to herself.

Among the features of this movement that distinguish self from other is the way that self and other are characterized by a different space and a different time. The self's time is open, "unfinfinished" (*nezaveršën*), whereas the other we conceive is "completed" (*zaveršën*) insofar as we see him as what he is. The self's place is not only here, insofar as it must be transgredient and not completely immersed in this environment if it is to have the perspective needed to constitute a whole out of the other and his environment. The other is completely here, insofar as I equate his self, his body, and his environment as a unified whole—insofar as I architectonically complete him.

A certain ambiguity of values characterizes these differences. To be open, becoming, is a good thing; it is inseparable from my privilege in existence because it is inseparable from the uniqueness of my self. But as a unique becoming, my I-for-myself is always invisible. In order to perceive that self, it must find expression in categories that can fix it, and these I can only get from the other. So that when I complete the other, or when the other completes me, she and I are actually exchanging the gift of a perceptible self. This is what Bakhtin means when he argues that we get our selves from others; I get a self I can see, that I can understand and use, by clothing my otherwise invisible (incomprehensible, unutilizable) self in the completing categories I appropriate from the other's image of me. As opposed to Lacan, Bakhtin conceives the mirror stage as coterminous with consciousness; it is endless as long as we are in the process of creating ourselves, because the mirror we use to see ourselves is not a passively reflecting looking glass but rather the actively refracting optic of other persons. In order to be me, I need the other. Thus, completing can also be a good.

This is another example of the constant struggle between the centripetal forces that seek to close the world in system and the centrifugal forces that battle completedness in order to keep the world open to becoming. "Self" and "other" are the names we give to the poles in the Manichaean struggle as it is present to consciousness. The "I" is the ground of openness, the "other" is the ground that ensures the possibility of completing.

This I/thou distinction was not original with Bakhtin. It had been present in classic philosophy since the late eighteenth century and reached Bakhtin through the Marburg Neo-Kantians. Cohen had posited holiness as the force joining men and God, which long before Buber led him to meditate self/other relations: "It is an intriguing [Aristotelian] illusion that the solitary thinker is most likely to attain full selfhood. We [Jews] know, however, that the isolated self exclusively engaged in thinking cannot be an ethical self. The ethical self must be engaged in action. For this self there exists no I without a thou. *Reah* [in Hebrew] means the 'other,' the one who is like you [specifically it means 'neighbor' or 'fellow creature,' which should not be confused with *aher*, "other," or *ruah*, "spirit"]. He is the thou of the I. Selfhood is the result of an unending relation of I and thou."[9] And since self is equated with consciousness and consciousness with consciousness of the other, the highest priority is given to society, or the particular ways in which people sort out self/other relations in history.

Although the self/other distinction is a recurring preoccupation of many other post-Romantic systems of thought, Bakhtin is the only major figure to frame the problem in terms of authorship. He is distinguished not by his emphasis on the self/other dichotomy as such but rather by his emphasis on the essentially authorial techniques of dialogue and character formation which permit the poles of consciousness to interact while maintaining their fundamental difference from each other. Ultimately, Bakhtin's thought is a philosophy of creation, a meditation on the mysteries inherent in God's making people and people's making selves, with the activity of people creating other people in literary authorship as a paradigm for thinking at all levels of creating.

The act of authorship dealt with in *The Architectonics* is the master trope of all Bakhtin's work. The encounter of authors with the heroes they weave into the world of their texts proves a successful form for bringing together and modeling all Bakhtin's other categories. This organizing role of authorship enables Bakhtin to focus his concerns in biology, linguistics, psychology, theology, and politics. A key problem in biology, for example, involved neurological integration and the identification of the system of systems that keeps the various electrochemical and mechanical forces at work in the human body operating together in a unity. What, in other words, is the seat of control, the author of each individual body's actions and reactions? This question had a strong resonance in Russia, where physiology of the brain was a popular and successful area of research.

In linguistics, fundamental questions had to do with semantic integration. Saussure's emphasis on the arbitrariness of the sign undercut assumptions dating back at least to Saint Augustine about the ability of personal intentions to control meaning. The problem was where to locate the seat of control directing meaning in language. Who, if anybody, is responsible for the semantic weight of any given statement? Who is or can be the author of utterances made in so impersonal a medium as the model of language proposed by structural linguists? In psychology, after Freud's emphasis on the unconscious, the question became: Who is master of the psyche? Who is the author of any action, the ego of the conscious person or the unconscious and impersonal forces of the Id? This problem continues to bedevil the judiciary.

In theology, the question was always one of ontological integration. Who in any given act is responsible, God's law or man's will? This problem is especially serious in versions of Christianity that highlight the free will of the individual, as does Russian Orthodoxy. Am I authoring this deed as an exercise of my free will, or am I merely articulating an aspect of a larger movement whose whole articulates the will of a higher, extraindividual plan? And in politics questions of authority and responsibility were most pressing. For this reason Bakhtin's discussions of such scholarly matters as monologue versus dialogue and the relations between authors and their characters may be read as latent political commentaries having a special relevance to his own time and place.

At the heart of all these questions is a recurring confrontation between one pole of individual personhood and the opposite pole of impersonal force. The two poles are nominated in different ways in these heterogeneous discourses, but in all cases they essentially designate the conflict between a radical self responsible for its actions and an impersonal other variously conceived as the source of accountability. These self/other relations or author/character relations, which are the major preoccupations of all religious systems, indicate the role of religion in Bakhtin's thought. He was strongly influenced by Christianity. But as always with Bakhtin, the influence was indirect and thus difficult to calibrate precisely. His thought in this area is more a philosophy of religion than a theology assuming faith as an *a priori.*

For Bakhtin, religious thought is not a narrow discipline. He refuses to cut religion off from all other kinds of concerns, especially those having to do with language, society, and the nature of the self. In this respect he contrasts with many other Russians who during this period devoted themselves to religious philosophy. For example, L. P. Karsavin, whose *On Personality* (1929) is strikingly similar to Bakhtin's early work, suffered from a failing to which Bakhtin never succumbed: the inability to translate theological categories into other discourses. Karsavin thus remains a minor figure in the history of Orthodox theology, while Bakhtin has international importance because he carnivalizes the languages of sociology, literary criticism, and linguistics by hybridizing their traditions with a radical Christology. In other words, what distinguishes Bakhtin is not his theories about the personhood of Christ but his way of using those ideas to refresh areas other than theology.

In this respect Bakhtin is not an exotic special case, an underground Christologist, but part of a much wider movement in modern thought to sustain the conceptual power of almost two millennia of Christian thought while still taking into account the challenge posed to traditional theology by post-Enlightenment developments in the sciences. Bakhtin's concern is to understand the mysteries of authorship not just of literary texts but of the texts constituted by speech in everyday life. This driving force leads him to take up questions of the relation between the self and other (who is authoring whom?) and of language and literature.

The relevance of theology for Bakhtin is shown by the parallels between his thought and the recurrent themes of Christianity, for even in secular epochs questions about the nature of creativity, authorship, and authority continue to pose problems that, in religious epochs, were addressed by thinkers who sought to understand God's authorship of the world. The traditional concern for Logos has many analogues with, and much conceptual power to bestow on, modern attempts to understand the word. As Kenneth Burke remarked, "statements that great theologians have made about the nature of 'God' might be adapted *mutatis mutandis* for use as purely secular observations on the nature of *words* . . . it should be possible to analyze remarks about 'the nature of God' like remarks about 'the nature of reason,' in their sheer formality as observations about the nature of language . . . such a correspondence between theological and logological realms should be there, whether or not 'God' exists." To think about language, even without invoking terms from theology, must in the nature of things engage some of the central issues with which religious thinkers have always wrestled, such as the nature of meaning, of the other, and of the subject (the person). As Burke added, "What we say about words in the empirical realm will bear a notable likeness to what is said about God in theology."[10] This is so because the inescapable dualities of theology (man/God, spirit/matter) are at the heart of language in the duality of sign/signified.

A word is a material thing insofar as it exists only by means of physical production, as by speech organs or ink on paper. But a word also is more than, or transcends, its sheer physicality insofar as it has a meaning. This duality of the word extends to its use: the sign is never what it signifies. The word *tree* is never a tree. If man is the language animal, he is fated to dualism, insofar as the order of signs never coincides with the order of things they name. The world is always other to consciousness, so alterity is in human nature. It is not only that a tree is never the same as the sign *tree*, but also that I am never any of the signs that name me, least of all the pronominal signs such as *I*. Nonlinguists ignore the fact that the world does not correspond to the system of language. But we all must confront the reality that *I* somehow does not correspond to *me*. In acting as if we were unitary identities, we create fictions of sameness, much as language operates with fictions of correspondence. This shared duality between consciousness and self, on the one hand, and language and the world, on the other, gives meaning to Peirce's formulation "Man is a sign."

In dealing with these dualities, Bakhtin emphasizes not so much the gaping dichotomies at the center of human existence as the strategies by which they might be bridged. This emphasis finds expression in Bakhtin's term for the condition of the world as it presents itself to consciousness, "addressivity," which implies that our relation to the world is essentially communicative. Thus, the nature of human beings is dialogic. The structuring force that organizes communicative relations—whether between self and self, self and other, different selves, or self and the world—is what Bakhtin calls "architectonics," the activity of forming connections between disparate materials.

It is difficult in the West to see the connection between Bakhtin's Christology and the major, apparently nonreligious concerns of his thought. This difficulty stems in part from Bakhtin's immersion in the Russian kenotic tradition, which emphasizes the degree to which Christ is a God who became a man, unlike most Western traditions. Bakhtin's theology is also grounded in a Christian tradition that honors the present, the human, the richness and complexity of everyday life. This tradition cannot comprehend a Pauline contempt for the here and now, a revulsion for the body. In fact, both of these factors—the immediacy of historical existence and the regard for matter—have long had a grip on the Russian religious imagination. As Nicholas Zernov observed, "The fundamental conviction of the Russian religious mind is the recognition of the potential holiness of matter."[11]

This concern for the materiality of things appears in Russian Orthodoxy's obsession with the corporeality of Christ, the emptying out of spirit when the Word took on flesh during the life of Jesus. From Saint Theodosius to Dostoevsky, the Russians have venerated Christ not as a pantocrator but as a man, and this tradition continued into the twentieth century in the Russian fascination with a God-manhood that cuts across all political boundaries. The canonization of the first two Russian national saints, Boris and Gleb, came about not because they had been martyrs for their faith. These two young brothers had in fact been murdered for cold-bloodedly political reasons, to ensure another brother's inheritance of their father's throne. However, when warned of their impending murder, the two brothers refused to avoid death. As Boris said in his last words: "Glory to Thee [O, God] . . . For Thy sake I am murdered the whole day, they treated me like a lamb for the eating. Thou knowest, my Lord, that I do not resist, I do not object." This humility, this following of Christ's example, is what served as grounds for the canonization of Boris and Gleb. According to George Fedotov, this peculiar class of saints, who greatly mystified the Byzantine clergy who had just converted the Russian nation, "did what was not required of them by the Church ... but they did what Christ expected of them and in the words of the Chronicle 'took away ignominy from the sons of Russia.' Through the lives of the holy sufferers ... the image of the meek and suffering Saviour entered the heart of the Russian nation as the most holy of its spiritual treasures."[12]

Saint Theodosius, too, established a central role for kenotic Christology. Although he founded the greatest monastery in ancient Russia, he was supremely disobedient throughout his life. As Fedotov explained, Theodosius did not conceive of love as the last and most difficult degree of perfection, like most Greek ascetic thinkers, but thought of it rather as "a simple, immediate and self-evident implication of Christ's love of man. Love of one's fellow man does not need to justify itself as if it were robbing something from the love of God. Indeed, Theodosius seems to ignore *eros* in the sense of God as celestial Beauty. *Agape* remained for him the only type of Christian love. That is why there is nothing mystical about him ... in this respect ... Theodosius is the spokesman of ancient Russia. Mysticism is a rare flower on Russian soil ... The terms in which he speaks ... of his love for Christ are quite remarkable: the Eucharistic bread and the land of Palestine speak to him not only of Christ, but especially of Christ's flesh. Theodosius' religion is not a kind of spiritualism, neither is Russian religion in general. The distance between the two worlds is not the gulf between flesh and spirit—as in Platonic mysticism—but between the fallen and the transfigured ... flesh."[13]

Two concepts that are bound up with the kenotic tradition had a powerful effect on Bakhtin's thought. The first of these is a radical communality (*sobornost'*); the second is a profound respect for the material realities of everyday experience. Emphasis on the humanity of Christ caused Russians to value community. In Anthony Ugolnik's words, "Christ is not our 'personal,' but our common saviour." Christ gave up the privileges of divinity, his uniqueness, to share the general condition of humanity, a model establishing the priority of shared as opposed to individual values. In Bakhtin's thought this concept is translated out of the discourse of theology into the more widely appropriable discourses of linguistics and social theory. He interprets the ancient Russian concern for community not only in terms of Christian love and charity but also as a kind of epistemological mandate: "To be means to communicate dialogically. When the dialogue ends, everything ends." Christ is important not only as an event in the cosmic history of human salvation from sin but also as an event in the development of human consciousness. This consciousness is the consciousness of the self's relation to the other. In *The Architectonics* Bakhtin traces different stages of self/other relations in antiquity as culminating in "the Christ of the Gospel. In Christ we find a synthesis—unique in its profundity . . . for the first time there appears an infinitely deepened I-for-myself, yet not a cold I-for-myself, but one which is boundlessly good toward the other."[14]

Christ is important for revealing for the first time the basis of all human consciousness and thus for supplying the key to understanding all things human. Politics, art, science—all are aspects of the self/other mechanism by which humans exist as conscious beings. God is a way to conceive the workings of alterity in everyday life, for "What I must be for the other [person], God is for me [for my I-for-myself]."[15]

The bond that holds the community together is conceived by Bakhtin to be language. And just as he appropriates communality for an innovative cognitive sociology, so he reconceives the kenotic tradition as the basis for an innovative translinguistics. In Christ the word was made flesh, and a primary feature of Bakhtin's concept of language is his emphasis on the materiality of the word: "Consciousness can arise and become a viable fact only in the material embodiment of signs." Meaning is not completely coincidental with the sign, but it is not possible without it. Bakhtin's understanding of the sign parallels a strain of Orthodox thought going back to the beginnings of patristic thought. As Anthony Ugolnik explained the connection: "Viewed in a dialogic light, the question of the trinity becomes a dynamic one. In the Word Become Flesh, we perceive the carnate, material grounding of the utterance. In discourse, Bakhtin notes, 'The Word is a two-sided act. It is determined equally by whose word it is and for whom it is meant.' Discourse is a communal engagement, and God Himself has engaged us. He has oriented His Word, incarnate and material, to us . . . It is God's relation to creation, after all, that allows Theophilus (of Antioch) to project the 'triad of God.' The Father orients His Word, His Son, to us."[16]

Bakhtin expresses this emphasis on materiality not only by

formulating a philosophy of language but by celebrating the body in ways that may seem difficult to associate with religiosity. The body for Bakhtin, even its "lower strata," which is his comprehensive term for the organs of sex and defecation, is tied up in the most immediate way with the self/other dichotomy. In *The Architectonics* he charts the difference that Christ's appearance in history wrought in perceptions of precisely the body. For instance, in the history of Christianity "we can trace two opposing orientations. In the one, Neo-Platonic tendencies are foregrounded and the other is conceived as being first and foremost the I-for-myself, for flesh in itself is an evil in both me and in the other. In a second orientation, both value relations are given their due and perceived as distinct, i.e., both one's relation to oneself and one's relation to the other," which is apparent in the way one prizes one's own and the other's flesh. The first tendency, which Bakhtin does not find sympathetic, stands opposed to the tradition in which he sees himself as working, one that is Russian and kenotic but is also associated with the commentaries of Bernard of Clairvaux on the Song of Songs and with Francis of Assisi, Giotto, and Dante. This is the tradition that says, "The body shall rise from the dead not for its own sake, but for the sake of those who love us, who knew and loved the countenance [the flesh] that was ours and ours alone."[17] Here, at the very outset of his career, Bakhtin is modeling the opposition between ideologies as an opposition between attitudes toward the body.

This fascination with the dialogical relationship between spirit and corporeality has taken different forms in Russian history, some of them extreme. The sect of the Khlysty, for example, a Slavic version of Tantrism, engaged in sexual orgies, which were highlighted in the central role played by Rasputin at the court of the last Romanov. The Symbolists, an early influence on Bakhtin, were also fascinated by the paradox of Christ's physicality, "the mystery of the flesh," as Merezhkovsky called it.[18] Bakhtin stresses the need for persons to take responsibility for their unique place in existence through the care that they exhibit in deeds for others and the world. The word *deed* is understood as meaning "word" as well as "act": *postupok* (deed) is how meaning is realized, how the word becomes flesh.

Authoring is the particular deed whereby Bakhtin shows the various ways in which meaning can take on flesh. That which in his epistemology is modeled as the I/other distinction becomes in his aesthetics the distinction between the author, who occupies a position analogous to the self, and the hero, who occupies a position analogous to the other. This movement is rehearsed each time the text is read, as the reader becomes the flesh of the author's meaning, a self transgredient to the text's otherness.

Such a movement renders the author invisible. Just as the self can never be completely imaged as a person like other persons, so the author can never be fully perceived as another person. The reason for the invisibility of the author is the same as that for the invisibility of the self: the author is not a single, fixed entity so much as a capacity, an energy. As such, the author-creator is no more coincident with the author-person than the self ever coincides with its projections.

What has importance is not who an author is but how, when, and where she is. The author-creator is not, first of all, the author when she is not creating. There was Tolstoy, the biological entity who was born in 1828 and died in 1910, who ate kasha for breakfast, raised horses, bought and sold property, and discussed his children's upbringing with his wife. "Author" was the description that the government and the man himself provided of his profession, much as a farmer might describe himself, even when he is not farming, as a farmer. Between that person and the being who participated in the process of creating *War and Peace* there is some kind of connection. As Bakhtin says, "The artist's struggle to achieve a well-defined and fixed image of his hero is, to a large degree, his struggle with himself."[19] But the connection is of a kind that the reader can no more than the artist directly perceive as a process, which is the ongoing act of creation during the period when the work actually is being produced. Readers may, as the author-person may, speculate about the historical causes, social conditions, and psychological reactions that went into the process. But in a systematic aesthetics readers cannot know these factors directly, least of all those pertaining to the author-person's psychology. Readers can know the author-creator in only one way, not as an open, unfinished process, as they know the self, but rather as a completed result, although coming to know the result is a process in its own right.

In the case of an author's own account of how he created a work or, as so often in Russian literature, an author's confession, the author-person is no longer being the author-creator. After he has stepped out of the process, he is in much the same position as those who regard his finished work. He can see the process only in the result it has given. Bakhtin explains: "The total reaction [of the author] creating the whole of the [work] manifests itself actively, but [such a total reaction] is not experienced as a reaction to anything specific. Its specificity is to be found precisely in the product it creates . . . the author serves as a reflector for the emotional and volitional position of the hero, but the author does not reflect his own position vis-à-vis the hero. He manifests this latter position; it is objectified, but does not itself become an object for scrutiny . . . The author creates but sees his creation only in the object which he forms, i.e., he sees only the product of creation as it comes into being, but not its inner, psychologically determined process."[20]

That is, the pure activity of authorship during the act of authoring is similar to the pure activity of self during any conscious moment, since it is the self that is the whole governing all the partial images we manifest of ourselves. Although the self is experienced, "the experience does not hear and does not see itself, but only the created product toward which it is directed."[21] As a result, not only do the characters take on a life of their own after completion of the work containing them, but so does the author-creator who gave them shape and direction. She separates from the author-person to become the secret legislator of the text that her energy has brought into existence.

In short, the author who determines the text is not a person. At the same time, he is not one of the characters, even when the text contains a figure who acts as, or is nominated as, "the author," such as a first person narrator. The mode of being of the author-creator in the completed text is different from that of a person, and it is different from that of the characters. Such an author is in a different place from a person who is not creating, because people are always, as people, outside the text. As Bakhtin stresses, art is other: "art is not life." The author-creator is in the text, but he is on a different plane from the characters who are in the text. Not only is the author of *War and Peace* not Pierre Bezukhov, and the author of *Notes from the Underground* not the first person narrator of that work, but even such an "omniscient author" as the one in *Madame Bovary* or such an interstitial narrator as the one in *The Ambassadors* does not constitute a presence whose figure is adequate to the wholeness of the author-creator's presence in the text. On a scale of visibility, Pierre and the underground man are easily seen, while the narrators of *Madame Bovary* and *The Ambassadors*, though harder to fix into an image, are nevertheless perceived in locutions and devices that are characteristic for them. These devices are more complex and diffuse than the leitmotiv of Helene's marble bosom in *War and Peace*, but they nevertheless conduce to a specific, limiting conception of the narrator that lets him ultimately be completed, be seen.

Bakhtin deals with the apparent contradiction in the author's being in the text but invisible by the same strategy that he deals with the apparent paradox of the self's inability to see itself. That invisibility is neither mysterious nor even metaphoric but rather structural, being a cognitive invisibility insofar as the whole of the self can never be fixed in any image of it, since it is in the nature of thought that such a figure will always be partial, incomplete. There will always be a noncorrespondence between the active self that makes signs and the signs of itself that it generates. The self/other distinction is at the heart of all cognition. *Alterity* is the name Bakhtin assigns to the logic that determines mind, in the sense that it grants the capability of imagining whole entities to some aspects of perception, namely to other selves that are not that mind, but it denies that capability to another aspect of perception, namely the self that is the mind.

The problem, once again, is to understand how the author may be in the text without being visible. A systemic analogue is needed to think through this paradox. One analogue is found in the complex operations of self-perception. A further analogy is found in the way subjectivity works in spoken speech, where the self is always present but never fully exhausted.

As Emile Benveniste pointed out, pronouns have a peculiar status among the nominal elements that constitute any language. Most nouns refer to something. The sign *tree*, for example, signifies a particular kind of natural growth. We may get very far from the apple tree in our backyard with such a sign, and a novel can be written called *The Tree of Man*. But even these uses of the sign contain some kind of reference to the sort of flora that *tree* nominates on less metaphoric occasions: "Each instance of use of a noun is referred to a fixed and 'objective' notion, capable of remaining potential or of being actualized in a particular object and always identified with the mental image it awakens. But instances of the use of *I* do not constitute a class of reference since there is no 'object' definable as *I* to which these instances can refer in identical fashion."[22]

That is, we can see the signified in such signifiers as *tree*. But what *I* refers to cannot be "seen." In fact, in order to perform its function as a shifter, indicating the "person who is uttering the present instance of the discourse containing 'I,' " the referent of *I* must logically be invisible, or it would not be capable of referring in a particular instance to "me." In order for my specific subjectivity to fill the structural slot of the first person pronoun, that pronoun must be cognitively empty, relative to the semantic plenitude of a word like *tree*, when it is not occupied by my self or the self of others. Stated in another way, *I* is a word that can mean nothing in general. The referent it names cannot be seen. But this invisibility is not mysterious; it is a systemic token of absence that is capable of being filled in any specific utterance. Only at the level of system can it not be seen; at the level of particular performance its meaning is always rendered visible. In other words, the pronoun *I* marks the axial point between the pre-existing, repeatable system of language and my unique, unrepeatable existence as a particular human being; "language is so organized that it permits each speaker *to appropriate* to himself an entire language by designating himself as 'I.' "[23]

This is what Bakhtin means in describing consciousness as being always on the border: it is on the border between the immediate reality of my own living particularity, a uniqueness that is only for me, and the purely abstract reality of the system that precedes me in existence and is intertwined with everyone else's ability to be a self in language. The instrument by which this dialogue takes place between the centrifugal forces of subjectivity, which are chaotic and particular, and the centripetal forces of system, which are rule driven and abstract, is the peculiar mode of being of the first person pronoun: "How could the same term refer indifferently to any individual whatsoever and still at the same time identify him in his individuality? We are in the presence of a class of words ... that escape the status of all other signs of language."[24] "I" is not simply the name of another part of speech but the very mechanism that permits a person to enter the world of signs; it is the portal between self and all that is not self.

This gate of the "I" is located at the center not only of one's own existence but of language as well. Language is not just metaphorically but systemically the "house of being," because in it the "I" is the benchmark to which all its spatial operations are referred and the Greenwich mean by which all its time distinctions are calibrated. "I" is the invisible ground of all language's other indices. "I" distinguishes this from that, here from there, now from then. The difference between all these markers is manifested as two different orders of proximity. The series this, here, and now lies close to the self, while the series that, there, and then lies farther from the self: "Language itself reveals the profound difference between these two planes."[25]

Not only does the first person pronoun structure differences between time (now/then) and space (here/there), but it also determines the fundamental I/you distinction. Consciousness of self is possible only if it is experienced by contrast. This is not merely a phenomenological speculation but a primary characteristic of language itself: "I use 'I' only when I am speaking to someone who will be you in my address . . . This polarity of persons is the fundamental condition of language, of which the process of communication in which we share is only a mere pragmatic consequence."[26]

The author-creator is thus to the text as the self is to consciousness. This means that the author-creator's residual presence in the text is that point, in absentia, from which the structure of all the text's space/time distinctions are calibrated *in praesentia*. Each character in the text, including the so-called omniscient author, is present as a distinct entity only by means of the series of pronominal axes it serves to motivate. Pierre Bezukhov is the sum of the placements that his subjectivity, his use of "I," marks off: when either he says "I" or the "author" says "he" for him, there is another point from which are controlled both Pierre's own "I" and the identity that the "author" ascribes to him in speaking of him in the third person. Pierre says "I did" or "I will," thereby giving the reader's consciousness the necessary temporal coordinates for fixing the difference between now and then within the other time governed by all the other characters' pronominally defined subjectivity. The same holds true for spatial distinctions within the text, where either one of the characters'

"I's" or one of the "author's" third person instances of the same character ("then Pierre . . .") marks the distinction between here and there: when the textual space is occupied by Pierre, readers know they are where he is, and if that is Moscow, no matter how readers evaluate the distinction, then Petersburg is *there*." The same holds true for all the characters. In other words, the author's mode of being extralocal to the text is similar to the way consciousness is always conscious of something. The "consciousness of" that defines the consciousness of the author-creator is the consciousness of the whole of which each other aspect of the text is only a part. Because the author is on a different plane of consciousness from all the other characters who can be "seen" in the text, he himself cannot be seen.

The mechanism here is parallel to that in effect when I "see" the whole of someone else from the vantage of my "surplus of seeing" an image whose completeness the other cannot have for himself. According to Bakhtin, when the mechanism of such a surplus is extended from operations of consciousness in lived experience to semantic operations in the world of the text, it becomes the bud in which sleeps the blossom of full-fledged aesthetic activity. I "live into" his consciousness; I see the world through his eyes. But the more successfully I do this, the more I fall prey to the limitations of the other's horizon. When I invest his unconsciousness as completely as I can, I am inside his horizon, and what he cannot see, I cannot see. The necessary second step is for me to return to my own consciousness, where I can now see not only from the inside, as he himself sees, but also from the outside, as I see him, thus not only as a subject, but as an object. It is in this return that my distinctively aesthetic activity begins. Because I live on the borders between my own subjectivity for myself and my status as object for others, I am able to cross this border and, in my imagination, see the other as subject and myself as object.

This movement governs self/other relations in lived experience. When the same procedures are applied to author-hero relations in the world of the text, certain modifications are needed in order to achieve a distinctively aesthetic result. A key difference between the dialogue of self and other in life and of author and others in the text is that in the latter case each word simultaneously signifies both the action of signifying another's identity as it is for her and the action of rendering the other complete, a deed possible only by someone who is not she. This is perhaps the deepest meaning of Bakhtin's claim that the word is always dual. The invisible glue that keeps each of these two aspects of every word in the text together is the cognitive bond of the author who is transgradient to all the text's features that are *in praesentia*.

Authorship is extendable to extraliterary categories because it is an architectonics of consciousness. Authorship is the primary activity of all selves in a world dominated by the self/other distinction. As such, it is the ground not only of these categories but of all the other dyads around which Bakhtin's work is organized. Self and other lie behind other characteristic dichotomies such as finalized/unfinalized, official/unofficial, monologic/dialogic, epic/novel, and inner/outer.

The centrality of the self/other distinction in all Bakhtin's work may obscure the originality of his thought, since many of his preoccupations are familiar through other thinkers who were working their way out of the same tradition of Cohen's Neo-Kantianism and Husserl's Phenomenology. Bakhtin's concept of responsibility has striking similarities to Heidegger's *Being and Time*, while Bakhtin's ideas about self/other and visual metaphors resemble Sartre's *Being and Nothingness*. Yet Bakhtin's *Architectonics* came first. Only the peculiarities of Soviet censorship and of Bakhtin himself kept it from being published until 1979. It had been written sixty years earlier, in 1919, eight years before the appearance of Heidegger's *Being and Time* and decades before Sartre's *Being and Nothingness* (1943). There could be no question of influence. The situation was rather one of a series of like responses to the same set of philosophical questions that were abroad in the early twentieth century.

CHAPTER 4

The Leningrad Circle
1924-1929

The five-year period from 1924 to 1929 was one of enormous activity for Bakhtin. During this brief interlude he completed four major books, on Freud, the Russian Formalists, the philosophy of language, and the Dostoevskian novel, in addition to a number of articles. At first glance, this burst of intellectual energy in the case of Bakhtin might appear to have been in neat congruence with the general frenzy on all fronts during this most seminal of decades in modern Russian history. But there was no such easy equivalence between the man and the age.[1] In fact, there was a dramatic incongruity between the shape of Bakhtin's career at this point and the characteristic outlines of the decade. This noncorrespondence included major differences not only between Bakhtin and "his age" or Bakhtin and "his peers" but also between Bakhtin and "his circle."

Most members of Bakhtin's circle were embroiled in the great intellectual debates of the age and in a daunting range of professional and cultural activities. The activities in which Bakhtin was engaged seem meager by contrast. The main record of his intellectual life during this period is found rather in his works. Yet because of the nature of the Bakhtin circle, the activities of his friends were in a sense his also; they were in his dialogic sphere.

Bakhtin returned to Leningrad in the spring of 1924.[2] Most of his friends had preceded him there. Yudina had returned to the conservatory in 1920; Pumpiansky and Sollertinsky had returned in 1921 to teach at the Tenishev school; Medvedev came back in 1922 to work at the State Publishing House; and Voloshinov returned around that time to reenroll at Petrograd University. Bakhtin never found a similar niche for himself in Leningrad. He had finally been able to return only because the increasing seriousness of his illness qualified him for a state pension, second class, so that he no longer had to work.

By the time of Bakhtin's return, Leningrad had recovered from the worst chaos and shortages of the Civil War. As early as 1921 the literary community was treating itself to tea and eclairs at the House of Arts.[3] The improvements in the lot of intellectuals were not only material but also professional, including greater opportunities for publication and dissemination of their work. A by-product of the New Economic Policy of 1921, permitting limited, small-scale capitalist enterprises, was the opening of private publishing houses. Until 1927 Soviets were also allowed to use Russian language publishing houses in Berlin. The end of the Civil War enabled the government to allocate more money, paper, and facilities to the arts.

An unfortunate consequence of these increased resources was an intensification of rivalries as the different schools competed to win a lion's share of the funds. Some groups, such as the self-styled "proletarian" bodies made up of party or working class members, even agitated for their right to hegemony in Soviet culture. As yet, however, they had not been shown special favor by those in the party responsible for culture. In literature, the only group that could be said to be in any favor at this time were the so-called "fellow travelers," those nonparty writers who were more or less sympathetic to the regime.

In the mad scramble for power, paper, and press, Bakhtin was far from the fray. He spent this most intense period in the history of Soviet theoretical debate largely at home in his private world. Yet at this very time all the subjects that he had been thinking about in Nevel and Vitebsk were being discussed with new urgency. In particular, his ideas about authorship were being tried in dialogue with two other theories of the text: the Formalist, on the one hand, and the Marxist, on the other. Bakhtin debated with representatives of both points of view not from the podium, as he had the Marxists in Nevel, but only in his writings, and then often obliquely.

The most logical place for Bakhtin to participate in the theoretical debates would have been the State Institute for the History of the Arts, particularly its Division for the History of the Language Arts, founded in 1920. This division was headed by V. M. Zhirmunsky, an associate of the Formalists, and was dominated by the Formalists, who made up most of its faculty. But its members were not narrowly partisan. The division thrived on challenge and believed in fostering debate. To this end, besides providing formal classes, it opened its doors to some of the best minds in the country who were not on the faculty. These outsiders were invited to give public lectures on any topic that interested them, no matter how unlikely. Meyerhold was one who lectured there. Work-in-progress seminars allowed faculty, students, and members of the public at large to debate one another. All of the major works written by faculty members in these years were debated in this way, which would have given Bakhtin an opportunity to confront the Formalists face to face. The division became what Shklovsky described as a sort of "Noah's ark," offering a platform to intellectuals who were disaffected or out of favor. For instance, Bakhtin's old mentor Zelinsky had been a professor there just before emigrating in 1921. And for a time the division organized literary readings by some of the most lively contemporary writers, such as Zamyatin and Ehrenburg.[4]

Bakhtin would have been expected to be attracted to the Institute for the History of Arts as a center of serious, independent-minded cultural and intellectual activity. Indeed, he notes in his Work Book that he lectured at the institute in 1926. Yet every eye-witness has categorically denied that Bakhtin was ever associated with the institute, either to lecture there himself or to attend any of its lectures or discussions open to the public. And the published reports of the institute include no record of his having lectured. This is surprising, since several members of his circle, including Medvedev, Sollertinsky, and Konrad, gave public lectures there.[5] Moreover, Sollertinsky was a student at the institute in the early 1920s and from 1926 to 1929 was simultaneously a graduate student and faculty member, while Pumpiansky's future wife, Isserlin, studied at the institute and was also related to Tynyanov, a prominent faculty member in the Division for the History of the Language Arts.

Until the late 1920s, Bakhtin was almost unknown in most Leningrad intellectual circles. He had no institutional affiliations, was obliged to publish under others' names, and was valued only by a small group of devoted friends and a few students. This experience contrasted sharply to his situation in both Nevel and Vitebsk, where he had worked for a variety of government institutions, given many public lectures, and participated in public debates. In Leningrad he not only did very little work for official bodies but also did very little public lecturing and no public debating, dramatic productions, or literary readings. Much of this difference must be ascribed to his poor health and limited mobility. Also, Leningrad was one of the nation's two cultural capitals, not just another provincial town like Nevel or Vitebsk, and Bakhtin simply did not have the contacts, publications, or name to make his mark in it, nor was he prepared to establish himself as an epigone of someone else who had. Moreover, for someone of his intellectual orientation it was getting harder to find work as the Revolution progressed.

In consequence, Bakhtin's life in Leningrad was one long battle to survive. His pension was very meager, and even that decreased gradually in the course of the annual reviews. In 1925 it was downgraded to third class, and in 1929 it was downgraded once more to fourth class. His wife made stuffed animals to help supplement their income. Bakhtin himself never knew where he might find work. It would suddenly turn up, but often paid only enough for his cigarettes. For example, he gave lectures to librarians on new works coming into their libraries, for which he had to read many trivial books, but he was grateful to be paid. His official Work Book also lists him as having performed certain other jobs, though these entries too may be fictitious, as in the case of his lecturing at the institute. He is listed as having served in 1927 on the staff of the literature section of the Leningrad State Publishing House, where Medvedev was then installed. Bakhtin reportedly did editorial work and wrote internal reviews. At the same time he is listed as working as a consultant at the Leningrad Industrial Bureau. The only other activity that Bakhtin cites in his Work Book for this period is "scholarly works on the history and theory of literature."

Bakhtin's other means of support was lecturing to unofficial groups which met in private apartments. Primarily, he lectured on aesthetics, philosophy, literature, and the history of culture. Sometimes he gave single lectures, and at other times entire courses. The two Mirkina sisters, who had taken private lessons from Bakhtin in Vitebsk but had since moved to Leningrad to study at the Institute for the History of the Arts, again took private lessons from him between 1925 and 1927. At the various private lectures a plate was usually put by the door, for offerings from the audience. People gave what they could, but the sort of people who attended were often themselves living in straitened circumstances. The Mirkina sisters volunteered as their contribution for each lecture the price of a trolley ticket to the farthest point in Leningrad. When they could, they paid double.

Thus, all Bakhtin's activities brought him very little income. Letters of 1924–1925 from Bakhtin's mother in Nevel to Nikolai in Paris express a constant refrain: "Help 'Misha' if you can. He is in desperate straits and makes only 15–25 roubles a month by lectures and lessons." At this time Bakhtin's father, who suffered from arteriosclerosis, was so unwell that he could not help financially.[6]

Bakhtin's quixotic attempts to make money from publications were often frustrated. As soon as he arrived in Leningrad, he began translating Lukacs's *Theory of the Novel*, but he gave up the project upon learning through a Hungarian acquaintance that Lukacs no longer liked the book. In 1924 an article by Bakhtin, "The Problem of Content," was actually accepted for publication in *The Russian Contemporary*, but that periodical was closed down by the government before the issue could appear, and the article was too long to be accepted elsewhere.[7]

In Leningrad Bakhtin was at first only able to afford to take rooms in friends' apartments. Initially he stayed in the apartment of the Rugeviches.[8] Then he moved to the nearby apartment of a new friend, Ivan Ivanovich Kanaev, whom he met through the Rugeviches.[9] The Bakhtins lived there from June 1924 until 1927, occupying a big room on an upper floor, but it was sparsely furnished with just two iron beds and a desk. One of Bakhtin's friends, Konstantin Vaginov, described this room in a 1926 poem: "Two motley blankets/Two shabby pillows/The beds stand side by side/But there are flowers in the window . . . Books on the narrow shelves/And on the blankets people/A pale, bluish man/And his girlish wife."[10] It was in this room that Bakhtin wrote his Dostoevsky book. Bakhtin was finally able to establish a separate residence when he began to receive royalties from publications. His last residence in Leningrad was a top-floor apartment, once again not far from where he had lived before.[11] Yet the illness was taking its toll, and life in top-floor rooms could not have helped someone with his bad legs. He had a tendency to spend the entire day in his armchair, where he read, thought, wrote, and received callers.

This was Bakhtin's most productive period in terms of publications, probably because he did not have any outside job. He also had his own sources of intellectual stimulation and better access to the books he needed than in Nevel and Vitebsk. Although he did not take much part in public intellectual life, the role he played in his private circle was even greater than before. The old group continued to meet, and Bakhtin emerged more and more as its leader. The Leningrad version of the Nevel school had at its core most of the oldtimers from Nevel and Vitebsk. Pumpiansky, Sollertinsky, Voloshinov, Medvedev, and Yudina were regular members. Kagan, who after the closing of the university in Orel had moved to Moscow and become a corresponding member at the State Academy of the Arts in the areas of philosophy and the philosophy of history, was able to visit only rarely. Zubakin too had moved to Moscow, where he became a professor at the Moscow Archaeological Institute, specializing in the history of primitive cults and art and the survival of superstitions, but he was occasionally able to attend.

In Leningrad the group acquired a number of new members who extended its range of intellectual and professional interests.

38 Preobrazhenskaya Street, Leningrad, where the Bakhtins lived with Kanaev in apartment no. 5, 1924–1927

Some of these attended only occasionally; others regularly. One of the occasional attenders was Nikolai Iusifovich Konrad (1892–1970), an expert on Chinese, Japanese, and Korean cultures. Konrad, who had been responsible for getting Kagan a position at the university of Orel, worked during the 1920s at both Moscow and Leningrad Universities and at the Asian Museum in Leningrad, the center for Eastern studies in the Academy of Sciences. One of his interests, as with many specialists on the East at this time, was the comparison of Eastern and Western cultures.[12] Another occasional attender, Vaginov (1899–1934), was the group's only recognized writer, although other members, such as Voloshinov and Pumpiansky, wrote poetry. Vaginov, who was primarily a poet, started in the late 1920s to write a series of experimental novels that were effectively *romans à clef* about Leningrad intellectual life.

Two other occasional attenders were closer in their intellectual profiles to Bakhtin's own sphere of interests. In particular, they were interested in contemporary German philosophy. One of these was A. A. Frankovsky (1888–1942), a philosopher and translator who was a neighbor of the Bakhtins when they lived with the Rugeviches. Frankovsky translated many books, including Spengler's *Decline of the West* (1923), which was much discussed among the Leningrad intelligentsia of the time, Wölfflin's *Basic Concepts in the History of the Arts* (1928), and works by Swift, Sterne, and Proust. The other occasional visitor, B. M. Engelhardt (1887–1942), had studied philosophy in 1909–1911 at Heidelberg and Freiburg before continuing its study at Petersburg University. His main interest in the 1920s was the philosophical basis for methodologies in literary theory, and he published a book on Veselovsky in 1924 and another book, *The Formal Method in the History of Literature*, in 1927, which Bakhtin later criticized in his own book on the Formalists.

Among the more regular new participants in the circle was Boris Vladimirovich Zalessky, who had the unexpected occupation of petroleum geologist. Although Zalessky was very quiet at the group's meetings, he rendered its members great services in later years when, after moving to Moscow, he worked in the Institute for Petrography, Geology, Mineralogy, and Geochemistry of the Academy of Sciences and thus became relatively affluent. Over the years he lent Yudina and Bakhtin money. Yudina ended up owing him 8,000 rubles, which she had borrowed for others and could never repay.

The most important new member of the group for Bakhtin was Kanaev, who was also in the natural sciences. Born in 1893, Kanaev was a biologist who later concentrated on the history of comparative biology. Kanaev was instrumental in interesting Bakhtin in questions of biology, especially those concerning the relationship of mind to matter and body to spirit. This interest led Bakhtin to write the review article "Contemporary Vitalism," which appeared in 1926 in the popular scientific journal *Man and Nature (Čelovek i priroda)* under Kanaev's name, the first of Bakhtin's articles to be published under a friend's name.[13] Vitalism maintains that there exists in the organism of plants and animals some special extramaterial force which controls the basic processes of life. In 1925 Kanaev took Bakhtin to a lecture by the physiologist Ukhtomsky on the perceptions of intervals of time and space, or chronotopes, by human cortical dominants, which would influence Bakhtin's later work on the theory of the novel.

The most important new member of the group in terms of playing a major role in its discussions was Mikhail Izrailevich Tubyansky, an expert on Tibet, Buddhism, ancient Indian and Bengali literature, and Indian and Mongolian languages. He was the first to translate Tagore, a popular writer at the time, into Russian. His main scholarly work of the 1920s was on a Buddhist treatise on logic. He taught in the Asian Museum of the Academy of Sciences and at Leningrad University. Tubyansky's interest in Eastern philosophy and religions was a common interest of the Leningrad intelligentsia at the time, including the Bakhtin circle. Pumpiansky made a serious study of Buddhism and Islam. Tubyansky himself was a founding member of the Institute for Buddhist Culture, which during the late 1920s became an island of broad-ranging intellectual inquiry. The Institute for Eastern Studies, which included the Asian Museum, was known for the religious leanings of its faculty, a high percentage of whom were later purged. The Leningrad orientalists by no means confined their interest to Eastern philosophy but studied Western as well, especially Bergson, an interest that the Bakhtin circle shared.[14] Tubyansky was a particularly contentious member of the circle and a consistent opponent of Bakhtin. He represented an even more abstract philosophical position than any other member of the group, and his idealism at times approached mysticism.

At the Rugevich dacha in Peterhof, 1924–1925.
From left: Bakhtin, Rugevich's sister, Rugevich,
Elena Aleksandrovna, and Anna Sergeevna Rugevich.

The Bakhtin circle was not in any sense a fixed organization. They were simply a group of friends who loved to meet and debate ideas and who had philosophical interests in common. Sometimes they all met together, but at other times just two or three of them met to discuss a particular work. Usually one of the group prepared a short synopsis or review of a philosophical work and read this to the circle as a basis for discussion. The range of topics covered was wide, including Proust, Bergson, Freud, and above all questions of theology.[15] Occasionally one member gave a lecture series to the others. The most famous of these was a course of eight lectures on Kant's *Critique of Judgment* given by Bakhtin in early 1925 to a group that included Yudina, Kanaev, Medvedev, Voloshinov and his wife, Vaginov and his wife, and Pumpiansky. Essentially the group divided into two categories of members, disciples of Bakhtin and his interlocutors. Yudina, Kanaev, Medvedev, Voloshinov, Zalessky, Vaginov, and their wives were generally disciples, while Tubyansky, Sollertinsky, Pumpiansky, and Kagan were for the most part interlocutors.

Despite the group's acquisition of new members in Leningrad, the tone of its meetings and the ethos of its members were established by the oldtimers. In Leningrad, as in Nevel and Vitebsk, members were high-spirited, energetic, ambitious, and eccentric. They also held the ideal of service to their society. Individual members proselytized for the ideas and values in which they believed and, with the exception of Bakhtin, looked for work where they might serve society. Most of those who found such work proselytized so single-mindedly that their careers came to represent a paradox in Soviet life, that of the nonconforming conformist, the eccentric person of nonreceived views who nevertheless survives, finds a place within Soviet intellectual institutions, and even makes an impact on Soviet intellectual life.

One striking example of the nonconforming conformist was Sollertinsky, the most versatile member of the group. A polyglot, he knew twenty-five languages, or thirty-two including dialects. He reportedly wrote his diary in ancient Portuguese to keep its contents from prying eyes. He had a prodigious memory and could recite an entire page of Sanskrit from memory after glancing at it only once. No mere bookworm, he was jovial and high spirited. He loved to ride the roller coaster in the Leningrad Fun Park, and he especially loved all forms of word play. At the same time, Sollertinsky did not suffer fools gladly and used his ready wit unsparingly. He was often unkempt in appearance. His artistic tastes and intellectual beliefs were largely outside the official canon. All these traits were not destined to make him the darling of the increasingly conformist intellectual establishment. And yet Sollertinsky was able to carve out for himself a successful and productive Soviet career.

Sollertinsky first went through a series of metamorphoses in terms of his intellectual interests and professional occupations. While still in Vitebsk he considered himself a philosopher, but he converted to philology, specializing in Spanish literature, at Petrograd University, from which he graduated in 1924. He simultaneously studied theater at the Institute for the History of the Arts, where he earned a graduate degree in 1929. During these years he also taught a curious range of subjects, from Middle Eastern history at the Tenishev Gymnasium to theater, Freudian psychology, and Japanese art at the Institute for the History of the Arts. Sollertinsky's primary interest gradually changed from theater to musical theater, ballet, opera, and finally to music itself. In 1927 he started a regular career in the arts by joining the Leningrad Philharmonic, first as a lecturer, than as head of its repertoire section, later as chief of publications, and ultimately as artistic director. He progressively acquired other posts which he held concurrently with his position at the Philharmonic, such as professor at the conservatory, lecturer at the Choreographic School and the Theatrical Institute, and head of the Musicology Section of the Composers' Union, the Section on Musical Theater at the State Institute of Theater and Music, and the Repertoire Section of the Kirov Theater of Opera and Ballet. Over his lifetime he produced around three hundred publications, most of them articles and reviews, and gave over two hundred and fifty lectures to introduce concerts of the Philharmonic. Sollertinsky's taste for modernist and Western music got him into difficulty in 1936, partly for his support of his close friend Dmitri Shostakovich's opera *Lady Macbeth,* and he had to recant on that issue, but he retained his positions, and thanks to him the opera and ballet were more exciting and imaginative in Leningrad during the 1930s than in Moscow.[16] His career was uninterrupted right up to his death from a heart attack in 1944. In short, Sollertinsky's career is remarkable when looked at in the context of a society that is often described as homogeneous. Even a Leonard Bernstein of America's "pluralist" society might envy the range of subjects on which Sollertinsky was permitted to pronounce and decide policy.

Another striking example in Bakhtin's group of a nonconformist who enjoyed a successful Soviet career was the pianist Maria Yudina. Yudina, who was more flamboyantly eccentric than Sollertinsky, as well as more outspoken and dissident, was also the more famous of the two. In 1921 Yudina graduated from the Petrograd Conservatory, sharing the gold medal with Sofronitsky, the noted interpreter of Scriabin. Shostakovich was another classmate. Yudina immediately joined the faculty of the conservatory, where in 1923 she was appointed professor. During this time she began to establish an outstanding concert career.

Yudina's intellectual interests ranged far beyond music. In the early 1920s she studied classics at Petrograd University. She was interested in avant-garde art and architecture, such as the work of Le Corbusier, and she was close to such artists as Favorsky, Glebova, Poret, Malevich, Filonov, Tatlin, Matiushin, and Sterligova. She also knew every important literary figure in Leningrad. Among her favorites were the avant-garde writers, such as the Oberiu or the Russian absurdists.[17]

Yudina was committed to the cause of the intelligentsia in its specific Russian meaning of concerned truth-seekers who flout conventional political constraints and bourgeois complacency in their effort to lead an honest, examined life and to promote just causes. She was particularly drawn to writers who were out of official favor. When the Mandelshtams were living in exile in Voronezh in the 1930s, Yudina contrived to give concerts there so that she could be one of their few visitors. She had a long association with Pasternak, who read his latest works to small gatherings of friends at which Yudina played the piano. When Pasternak's poetry was banned in the 1930s, Yudina sandwiched in a reading of it between Bach and Beethoven in one of her concerts, for which she was temporarily banned from performing in Leningrad.[18]

Yudina seemed fearless in the face of political pressures against her convictions. As a musician, she was best known as an interpreter of Bach, but beginning in the late 1920s, precisely when contemporary avant-garde music, especially from western Europe, was out of favor and thus difficult to schedule, she became its champion. She played pieces by Shostakovich, Křenek, Hindemith, and Bartok, even though the halls were half empty. Stravinsky became her idol, and later Stockhausen. In her zeal to spread the light, Yudina gave lectures before most of her concerts, and if an audience did not respond correctly to a particular piece, she often chided them and played the piece over again so that they might respond better. Her missionary activities were not confined to music. For instance, she introduced many poets to the work of the trans-sense poet Khlebnikov, and she urged everyone to read Lev Vygotsky's *The Psychology of Art* at a time when it was not well known.

One of Yudina's major contributions to intellectual life was as the host to unofficial lectures and readings. Her apartment in the 1920s was centrally located, right on the Neva River near the Winter Palace and across from the Peter and Paul Fortress.[19] Her rooms were sparsely furnished, more from antimaterialist conviction than from need, as in Bakhtin's case, except that their walls were hung with huge talismans. One huge room became the scene for her literary evenings. Many writers read their work there, including the peasant poet Kliuev, who had to rely on such private venues after 1924 when his long poem "Lenin" got him into political trouble.[20]

Yudina also organized philosophical evenings in her apartment. At one such evening Bakhtin lectured on Vyacheslav Ivanov. He stood before the audience in a huge, hooded cape, worn not so much for achieving dramatic effect as for hiding his threadbare suit. The large audience found his lecture, according to Mirkina, "strenuous but exhilarating." At the end someone said: "What a lecture. He has outlined all of culture." There was no discussion because everyone was so stunned.[21]

In addition to helping disseminate ideas that no longer had a public forum, Yudina assisted intellectuals in distress. She used all her contacts to help those who had been arrested or could no longer get published. She collected or borrowed money to support intellectuals out of favor. Rumor has it she even used to beg outside churches and then ride off in a taxi.

Yudina's courage was legendary. According to one story, when Stalin heard Yudina playing Mozart's Piano Concerto no. 23 over the radio, he liked it so much that he telephoned the station and asked them to send over the record. This caused great consternation, because the performance had been a live one and there was no record. It was decided to make him one on the spot. Yudina and an orchestra were summoned to the studios. The conductor was so nervous that he had to be replaced, but his replacement was no better, and only with a third conductor did they manage to make a record. Yudina was unruffled throughout. Stalin was so pleased with the record that he sent her a large sum of money. In her thank you note, she told Stalin that she had given the money to her church and then declared, "I will pray for you day and night and ask the Lord to forgive you your great sins before the people and the country." Everyone expected Yudina to be arrested forthwith, but Stalin, who perhaps had a weak spot for people of the church as a holdover from his seminary days, did not react. Her recording of the Mozart was reportedly found on the turntable in Stalin's dacha when he died.[22] This story, which may well be apocryphal, nevertheless illustrates the place that Yudina occupied in the imagination of the intelligentsia of her day.

Yudina did not go through the Stalin era completely without trouble. In 1930 she was fired from the Petrograd Conservatory, the official grounds for her dismissal being that she had absented herself without permission to attend a concert in Kiev. But she was able to get a job at the Tiflis Conservatory in 1932 and in Moscow in 1936, and she was not repressed further.[23] Moreover, her dismissal in 1930 seems to have been largely because of her openly espoused religious beliefs and not because of her other views.

Yudina's ostentatious religiosity indeed offended many people. Shostakovich derided her as a "religious hysteric." Her disregard for the conventions of dress also offended many. At one concert in the 1920s she forgot to change out of the big fur slippers that she usually wore around the house. The box office attendant lent her some shoes for the concert, but they were so uncomfortable that Yudina slipped them off under the piano. The audience was shocked to see her pedal in bare feet. In the 1930s, after she had been dismissed from the conservatory, she began to dress more conventionally. But she still wore an old raincoat of her father's, a beret, and tennis shoes, and she was so absent-minded that she invariably left some item of clothing behind after visits.[24]

This unconcern for external appearance was one of the many traits that Bakhtin and Yudina had in common. Another common characteristic was a love of music. In the 1920s Yudina often played for Bakhtin for hours on end. But there were major differences between the two in both ideas and temperament. Yudina was a doer, while Bakhtin was a thinker. She was a bundle of energy, rushing around town to see people and proselytize for her adopted intellectual causes, while Bakhtin preferred staying at home in his armchair to read, write, and think. Yudina was headstrong, quick to express her opinions, and intransigent. Whenever people made political compromises in their scholarly work, she castigated them with vehemence. Bakhtin was more subtle and flexible both in his thought and in his approach to others. For instance, he was a sincere Christian but could happily analyze the Orthodox Easter as yet another folk ritual.

For all Bakhtin's apparent passivity and accommodation, he was in his way no less fervent a proselytizer for the life of the mind and for free inquiry than was Yudina. But he did so in his writings, and even then obliquely. Most members of the Bakhtin circle were extremely active, and some, such as Medvedev and Sollertinsky, published prolifically, yet not one of them other than Bakhtin realized the promise of his brilliance in a major work that is read

Bakhtin, c.1924–1925

widely today. Perhaps as a result of their zeal, other group members were more successful than Bakhtin in making a Soviet career, although for many this career ended in their repression. But Bakhtin's writings remain to carry the ideals of his circle beyond its time and place.

Pumpiansky was, with the exception of Bakhtin himself, the only member of the group who was unsuccessful in pursuing his career in the 1920s. He began by teaching in the Tenishev School but after 1923 had no regular employment. Like Bakhtin, he was obliged by his straitened circumstances to live in the apartments of friends. For a time he lived with Medvedev. He earned an income largely by giving lectures to librarians about their new acquisitions or to private groups.

Pumpiansky's lack of regular employment did not concern him unduly, for it freed him to pursue the life of the mind. This insouciance was typical of Bakhtin and his friends. It perhaps explains why some of them were able to enjoy successful careers and yet remain relatively uncompromised. When Pumpiansky worked, he led a monklike existence. During hard times he frequently had nothing to eat, but his remedy was to sit and write for hours on end. He often wrote an entire article in one day. Unfortunately, little of his output has been published. His main publication of the period, *Dostoevsky and Antiquity* (1922), was subsidized by a disciple. Otherwise he was mainly able to publish only introductions to collected works of Russian writers.[25]

Pumpiansky's scholarship ranged over the areas of humanities, philosophy, and political thought, but his main interest was poetics and literary history. He was widely read in the classics, and one of his pet themes was to find classical antecedents for the poetry of Russian writers. He believed that the "Russian classical literary tradition," which comprised Lomonosov, Derzhavin, and Pushkin, formed a paradigm for Russian historical consciousness in general. He was the first to apply the term *Baroque* to Russian literature as a style and as a period. Yet he also kept up with the latest literary developments in French, German, English, and American literature. He wrote on Romain Rolland, started a book on James Joyce, and completed one on American literature. When the latter manuscript was sent back by the publishers for corrections, Pumpiansky just shrugged the matter off and didn't pursue it further. This was typical of Bakhtin's friends, who generally set little store by publication.

Two other old members of the Bakhtin circle, Medvedev and Voloshinov, had conventional Soviet careers in the 1920s. Voloshinov graduated from the Philological Faculty of Leningrad University in 1927 and went on to graduate work under V. A. Desnitsky and N. Yakovlev in a group working on literary methodology at the Institute for the Comparative History of Literatures and Languages of the West and East. This institute represented a "new Marxist approach" to linguistic study which challenged such undesirable approaches as the Formalist. The topic of Voloshinov's dissertation was probably "the problem of how to present reported speech" (*problema peredači čužoj reči*), which was cited as the topic of his research in an article on the institute published in 1928 in *Literature and Marxism (Literatura i marksizm)*.[26] Voloshinov lectured on the history of music at various institutions of popular enlightenment. He also published articles, book reviews on musical subjects, and derivative Symbolist poems in the journal *Notes of the Traveling Mass Theater of Gaideburov and Skarskaya* (*Zapiski peredvižnogo obščedostupnogo teatra Gajdeburova i Skarskoj*) until its closing in 1924. Afterward Voloshinov's output dropped off, though he was able to publish some book reviews in the Leningrad literary journal *The Star* (*Zvezda*). Several major articles and books on Freud, linguistics, and literary theory published in the 1920s under Voloshinov's name were probably written largely by Bakhtin.

Medvedev, by contrast, published the most actively of the group. He had always been a Soviet establishment figure, and in Leningrad he expanded his career as a cultural bureaucrat. Medvedev worked first in the Museum for Extramural Education and in the literary and artistic section of the State Publishing House. In 1927 he became a docent at the Herzen Pedagogical Institute, where he gave courses on twentieth century and Soviet literature. He also did research at the Leningrad Institute for Russian Literature of the Pushkin House, conducted a graduate seminar at the State Academy for Fine Arts, and lectured on Russian literature at the Tolmachev Military Academy. He did a good deal of public speaking, such as giving lectures before mass audiences of the Soviet army and fleet.[27] Like Bakhtin, he was able both to lecture brilliantly to academic audiences, earning himself a devoted student following, and to captivate the imagination of relatively uneducated audiences.

Medvedev published little that was imaginative or creative. His scholarly activity consisted largely of editing and recording biographical materials and writing introductions to contemporary writers' works. His main work of the 1920s was editing the notebooks and diaries of Blok. Like Bakhtin, Medvedev was interested in theories of authorship, which resulted in his book *In the Writer's Laboratory* (*V laboratorii pisatelja*, 1933). In this decade he also published under his own name a book polemicizing with the Formalists which was probably written by Bakhtin.[28]

Of all the regular members of the group, Medvedev was the only one who was really involved in contemporary literature. Over the years he became close to major Leningrad writers, such as Aleksey Tolstoy. Medvedev played an organizational role in a series of Leningrad writers' societies and ultimately in the Writers' Union itself. In particular, he was a member of a small Leningrad writers' organization known as The Fellowship (*Sodružestvo*), founded in 1923. Although The Fellowship comprised only about a dozen writers, it included both distinctly Soviet writers, such as Boris Lavrenev, who wrote the Soviet classic *The Forty-First*, and writers who were closer to pre-Revolutionary movements, such as Vsevolod Rozhdestvensky. Its philosophy held that all the members must help each other improve their writing in a spirit of comradely fellowship, without regard for their ideological differences. Medvedev became quite powerful within Leningrad literary life, rising to head of the literary section in the Leningrad branch of the State Publishing House by the end of the decade.[29]

Medvedev was active as a literary journalist. From the 1920s he was a frequent contributor to *The Star* and to *Literature and Marxism*. In the main he wrote book reviews that were in the Belinsky school of hack and slash. One review opens, "What a muddle-headed book!" Another review laments, "The mountain gave birth to a mouse."[30] Unlike Bakhtin, Medvedev was quick to turn out a publication, and his book reviews appeared very shortly after the book in question.

Medvedev has been described as a "businessman of literature," an "operator," and a "functionary," who essentially used materials to further his career prospects. Indeed in many superficial respects he conformed to the careerist type usually found in Soviet fiction. For instance, he was always stylishly dressed, in sharp contrast to the others in the circle, and he was known as a ladies' man. By the end of the 1920s Medvedev emerged as a sort of Soviet organization man of intellectual life, and Voloshinov too seemed to be leaning in that direction.

But actually neither Medvedev nor Voloshinov was a party member. Moreover, the theatrical journal *Notes of the Traveling Mass Theater of Gaideburov and Skarskaya*, which Medvedev edited from 1922 to 1924, conveyed a very different picture from the Marxist outlook. This journal was the mouthpiece of an experimental theater founded in 1903 which stood for two ideals common to the circles in which Bakhtin and his friends moved. One ideal was to bring theater to the lower classes and provincials who would not otherwise see it. This intent coincided with official policy in the early post-Revolutionary years, and the theater played a major role in the cultural life of the Bolshevik regime. But the other ideal was to explore questions of religion and religious experience. Perhaps the most popular play in the theater's repertoire was the Norwegian Bjørnstjerne Bjørnson's *Over Aevne* (*Svyše našix sil*, 1883), which concerns a clergyman who is capable of working miracles but cannot respond to his wife's love.[31]

Medvedev was more to the Traveling Mass Theater than simply the editor of its journal. His wife was an actress with the theater, while he was its spokesman on matters of literature and often gave introductory lectures before performances or occasional addresses marking a writer's anniversary. An ambitious man, Medvedev also made the journal more than a theater organ. Under his editorship, many of the more interesting nonparty intellectuals of Leningrad published there, including several from the Formalists' circle and poets such as Vaginov, Rozhdestvensky, Piotrovsky, and Kliuev.

Medvedev himself contributed articles and book reviews, mostly on drama and contemporary poetry. These are benign and sentimental, far from the hack-and-slash approach that would be his later style. Medvedev's position in these reviews is that of an epigone of his idol Blok, on the one hand, and of his mentor Bakhtin and, via Bakhtin, of the Kantians and Neo-Kantians, on the other. Like Blok, he argues that the true artist is inevitably drawn to the Revolution and to its violence. The artist knows the attraction of its "music" and can "hear the Revolution with his entire body" because it is a "creative act." Thus, for the artist the Revolution brings an explosion of creative energies and renewal. In other articles, however, Medvedev offers crude reformulations of Bakhtin's ideas. Medvedev declares, for instance, that everyone must not follow prescribed patterns in life but must "create" it, as Tolstoy did: "Thus Leo Tolstoy and his example should represent for us not some canonized man of virtue, not some abstract dogma, a rule or measure, but a symbol of true living creativity [*žiznetvorčestvo*] . . . Tolstoy was not something given, but something achieved [*ne dan, a zadan*]."[32]

Despite Medvedev's enthusiasm for the Revolution, he was not at this time a Marxist. In fact, he periodically emerged as a religious mystic in the Symbolist vein. In describing a production of Bjørnson's *Over Aevne*, for instance, he claims that "No other theater can provide this dynamic spirituality which infuses all aspects . . . of the Traveling Mass Theater, nor its consequent uplifting, purely religious experience . . . this production is indeed 'beyond human power' . . . If people had more faith and active spirituality, such 'spectacles'—a more appropriate name for them would be mysteries—would be able to perform real miracles."[33]

Voloshinov's contributions to the journal also include religious-mystical passages. For instance, a 1922 poem opens, "Drawn by the miracle and mystery of Nazareth," and goes on to talk of the "Midday prayer to the Lord." He also writes that in Beethoven the "tragedy of the soul was transformed into the mystery of the spirit of the body crucified on the cross."[34]

By 1924 the powers that be were less tolerant of religious quest, and the Traveling Theater and its journal were closed by order of the local Committee for Political Enlightenment. The theater itself reopened a year or so later, but not the journal. By 1925, when Medvedev found a new outlet for his journalistic zeal by becoming a regular contributor to *The Star*, he had acquired a fairly acceptable public persona and sloughed off all his religiosity, mysticism, and even sentimentality, to become the hard-nosed journalist that was fashionable in the mainstream press of the day. But some activities of his still gave intimations of the former Medvedev. For instance, in 1922 Medvedev had prepared the autobiography of the rebellious and religious village poet Kliuev, and in 1927, when this sort of thing was more consequential for one's career, he nevertheless published an article on another village poet, Sergei Esenin, who was then in official disfavor for his general rowdiness and anarchic tendencies prior to his suicide in 1925, and Medvedev included with the article Kliuev's poem "Lament for Esenin," which was officially considered anti-Soviet.[35]

Thus even Medvedev, the Soviet careerist, turns out to have been multifaceted and somewhat idiosyncratic in his activities of the 1920s. Only in the context of Bakhtin's friends could he have seemed conformist. What distinguished Bakhtin's group—though in this decade the distinction was by no means unique—was the eccentricity, brilliance, and intellectual range of its participants. Bakhtin in Leningrad may not have had a brilliant career, but he was surrounded by colorful people of unusual talents: the literary specialist Pumpiansky, rarely seen without his cast-off, ill-fitting uniform coat, whose braided loops and knots gave him the appearance of an early-blooming Sergeant Pepper; Medvedev, a bearish, round-faced man of exquisite taste and elegant dress, flitting between the world of theaters, writers, institutes, and editors' offices; Sollertinsky, Bakhtin's equal not only in erudition but in

The Bakhtin circle in Yudina's apartment, Leningrad, c.1924–1926.
Seated from left: Bakhtin (with cigarette and teapot), Yudina,
Vaginov, Pumpiansky, and Medvedev. Standing:
Vaginov's wife, Elena Aleksandrovna Bakhtin, and an unidentified man.

love of jokes; and Yudina, the mystic Christian and supreme eccentric who shocked the public by wearing at all times a loose-
fitting black garb reminiscent of a nun's habit. These people were
all verbal and contentious. None could have been called a passive
disciple. Moreover, the thread of theatricality bound them all,
from Pumpiansky's tendency to dress in costumes, to the entire
group's love of charades and word games, to Medvedev's close involvement with the theater itself.

Such colorful, self-consciously theatrical personalities lent
themselves naturally to being written up in literature. Vaginov in
his novel *The Satyr's Song* (*Kozlinaja pesn'*, 1927) satirized the
group's activities in Vitebsk, in Leningrad, and at Pumpiansky's
rented summer dacha in Peterhof outside Leningrad. Vaginov
emphasizes the isolation of Bakhtin's group from Soviet society
and the members' complete immersion in their own ideas. Most of
them are depicted as ineffectual and quixotic. The central charac-

ter, Teptelkin, who represents Pumpiansky, is often seen "head-
ing for the communal dining room for hot water, surrounded by
nymphs and satyrs."[36]

But the eccentricity of the members of the Bakhtin circle,
their wide range of intellectual and professional interests, and
their contentiousness, energy, and exuberance were not merely,
as Vaginov implied, quaint and endearing personality traits. They
were also the products of a nexus of shared values. Bakhtin and
his friends valued above all variety, difference, free inquiry, dialogue, and debate. They believed in being free of conventional
norms and the traditional bounds of a given discipline and in pursuing a life of the mind that was as rich and lively as possible. In
their different ways they were almost all independent spirits who
cared little to conform to the expectations of their peers, whether
of the right or the left, of the Soviet establishment or of its opposition. And so when they met, it was for spirited discussion. Each
sought to learn something from the discourse of others who
worked in different intellectual fields. Their debates ranged over
the religious and philosophical systems of the East and West, of
the ancients and the moderns, and over topics from the humanities to the natural sciences.

The spirit of free inquiry was easy enough to live by during
the first confused, iconoclastic years after the Revolution, when
the czarist order was being dismantled and people sought con-
sciously to overcome the old bourgeois morality, materialism, and
conformism. As the 1920s progressed, however, and the confusion
of the early years gave way to an increasing conformism and
bureaucratization in Soviet intellectual life, free inquiry became
harder for the Bakhtin group. The reason was not just that most
members were not Marxists, for until late in the decade a non-
Marxist orientation was not necessarily an obstacle to an intellectual career. The Formalists, for instance, made their
careers under the Soviets. Moreover, until 1927 there was not
a single party member in the Academy of Sciences.[37] Bakhtin
and his friends, in fact, felt increasingly alone and isolated vis-à-
vis all prevailing intellectual groups, both Marxist and non-
Marxist.

In Vaginov's The Satyr's Song, which focuses on the years
1925 to 1926, the individual group members experience a crisis of
existential Angst and depression as they recognize that their past

intellectual stance will doom them in the new era to unpublishability. They also have grave doubts about the intrinsic worth of their past position. Several characters, such as Teptelkin and Asphodeliev, who represents Medvedev, find a makeshift resolution of their dilemma by working within the system. Asphodeliev is a sinister name, derived from asphodel, a flower that grows in places associated with death, and Asphodeliev is depicted as one who cynically compromises with the regime to his own material advantage. He therefore has no trouble publishing and is "on a first-name basis with the proletarian writers."[38] By contrast, the figure most nearly representing Bakhtin—"the philosopher"—commits suicide.

In reality, however, the contrast between the various responses to the crisis in the Bakhtin circle was not so dramatic as Vaginov made it. At about this time many non-Marxist intellectuals were under pressure to modify their intellectual stance, and many did so. For instance, in 1927 the Leningrad Formalists published articles demonstrating that they had become less intransigent about the role of extraliterary factors in literature and had adopted a more "sociological" approach. It is impossible to ascertain to what extent this change was made in response to political pressure and to what extent it represented a recognition of the limitations of their militant rejection of context.

At about the same time, many members of the Bakhtin circle also experienced difficulties and changed their public, if not their private, intellectual position. For instance, Voloshinov became a sincere Marxist in 1927.[39] Somewhat later Pumpiansky moved to a more Marxist position, which in 1934 finally enabled him to be employed as a professor at the Leningrad Conservatory. In Bakhtin's case, his recognition in 1924 that he was not going to be able to publish under his own name propelled him to begin publishing under others' names in 1925. Perhaps this was what Vaginov meant by his "suicide." At the same time, however, Bakhtin modified his intellectual stance and became more sociological in his approach. This change came about partly because he wanted his writings to be published, but also because his own intellectual interests and reading were taking him in that direction, as they were taking many others at the time.

Medvedev's response to the crisis was not all cynical compromise. There is even evidence that he might not have been "on a first-name basis with the proletarian writers," as Vaginov implied. In 1927 the proletarian camp took such exception to a review by Medvedev of an anthology of proletarian literature that the editors of *The Star* had to publish a formal recantation. As a consequence, articles by Medvedev which had already been announced as forthcoming in *The Star* for later that year did not appear. When Medvedev returned to print in *The Star* in 1928, his first piece was a favorable review of another proletarian anthology.[40] After this experience some of the confidence went out of Medvedev's journalism. He became much tamer.

Whatever was the accommodation or conversion that members of the Bakhtin circle made to the regime, it was only a partial one, and they were all in some danger of repression once Stalinism became entrenched at the end of the decade. Yet it was at precisely this time that most of them also advanced in rank or status. Even Bakhtin seemed on the point of making a career for himself and ending his marginal financial and intellectual existence. In late 1928 Bakhtin somehow managed to organize for himself a lecture series at the former Yusupov mansion. Although the initial turn-out was poor, Bakhtin's performance was so impressive that for the second lecture he attracted a crowd. But by a cruel irony, before the third lecture could be held, he had been arrested. Had he not been arrested, his popularity as a public lecturer, together with the publication of his Dostoevsky book a few months later, would surely have brought him some sort of work, if only occasional lecturing.

Even "careerist" Medvedev remained in danger, although he continued to rise in rank and status. In 1933, for instance, he was appointed full professor at the Leningrad Historico-Philological Institute, yet the 1934 entry on him in the *Literary Encyclopedia* calls his critical work "uneven" and charges him with a tendency to "Neo-Kantianism" in *The Formal Method in Literary Scholarship*, which is, ironically, almost certainly Bakhtin's book.[41]

Yet in the mid-1920s it was not their Neo-Kantianism that made Bakhtin and his friends so vulnerable and isolated, for most of them had by then outgrown its influence. Their involvement in religious questions, more than any other aspect of their activity, was what gave them a sense of isolation. By this time not only the Marxists but also the most impressive non-Marxist schools of thought, such as the Formalists, tended to be atheistic or agnostic.

The Bakhtin circle was tormented by the fear that they represented a superseded philosophical era. This sense is poignantly conveyed in *The Satyr's Song*, where the members of the circle compare themselves to the last of the pagan philosophers who were trying to continue their work in the new Christian era.[42]

against the grain of hegemony

CHAPTER 5

Religious Activities
and the Arrest

Bakhtin was a religious man. In his childhood he had had a conventional upbringing as a Russian Orthodox. By the 1920s, religious thought had become one of Bakhtin's central interests. He was known in intellectual circles of those days as a *cerkovnik*, a "churchman" or "adherent of the church."[1] This term does not mean that he was a churchgoer but implies simply that he was ideologically committed to the church. Although he later became less involved in religion, he remained a believer in the Orthodox tradition all his life.

The palpable anticlericalism of his Rabelais book has made it hard to see connections between Bakhtin's published work and his religiosity. But Bakhtin was never a conventional Russian Orthodox in the sense of conforming to an organized religion. Rather, he was a religious intellectual from the Orthodox tradition. His religious views came not so much from traditional Orthodox thinking within the church as from the religious revival in the early twentieth century among Russian intellectuals who sought to break new ground in theological thought. Bakhtin's Orthodox theology was not the theology of the run-of-the-mill seminary but of the highbrow intelligentsia. Indeed, he was not interested so much in religion as in the philosophy of religion. He and the other members of his group did not separate religious from other philosophical concerns. Their aim in conducting their philosophical nights was an extremely ambitious one, which, as Pumpiansky characterized it, was to rethink all the categories of modern thought in terms of the Russian Orthodox tradition. Although the Russian Orthodox tradition was not the point of orientation for all members of the group—Kagan, for instance, being more interested in the Judaic tradition—Pumpiansky's characterization highlights the universalist spirit that they all brought to their theological inquiry.

The Bakhtin group, along with other intellectuals of the time, sought to realize an ideal rather like that of the nineteenth century German idealists Fichte and Schelling, which was to synthesize all human experience, including the religious. They believed that it was not enough to be a theologian; one should also work in and draw on a broad range of fields of inquiry, including the so-called hard sciences. Thus, many Russian theologians of the early twentieth century were also educated as scientists, such as the physicist and mathematician Florovsky and the chemist and philosopher Askoldov; and the physiologist Ukhtomsky had originally trained in theology.

The most striking example of this phenomenon was Father Pavel Aleksandrovich Florensky. He was a physicist, mathematician, inventor, philosopher, historian, archeologist, theologian, philologist, and art historian, who was also interested in all varieties of nonreceived, nonpositivist science and dabbled in parapsychology, astrology, magic, and alchemy. Born in 1882, Florensky had trained in both mathematics and theology before being ordained a priest in 1911, and before the Revolution he both taught the history of philosophy at the Moscow Theological Academy and edited the journal *The Theological Herald* (*Bogoslovskij vestnik*). But it is his career after the Revolution that illustrates most spectacularly the sort of universalism to which many religious intellectuals aspired. Upon the closing of the Theological Academy in the summer of 1918, Florensky moved into a successful career in the natural sciences. Indeed, the Soviets labeled him a scientist rather than a theologian. He worked for GOERLO, the body set up in 1920 to realize Lenin's dream of electrifying all of Russia. He gave lectures on the theory of perspective to the Higher Art Studios from 1920 to 1927, and in the late 1920s he held a post at the All-Russian Electrotechnical Institute. He made several inventions, including a noncoagulating machine oil. Legend has it that he used to astound delegates at Soviet scientific conferences by appearing on the rostrum in his priest's garb. Florensky published in a number of fields, including dialectrics, electricity, theory of perspective, and musical polyphony, as well as in more predictable areas, such as iconography and theology. Even on the latter subjects, however, he always brought to bear scientific and other extratheological ideas.[2]

This intellectual versatility appeared in less dramatic version in Bakhtin and most other members of his circle. Bakhtin was attracted by the work of the physiologists Kanaev and Ukhtomsky, both of whom were scientists and believers. He himself published on the theory of Vitalism and frequently touched on physiological issues in his writings. Kagan was not only a philosopher and religious thinker but also an accomplished mathematician who underwent a spiritual crisis at the end of the 1920s and decided to engage in the practical task of building the country. To this end, he left his job at the State Academy of the Arts and went to work for the National Economic Council, where he could use his mathematical expertise. At the time of his death in 1937, Kagan was working at the Energy Institute of the Academy of Sciences, where he had just completed a monumental atlas of the country's energy resources. Others in Bakhtin's group, like Yudina and Sollertinsky, were not involved in the natural sciences but worked in an impressive range of fields within the humanities and fine arts. The group did not confine its spiritual quest to Russian Orthodoxy or even to the Judeo-Christian religion, but kept also in its purview Eastern religious and philosophical traditions, as well as the wide body of issues raised in the philosophical debates of early twentieth century Europe about the nature of experience, in which such figures as Kierkegaard, Husserl, and the Neo-Kantians loomed large.

Bakhtin and his group not only did not separate religious issues from other philosophical concerns but also did not perceive any necessary opposition between religion and a socialist revolution. Thus in the 1920s, at a time when religion was being compressed and politicized into a "reactionary survival" not only by the powers that be but also by leading intellectual groups, such as the Futurists, Bakhtin and his circle were more isolated in intellectual life than they had been during the previous decade, when leading Marxists had been able to debate with Religious-Philosophical Society members under the society's own roof. Because of this growing sense of isolation, as well as for reasons of censorship, Bakhtin's works of this period address the broad philosophical issues which concerned him in a language that is both distinctly "sociological" and devoid of any manifest reference to religion. This accorded with Bakhtin's sense of religion as an integral part of a dialogic world view which is ever changing, ever responding to current reality.

The Bakhtin circle with its religious orientation did not become totally isolated, however, during the 1920s, especially in the *1917-1922* first five years after the Revolution when there was a remarkable amount of public religious debate and religious interest among intellectuals of all persuasions. For instance, there was a revival of interest in the Orthodox Church itself. A number of intellectuals rejoined the church, and some even took holy orders as a gesture of independence or protest or as an expression of concern at the lack of a spiritual dimension in Bolshevik ideology. In literature a popular interpretation of the Revolution was as an uprising of the Russian people to overthrow the sterile Western order that had been imposed on them and to return to their native traditions. Many writers in this vein were religious, such as the peasant poet Kliuev, who had connections with the Bakhtin circle through Yudina and Medvedev. Religion in these years was not even denied a public forum. Public debates took place between leading Bolshevik and religious intellectuals about the existence of God, the most famous of these being the debates between Lunacharsky and Vyacheslav Ivanov in the Polytechnic Museum in Moscow. Bakhtin and his friends had been involved in a provincial echo of the same phenomenon in 1918–1919 when they debated the local Marxists in Nevel.

While Bakhtin and his friends were conducting private religious-philosophical discussions in Nevel and Vitebsk, there was considerable public and semipublic activity among religious and God-seeking intellectuals in the two capital cities. Several new religious organizations were founded in Petrograd, to which members of the Bakhtin circle had links or in which they participated. Bakhtin himself was not a member of any particular religious group at this time. His nonparticipation was in keeping with both his phlegmatic character and his distaste for dogma and organization. However, he was close to several religious organizations in Petrograd in the sense that he knew their members, read their writings, and possibly attended an occasional meeting on one of his trips. The kind of religious thought favored by these organizations influenced Bakhtin, even if in some instances only as a position against which to define himself.

Some of the post-Revolutionary religious organizations in Petrograd were born of a sense that the times demanded a new direction, but others came about because of political pressures, especially those organizations that were specifically Russian Orthodox, for after October 1917 the position of the Orthodox Church in Russia became difficult, given the militant atheism of the new Bolshevik government. From the very beginning the government made efforts both to curtail the church's activities and to turn what was left of the church into an official Orthodox Church, tied to the Soviet government. These aims were opposed by most Orthodox intellectuals, and many of those involved in the religious revival had long advocated an end to the traditional subordination of the Orthodox Church to the Russian state, a goal that had briefly been realized in the February Revolution. For these reasons there were growing tensions between the Bolsheviks and leading Orthodox intellectuals and theologians.

In 1918 the Orthodox Theological Academy in Petrograd was closed by the Bolsheviks, and public discussion of theological questions in venues other than official debates became extremely difficult. Yet religious thinkers in Petrograd showed considerable ingenuity in finding other public outlets for their ideas. For instance, during 1921–1922 a series of thinly disguised religious lectures was given by Orthodox thinkers at both the House of Writers and the House of Scholars. Prominent university professors also rallied to the cause in 1920 by founding, together with former teachers from the theological academy, a private center of instruction, the Theological Institute. Most of the faculty of the new institute were also members of an organization known as the Brotherhood of Divine Wisdom, or Brotherhood of Saint Sophia, which met to discuss both the gospels and contemporary church issues. Several members of the Bakhtin circle, including Bakhtin himself, had connections with members of the Brotherhood of Saint Sophia. For instance, the founder of the brotherhood, A. Kartashev, later Minister of Confessions under Kerensky, had introduced Bakhtin to the Religious-Philosophical Society in 1916. Both Bakhtin and Pumpiansky used to meet in the home of another brotherhood member, L. P. Karsavin, to discuss the works of Saint Augustine. Later in the 1920s Bakhtin gave lectures in theological courses organized by another member, Professor Scherbov. And in 1920 Yudina became an enthusiastic student at Petrograd University of two brotherhood members, I. M. Grevs and L. P. Karsavin.[3]

Although Bakhtin knew and admired individual brotherhood members, the circle itself was probably too conservative in orientation to have attracted him. The religious revival after the Revolution was by no means confined to Orthodox thought. Among Jewish intellectuals there was a heightened interest in Judaism and the Judaic heritage, prompted by the release of restrictions on Jews and on practicing Judaism after the February Revolution. In the early 1920s Kagan was actively engaged in this movement. He gave lectures in institutions set up to study the Jewish heritage, such as the Moscow National Jewish University and the Petrograd Jewish University, and he talked about the Judaic tradition to non-Jewish religious-philosophical organizations, such as the short-lived Free Academy of Spiritual Culture in Moscow, whose members included Florensky and the religious thinker Berdyaev.[4]

Though Kagan was active in the Judaic revival, he was not a Zionist. Like Cohen before him, Kagan saw the way forward for Jewry rather in taking a more active part in European cultural and intellectual life. Similarly, the Christian members of the Bakhtin circle did not wish to be narrowly Orthodox. Indeed, in the early 1920s several members of Bakhtin's group were involved in a philosophical society in Petrograd that was especially interested in the philosophy of all belief systems, including the Christian. It was officially called the Free Philosophical Association but was generally known as Volfila (Freephila).

Volfila, which had been founded in 1918 but did not begin meeting until November 1919, originally defined its aim as to work in philosophy with a socialist orientation and also to respond to topical issues of the day. The association saw its role as providing a forum for debate in all areas of intellectual inquiry for those concerned with "spiritual quest." Thus it was not specifically religious. The founders, who were of various political and intellectual persuasions, included the Symbolist writers Blok and Bely, the artist Petrov-Vodkin, the theatrical director Meyerhold, and the socialist revolutionary writer Ivanov-Razumnik. It is possible that Bakhtin attended occasional meetings of the association on his visits to Petrograd. At any rate Pumpiansky, Tubyansky, and Kagan of his circle all lectured there.[5]

The word "Free" in the association's title stood for free discourse, in the sense of being both wide-ranging and unconstrained by preconceived notions or dogmas. This aspect of Volfila's philosophy, which was similar to Bakhtin's thinking at the time, was expressed in a 1923 report by the group. The report stressed the Bakhtinian theme of the perennial need to debunk received truths and canons, including not only "the dogmatic trumpeting forth of definite, absolutely unambiguous answers and approaches" (perhaps a hint at the loud sloganeering of the regime) but also all forms of "ossified thinking," which must be combated by "strengthening habits of critical thought and acute self-analysis."[6]

Although Volfila hosted literary evenings and organized study circles and papers on a wide range of specialized topics ranging from individual Russian writers and radicals to the theory of relativity, its main interest was the philosophy of beliefs. Thus it organized individual study circles on Marxism, communism, anarchism, populism, anthroposophy, and religion itself. A lecture series on "the crisis in culture seen as a crisis in religion" was organized in 1920 under its auspices, and it occasioned papers on religious topics by prominent intellectuals, including Bely and the religious thinkers N. O. Lossky, S. A. Askoldov, and A. A. Meier.[7]

A special circle on the philosophy of religion was run by Meier, who in the pre-Revolutionary period had been a mystical anarchist and leading member of the Petersburg Religious-Philosophical Society. Meier was an important figure for Bakhtin, who read his writings extensively and sought him out sporadically for dialogue until the end of Meier's life. In 1917 Meier had also founded a religious circle known as Voskresenie, which means "resurrection." Bakhtin was not definitely a member of Voskresenie, though Yudina and Pumpiansky attended meetings from the fall of 1920.[8] The group's ethos and practices were nevertheless close in many respects to Bakhtin's own religious position at the time.

Many members of Voskresenie were former members of the Petersburg Religious-Philosophical Society, of which they represented more or less the left wing. They were anathema to the former leaders of that society, the Symbolist poets Merezhkovsky and Gippius, who had been closely associated with Meier but now attacked Voskresenie as being too accommodating toward the Revolution. In addition to Meier, Voskresenie's leaders were Kseniya Anatolievna Polovtseva, in whose apartment the meetings were originally held, Nikolai Pavlovich Antsiferov, a writer and expert on the cultural milieu of Petersburg, and Georgii Petrovich Fedotov, a religious thinker and former revolutionary who emigrated in

1925 and later became a Harvard Professor and author of *The Russian Religious Mind*, a basic text on Orthodoxy.[9] Meier, Fedotov, and Antsiferov had met in the Leningrad Public Library, where all three worked after the Revolution.

As with the Bakhtin circle, the Voskresenie group attracted people with a range of professional and intellectual interests. The members of Voskresenie likewise did not represent a consensus on most points, though they did have a distinctive ethos. The members represented such a variety of persuasions and religious backgrounds that the group could in no way have been called a church group, or even Orthodox. In the early years, Voskresenie included two Protestants, two Roman Catholics who were formerly Russian Orthodox, and several unbaptized Jews. Most of the other members, though Orthodox by birth and orientation, were not communicants. Pumpiansky and Yudina, who were ethnic Jews, had converted and been baptized. But all members, even the unbaptized ethnic Jews, put Christ at the center of their life and thought. The group was also variegated in terms of its political orientation. It included a monarchist, who was also the group's only proletarian, and two religious communists. Most of the other members were socialists of various hues.[10]

Christo-centric lives

The leaders of Voskresenie set its political tone. Two of them, Meier and Fedotov, had a common past in the revolutionary underground. Unlike other intellectuals who had come from revolutionary politics to a religious position, they had not abandoned their faith in socialism. Fedotov believed in a kind of democratic socialism that was in favor of worker control of the factories.[11] Meier, who according to Bakhtin was a "very tough Marxist," saw his task as showing how religion and revolution could dwell together in man. Antsiferov was presumably also socialist because his wife served on the local revolutionary committee.

The majority of the members were not especially antagonistic toward the Bolsheviks. Although they were unhappy at the bloodshed and hoped the regime would in time become less extreme in its practices, they agreed with many of its stated socialistic aims. Their actual sense of what socialism entailed, however, differed somewhat from that of the Bolsheviks. Several members dreamed of becoming the kernel of a new Saint-Simonianism in Russia, continuing the work of such French utopians as Pierre Leroux, Lamenais, about whom Antsiferov wrote, and Georges Sand.[12]

The aims of Meier and Polovtseva were more radical: to link religion and revolution, communism and Christ. In 1917 they had formulated a set of theses called "The Revolution and Christ," which represented a point of view similar to the one Blok would shortly express in his poem "The Twelve," which portrays Christ at the head of a band not of twelve apostles but of twelve rough and ready revolutionaries. After the Revolution, Polovtseva accepted the economic policies of the Bolsheviks but argued that religion was also needed for the renewal of man. She even insisted that May Day should be celebrated on Easter Sunday. But the group's basic philosophy remained as it was first set forth by Fedotov in 1918: "We acknowledge the truth and justice of socialism but seek some spiritual basis for it . . . This aim is a bold one, but the times demand daring deeds: we must save socialist truth with spiritual truth, and save the world with socialist truth."[13]

Bakhtin had much in common with the thinking of Fedotov and Meier. For example, Fedotov gave a central role to the Orthodox concept of kenoticism, as did Bakhtin. Both Fedotov and Meier were antiauthoritarian and stressed the need for freedom. The motto of the inner group of Voskresenie was in fact "Christ and Freedom." Moreover, the leaders of Voskresenie stressed that their meetings should be free of any use of "standard ideas or concepts." These sentiments were close to the heart of Bakhtin, who decried all ideological monism.[14]

Another area of common ground between the Voskresenie leaders and Bakhtin was their ecumenical, internationalist spirit. Fedotov, for instance, rejected all Russian varieties of messianism. He was against narrow nationalism, in both religion and politics. He posed instead the ideal of a "new fatherland," a sort of universal nation of kindred spirits which cut across national borders. For this "Westernism" Fedotov was looked at askance by many Orthodox contemporaries who did not consider him of their number. Yet Fedotov also rejected Western bourgeois forms of government as failures. He saw in communism the seeds of a superior social order, claiming that "in revolutionary Marxism, especially its Russian versions, there lurks a religious idea, albeit a vague one: in its structure revolutionary Marxism is a Judeo-Christian apocalyptic sect . . . Marxism in its social and class consciousness and the dogmatism of its system hides a potential for Orthodoxy: this was revealed by the leaders of a new theological school which emerged from it." Thus, Fedotov did not see Marxism and Christianity as irreconcilable systems. The singularity of Fedotov's thought has in fact been described as its "intertwining of Christian truth and Marxist sociology."[15]

Neither Fedotov nor Bakhtin, however, came close to endorsing communism in its Bolshevik interpretation. Fedotov and most other Voskresenie members wanted a religious basis for the new social order and, like so many in the Religious-Philosophical Society before them, envisaged something like the communistic ideal of the early church fathers. Central to their thinking, as to Bakhtin's, was the concept of *sobornost'*, "togetherness" or "true sense of community." The Voskresenie members looked to an ideal community where each individual personality would flourish, there would be no absolute authorities, and yet all would have a sense of common bond—something like the Bakhtinian polyphony or heteroglossia translated into social terms. Indeed, the ideal of heteroglossia is reflected in the title for the group's short-lived journal, *Free Voices* (*Svobodnye golosa*), where the plural was deliberately chosen to emphasize the pluralism of the group and the fact that the journal was the product of *sobornoe* or "joint" creativity.[16]

The ideal of community also influenced the format of the group's weekly meetings. Usually the theme for discussion was decided on collectively at the previous week's meeting. Each meeting began with the ritual of everyone shaking hands. One of the leaders of the group, such as Fedotov, Meier, or Antsiferov, then made a short, introductory remark on the topic, after which every member of the circle was obliged to say something on it, even if only a few words. The interest in community was also reflected in the topics chosen, such as "patriotism and internationalism," "the interrelationship between the concepts of freedom, equality, and brotherhood," and "comradeship and friendship."[17]

The ideal of community went along with the ecumenical spirit of the group. The Voskresenie members were interested in church unification, and so they recited the Our Father in their opening prayers in three languages—Old Church Slavic, Latin, and German. The group was careful to keep itself independent of the institutionalized Orthodox Church, and it never admitted priests as members, though it celebrated the Russian feast days with pomp and ceremony. The members' church life was not con-

sidered an affair of the group, and they never took communion together.

The ideal of community inspired several members of Voskresenie to found short-lived communes of their own, largely in
places on the periphery of Petrograd, like Detskoe selo and Peterhof. Yudina may have founded such a group. Bakhtin was not
taken by this aspect of the group's beliefs and charged that these
members were ignoring the real social conditions in which they
lived. In the Dostoevsky book he attacked as naive the idealized
sense of community shared by Meier and his friends.[18] But in
other respects Bakhtin was generally close to the group in his religious orientation.

During the early 1920s these three groups—the scholarly
Brotherhood of Saint Sophia, the public and eclectic Volfila, and
the more private Voskresenie—were important to members of the
Bakhtin circle living in Petrograd, but by the time Bakhtin returned in 1924 the situation of intellectual religious-philosophical
groups and the whole tenor of religious inquiry among intellectuals had altered radically. In the main, the reasons for this
change were political, having to do with increasing government
repression. For instance, in 1922 the Soviet Union expelled over a
hundred intellectual families, most of them religious, including
such well-known thinkers as S. Bulgakov, Berdyaev, Lossky,
Frank, and Karsavin. Between 1922 and 1923 most public religious associations were forced to disband. The Brotherhood of
Saint Sophia was dissolved in 1921 or 1922, and the Theological
Institute was closed in 1923. Ecumenical organizations lasted
a little while longer. Volfila, for instance, was not closed until
1924. As a consequence of these events, religious associations
among the intelligentsia tended either to go underground or to
become very informal and to meet in private homes. Only occasionally were semipublic glimmers of religious discussion seen.
For instance, in the summer of 1924 leading religious thinkers
conducted religious debates and discussions with intellectuals in
the gardens of the sanitarium of the House of Scholars outside
Leningrad.[19]

The situation of the Voskresenie group was not altered radically by these events. Its members had always met informally in
private homes and were mostly well disposed toward the Revolution. At this time, however, Voskresenie underwent a change in

the direction and tenor of its religious-philosophical quest. While the group remained ecumenical in spirit, it drifted closer toward identification with Russian Orthodoxy. In earlier years the topics discussed had been primarily social, but now they became more exclusively religious. Individual members of the group also drew closer to the church. Several Jewish members were baptized, which was quite common in Leningrad at this time. Their baptisms were accompanied by great celebrations in the group. Although Fedotov lamented that those baptized soon fell under the influence of the priests, he himself eventually rejoined the church, as did Meier.[20]

This trend in Voskresenie had its parallel among members of the Bakhtin circle. Their interest in religious questions, particularly in Russian Orthodoxy, became more pronounced, Sollertinsky being the only definite exception. Pumpiansky reported around 1926 that the circle had been studying theology intensively: "This year my theological position has been established definitely and clearly: The Eastern Orthodox Church . . . [and I have come to] the conviction that the philosophy of religion of both Kant and H. Cohen are completely unsupportable."[21]

Those heady post-Revolutionary years, in which a marriage was thought to be possible between communism and Christ, were now over. For most members of Bakhtin's circle the mid-1920s were a time of intellectual crisis. Even as they were becoming more immersed in religious questions and Russian Orthodoxy, they had to confront the reality not only that work reflecting these interests was virtually unpublishable but also that, as a result of the migrations, expulsions, and dissolutions of religious forums, few organizations or individuals were left with whom they might find a dialogue. Most members coped with this crisis by making some accommodation to the prevailing directions of Soviet intellectual life. Bakhtin himself reoriented his approach in his writings and largely abandoned his Neo-Kantian vocabulary for one that was more secular and sociological.

Although Bakhtin's change of approach may well have come about in response to changed political realities, it did not merely represent a compromise on his part. Rather, it represented a development in his antimetaphysical, anti-idealist standpoint. In this respect Bakhtin was untypical of religious thinkers in the Soviet Union at the time, most of whom did not develop a more sociological approach until the 1930s, and then only as a compromise. Bakhtin's adoption of a sociological approach also did not mean any abandonment of his faith. He was therefore in a singular position vis-à-vis most religious thinkers in Leningrad, and he polemicized indirectly with their idealism and some of their utopian programs. Yet this stance neither ostracized him nor caused him to distance himself from his opponents, for he always loved dialogue and was unusually successful in charming opponents.

Albeit Bakhtin was by now in some senses to the left of the left wing of free religious inquiry as represented by Voskresenie, he was also loosely associated with groups farther to the right. In particular he was linked with the Brotherhood of Saint Seraphim, a group that was both more specifically Russian Orthodox and more underground than Voskresenie. Named after Saint Seraphim of Sarov, the last canonized saint of Russia, the brotherhood was a circle of intellectuals committed to furthering theological knowledge. It organized religious discussions and courses that attracted young scholars, graduate students and priests. It also conducted missionary activities, especially among young Jews. The brotherhood's membership included the literary scholar Vasily Leonidovich Komarovich, who published on Dostoevsky and was interested in Freud; Ivan Mikhailovich Andreevsky, a specialist on mental illness and children's medicine who later migrated to the West and published under the name I. M. Andreev, and the historians Tarle and Platonov. Several members of Bakhtin's circle were associated at some time with brotherhood members. Yudina, for instance, was a friend of Tarle's, living in the same apartment house as he did in the early 1920s.[22]

The brotherhood had been founded in 1921 by Sergei Alekseevich Askoldov and was originally known as Askoldov's circle, but in 1926 it was renamed the Brotherhood of Saint Seraphim. Askoldov, the pseudonym of S. A. Alekseev (1870–1945), was a religious thinker and philosopher who particularly interested Bakhtin. Before the Revolution he had achieved a name for the independence of his thought. He was thoroughly at home in all the current schools of philosophy but subscribed to none of them. In his *Thought and Reality* (1914), he criticized Neo-Kantianism in general and the Marburg school in particular. The basic proposition of the book, that the Neo-Kantians were not terribly original and the most interesting features of their work were more profoundly present in Kant himself, was one to which Bakhtin would subscribe in the 1920s as he became more critical of Hermann Cohen. Askoldov's *Consciousness as a Whole* (1918), particularly the fourth section devoted to "Depth of Consciousness and the Personality," dealt with the status of I/not-I relations at a time when Bakhtin himself was just beginning his lifelong exploration of the same topic. Askoldov was more helpful to Bakhtin in his attempts to get beyond Cohen's thinking about this topic than any other Russian philosopher, including such obvious candidates as A. Vvedensky, Bakhtin's teacher at Petrograd University, whose book *On the Limits and Characteristics of Becoming Conscious* (1892) deals with the problem from a Kantian perspective, or F. P. Lapshin, whose *The Problem of the I and the Other* (1910) is merely a review of other treatments of this topic.[23]

There is no conclusive evidence that Bakhtin was a member of the Brotherhood of Saint Seraphim, although he was later accused of it. At this time Bakhtin did keep a bust of Saint Seraphim in his room. Seraphim was an extremely popular saint among Russian religious intellectuals in the early twentieth century, and it was somewhat under his banner that the movement among intellectuals for a return to the church was conducted. But the meaning of the bust in Bakhtin's case is not self-evident, for like so many popular symbols, Saint Seraphim meant different things to different people.

Seraphim, who had been born Prokhor Moshin in 1759, belonged to the Russian Orthodox tradition of the ascetic elder. After taking the priesthood, he joined a remote monastery at Sarov. Not content with that isolation, Seraphim made himself a hut farther into the woods, where he spent seventeen years in seclusion and prayer, living on bread from the monastery and vegetables he grew himself. In addition, in the tradition of Simon Stilites, he spent one thousand days and nights on a rock. For the last four years of this period he took a vow of silence and ate only wild grasses. Being thus purified, he opened the doors of his cell in 1825 to all who wanted help, somewhat in the manner of Dostoevsky's Father Zosima in *The Brothers Karamazov*. Pilgrims poured in until his death in 1833. He was finally canonized in 1903.[24]

For some Russian intellectuals, Saint Seraphim was a symbol for Russia. Others associated him with loyalty to the old monarchist regime. According to one story, Seraphim, who always blessed everyone who approached him, once explained his refusal to bless a group of young officers by pointing to some waters which had become murky. It later developed that these officers had been plotting the Decembrist uprising. Seraphim also foretold that the czar would come to a nearby nunnery that Seraphim guided and there would be a great "Easter" in summer. This prediction was realized in July 1903 when the czar along with a great multitude descended on the nunnery for the canonization ceremonies. Seraphim further foretold that the czar's visit would be followed by a period of great upheaval and bloodshed, when many Russians would leave for points all over the globe. But this trouble would lead ultimately to the triumph of Orthodoxy in the world.[25]

The narrowly monarchist and chauvinist views of Seraphim were among the many aspects of his teachings and example that were diametrically opposed to Bakhtin's views. Another conservative aspect that would not have appealed to Bakhtin was Seraphim's altogether too mystical, or what the Soviets would call "obscurantist," approach to religion. For instance, Seraphim reputedly had visions of the Virgin Mary, who showed him the way out of difficult situations. He was said to have glowed with a special aura, to have discovered a spring with healing powers, and to have healed people by the laying on of hands. He advocated saying certain prayers a specified number of times and using the rosary, whereas Bakhtin objected to external exultation and religious "hysteria." Two other aspects of the saint's teachings that would not have appealed to Bakhtin were his striving to be full of the Holy Spirit as a nonmaterial presence and his preaching about another order of time from this-worldly time.[26]

Yet many aspects of Seraphim would have appealed to Bakhtin, such as his scorn for material possessions, his populist streak, and his belief in prayer as a means of direct contact with God—dialogue, if you will. Seraphim stood for the man whose clerical career did not take the normal route. He kept minimal contact with the organized church and, while staying within the recognized Orthodox tradition of the ascetic "elder," eschewed most of the superficial, formal trappings of the religious life.

As for the brotherhood itself, Bakhtin could not have been close to many of its members in his philosophical-religious views. But several members of the Bakhtin circle had connections with

the brotherhood, which was one of the few places where theological discussions of any intellectual caliber were then taking place,
and Bakhtin needed that dialogue. He polemicized with Askoldov,
and if he attended brotherhood meetings at all, it would have been
to argue and debate rather than to commune with persons of a like
mind. At this time Bakhtin was reorienting his own position, and
he may have done so by sounding off against the members of the
brotherhood, who represented variants on common pre-Revolutionary views that had formed Bakhtin's own intellectual environment in his student years.

The Brotherhood of Saint Seraphim was heavily influenced
by Florensky, the priest whose career as a philosopher, mathematician, art historian, inventor, and physicist during the 1920s was
a spectacular example of how broad-ranging religious thought was
at that time. Florensky's influence with the brotherhood rested
not only on the intrinsic power of his thinking but on the fact that
he best represented a synthesis between ancient concerns unique
to the Russian Orthodox tradition and ideas from German philosophy and the classical heritage of Greece and Rome that were close
to the interests of the brotherhood. Florensky was also admired by
Bakhtin and others around him. For instance, Pumpiansky read
Florensky to Yudina on the night before her baptism to the Orthodox faith. The parallels between the thought of Bakhtin and
Florensky are significant, and currently the two men are perceived by many intellectuals in the Soviet Union as the major
Russian thinkers of the modern period.

Both men were unusually cultured, particularly in classical
and modern European philosophy. Both were eager to strip away
the layers of self-importance, ignorance, and parochialism of the
autocephalous Russian Church in order to restore the great religious truths that both believed the Russian tradition contained.
But these truths had to be sought in new ways, which could bring
charges of heresy. In 1904, for instance, Florensky, although a
priest, was arrested by the government police and briefly detained
on charges of delivering antichurch and therefore antigovernment
sermons. Both Bakhtin and Florensky were enemies of clerical-
ism. Florensky invoked a more personal and immediate sense of
God's presence by emphasizing Christ's saying, "When two or
more are gathered in my name, there shall I be." Much as Bakhtin
was interested in the communal utopian aspects of the early

Christians, Florensky was favorably impressed by this early form of communism.[27]

The closeness between the two thinkers was even reflected in their distinctive styles. Each was given to coining terms, and both were drawn to words that use the Russian prefix for sharing, *so-*, often expressed in English as *co-*, as in *cohabit*. The central role of such words in the thought of each was dictated by their common effort to oppose monism, that radical emphasis on the ego or the isolated subject, which both saw as typical of the West. Florensky believed in the need to go beyond *samost'*, or "self-centeredness," to reach out to an other, a thou. Love was for both the major factor propelling a flight out of solipsism.[28]

In all these views, particularly in their emphasis on communality, anticlericalism, and the I/thou distinction, both men were typical of the unorthodox Orthodoxy abroad in the 1920s. But in other respects they had important differences. Florensky, who was of a slightly earlier generation than Bakhtin, was generally closer in thought to both traditional Orthodoxy and pre-Revolutionary thought, especially Symbolist. The crucial difference between the two was that while Florensky stressed the need to get out of the palpable world of the senses to a higher spiritual reality, Bakhtin emphasized the material things of this world and physical experience. Hence, while Florensky dreamed of an end to time, of a stasis that would come when we get beyond the flux of this world and history ends, Bakhtin believed that there should be no end to becoming, and he was an enemy of all that is finished (*zaveršen*). Similarly, while Florensky believed that we should transcend the bodily in the interests of attaining a higher, religious truth, Bakhtin celebrated the joys of the flesh, praising good food, strong drink, and abundant sex. Even the two thinkers' analyses of the I/thou dynamic were effected by this crucial difference. Florensky's concern with the I/thou dynamic was ultimately directed at overcoming the dichotomy. He sought ways to make all contradictions between "I" and "not-I" fall away as both transcend themselves; he looked to a One that would resolve all differences.[29] For Bakhtin, however, all that is living is alive precisely because of a noncorrespondence with others. Cacophonous difference is what he valued most, not the endless silence of a homogenizing harmony.

While Bakhtin's thinking showed the influence of Orthodox

tradition, especially in its emphasis on community and kenosis, his Christology was in essence noncanonical and nonsectarian. Although Florensky at times played down the importance of Orthodoxy's formal trappings, his thought followed central features of Orthodox dogma. For instance, his theory of the iconic sign, which has attracted the attention of contemporary Soviet semioticians, was based on the traditional Orthodox view that the church's altar is not of this earth. It is a locus for divine grace, with the screen of icons found in Orthodox churches serving as a border between an area of this earth and another not of this world.[30]

Florensky, like his contemporaries the Neo-Kantians, never succeeded in fusing his insights into the nature of the sign with current work being done in linguistics so as to produce a philosophy of language. This aim of working out a philosophy of language was a preoccupation of intellectual activity in the 1920s, when thinkers from a range of disciplines—physiology, literature, psychology—tried to reconceive their disciplines by rethinking the relation that each bore to language. Unlike Florensky, Bakhtin succeeded in translating his theological concerns into a philosophy of discourse. Whereas for Florensky Orthodoxy remained in the category of what Bakhtin called "authoritative discourse," for Bakhtin Orthodoxy was transformed into the discourse of "inner persuasiveness," a form of communication in which there remains open "a zone of contact with unresolved contemporaneity." The word in such discourse has been reclaimed for contemporaneity; such a word relates to its descendants as well as to its contemporaries as if *both* were contemporaries.[31]

Thus, as the decade progressed and Bakhtin became more involved in the discourses of linguistics and sociology, his writings drew away from the discourse of Florensky and other such leading religious thinkers of the day. But he did not lose contact with Orthodox intellectual circles, and he even became involved, if peripherally, with a schismatic group in the Orthodox Church. The 1920s were a period of great confusion in Orthodox circles, with several schisms and competing factions within the church, each with its own parishes and priests. The schism with which Bakhtin was connected had come about in response to a declaration by the Soviet patriarch Sergii in July 1927 affirming the positive role of the Soviet state as the church's temporal power or, in other words, once more subordinating the church to the state. A number of parishes and prominent priests broke with Sergii and refused to accept the declaration. The most notable of these schisms was the Josephite schism of January 1928, named for the rebellious Metropolitan Joseph of Leningrad.[32]

The Josephite schism did not become a mass movement, and it was limited in its influence to the principal cities of Russia and some concentration camps. In its center, Leningrad, five churches joined the schism, as well as part of the brotherhood in the Alexander Nevsky Monastery. The main church of the schism was Spas-na-krovi, and among the priests attached to this church, as to the Sergii cathedral, was Archpriest Fedor Konstantinovich Andreev, a former professor at the Moscow Theological Academy and a friend of Florensky, who is also said to have been a Josephite. Andreev, who had been a member of the Brotherhood of Saint Sophia, was associated with Yudina, whom he had baptized in 1919, and also with Bakhtin. He was a superb preacher and attracted many to his services. His orientation was toward the less orthodox intellectual religious thinkers, such as Vladimir Soloviev, who preached ecumenism, and Karsavin.[33]

The three religious-philosophical groups with which Bakhtin was associated in the 1920s—Voskresenie, the Brotherhood of Saint Seraphim, and the Josephite schism—were not entirely separate. There was some overlap both in membership and in ideas. The pool of Orthodox intellectuals in Leningrad at this time who did not identify with the Soviet Orthodox Church was quite small, and they tended to know each other. One of their greatest concerns was the fate of theological or spiritual knowledge, and many of their efforts in both discussion groups and study circles were directed at keeping it alive in post-Revolutionary Russia. Theological education again became a problem for the Orthodox factions in Leningrad after the closing of the Petrograd Theological Institute in May 1923, but its rector, Chukov, found a way to carry on instruction by setting up a series of courses in private homes, for which he finally received accreditation in 1925. These courses continued until August 1928. The factionalization of the church at this time was typified by the existence in Leningrad of yet another focus of theological instruction, the so-called "pastoral courses" run by Chukov's former colleague, Scherbov. The faculty in this case, who identified with the Josephite schism, were repressed in 1928, shortly after Scherbov's own death.[34]

Bakhtin claimed to have taught "under Professor Scherbov," which would indicate that he taught in the "pastoral courses," the ones that attracted the most official displeasure. He may have taught the history of philosophy, logic, or possibly both. In any event, although these might seem to be relatively innocent subjects, his involvement in the courses would later prove fateful.

Over the next few years the sort of political pressures that had given rise to the Josephite movement became worse, and they were by no means confined to the church. Stalin was now in power, and his First Five-Year Plan, instituted for the years 1928–1932, introduced sweeping changes on the economic, social, and cultural fronts. An all-out drive was launched to industrialize the country and to collectivize its agriculture. These programs were accompanied by what was called a "cultural revolution." In its mildest form this revolution meant programs to eradicate illiteracy and to combat alcoholism. But in its more extreme interpretation, cultural revolution meant what was called "proletarianization" in all areas of cultural life. At a series of trials, such as the Shakhty trial and the Industrial Party trial, "bourgeois" specialists in industry were found guilty of sabotage and conspiracies linked with capitalist powers. Soviet officials drew lessons from these trials by replacing bourgeois professionals and students at factories, universities, and other institutions with people from the party, peasantry, or working classes.

For many in literature and literary theory, this was an especially hard time. Writers were required to write works for and about the workers and the national industrial effort. The niches that such non-Marxist groups as the Formalists had found for themselves in Soviet institutions suddenly became precarious with the founding in 1929 of a Committee for the Purging of the Institutions of the Commissariat of Enlightenment—Lunacharsky's old ministry. This committee set about attacking the alleged "reactionary social strata" which had "penetrated" the State Academy of the Arts, home of Kagan, and the Institute for the History of the Arts. Under such pressure, the Formalists were obliged to leave the institute in 1930.[35]

The campaign to proletarianize Soviet culture was accompanied by intensified assaults on the church. The years 1928–1930 mark the time of its worst persecution in the Soviet Union. The League of Militant Atheists, an organization founded in 1925, reached the peak of its activity in 1929 when, along with the Komsomols, it conducted raids on church services, trying to intimidate the worshipers. The government also passed decrees making it harder for the church to proselytize and calling for antireligious education. During these years there were mass arrests of priests and bishops, and churches were closed down. The last of the unofficial religious organizations, including the Brotherhood of Saint Seraphim, Voskresenie, and the Josephite schism, were repressed in 1928–1929. With the rout of the Josephite schism, the Orthodox faithful who opposed ties with the Soviet regime went underground and joined the so-called True Orthodox Church, also called the True Orthodox Catacomb Church.[36] But Bakhtin is not known to have been a member of it.

Andreev, the Josephite priest closest to Bakhtin, was arrested on December 11, 1928. In the spring of 1929 he was sentenced to be shot, but this sentence was commuted to ten years in the dreaded Solovki prison camp on the Solovetsky Islands in the far north. He was then found to have an advanced case of tuberculosis and was released to die at home. His funeral in 1929 became the occasion for a mass demonstration of sentiment. Such a crowd had not been seen since Dostoevsky's funeral in 1881. When permission was refused to proceed from Spas-na-krovi Cathedral to the cemetery by way of nearby Nevsky Prospect, the crowd took to the side streets instead, causing immense traffic jams.[37] As in this incident, the repression of intellectuals and religious people during the First Five-Year Plan sometimes met resistance. There was more resistance then, in fact, than in the later, more sweeping purges of the 1930s.

Bakhtin himself was arrested as a minor figure in one of these dragnet operations, which lasted over two years and brought in large numbers both of members of religious groups and of intellectuals. So curiously interconnected were the two categories in this particular operation that in some cases it was difficult to say whether an individual had been arrested for religious or intellectual affiliations or both. The purge began in December 1928 with the arrest of several members of Voskresenie, including Meier, Polovtseva, and Pumpiansky. Although the Voskresenie group was itself quite small, comprising some eleven or twelve members, one hundred people were arrested as members, and about seventy were charged and given sentences of five to ten years, mostly in the Solovki camp on the Solovetsky Islands. The nonmembers were largely friends of members. And then in successive waves their friends were arrested, probably because an even larger number was needed to justify the original arrests as members of a dangerous conspiratorial group.[38]

The roundup of the alleged Voskresenie conspirators was meant to be more than the purging of a religious organization. The senior interrogator at the Leningrad OGPU in the late 1920s and early 1930s was V. Alexander (Albert) Robert Stromin, who told Antsiferov at the time of his arrest on Palm Sunday, 1929 that this round of arrests was merely a dry run for a much bigger show that Stromin hoped to choreograph in the near future, a "Shakhty-type trial for the scholarly intelligentsia." In fact, a commission was shortly set up to purge the Academy of Sciences of those with dubious social origins, including bourgeois, aristocratic, or foreign connections. This purge culminated in 1931 with the arrest of the historians Tarle and Platonov, accused of anti-Soviet activities, monarchism, and plans to become ministers in a new government.[39]

Tarle had many friends among those arrested as Voskresenie members, establishing one connection between the academic and religious arrests. Moreover, in the summer of 1930 Meier, Polovtseva, and Antsiferov, who had already served eight months of their sentences in the camp on the Solovetsky Islands, were returned to Leningrad to be retried in connection with the purge of academics. Months of harrowing interrogation by Stromin followed, during which they refused to give false testimony regarding conspiracies in academic institutions. As a result, the three were sentenced to new ten-year terms working on the Belomor Canal.[40]

Confirmation of the role of the Voskresenie affair as a dry run for the trials of professional intellectuals came from the fact that the accusations leveled at both groups were couched in much the same terms. As one Soviet publicist described the activities of Voskresenie, "Under the camouflage of religion all kinds of hardened counter-revolutionaries conducted anti-Soviet work. They had overseas connections and hatched plots against the Soviet regime." Most of the Voskresenie arrests were made only a day after the arrest of a group of so-called "saboteur engineers" from the Leningrad shipbuilding yards. Much was made of the group's name, Voskresenie, a word that means both "Sunday" and "resurrection" and which was interpreted as signifying that the group sought the return of the old regime.[41]

Bakhtin fell an early victim to Stromin's drive to make a

name for himself as the prosecutor of intellectuals. Bakhtin was arrested around January 7, 1929, on a number of charges. One charge, which was later dropped, was that of being a member of the Brotherhood of Saint Serafim. Another charge was that a list of members of a future anti-Communist Russian government, published in Paris, included his name along with those of Tarle and Platonov.[42] Still another charge was that in his private lectures in the pastoral courses around Leningrad Bakhtin had engaged in the Socratic crime of "corrupting the young."

Bakhtin was initially put in the Prison for Preliminary Detention, as were all the others arrested in the Voskresenie and Academy of Sciences purges. Conditions in the cells were not bad, and he was able to write. During the couple of months that he was held there, he was never tried, he was questioned infrequently, and his interrogators spoke to him with respect. Although one of them, Petrov, was not accommodating, the other, Stromin, was rather nice. When Stromin saw that Bakhtin was reading Hegel, they had a discussion about Hegel's works. Antsiferov had a much harsher recollection both of conditions in the prison and of Stromin's interrogations. Probably some of the disparity is due to Bakhtin's good nature and adaptability, as well as to the fact that he was not so central a figure for Stromin as were the others and therefore was not subjected to so intense an interrogation. When Tarle years later wrote to Bakhtin in triumph to report that their interrogator had been liquidated, Bakhtin, slow to condemn, thought ill of this attitude, since Stromin had been polite.[43]

Another factor that may have afforded Bakhtin better prison conditions was his deteriorating health. By June 1929 his leg condition was complicated by paranephritis in the kidneys. His medical condition was reevaluated, and his disability rating was upgraded to second category, which made it legally possible to transfer him from the prison to the Uritsky Hospital on July 9 for an operation the next day. The specialist, Professor Shak, kept Bakhtin there as long as he could and then had him transferred on August 8 to the Erisman Hospital, where Bakhtin remained until autumn.

In the meantime, a campaign had been started for Bakhtin's release. Yudina used every contact she could muster. She also approached Kagan's wife to help her with authorities in Moscow, where the Kagans lived. At that time E. P. Peshkova, the ex-wife of

Gorky, and a lawyer named Vinaver ran an agency of the Red Cross in Moscow to help political prisoners.[44] Yudina came down from Leningrad and, together with Kagan's wife, approached Peshkova about influencing Gorky to send a telegram to the authorities supporting Bakhtin's case. Gorky actually sent two such telegrams. Aleksey Tolstoy, the novelist, also sent one, presumably arranged by Yudina, who knew his circle at Tsarskoe selo.

Lunacharsky also helped Bakhtin's case inadvertently. Bakhtin's Dostoevsky book came out *after* his arrest, in May 1929, and Lunacharsky published a favorable review of it.[45] Bakhtin later objected that Lunacharsky had not understood his book and had found examples of polyphony in literature much earlier than the concept applied, but this was somewhat ungrateful of him, since Lunacharsky's article, together with Gorky and Tolstoy's telegrams, helped considerably in getting Bakhtin's sentence lightened, although Lunacharsky's help came almost too late in the sense that he himself was replaced as Commissar of Enlightenment in the fall of 1929.

An appeal for clemency on medical grounds was also made. On September 2, 1929, Bakhtin, then still in the hospital, sent an application to the Commissariat of Health requesting that a medical commission examine his physical condition and provide evidence in support of his application for a review of his case. At this time Bakhtin reported that he understood that he was being sentenced to five years on the Solovetsky Islands, and he protested that his health could not survive such a sentence.[46] Later he observed that the sentence was ten years, and it says something about the confusion of the times that Bakhtin's wife wrote to Kagan's wife requesting that she see Vinaver and find out exactly what Bakhtin's sentence was, since they were not sure, and ask if he could organize medical help. On October 24, 1929, Bakhtin's wife again wrote to Kagan's wife asking her to go to the Red Cross agency to find out if an answer had come through to Bakhtin's petition, which she had sent on September 5–7, for a change in the sentence on the grounds of his illness. Peshkova and Vinaver reported that the request for the review had been rejected "some time ago."

Later, possibly on December 23, Bakhtin was released from preliminary detention to recuperate at home. While there, he was visited by investigators, who politely asked him about the author-

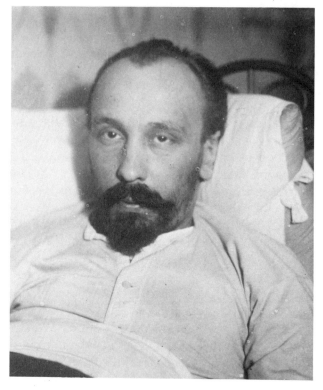

Bakhtin after his arrest, when he was suffering
from osteomyelitis and about to set off for exile
in Kazakhstan, March 1930

ship of the three books published under the names of Medvedev
and Voloshinov, but which were rumored to have been written by
Bakhtin. The investigators said, "We know you know Marxist
methods," which meant that he could have written these books
which seem Marxist. They promised not to tell or to harm the
others if Bakhtin admitted authorship. Bakhtin later remarked
ruefully that the investigators had kept their word, but that intellectuals closer to him had not and had told others of Bakhtin's authorship.

The secret police also called in Bakhtin's wife to inform her
that they had intended to sentence Bakhtin to ten years on the Solovetsky Islands but had changed the sentence to six years in exile
in the town of Kustanai in Kazakhstan. At Bakhtin's request, he

would be allowed to travel to Kustanai at his own expense, without an escort. They also gave him the right to choose his own work there, though he would not be allowed to teach in the schools. When Bakhtin's wife asked the police what life in Kustanai would be like, they replied, "The climate is severe but healthy." Certainly the climate there would be much better for Bakhtin's poor kidneys and osteomyelitis than the rigors of Solovki. The Bakhtins set out for Kustanai early in 1930.

CHAPTER 6

The Disputed Texts

There is irony in the fact that Bakhtin, who spent so much of his life meditating the concept of authorship, was himself the subject of disputes about authorship. Three of his books and several articles appeared in the 1920s under the names of his friends. Kanaev was given credit for "Contemporary Vitalism"; Medvedev was given credit for *The Formal Method in Literary Scholarship;* and Voloshinov was given credit for *Freudianism: A Critical Sketch, Marxism and the Philosophy of Language,* and the articles "Beyond the Social," "Discourse in Life and Discourse in Art," and "The Latest Trends in Linguistic Thought in the West." Bakhtin's authorship of the "Kanaev" article has never been disputed, but his authorship of the other texts, those published under the names of Medvedev and Voloshinov, has been variously denied and accepted. At times both Bakhtin and the two official authors have been assigned different roles in a kind of collaboration.[1]

The controversy is a recent one. For almost five decades only a handful of people suspected any connection between the literary journalist and cultural bureaucrat Pavel Medvedev, the linguist and sometime musicologist Valentin Voloshinov, and the literary specialist Mikhail Bakhtin. The relationship of these men had gone unperceived for so long partly because two of the individuals involved, Medvedev and Voloshinov, were relatively obscure, and by 1938 they had both died. But in the wake of the rediscovery of Bakhtin in the early 1960s Soviet scholars began to learn that the scope of his work was broader than the Dostoevsky and Rabelais books suggested. In 1967 the psycholinguist A. A. Leontiev mentioned the existence of a "Bakhtin circle," and in 1969 he quoted from *Marxism and the Philosophy of Language* to indicate the position of that circle. A year later the linguist Vyacheslav Ivanov for the first time in public unequivocally identified Bakhtin as the author of the texts by Medvedev and Voloshinov. He subsequently amended this statement by saying that Voloshinov and Medvedev had made "only small insertions and changes in particular parts."[2] Since then, recognition of Bakhtin's authorship of the disputed texts has widened. Translations of the books in Japan, Germany, and the United States now list Bakhtin as an author together with Voloshinov and Medvedev. VAAP, the Soviet copyright agency, officially requires that Bakhtin's name appear on any new edition of the disputed volumes. And most scholars both in the Soviet Union and abroad believe that Bakhtin played the central role in the production of these texts.

Unfortunately, there is nothing on paper to resolve this controversy once and for all. There is no absolutely unambiguous evidence that is the documentary equivalent of the smoking pistol. None of the manuscripts is still extant. Nor is any correspondence available of Medvedev, Voloshinov, or Bakhtin concerning these publications: Medvedev's papers were almost all confiscated by the secret police when they arrested him in 1938; Voloshinov's papers were destroyed in the Second World War when the building in which he had lived was bombed; and Bakhtin probably left his papers behind in Leningrad when he departed for Kustanai, or at any rate nothing relevant survived his subsequent moves. In 1975 Bakhtin assented to the preparation of a document to clarify matters for VAAP, which states that Bakhtin wrote the three disputed books and one of the articles, "Discourse in Life and Discourse in Art." But when this document was presented to Bakhtin for his signature, he refused to sign it. At the level of legal evidence, this only deepens the mystery.

As a result, no account of how and by whom these texts were written can ever be indisputable. Yet there is good reason to conclude that the disputed works were written by Bakhtin to the extent that he should be listed as the sole author, Medvedev and Voloshinov having played a largely editorial role in each instance. For one thing, nothing has established that Bakhtin could *not* have written the disputed texts and published them under friends' names. More important, many eyewitnesses have said that he was the author, as did both Bakhtin and his wife on private occasions. Neither the disparity between Bakhtin's private claims of authorship and his public utterances nor the disparity between the documented and oral evidence is a compelling counterargument, for a man as cautious as Bakhtin would hesitate to make public statements on this tricky issue. Indeed, during the 1960s and 1970s most people found that if they asked Bakhtin directly about whether he authored the disputed texts, he either avoided the question or was silent. At first he did not even admit authorship to his literary executors, and when he later did admit it, he did not like to talk on the subject.[3] This is yet another instance, like Solzhenitsyn's *Gulag Archipelago*, where Soviet history must, for lack of documentary sources, be put together from eyewitness, oral accounts. Although these accounts cannot be verified and may in some instances be inaccurate, in their totality they suggest the shape of events.

The accounts by Voloshinov and Medvedev's heirs of what happened are ambiguous. Voloshinov's first wife flatly disavows her husband's authorship and claims that Bakhtin wrote the two books in question, but Medvedev's son and daughter claim that their father did write the book on Formalism. As his son Yury Pavlovich Medvedev put it, "My father wrote the book as such, although he consulted with Mikhail Mikhailovich Bakhtin." Neither assertion by the Medvedevs can be considered conclusive evidence, since the daughter Natasha has little familiarity with her father's scholarly work and had never before known that there was such a disputed text, while the son was only ten months old at the time of his father's arrest and is unable to advance any material as evidence of his position.[4] Nevertheless, these assertions cannot be discounted out of hand and are reminders that a conclusive answer to the question of Bakhtin's authorship cannot be found.

There is no way to counter the sentiments of Medvedev's children. But the opinions of Western scholars who dispute Bakhtin's authorship are another matter, since they are based on less than a complete review of Bakhtin's life and work. One objection raised to Bakhtin's authorship is the difficulty of writing four books, each covering a different field, and several articles all during the brief period from 1926 to 1929. In reality, however, these works were all merely published during that period and were actually written over a much longer period. For instance, Bakhtin had already completed a book on Dostoevsky as early as 1922 and probably only revised it for later publication.[5] His article "The

Problem of Content," which had been accepted for publication in 1924, contains the basic argument of *The Formal Method in Literary Scholarship*. Moreover, it would not even have been impossible for him to write all these works in the space of a mere four years, for they do not represent major treatises in psychology, linguistics, and literary theory, which would imply a bewildering and unlikely atomization, but rather raise a single set of questions about the nature of language within a number of different contexts. A profound unity of concern informs all these books, despite their external differences. Bakhtin himself spoke of the unity of concern in all his works in an unfinished preface intended for a future collection of his writings.[6]

Most of the conditions of Bakhtin's life in the late 1920s were also conducive to productivity. He had no children and few job obligations. He was not ambitious, nor was he professionally active in the sense of making contacts and going to meetings. The practical side of his life was taken care of by his wife, who also handled much of the drudgery of manuscript preparation. Although Bakhtin was chronically ill, he had a remarkable intellectual energy, which lasted until the end of his life. Indeed, the explanation he gave to Yudina as to why he had published under his friends' names included the statement: "We were friends. We would discuss things. But they had jobs, while I had the time to write."[7]

The most important reason that Bakhtin was able to publish so prolifically in such a short period is that he did not write the works in question so much as he assembled them. Bakhtin's main method of work was to keep extensive notebooks in which he worked out his ideas. By this time, his thinking had cohered to the point of providing him with an entire philosophical system, albeit a loose one. Thus he had a major set of strategies and categories capable of processing almost any topic that interested him. He could simply rifle his notebooks for material about a given topic and prepare something on it for publication. The key to the disputed texts lies in this use of notebooks. Not only Bakhtin but several other members of his circle used the notebook method of composition. People who came into contact with Bakhtin and were impressed with his ideas usually kept notes on what he said, as Medvedev and Voloshinov undoubtedly did. The material that Bakhtin put in his notebooks was often stimulated by discussions he had had with other members of his circle. It seems highly likely, then, that much of the material in the disputed texts is worked over from notebooks, either from Bakhtin's, or from Medvedev's, or from Voloshinov's.

The actual method of composition may have resembled that found in a Renaissance artist's studio: the master, Bakhtin, would draw the main sections of the canvas, while his disciples did some of the less important painting, following his directions. This analogy, however, does not apply strictly in the case of Bakhtin and his disciples, since all three were obliged to alter their style to meet the political demands of the age, and the two disciples, Voloshinov especially, were more than mere epigones and possibly contributed material of their own. Also, as Bakhtin said, "Agreement [*soglasie* or "co-voicing"] is very rich in varieties and shading" when conceived dialogically.[8]

Another puzzle is why Bakhtin would have let so many of his major works see the light of day not only under other names, but under names that were not mere pseudonyms but belonged to real men who published under their own names works undeniably theirs. This willingness is so rare in the West that there is no term for the situation, unless it be reverse plagiarism. In Soviet Russia, however, the practice is not so rare. Several writers who have been blacklisted, such as those who signed letters of protest over the invasion of Czechoslovakia, have published under friends' names. In the main, they did so in order to receive royalties and thereby keep afloat financially, royalties for academic books being much more considerable in the Soviet Union than in the West. The desire to see the book in question in print was often a secondary consideration, and the book was written deliberately in a manner felt to be publishable. Although Bakhtin was not blacklisted, it was extremely difficult for him to publish because of his lack of an organizational affiliation or a previous publishing record, except for a short piece in a Nevel newspaper, and above all because of his known views. Indeed, the question of how Bakhtin could have written so many books and articles over the years 1926–1929 should more appropriately be reformulated to ask how Bakhtin, with his tenuous position in Soviet intellectual life, could have possibly published so many books and articles under his own name in those years when the political situation was worsening for intellectuals of his ilk. It would have been nothing short of a miracle if he had done so, especially on such subjects as Marxism, philosophy of language, and Freudianism. The Dostoevsky book, which was ostensibly about quirks of Dostoevsky's compositional method, was more publishable, though even there Bakhtin needed a lot of help for it to see the light of day.

After the closing of the *Russian Contemporary* in 1924, Bakhtin realized that he was not going to be able to publish his work. He thus had no other adequate source of income unless he published under others' names. Medvedev and Voloshinov were sufficiently cynical to see no harm in such a thing. Moreover, Medvedev, who was already helping Bakhtin out financially, was ambitious for his own academic and publishing career and wanted an impressive book to add to his dossier. An attack on the Formalists would be especially timely. He therefore contracted with Bakhtin for Bakhtin to write the Formalism book, in return for which Medvedev undertook to help get Bakhtin's Dostoevsky book published. Bakhtin later declared that the Dostoevsky book would never have been published in 1929 if it had not been for Medvedev's help.[9] The cynicism was not all on Voloshinov's and Medvedev's side. Bakhtin was himself a great lover of rascals and would have taken delight in pulling off so large-scale a hoax.

Bakhtin's involvement in this reverse plagiarism appears credible in view of other peculiar aspects of his character, which in his work were transformed into major constituents of his philosophy. The first idiosyncrasy, which in a sense subsumed all the others, was Bakhtin's love of conversation, the give and take of good talk. This is the keystone of his dialogism. Meaning is always a function of at least two consciousnesses. Thus, texts are always shared, or as he put it in explaining the reverse plagiarism, "creativity is in essence anonymous."[10]

Another idiosyncrasy was Bakhtin's love of eccentricity, peculiar people, and recherché jokes. In those turbulent, post-Revolutionary years, Bakhtin forged bonds with people who had a common flair for theatricality, disguises, and pranks. These qualities permitted them to transcend the restrictions that ordinarily close people off from one another and to create a kind of communism of the spirit that rendered immaterial, if only briefly, the differences between commissar, actor, philosopher, and musician. In this respect the Bakhtin circle resembled the medieval world of carnival where, according to Bakhtin, "civil and social ceremonies and rituals took on a comic aspect . . . All these forms of protocol

and ritual based on laughter . . . were sharply distinct from the serious, official, interiorated, feudal, and political cult forms and ceremonials."[11]

Still another key aspect of Bakhtin's character was his unwillingness to consider his texts complete, no matter how long he had
been working on them or how voluminous they had become.
Whenever he contracted to publish a work, it was only with the
utmost difficulty that friends could drag the manuscript away
from him and get it to the press. He gave permission to republish
his Dostoevsky book in the early 1960s only after an agreement
had been reached that he could add to the original version,
thereby making it clear that the 1929 book had indeed not been
finished. Even in the third edition of 1972 Bakhtin insisted on the
incompleteness of the book: "The second edition . . . had corrections made in it and was significantly expanded. But, of course,
even in its new edition the book can have no pretensions to being
a complete investigation of the problems posed."[12] He also
changed the Rabelais manuscript from the 1940s version when he
finally published it in 1965.

Bakhtin's method of composition was affected by this attitude
toward completion. Much of his work is simply a notation of ideas,
often without connecting syntactic links. Of the last book that he
saw through the press, the anthology *Questions of Literature and
Aesthetics*, he remarked that it was "unified by a single theme at
different stages of its development. The unity of an idea in the process of becoming. As a result, a certain *internal* open-endedness
(*nezaveršënnost'*) to many of my ideas. But I do not wish to make
a virtue out of a shortcoming . . . there is also a good deal of external incompletedness (*nezaveršënnost'*) not only of thought but of
its expression and articulation. It is sometimes difficult to separate
the open-endedness from the incompletedness."[13]

Bakhtin was an enemy of anything that had ceased to be in
process, which was no longer open to correction, addition, or contribution from the outside. He was ambivalent about the status of
writing as opposed to speech, and some of the subtlest of his own
applications of his theories open up other written texts to the kind
of give and take usually thought to obtain only between two people
engaged in conversation. Another reason, then, for publishing
works under other names was that he was not ready to concede
that those texts were finished, particularly since all of them were

devoted to complex issues that he continued to ponder throughout his life.

Motives of caution or fear undoubtedly played a role in Bakhtin's decision to let his thoughts enter these debates in, as it were, disguise. In the Rabelais book Bakhtin seems to be commenting on his own approach to publication when he says of Rabelais, "In spite of the frankness of his writings he not only avoided the stake but suffered no serious persecution or vexation." This was the case with Bakhtin as well, for he was arrested not for his publications but for his religious activities and lectures. Although Rabelais had "to take certain precautions, to disappear for a time," as Bakhtin himself would later do at the time of writing this work, "generally speaking everything ended well for him." In comparing Rabelais' approach with that of his friend Etienne Dolet, Bakhtin could almost have been comparing the fate of Medvedev, who was purged, with his own: Dolet "perished at the stake because of his statement which, although less daring, had been seriously made. He did not use Rabelais' methods."[14]

Bakhtin was an astute student of his own time and place. He studied them like a scholar, marking *Pravda* editorials with colored pens to bring out the hidden meanings behind the different levels of discourse. One goal in his own work, to develop more refined techniques for analyzing in different historical periods the specific mix of ideologies and of languages in which they were couched, was a reflection at the theoretical level of a more practical concern. Soviet citizens are perforce semioticians, constantly scanning the political horizon for signs of which way the breeze of the permissible will next blow. The Soviet Union, rather than Japan, is the true *Empire des signes,* and the wages for failing to read the signs correctly can be dire indeed.

Yet another objection to Bakhtin's authorship of the disputed texts is based on their alleged Marxism. The argument goes that Bakhtin was a non-Marxist and would not have wished to associate his name with texts which had for reasons of political tact been given a Marxist coloring. Moreover, as one scholar put it, "The Marxist orientation (however unorthodox from some points of view) that permeates all the writings signed by V. N. Voloshinov (and Medvedev as well) is conspicuously absent from Bakhtin's [Dostoevsky] book."[15]

But Medvedev and Voloshinov did not have a Marxist orientation in all their writings. Moreover, Bakhtin did in fact use Marxist terminology in most of his published works, including the Dostoevsky book. Thus, the difference between texts is not a question of the presence or absence of Marx but of how much of his terminology is used. For instance, in the first edition of the Dostoevsky book Bakhtin explains that the polyphonic novel could have "been realized only in the capitalist epoch. The most favorable soil for it was moreover precisely in Russia, where capitalism set in almost catastrophically and where it came upon an untouched multitude of diverse worlds and social groups which had not been weakened in their individual isolation, as in the West, by the gradual encroachment of capitalism."[16] The language in which this point is cast, with its assumptions about capitalism's near-catastrophic arrival, the widespread leveling out of differences, and the atomization that accompanies alienation, is in a general sense Marxist.

A more sustained Marxist orientation is evident in the two works that Bakhtin published under his own name in 1929 and 1930, the introductions to two of the thirteen volumes of the *Collected Literary Works* of Tolstoy that began to appear in 1928 under the general editorship of Konstantin Khalabaev and Boris Eikhenbaum. Only two other volumes in this edition were published with introductions, and these essays were written by two well-established Bolsheviks, Akselrod-Ortodoks and Lev Voitolovsky. Bakhtin adapted his voice convincingly to fit the rest of this Marxist choir. The first of his essays, dealing with the plays that Tolstoy had written before 1880, is grounded in a thesis taken almost unchanged from the conventional party line. Tolstoy is seen as a nobleman who, aware that the newly emerging Russian capitalism was destroying his cherished aristocratic ideals, retreated in *War and Peace* from the hurly-burly of his own age back to the patriarchal life of his forebears. Tolstoy misrepresented the peasants, showing their strivings from his own point of view, which were not at all "the class aspirations of the peasants themselves . . . The socioeconomic base, everyday peasant reality, is left completely out of these plays. The capitalistic disintegration of the countryside, their struggle with the kulak-bloodsuckers [*bor'ba s kulakom-miroedom,* one of the party slogans during this period of collectivization], with officials, landlessness, the threat of arbitrariness in civil law—none of this is anything like reflected in Tolstoy's drama."[17]

In his second essay, an introduction to *Resurrection,* Bakhtin goes even further, accusing Tolstoy of lacking a "dialectical sense of history." To support this thesis, he cites the reservations earlier expressed in Plekhanov's essay "Karl Marx and Lev Tolstoi," as well as in the party's canonical statement on the subject, Lenin's 1906 essay "Lev Tolstoy as a Mirror of the Russian Revolution," from which the view of the patriarchal Tolstoy derives. By now Bakhtin has learned the language not only of Marxist but of Soviet Marxist literary criticism: "Our Soviet literature has recently worked unyieldingly to create new forms of the socioideological novel. This is perhaps the most important and vital (*aktual'nyj*) genre in our literature at the current time. The socioideological novel is ultimately a socially tendentious novel, a completely legitimate artistic form. An unwillingness to admit its purely artistic permissibility is the naive prejudice of a superficial aestheticism which it is long past time to eliminate . . . As a model for the socioideological novel, *Resurrection* may have a not inconsiderable value for the contemporary literary quest."[18]

This remark by Bakhtin may have a subtext. In the late 1920s as Soviet literature was tending toward its ultimate canon of socialist realism, Lunacharsky had coined the term *socioideological* to identify the sort of tendentious writing he favored for Soviet literature. But this comment by Bakhtin, praising *Resurrection* as such a model, must be viewed in context with the lack of enthusiasm that he expressed for Tolstoy in many of his other writings. The statement may therefore have been a mask over one of his jokes. He may have been taking a dig at what would become known as socialist realism by identifying it with a novel from Tolstoy's religious phase.[19]

On the surface of these two essays, however, Bakhtin shows great tact in giving his nod to the establishment view of what should happen to Soviet literature. Taking his cue from Lenin, he also shows great skill in both condemning and defending Tolstoy within the language and system of the party. In this sense, Bakhtin was just like other party-minded scholars working on literature during this period, including Medvedev and Voloshinov. Thus the reality is that all three, Bakhtin, Medvedev, and Voloshinov, became more Marxist in their writings of the late 1920s, as was necessary to ensure publishability.

Bakhtin's religious persuasion has also been proposed as

ground that he could not have written such Marxist texts as the disputed works. This charge raises questions of how Marxist the texts in question really are, and how incompatible with Bakhtin's religious position is the Marxist terminology used. Many members of the religious circles around Bakhtin in his early adulthood used discourse that combined "Christian truth with Marxist sociology," and in the early 1920s some members of the Voskresenie group even wanted to reconcile communism and Christ, not then for reasons of political expedience but out of conviction.[20] There is much common ground between Marxism and certain Russian strands of radical Christianity. In particular, Marxism's stress on collectivity fits with the antisubjectivist position of Orthodox theology. For many who participated in the religious revival of the early twentieth century the principle of true communality was combined with the intelligentsia's traditional emphasis on social justice and their traditional distaste for both the "spirit of property" dominating the "bourgeois" West and the ruling classes' desire to impose a single set of values. In fact, much of the purportedly Marxist terminology used in the disputed texts was not exclusively the property of Marxists but was commonly used by leftist intellectuals in Russia in the late nineteenth and early twentieth centuries.

Thus Bakhtin was frequently able to capitalize on the common ground between Marxist terminology and his own thought. Much of the supposedly Marxist terminology he uses can readily be translated into his own characteristic terminology without conceptual violence. For instance, the "base/superstructure" distinction can stand for the "given/conceived" distinction that Bakhtin took from Neo-Kantianism, and the Marxist stress on the collective can translate into Bakhtin's insistence on the primacy of the social in human development.

Bakhtin was trying above all in this period to articulate a philosophy that accommodated traditional subjects of religion in secular terms and which also gave language a central place. The particular Marxist terms that he used in the disputed texts made it possible not merely to express views that did not clash with his religious convictions but also to articulate his own linguistic theories. For instance, as a philosopher of dialogue, Bakhtin opposed any tendency that in his judgment gave insufficient weight to the social nature of human existence, which in *The Architec-*

tonics he called the "sharing/event of being" (*sobytie bytija*). While Marx advanced the collective in the service of a particular ideology, Bakhtin, a philosopher of language, emphasized the shared nature of communication. In his analysis of speech operations the collective is not simply a posited construct but an actual reality which cannot be doubted by anyone who uses words.

The dominance of the collective over the individual that characterizes both Marxism and linguistics doubtless accounts for the fact that Leonard Bloomfield, after reading *Das Kapital* in the 1930s, "was impressed above all by the similarity between Marx's treatment of social behavior and that of linguistics."[21] In all Bakhtin's writings, language is that which makes humans human. But language is in its nature collective, and therefore people are in their essence social.

Vladimir Propp, another literary theoretician and Bakhtin's contemporary, cautioned in his *Morphology of the Folktale* (1929) against overinvesting meaning in the coloration given a particular protagonist in a folktale and suggested that the protagonist's function was more crucial. By analogy, one should concentrate more on the functions performed by the Marxist terminology in the disputed texts and not assume a one-to-one relation between their brute presence in the texts and the political convictions of the putative authors. The Marxism generally serves two functions. On the one hand, it acts as a safety measure, encoding potentially explosive ideas. On the other, it legitimizes Bakhtin's own theories by capitalizing on the common ground between them and Marxism. Marxism takes three forms in the disputed texts, none of which is itself unambiguous. It is present in the form of direct quotations from Marx, of terms taken over from the Marxist tradition but found outside Marxism as well, and of Marxist ideas or values. All three forms of Marxism are used to assign or deny validity to claims made from other points of view. For instance, Marxism's opposition to Monism is used to validate Bakhtin's own anti-Monistic position.

Bakhtin's authorship of the disputed texts is confirmed by the texts themselves, especially in comparison with other texts by Bakhtin, Medvedev, and Voloshinov. There is a superficial but nonetheless significant feature which all the disputed books and several of the articles have in common, an authorial strategy which was a hallmark of Bakhtin's longer publications, such as the Dostoevsky book, and several other writings of his whose authorship is not in dispute, such as "The Problem of Content." This feature is an opening section which sets up two contrasting approaches to the subject at hand, such as idealism versus positivism in the case of *The Formal Method,* and then advances the author's own position as one that avoids the mistakes of either extreme.

Although Medvedev was much more prolific in his publications of the 1920s than was Voloshinov, there are fewer disputed texts by "Medvedev" than by "Voloshinov." The dispute in Medvedev's case centers around three texts that deal with the Formalists: "Scientific Salierism" (1924), *The Formal Method* (1928), and *Formalism and the Formalists* (1934). Medvedev is generally regarded as not having had the intellectual caliber to have written one of these texts published in his name.[22] Of the three in dispute, Bakhtin wrote only *The Formal Method.* Of the other two, only "Scientific Salierism" seems even remotely likely to have been by Bakhtin. It contains much of the distinctive vocabulary of his Neo-Kantian period, such as *dannost'/zadannost', postupok,* and *arxitektonika,* and it presents a similar argument to the one offered in Bakhtin's "The Problem of Content," which was to have been published in the same year, and in *The Formal Method.* For example, the author describes the Formalists' absolute insistence on form to the detriment of content as a *reductio ad absurdum,* which obliges them in the end to reintroduce content anyway. However, this article was more likely influenced by Bakhtin but executed by Medvedev, because it is more superficial than Bakhtin's work. There is no philosophical depth, and its parade of learning amounts to name dropping. Above all, the article is more polemical and vague than Bakhtin's writings. It is a relentless and self-righteous monologue. The author descends to name calling as his method of attack, a technique commonly used by the literary journalist but never by Bakhtin until the late 1920s when he was obliged to use certain standard terms of abuse from that time, like "kulak bloodsucker."

The Formal Method, however, is largely by Bakhtin. The book's philosophical orientation and the seriousness and rigor of its arguments are his. Once again, the more heavy-handed Marxist passages of the book have the air of interpolations, being the sort of window dressing deemed necessary to get the book past censors and editors. The author's periodic assertion that "only Marxism" or "dialectical materialism" provides a valid methodology for pursuing issues that the Formalists had pursued erroneously does not prevent him from taking a theoretical position substantially like the one Bakhtin adopted in *The Architectonics*.[23] These "Marxisms" do not represent mere random obsequies to the language of the age but follow a shrewd, well-worked-out strategy. Moreover, much the same strategy characterizes the "Voloshinov" book *Marxism and the Philosophy of Language*. Both these factors suggest that the passages were added to the completed text in an effort to get the book past the censor, either by Bakhtin himself, shrewd follower of signs of the times as he was, or by Medvedev, or by the three friends working together. The interpolations may also have been suggested by another party altogether. When Medvedev was arrested in 1938, one of the letters written to the security police in his support came from V. A. Desnitsky, an old Bolshevik and Marxist literary theoretician, who was Medvedev's superior at the Herzen Pedagogical Institute and had had a long association with him since the days when they both worked in Extramural Education, and who was also Voloshinov's superior at the Institute for the Comparative History of Literatures and Languages of the East and West when Voloshinov was in graduate school there. In this letter Desnitsky stated that Medvedev had consulted him about the manuscript for *The Formal Method*, and Desnitsky had suggested changes.

Even if Medvedev and Voloshinov sought authoritative outside help in preparing the disputed texts to pass the censors, they probably used their advice selectively, for the Marxism in these texts is of a singular kind. In *The Formal Method* it is opposed both to positivism and to what in the Soviet Union was labeled in the late 1920s "vulgar sociologism," the notion that literature can directly reflect such extraliterary factors as ideologies, socioeconomic conditions, or class situations. Indeed, the book maintains that literature does not reflect external reality directly at all. At the same time, it criticizes leading Marxist literary theoreticians of the day and even goes so far as to criticize the attacks of Soviet Marxists on the Formalists. It also slips in a not unfavorable mention of the Neo-Kantians and commends the religious thinker Askoldov's earlier criticisms of the Formalists.[24] Certainly this is not Marxism in the sense used conventionally in Soviet literary criticism of the day. The philosophy of the book is dominated by a concern more for the nature of signs than for any Marxism as such.

Eight years later Medvedev published another book on the

Formalists, *Formalism and the Formalists,* when Bakhtin was already in exile, so that there cannot have been much contact between the two men. In this work the function of the Marxist rhetoric is almost exclusively polemical, part and parcel of a virulent personal attack. The author is unmistakably Medvedev. Marxism is invoked as a self-evident truth in a way that is foreign to *The Formal Method.* No one has ever suggested that Bakhtin had anything to do with this later text.

It is much easier to determine which of the "Medvedev" publications is written by Bakhtin and which are by Medvedev himself than is the case for the disputed "Voloshinov" publications. For example, there is a greater contradiction between works actually written by Medvedev and the one now ascribed to Bakhtin than there is between works actually written by Voloshinov and those now claimed to be by Bakhtin. Voloshinov's undisputed publications of the late 1920s also show greater depth, erudition, and intellectual caliber than do Medvedev's undisputed publications of the same period. Though Voloshinov cannot match Bakhtin's brilliance, he comes closer to it than does Medvedev. Moreover, with his training in linguistics, Voloshinov was better equipped than Medvedev to pronounce on certain theoretical questions that Bakhtin tackled. Also, there is a much larger body of disputed "Voloshinov" material, which includes not only *Freudianism, Marxism and the Philosophy of Language,* "Beyond the Social," "Discourse in Life and Discourse in Art," and "The Latest Trends in Linguistic Thought in the West," but also two other articles, "Stylistics of Literary Discourse" and "On the Borders of Poetics and Linguistics." All these publications constitute a recognizable whole, inasmuch as the same key concerns are found throughout. In particular, they advance a theory of utterance as a dialogic process in which not only the speaker or writer is involved but also the implied or actual listener or addressee. They stress the importance of context in meaning, as well as the crucial role of intonation both in giving an utterance its evaluative coloring and in reflecting the force of its context. All the "Voloshinov" texts attack Formalism and other approaches to poetics that similarly treat a text as a grammar of signs rather than as a dynamic interplay. One of the hallmarks of these texts is a section in each demonstrating that a particular utterance can mean many different things, depending on the context in which it occurs. Most of the differences between the texts can be ascribed to the changing times in which they were published, starting in 1925 and ending in 1930. For instance, beginning around 1928 and intensifying in 1930, the "Voloshinov" publications become even more redolent with quotations from Marxists, especially Engels, which may reflect the increasing political pressure on writers and scholars and the increasing emphasis on the class nature of culture during the cultural revolution of those years. They also display an increasingly linguistic bias, most obviously from 1927, the year in which Voloshinov himself turned to linguistics as his specialty.

Most of the stylistic differences between the publications can be accounted for in terms of function. For instance, "Stylistics of Literary Discourse," a three-part article published in *Literary Study* in 1930, is somewhat simplistic and didactic, as articles published in that journal for beginner writers were intended to be. Other articles, such as "On the Borders of Poetics and Linguistics" of the same year, are more crudely polemical than the earlier works. But these differences in the various "Voloshinov" works are not so great as to make it impossible that the same person wrote them all.

These features do not prove that all the articles were written by Voloshinov, for they are characteristic as well of Bakhtin's writings of the 1920s. Most of the recurrent themes and ideas of the "Voloshinov" publications, for example, are found in *The Architectonics*. Moreover, much of the vocabulary of *The Architectonics* appears in the "Voloshinov" publications, where it is used in the same distinctive way. Examples include Bakhtin's proclivity for using the prefix *so-* in words like *so-vybor* (co-choice) and *so-tvorčeskoe* (co-creative), and his idiosyncratic use of *sobytie* (event/co-being), *vzaimodejstvie* (interaction) or *vzaimootnošenie* (interrelationship), *krugozor* (horizon), *ocenka* (evaluation), and *cennostno-ierarxičeskij* (evaluating and hierarchical). Also, the later "Voloshinov" articles include words from Bakhtin's new vocabulary of the end of the 1920s, such as "monologic" and "dialogic." Some characteristic features of the disputed "Voloshinov" texts resurface in Bakhtin's writings only in his later period, most strikingly in his notes of the 1970s where he adduces examples of polysemy in even the simplest utterances, such as, "What is the time?"[25] Both within and between individual "Voloshinov" texts there are variations in the degree to which statements read as pure Bakhtin, but even these variations do not indicate that the Bakhtinian sections were written by Bakhtin and the non-Bakhtinian by Voloshinov, because Bakhtin himself was fully prepared to compromise in the interests of publishability, and Voloshinov the disciple was wont on occasion to ape Bakhtin.

The many resemblances between the "Voloshinov" texts and others indubitably by Bakhtin prove, minimally, that Voloshinov was a disciple of Bakhtin or at least a fellow member of the old Nevel School and, maximally, that Bakhtin wrote all the works in question. As it happens, Bakhtin himself told his literary executors that he wrote all of them except "Stylistics of Literary Discourse." This statement does not really resolve the issue, for several of the articles beg the question of the extent of collaboration in working over the notebooks for publication.

The earliest "Voloshinov" text that seems a candidate for Bakhtin's authorship is "Beyond the Social," which was published in *The Star* early in 1925. Many sections in this article are similar to sections in "Voloshinov's" later *Freudianism,* published in the summer of 1927, which is also by Bakhtin. In particular, much of the first half of the article reads as a précis of the book. Where the two texts are more or less parallel, there are only minor differences in the wording of most of the sentences. For instance, the paragraphing, word order, and emphasis are often changed; sometimes a verb is given in the passive voice in one text and in the active in another; and frequently a different adjective is used. Some differences are even slighter. The only difference in one sentence is that in rendering the instrumental singular of the word "form," the article uses the standard form -*oj,* while the book uses the less common form -*oju.*[26]

The book is generally assumed to represent an expanded version of the article, but it is very possible that both are based on a third, preexisting text, Bakhtin's notebooks. The largely inconsequential differences between the book and the article can be explained not as a reworking of the article but rather as a reworking of the notes on Freud. Bakhtin probably rifled his notes on Freud to produce the article as a sort of first foray into print with his ideas under another's name, in the hope that a larger version of the material in his notebooks could later see the light of day as a book. The article must have been written in 1924 at the latest. By the time Bakhtin came to writing the book, which was probably in

1926 because of the citations to works published in that year, he had brought his own thinking and reading on the subject a little further, and there had been further discussions on Freud in his circle. Sollertinsky, for instance, lectured on Freud at the Institute for the History of the Arts in 1926. Bakhtin's notebooks on the subject would thus have been expanded. The further development of Bakhtin's thought is reflected in some differences between the two published texts, such as the introduction in the Freud book of the concept of "official consciousness."[27] The most important of these differences stems from Bakhtin's own changing interests over the years, since by 1926 he had already turned his attention to linguistics. In consequence, the book criticizes Freud's theories of the subconscious in terms of Bakhtin's own theories of language acquisition, a dimension that is completely absent from the article.

Whereas the emphasis in the Freud book is linguistic, the article reflects Bakhtin's interest at the time in the physiology of the brain, which was at its height in 1924–1925. This physiological aspect becomes most marked when "Voloshinov," in trying to substitute something concrete for Freud's woolly concept of the subconscious, posits "mechanisms analogous to those now familiar to us as reflexes (academician Pavlov and his school), and partly also as tropisms (Loeb) and as other chemisms, in short, processes which are purely somatic, materialistic." This reference to reflexology and the physiology or chemistry of the brain was presumably designed in part to make the critique of Freud more "materialist" and "positivist" for the authorities. But it was not an entirely cynical gesture, because the article continues, "any scientific definitions of the Freudian phenomena of the subconscious must be made at this level. And yet, of course, we are not able to translate them into this materialistic language, but at least we already know in which direction the translation can be made." Bakhtin's burgeoning interest in the physiology of the brain was also manifest in the next article that he prepared for publication under another's name, his "Kanaev" article on Vitalism, which appeared early in 1926 and to which, incidentally, he referred in a footnote of his Freud book.[28]

The Freud book might seem to have reversed Bakhtin's earlier position by its condemnation of the reflexologists: "*In psychology a simplistic, mechanistic materialism could well play a disastrous role.* Just such a turn in the direction of primitive materialism . . . is detectable among the American behaviorists and the Russian reflexologists." Yet this statement does not represent a volte-face so much as an elaboration of ideas that could be expressed only cryptically in the earlier article. The book repeatedly chides Freud for producing an account of the psyche which, while deceptively peppered with terms from biology, is in fact a "psychologized and subjectivized" version of biology.[29]

Bakhtin develops this idea in the book by restating the passage about Pavlov and Loeb from the article. The revised version asserts the value of looking into the objective findings of physiologists like Pavlov and Loeb for more satisfactory explanations of the phenomena that Freud had attempted to explain, but immediately adds that this is "in itself inadequate to explain human behavior." Since verbalization is so central to the workings of the psyche, economic and social factors have to be taken into account, and this can best be done by using the "versatile methods of dialectical materialism."[30] This statement, while as politically cautious as the earlier version in stressing the need to know economic factors, also reflects Bakhtin's own changing views and his heightened awareness of the centrality of language in all human activity.

The Marxist aspects of *Freudianism*, which have been cited to prove that it was not written by Bakhtin, have been exaggerated, as symbolized by the fact that the English language translation is called *Freudianism: A Marxist Critique*, although the Russian title, *Frejdizm: Kritičeskij očerk*, does not include the word *Marxism*. The attack on Freud, while couched in the clichés of Marxist rhetoric, such as "socioeconomic forces," "class disintegration," and "bourgeois philosophy," is not in essence dependent on a specifically Marxist point of view. Bakhtin's main charge against Freud is that he is a subjectivist, who values the individual psyche over collective experience. Such an attitude toward Freud logically follows from the philosophical point of view that Bakhtin had already worked out in *The Architectonics*. Similarly, the only specific reference to Marx is a quotation from the *Six Theses on Feuerbach*: "The essence of man is not an abstraction inherent in each separate individual. In reality it is the aggregate of social relationships."[31] This statement emphasizes the collective and social in man, a position that accords not only with Marxist thought but with any other position, such as Bakhtin's, that assigns a central place in consciousness to language.

When Bakhtin appears to be speaking most authoritatively in the name of Marxism itself, he in fact makes statements that many orthodox Marxists and certainly most Soviet Marxists would find debatable, if not downright heretical. At the very time, for instance, that he was writing "Marxism is far from denying the role of the subjective-psychical," such leading spokesmen for Soviet psychology as A. G. Kornilov were making speeches at the All-Russian Congress of Psychoneurology denying any subjective content in the psyche and claiming that what bourgeois science called "the subjective psychical" was merely an illusion which "a truly objective" Marxist psychology must ruthlessly expose. Moreover, when Bakhtin invokes the sacred phrase "dialectical materialism," it is to bolster an argument that he had already been making for several years in the service of his own epistemological theory. "Dialectical materialism," he asserts, demands that "human psychology be socialized."[32] This is a demand not only of dialectical materialism but also of Bakhtin's Neo-Kantian system of ethics, in that there is no "I" without the "other," and existence is defined as the sharing of experience with others.

In short, both the article and the book on Freud were probably written by Bakhtin in the sense of being based on his notebooks. This does not, however, say who actually wrote down each text and prepared it for publication. According to Voloshinov's widow, Bakhtin wrote out *Freudianism* himself. Whether he did or not is in any case of no great significance, since both texts are fundamentally Bakhtin's.

The next disputed "Voloshinov" article is "Discourse in Life and Discourse in Art," published in 1926. Although this article was included in the declaration of authorship of disputed texts that Bakhtin refused to sign, it is unquestionably his. Its language is distinctively Bakhtin's, and it opens with the tell-tale Bakhtinian practice of playing two opposites off against each other. It is a nodal work, with links to most of the major texts that Bakhtin wrote in the 1920s. Principal arguments in *The Architectonics*, such as the shared nature of language, the importance of its hierarchical and evaluative aspects, and the interrelationship between author, addressee, and hero, are aired again in "Discourse in Life and Discourse in Art," using much the same idiosyncratic terminology. At the same time, the article stresses the importance of context and intonation in giving meaning to utterance, a point that is a hallmark of all the disputed "Voloshinov" texts. Additionally, the relationship between author/hero and addressee treated in the article is further developed in Bakhtin's *Problems of Dostoevsky's Creative Works* (1929), while the article's critique of Formalism is offered less cryptically in his *The Formal Method*. In short, "Discourse in Life and Discourse in Art" in some ways provides a key to the essential Bakhtin of the 1920s.

The next "Voloshinov" publication, "The Latest Trends in Linguistic Thought in the West," was published in 1928. It is presented as a synopsis of three chapters of "Voloshinov's" forthcoming book *Marxism and the Philosophy of Language*. Inasmuch as the book is Bakhtin's, the article is presumably his likewise, though Bakhtin could have assigned to Voloshinov the onerous task of preparing a synopsis.

The authorship of *Marxism and the Philosophy of Language*, published in 1929, is clearly Bakhtin's. Aside from the title, the passages reputedly expressing Marxism, as in the declaration that only a Marxist approach can provide a cogent account of the nature of language, and the use of Marxist terms, such as *base* and *superstructure*, occur primarily in the first twenty-five pages of the book or in the final summarizing paragraphs of subchapters—namely in the very places to which a censor or publishing house editor's attention would be most alerted. The farther one reads in the book, the more the Marxist terminology fades from view. Moreover, although Marxist terminology appears periodically in declarations about the methodological approach, the book is singularly lacking in the sort of economic or class analysis that such declarations would suggest. The author is careful to justify this absence by criticizing the "vulgar sociologism" that was conveniently under attack at the time and by proposing that "class does not coincide with sign community." In some places, however, Marxist terminology gets confused. In one case the "base" is equated with "actual existence," and in another place a "typology" of forms of verbal communication is called "the most urgent task of Marxism." Another incongruous identification is implied between "production relations and the sociopolitical order" and "the hierarchical factor in the process of verbal exchange."[33] The book is thus a Marxist study of the science of ideology in only the most unconventional sense.

The last two disputed "Voloshinov" texts, the three-part "Stylistics of Literary Discourse" and "On the Borders of Poetics and Linguistics," were both published in 1930. Circumstantial reasons would militate against Bakhtin's having written either of them. He was arrested in January 1929; "On the Borders of Poetics and Linguistics" is dated November 13, 1929; and *Literary Study,* the journal in which "Stylistics of Literary Discourse" appeared, did not begin publication until 1930, so the article is unlikely to have been commissioned before Bakhtin's arrest. It would have been possible, however, that both articles were written before Bakhtin's arrest, or that Voloshinov was able to consult with Bakhtin or even get him to write the articles during the fall of 1929, when Bakhtin was released from prison to recuperate at home before setting off for exile.

Only Part Two of "Stylistics of Literary Discourse," titled "The Construction of an Utterance," has ever been claimed to be Bakhtin's, based on the degree of Bakhtinianism represented in it as compared with the crude Marxism of the other two parts. The first part, "What is language?" opens with a review of the history of language development, which takes as its guideline a "brilliant finding" from Engels and stresses the important role played in language development by such factors as the organization of labor and the advent of private property. At the end of the article, however, this heavy Marxist barrage gives way to the more familar Bakhtinian territory of inner speech and implied addressee. The second part, while not free of Marxist declarations, seems more purely Bakhtinian in its stress on context and intonation in meaning and its analysis of the different speech levels used by Chichikov in *Dead Souls* with different addressees. Moreover, the use of Marxism here displays the familiar casuistic patterns from *Marxism and the Philosophy of Language.* For instance, first the economic organization of society is called a crucial factor in language change, and then the subject its blithely abandoned. In another apparent attack on vulgar sociology, the author asserts, "You can't go directly from the economic and political conditions to the type of social discourse in a particular work." The third part, "Discourse and Its Social Function," is the most crudely Marxist of any work by "Voloshinov." Throughout, it insists on class as a crucial factor in the different meanings of words and even makes such claims as that "the proletariat, whose subjective point of view comes closest to the objective logic of reality, naturally does not have to distort that reality in its utterances."[34]

The varying degrees of Marxism in the three parts of this article are not sufficient reason for claiming the least Marxist to be Bakhtin's and the more Marxist Voloshinov's. For one reason, the apparent style of the three parts seems much the same, suggesting a sole author in the sense of the one who did the actual writing. For another reason, the years 1929–1930 were the most class-conscious and proletarian-oriented in the entire history of the Soviet Union, and all those who wished to publish at this time knew how they should color their writings. The two texts that Bakhtin published in 1930 under his own name, the introductions to Tolstoy, are striking examples of adaptation to the class hysteria of the time. A highly speculative but possible publication scenario for these three articles is therefore that the author, sensitive to the times in which he was writing, used a great deal of Marxism to ensure publication for his first article but, once it had been accepted, felt free to tone down the Marxism for the second. When the second then occasioned some problems, the third article had to be revamped in even more crudely Marxist terms, and consequently it missed being published in the next issue of *Literary Study*, no. 4, and did not appear until no. 5.

Bakhtin never claimed authorship of the article, and indeed the argument in many places does not reflect an intellect of his stature. At the same time, the article is Bakhtinian in the sense that, were it to be pruned of its Marxist window dressing, it would present many of Bakhtin's most characteristic ideas on language. Voloshinov most likely wrote it from his own notes.

The last disputed "Voloshinov" text is "On the Borders of Poetics and Linguistics." This text is more crudely polemical than anything Bakhtin ever wrote, the main butt of its attack being the Formalists in general and Vinogradov in particular. It is also more parochial, centering on the theoretical debates of the time in the Soviet Union, and it lacks the breadth of Bakhtin's writings, such as his own attack on the Formalists in *The Formal Method*. The author does occasionally invoke non-Soviet theoreticians and even embarks on a history of poetic language, but these subjects are not well integrated into the text, and the history never gets farther than the Greeks and the Indians. Nor is the Marxism as deftly or ambiguously deployed in this work as in earlier "Voloshinov" texts. For example, to illustrate how even the most reduced utterances depend on context and speaker for meaning, the article abandons such politically neutral examples as Bakhtin's *tak* (well) in "Discourse in Life and Discourse in Art," in favor of the expression, "I want to be like Lenin, like Vladimir Ilich."[35]

Despite all this, the article manages to be very Bakhtinian. It includes much of the familar Bakhtinian vocabulary, such as *sobytie, vzaimodejstvie, vzaimootnošenie, krugozor,* and *ocenka,* together with many characteristically Bakhtinian ideas and formulations, such as the notion that meaning resides not in the word itself, but in its relationship to author, addressee, and hero.[36] The article also has the air of having been written by someone from Bakhtin's circle in that it prominently cites *Marxism and the Philosophy of Language* and *The Formal Method.*

As it happens, Bakhtin told his literary executors that he wrote this article. The very fact that Bakhtin is one of the few people to claim that this last, and least Bakhtinian, of all the "Voloshinov" texts was written by him raises major problems in trying to decide who is the "real" author of these texts. Does authorship amount to preparing a manuscript for publication? Does it amount to translating ideas into a form and vocabulary acceptable for publication? Or does it mean providing the original ideas, along with the highly idiosyncratic vocabulary in which they are couched? These questions obsessed Bakhtin all his life. In a very real sense, then, the problem of answering the apparently naive question of who wrote which of the disputed texts addresses the same set of complexities that Bakhtin placed at the heart of his theories. If, as he maintained early and late, the relation between self and other is the key to all human understanding, and if "Quests for my own word are quests for a word that is not my own," then how can one ever assign responsibility for the acts that words are? If one's "own" word can never be the ultimate word, how is one answerable for what one says? Conversely, how is Bakhtin answerable for the texts that saw the light of day under the names of his friends?[37]

This is not the same as asking who is the "real" author of the disputed texts, which is unanswerable for technical reasons. It is also unanswerable for theoretical reasons, as Bakhtin implied when he wrote near the end of his life, "There are no pure texts, nor can there be."[38] But within Bakhtin's terms, he is still answerable for the texts that appeared under others' names in the sense that there is more of his self in them than of any of the other selves to whom they have been ascribed. Bakhtin argued from the first that any utterance is a shared text, partly one's own, partly the other's to whom it is addressed. The question is, whose part is the determining one, the author's or the addressee's? How much of one's self and how much of the other is present in the utterance? This is a question about proportion and ratio rather than about identity as such.

The architectonics of Bakhtin's answerability for his own self resulted in a search for meaning in the difficult years following the Revolution that required a style, a genre, that made the otherness of his friends obligatory. In these terms, Bakhtin may be said to be the author of the disputed texts, while at the same time avoiding "the false tendency to reduce everything to a single consciousness." Voloshinov, Medvedev, and Kanaev were coauthors in the texts published under their names, but so were Dostoevsky, Goethe, and Rabelais in other works. And the name "Bakhtin" itself is on occasion such an authorial other. With these complexities in mind, it is fitting to let Bakhtin himself have the last word as he asks himself in his notebooks, "In which utterance is there ever a face—and not a mask?"[39]

CHAPTER 7

Freudianism

Bakhtin began reading Freud systematically soon after his return to Leningrad in 1924, when Freud was very much in the air.[1] And just as Bakhtin felt compelled to join the debate surrounding the Formalists in literary theory, he felt called upon to engage the issue of Freud's place in psychological theory. Though long since a discredited name in the Soviet Union, Freud was in those years at the center of attempts to found a Marxist psychology. The All-Russian Congresses of Psychoneurology in Moscow in 1923 and 1924 focused almost entirely on Freud, and in 1925 the Communist Academy itself organized a conference on "Freud and Art." Bakhtin's contributions to these debates, which include three articles and a book, were all written under the names of others. As "Voloshinov," Bakhtin published the article "Beyond the Social," dealing openly with Freud. Under the name of his biologist friend Kanaev, Bakhtin published a two-part article on Vitalism, which directly attacks Henri Bergson and Hans Driesch, leading proponents of the idea that life is a force larger than mere biological determinants, but which is covertly aimed at Freud. And in 1927, once again as "Voloshinov," Bakhtin published *Freudianism: A Critical Sketch,* which sums up and extends the arguments against psychoanalysis contained in the earlier pieces.[2]

Bakhtin's interpretation of Freud came at a crucial point in the career of both men. Freud had begun his career as a "hard" scientist doing physiological research in the laboratory of Ernst Brücke, whose credo was, "No other forces than the common physical-chemical one are active within the organism."[3] The biologically deterministic principles of this early training continued to color Freud's later work in psychoanalytic theory and were responsible for Bakhtin's major criticisms. In Freud's last period, in such works as *Civilization and Its Discontents* (1930) and *Moses and Monotheism* (1939), he demonstrated a concern for precisely those issues of history and culture that Bakhtin charged him, in the 1920s, with ignoring.

Bakhtin also wrote about Freud at a particular juncture in his own thinking, when the early influence of German philosophy was increasingly complicated by his interest in recent advances in physiology. In other words, Bakhtin was moving from philosophy to physiology at roughly the point when Freud was moving from physiology to philosophy, although the physiology that occupied Bakhtin after 1924 was heavily freighted with metaphysics and even theology. Thus Bakhtin's view of Freud was influenced by developments in physiology, which accounts for the particular emphasis of his critique. Although in his Freud book, as in all his other works of the 1920s, Bakhtin formulates his argument on the basis of the general categories that he had already worked out in *The Architectonics,* his idiosyncratic, metaphysical style is here transformed into a simpler mode more attuned to the expectations of the wider audience he was now seeking. And his basic categories, such as the I/other, given/conceived, and inner/outer body, are translated from the language of philosophy into a more popular discourse that is engaged with more immediate social issues.

The first in this series of texts on psychology was the 1924 article "Beyond the Social." While there are differences, it hints at the final chapter of the Freud book. That chapter is a critique less of Freud himself, although he is given harsh judgment, than of Soviet psychologists who sought to appropriate Freud into a new science of the mind that would be not only revolutionary but Marxist. The one feature common to all these scientific attempts was the claim that Freud was not an idealist or subjectivist, as some Marxists had charged, but that on the contrary he fit in very well with the purely objective demands of dialectical materialism. The claims made on this point by A. B. Zalkind struck a particular nerve in Bakhtin. Zalkind argued that Freud had been misunderstood because no one had perceived that he was essentially a reflexologist, who was trying to do many of the same things that Pavlov in his experiments with dogs was trying to do. In order to arrive at this curious conclusion, Zalkind had to deny that sex was at the center of Freudian theory and that there was. any such thing as an unconscious or an ego/id opposition. Zalkind thus produced, according to Bakhtin, "a Freudianism without Freud." What Bakhtin finds most objectionable about this argument is not its crude reductivism of Freud but the relation of body to mind that it takes for granted. Although Bakhtin feels that Freud could not legitimately be claimed by reflexologists in their terms, he also believes that the work of Pavlov and Freud were parallel insofar as both reduced the complexity of psychic operations to overschematized biological mechanisms. Bakhtin attacks Freud's theory of libido as much as Pavlov's theory of reflexes when he says, "as a purely physiological method, reflexology is capable of mastering the major components of human behavior only in a very abstract way, but it cannot understand that behavior in its entirety because human behavior is not only a physiological fact."[4]

Whereas these attempts to wed Freud and Pavlov overvalued the role of sheer biology in psychic life, the Vitalists, whom Bakhtin took on next, undervalued the role of biology in their attempts to sneak free will back into discussions of human motivation through the back door of the life sciences. The "Kanaev" article entitled "Contemporary Vitalism" appeared in different numbers of the popular scientific journal *Man and Nature* for 1926. The article begins with a bang. "What is life?" asks the opening sentence. This calculatedly journalistic means of launching into a discussion, so at odds with Bakhtin's earlier philosophical style, is an example of Bakhtin's new attempt to reach a wider audience. The article is essentially an attack on the theories of Hans Driesch, who maintained that the difference between life and nonlife was that the living organism had the capability to repair and restore itself. Driesch took the concept of homeostasis to a radical extreme. He completely ignored the give and take between an organism and its surrounding environment, leaving out of account the impersonal forces of nature and assigning a primary role to the inner workings of the individual organism, in other words, to free will. As Bakhtin says, "choice unrestricted by environment leads to the subjective schematization of the free act . . . I could have visited friends, have gone to the theater, taken a walk. But instead I decided to stay home and work. Out of all my possibilities I *preferred* to work. And this is the scheme at the heart of Driesch's whole conception . . . But, of course, this scheme, this 'I wanted to do X, so I did X,' flies in the face of any scientific explanation."[5]

The concern that Bakhtin here expresses for a valid scientific explanation is not simply a device to convince the reader that this article was written by the biologist Kanaev. Rather, it is evidence of the continuing influence on the general cast of Bakhtin's thought of the Marburg school and its intention to wed the natural sciences with philosophy once again after the two had been completely divorced in the work of such post-Kantian Idealists as Hegel.[6] Cohen and his followers had originally been attracted to Kant because he appeared to them to be the last philosopher to take science seriously; indeed, for the first twenty years of his career he was a scientist. Since the most influential of the new sciences, such as physics, chemistry, and even biology, had their basis in mathematics, Cohen devoted a good deal of time, as had Kant himself, to a philosophy with a basis in mathematical logic.

Bakhtin was never as preoccupied with pure science as was Cohen or Natorp, but he was eager that his philosophical conclusions should at least not flout the logic of the natural sciences, for which he had great respect. This was particularly true of experimental biology, which had been assigned a privileged status by the Russian intelligentsia since the 1860s, when all factions in society had looked to physiology for answers to the social and ethical questions plaguing Russia. This tendency had led Turgenev in *Fathers and Sons* to portray Bazarov in constant search of new frogs to decapitate for use in his experiments on reflexes.[7] This tradition was given specific focus in Bakhtin's thinking during these years through his close friendship with Kanaev and his encounter with the Leningrad physiologist A. A. Ukhtomsky.

In July of 1925 Kanaev took Bakhtin to Peterhof, where Ukhtomsky directed an experimental laboratory, to hear the scientist lecture on his theory of the "chronotope." This concept is tied up with another of Ukhtomsky's theories, his idea that nervous activity in the body was integrated by a cortical "system of systems" which he called "the dominant." Bakhtin was fascinated by Ukhtomsky's ideas, especially after he learned that Ukhtomsky was a believing Christian who had finished the prestigious Moscow Theological Academy before turning to science. A further bond between them was the passion that both Bakhtin and Ukhtomsky brought to their study of Kant, on whom Ukhtomsky had written his dissertation at the academy and whose ideas on the nature of perception never failed to inspire Ukhtomsky's physiological research. And both Ukhtomsky and Bakhtin were greatly influenced by Dostoevsky, from whose novel *The Double* Ukhtomsky derived impetus for research in the area of another of his concepts, "the law of the worthy interlocutor."

Ukhtomsky played an important role in Bakhtin's development because, first, although Ukhtomsky was a workaday scientist whose research was rigorously empirical and highly respected by other scientists, his experiments were all performed in the service of answering the great questions of philosophy. He was able to maintain a balance between physiology and metaphysics that kept both in harmony without doing violence to the seriousness of either. Second, Ukhtomsky's work helped Bakhtin to see ways for conceiving the relation of mind and world as a dialogic continuum rather than as an unbridgeable gap. The body's relation to its physical environment provided a powerful conceptual metaphor for modeling the relation of individual persons to their social environment. In both cases, the emphasis is on ceaseless activity. The body is seen as a system by which the individual answers the physical world. In order to do so coherently, the body must model its environment, track and map it, and translate its data into a biological representation of it.[8] The body answers the world by authoring it.

Analogously, mind is seen as a system by which the individual answers the social world. By responding strongly or weakly to some impulses and screening out others, consciousness constantly tracks its place amid the axiological options among which it must make choices. It responds to social stimuli by authoring its own responses. Homeostasis is the body's mechanism for actively responding to the other, and utterance is similarly the mind's mechanism. In both cases authorship is a means for shaping meaning in a long and complex chain of architectonic operations.

When Bakhtin attacks the Vitalists for being "unscientific," then, he is using as his basis of judgment the kind of science represented by Ukhtomsky. Bakhtin's vision of science plays a central role not only in his articles on reflexology and Vitalism but in *Freudianism* as well, where Bakhtin links the founder of psychoanalysis with the Vitalists on the basis of the false scientific claims made by each. Both overestimated the biological aspects, crudely conceived, of life. Bakhtin attacks Freud's dehistoricizing emphasis on sex and his insistence on the purely physical, which had the effect of dematerializing the living physical body into abstractions. In this sense Freud was like the Vitalists, especially Driesch. Although Driesch was an important figure in the attempt to deny history and flee the social, Bakhtin chose rather to write about Freud than Driesch because Freud was even worse. His "notion of the sexual is the extreme pole of this fashionable biologism. It gathers and concentrates in one compact and piquant image all the separate elements of modern-day antihistoricism."[9]

At this point in *Freudianism* there is a curious, almost unique, instance of one Bakhtin mask alluding to another. Bakhtin-"Voloshinov" cites Bakhtin-"Kanaev" and then incorrectly ascribes the Vitalism article to N. I. instead of I. I. Kanaev. This may be nothing more than a typographical error, but the irony of Bakhtin's citing under one pseudonym an article he had written under another pseudonym and getting the author's name wrong makes one believe it was intentional.

Freudianism establishes the place of psychoanalysis among other ideologies dominant in the 1920s, such as the philosophies of Bergson and Spengler. Freud expressed most powerfully tendencies that were nevertheless diffusely present in these other thinkers. As Bakhtin explains, "A *sui generis* fear of history, an ambition to locate a world beyond the social and the historical, a search for this world precisely in the depths of the organic—these are the features that pervade all systems of contemporary philosophy and constitute the symptom of the disintegration and decline of the bourgeois world."[10]

In focusing on Freud's place, not among other philosophers but among other psychologists, Bakhtin uses his characteristic device of exposition, setting up an opposition between two extremes, showing the inadequacy of each, and then proposing his own third, mediating way of approaching the same set of problems. Here the two extremes are objective and subjective psychology. The objective school is typified by the work of physiologists such as Pavlov, who placed too much emphasis on sheer biology, and the subjective school is represented by Freud, who in Bakhtin's view overvalued purely individual features of psychic life.

Bakhtin offers three essential criticisms of Freud. First, psychoanalysis transferred into its constructs all the fundamental defects of the subjective psychology of the time. For example, "if we look at the *elementary* makeup of the psyche, as Freudianism conceives of it, we find that it is composed of sensations, presentations, desires and feelings, that is, of exactly those elements out of which the old psychology (going back to Kant) had built the 'mental life of man.' " Freud's novelty consisted in transferring these elements to the unconscious, but this translation did not fundamentally change the meaning of desires, feelings, representations; they all still existed "for consciousness." Freudian methodology was based merely on introspection, and "introspection is possible only from a conscious point of view."[11]

The Freudians claimed that their map of the psyche was objective insofar as it charted the operations of mind as a mechanism. But the "laws" by which the Freudian machine operated were all suspiciously human and willed; they did not evidence the quality of extrapersonality associated with the laws of nature. Psychological operations as Freud described them "belong not at all to the realm of physical nature; they are not naturalistic, but ideological." He attempted "to psychologize the organic" by reducing all instincts other than the sexual to a single set of ego instincts (*Ich-triebe*), but "such a classification is inadmissible from the rigorous biological point of view . . . [and] is in no way superior to Bergson's *'élan vital'* . . . Viewed in terms of fundamental methodology, it does not differ in any essential way from the psychology of consciousness. It is another species of subjective psychology."[12]

Bakhtin's second criticism of Freud involves the distinctive manner in which Freud arranged the traditional categories of desire and will into a scenario of constant struggle. The categories remained the same but were shaken into a new dramatic configuration: "Mental life for the old psychology was all 'peace and quiet': everything put right, everything in its place, no crises, no catastrophes; from birth to death a smooth, straight path of steady and purposive progress, of gradual mental growth, with the adult's consciousness of mind coming to replace the child's innocence." This optimistic scenario, characteristic of all pre-Freudian psychologies, was a legacy of the biological optimism "that reigned in the life sciences before Darwin, a notion finally replaced by the Darwinian doctrine on the struggle for existence . . . a strict concept of natural necessity came to prevail in all domains of post-Darwinian biology."[13] The psyche was all that remained as a last refuge of harmony and order in contrast to the laws of nature, red in tooth and claw.

Freud, by emphasizing the agon of psychic life, the ceaseless war of appetite and ego, eliminated this last outpost. The psyche, too, took its place on the great battlefield of natural forces: "The human psyche belongs to the realm of nature, human psychical life is part of elemental life—that above all was the message the public at large seized upon out of the entire doctrine of Freud." But Freud overlooked a crucial fact, as he himself hinted when he ruefully accepted one of his patients' characterizations of his methodology as the "talking" cure: "Freud's whole psychological construct is based fundamentally on human verbal utterance: it is nothing but a special kind of interpretation of utterances."[14]

Today it is customary to think of Freud in connection with language because of the work of Jacques Lacan and others, or to think of Freud as providing a new theory of hermeneutics because of the work of Paul Ricoeur and others. But in 1927, when Freud was still perceived primarily as a clinician, this was a new and radical point of view. Bakhtin was able to perceive the central role of language in psychoanalytic theory in part because he had already worked out a systematic world view of his own in which the key element was language. Thus he was sensitized to see the crucial role it played in other systems. Moreover, Bakhtin was in the process of further refining his theory of language into a method of interpretation during the very period in which he was reading Freud. His criticism of Freudianism is thus an attack by the formulator of one hermeneutic on another.

Bakhtin's third and most serious charge against Freud is not that he concerned himself with language, which was in fact a sign of Freud's power and of the degree to which he must be regarded as a serious opponent. Freud erred not in his overvaluation of language but in the inadequacy of the concept of language to which he was wedded. Freud was first of all wrong in assuming that he could achieve "objectivity" by means of so ideologically charged a medium as language. It was inevitable that in Freud's doctrine the interrelations prevailing between the conscious and unconscious should be so thoroughly unlike the relations prevailing between two material forces that allow a precise objective account. Even Freud's "conscious" and "unconscious" were at odds: "between them prevail mutual hostility and incomprehension and the endeavor to deceive one another. Surely interrelations of this sort are only possible between two ideas, two ideological trends, two antagonistic persons, and not between two natural forces. Is it conceivable, for instance, that two natural forces should engage in mutual deception or mutual nonrecognition?"[15]

Bakhtin argues that Freud was correct insofar as he emphasized the aspect of struggle in his model of the psyche. The workings were properly identified, but the energy that fuels the movement of thought was incorrectly labeled. This agon is not kept in tension by forces of nature, such as electricity or chemistry, although Freud sought to put language on the same "objective" level. His error was to take language, the most highly charged medium of specifically human—not natural—dynamics, as the extrapersonal element that grounded his "objective" account of behavior. Bakhtin earlier argued that Freud took something that is objective, namely biology, and, by "psychologizing" it, turned it into something that is subjective. He now argues that Freud did the opposite with language; that is, he took something that is subjective and gave it specious objectivity.

Language indeed lies at the core of consciousness, but not the objective dream of language with which a linguist, or a Freud, works, which is language conceived as an aspect of givenness. Language is at work in mind as it is revealed in the conceptual world created by the actual give and take in historically and existentially instanced dialogues. Freud's error in assuming that language can serve as the objective basis for his methodology was the result of a logical mistake, a failure to recognize the degree to which language is socialized and belongs not to the individual but to the group. Freud sought to monologize the nature of language, which was a necessary step if language was to be internalized in the consciousness as Freud described it. He saw the language of the unconscious as being at war with the language of consciousness, but the battle was fought out within the individual psyche. Bakhtin agrees that there is indeed a struggle of language, but "what finds expression [in the struggle] is the extremely complex *social interrelationships between doctor and patient* . . . A patient wishes to hide from the doctor certain of his experiences and certain events of his life. He wants to foist on the doctor his own point of view on the reasons for his illness and the nature of his experiences. The doctor, for his part, aims at enforcing his authority as a doctor, endeavors to wrest confessions from the patient and to compel him to take the 'correct' point of view on his illness and its symptoms. Intertwined with all this are other factors: between doctor and patient there may be differences in sex, in age, in social standing, and moreover, there is the difference in their professions. All these factors complicate the struggle between them."[16]

It is in the midst of this complex and very special social atmosphere that "the verbal utterances are made—the patient's narratives and his statements in conversation with the doctor—utterances that Freud placed squarely at the basis of his theory ... These utterances are not expressions of the patient's individual psyche. What is reflected in them is not the dynamics of the individual psyche but the *social dynamics* of the interrelationships between doctor and patient. Here is the source for that dramatism which marks the Freudian construct ... Here indeed, people, not natural forces, are in conflict." The basic opposition in the mind is ultimately what Bakhtin said it was in *The Architectonics,* an agon between the I-for-myself and the other (*ja-dlja-sebja i drugoj*): "The psychical mechanisms readily disclose their social derivation to us. The 'unconscious' stands in opposition not to the individual conscious of the patient but, primarily, to the doctor, his requirements and his views. 'Resistance' is likewise primarily resistance to the doctor, to the listener, to the *other* person generally." Freud's system thus projects the entire dynamics of the interrelationships between two people, the I and the other, into a single, individual psyche. Bakhtin reiterates the "nature/culture" (*dan/zadan*) distinction that Freud failed to take into account: "What we call 'the human psyche' and 'consciousness' reflects the dialectics of history to a much greater degree than the dialectics of nature. The nature that is present in them is a nature already in economic and social refraction."[17]

Bakhtin does not introduce "a positive program" with which to substitute Freud's misconceived theory concerning the motives and conflicts of verbalized behavior. But Bakhtin does point out a direction for further research, based on the metalinguistics that he was blocking out for himself. He boldly reformulates the distinction between the unconscious and the conscious as a difference not between two kinds of reality, since both concepts are variants of the same phenomenon, consciousness. The difference between the two is ideological rather than ontological. The unconscious is a suppressed, relatively idiosyncratic realm, insofar as ideology can ever not be shared, whereas the conscious is a public world whose ideologies may be shared openly with others. Freud's unconscious can thus "be called the 'unofficial conscious' in distinction from the ordinary 'official conscious.' "[18] This opposition between official and unofficial politicizes categories that less global thinkers would have felt were far from politics of any kind.

The language of the unofficial conscious is inner speech, and the language of the official conscious is outward speech, but they both operate according to the general rules of all human verbal behavior. And "the verbal component of behavior is determined in all fundamentals and essentials of its content by objective-social factors." Therefore, nothing verbal in human behavior, inner and outward speech equally, can under any circumstances be reckoned to the account of the individual subject in isolation: "the verbal is not his property but that of his *social group* (his social milieu)."[19]

This observation that economic factors of being determine consciousness sounds at first like the most orthodox kind of a-priori Marxist thinking brought to bear on the specific topic of language, but it reads just as easily as a restatement of Bakhtin's thesis in *The Architectonics* that human existence is the dual interaction between a world that is always already there (*uže stavšee bytie*) and a mind that is conjoined (*priobščën*) to this world through the activity (*postupok*) of enacting values. In *Freudianism* Bakhtin changes the names of the players, but the game and its rules are still the same. The particular way in which what is on hand (*naličnost'*) confronts a specific consciousness, a real person in a geographically locatable place and a historically fixed time, was stressed in *The Architectonics,* where the formula for such particularity was "the unitary and unique event of existence."

In *Freudianism* the particularity of what is always-already-there is called "socioeconomic." Marxist terms are used to argue both the impossibility of conceiving individuals in isolation and the primacy of the social conditions obtaining at any particular point in history in shaping consciousness. Beyond these general meanings, there is no specifically or exclusively Marxist significance in such terms as "socioeconomic base" or "class groundedness."

Bakhtin's old argument for socializing epistemology in the master distinction between self and other is integrated into the

Freud book with almost no modification: "We shall never reach the real, substantive roots of any given single utterance if we look for them within the confines of the single, individual organism, even when that utterance concerns what appears to be the most private and most intimate side of a person's life (*ja-dlja-sebja*). Any motivation of one's behavior, any instance of self-awareness (for self-awareness is always verbal, always a matter of finding some specifically suitable verbal complex) is an act of gauging oneself against some social norm; social evaluation is, so to speak, the socialization of oneself and one's behavior. In becoming aware of myself, I attempt to look at myself, as it were, through the eyes of another person, another representative of my social group, my class." Although a hierarchy of causes and effects stretches from the content of the psyche, which is understood as individual but never isolated, to the content of a large-scale system of culture, the route between the two extremes is a highway governed by the same rules of the road: "At all stages of this route human consciousness operates through *words.*" It follows that "any human verbal utterance is an ideological construct in the small. The *motivation* of one's personal behavior is juridical and moral activity on a small scale; an exclamation of joy or grief is a primitive lyric composition; pragmatic considerations of the causes and consequences of happenings are germinal forms of scientific and philosophical cognition; and so on and so forth. The stable, formulated ideological systems of the sciences, the arts, jurisprudence, and the like have sprung and crystallized from that seething ideological element where broad waves of inner and outward speech engulf our every act and our very perception."[20]

But while there are important similarities between the *modus operandi* of individual psyches, on the one hand, and of whole culture systems, on the other, there are also important differences, which explain Bakhtin's substitution of unofficial/official consciousness for Freud's unconscious/conscious distinction. While the systems of both individual psyches and whole societies are ideological through and through, ideology has a different status in each. The primary difference consists in the achieved, stable quality of an official ideology that is shared by the group as a whole. It is, in Bakhtin's terminology, "finalized" (*zaveršen*). Because of its rigidity, the official ideology is always already there; it is "prelocated discourse" (*prednaxodimoe slovo*), the language of the fathers, of a past that is still very present.

Over against this fixed system of values Bakhtin poses another individual or personal system, which he calls "behavioral ideology": "that inner and outward speech which permeates our behavior in all its aspects." As opposed to broad-based social values, behavioral ideology is "more sensitive, more responsive, more excitable and livelier" than an ideology that has undergone formulation and become 'official.' " It is not finished off, not completely formulated, because it is the world ideologized from the point of view of a still-developing individual consciousness that lives in "the absolute future" of possibility.[21] Behavioral ideology is shaped by the laws of what Bakhtin earlier called "horizon," while societal ideology is shaped by the laws of "surroundings."

The opposition that Bakhtin sets up here, though carefully camouflaged in Marxist terminology and neutral adjectives such as "social" and "behavioral," is still the same opposition that lies at the heart of *The Architectonics*: the conflict between a set of values grounded in the self and a set of values grounded in the other. Bakhtin is saying that there is a gap between behavioral ideology—a euphemism for the operation of the I-for-myself—and social ideology—a euphemism for the operation of alterity. Individual consciousness never fully replicates the structure of society's public values, even among the most wholly committed ideologues. This was the great mistake of the "vulgar Marxists" who believed that everything about even such idiosyncratic figures as Gogol and Dostoevsky could be explained by their social origin because there was no gap between individual and class consciousness. In *The Architectonics* Bakhtin explained this gap in ontological terms: The self and the other constitute two different realities that can never fuse on a single plane. In *Freudianism* the explanation for the gap is developmental: the more primitive behavioral ideology is still inchoate, but when it finds its highest expression, it will be fixed in the shared values of an official ideology. But the implication is clearly that the traffic between the social and the individual is not all one-way. An ideology, once formulated, has an enormous impact on the individuals comprising the society whose values it defines, but the opposite is also the case, for "in the depths of behavioral ideology accumulate those contradictions which, once having reached a certain threshold, ultimately burst asunder the system of the official ideology."[22]

What Freud called "consciousness," Bakhtin renames "official consciousness," because its content is in relatively close accord with the socially approved values of the culture as a whole: "On these levels of behavioral ideology, inner speech comes easily to order and freely turns into outward speech or, in any case, has no fear of becoming outward speech." But "other levels corresponding to Freud's unconscious lie at a great distance from the stable system of the ruling ideology. They bespeak the disintegration of the unity and integrity of the system, the vulnerability of the usual ideological motivations."[23]

Bakhtin thus translates Freud's metaphor of censorship into a recognizably Russian scenario. The unconscious, as the official conscious, operates like a minority political party opposed to certain aspects of the reigning politics of a culture. The more of these it opposes, the more "censored" it is, because the difference between its values and those of the majority is expressed as a difference of language. The less the unofficial party has in common with the official ideology, the more restricted are its expressive means. Insofar as the minority cannot share official values, it is condemned to relative silence. If, for example, an Eskimo revolutionary group seeking independence from the United States were to flood New York City with manifestoes written in an Eskimo language it would be in a similar situation. Even though willing a conflict with the majority culture, the group would be condemned to inaction by the structure of communication, the architectonics of value.

Bakhtin's approach here resembles that of the early Christians who sought to spread their message by parable. This parabolic intention explains why at one level Bakhtin felt compelled to revise Freud's scenario of conflict between conscious and unconscious into the openly political terms of a conflict between official and unofficial conscious. When Bakhtin writes, "the wider and deeper the breach between the official and unofficial conscious, the more difficult it becomes for motives of inner speech to turn into outward speech . . . wherein they might acquire formulation, clarity, and vigor," he is describing his own dilemma, the increasing gap between his own religious and metaphysical ideas and the Soviet government's ever more militant insistence on adherence to Russian communism. When Bakhtin observes, "Motives under these conditions begin to . . . lose their verbal countenance and little by little really do turn into a 'foreign body' in the psyche," he means as well that they become foreign bodies in the state.[24]

Bakhtin's daring insistence on the uniplanar coexistence of the rules of governance in the psyche with the rules of governance in the state is not only a new way to conceive Freudian theory but also a new way to send out coded messages from the catacombs. The gap between official and unofficial conscious can become so great that the official finally snuffs out the content of the unofficial. But since the traffic between the terminus of an individual psyche and that of a whole culture moves in both directions, a more optimistic scenario can be conceived for the unofficial force. It is not true "that every motive in contradiction with the official ideology must degenerate into indistinct inner speech and then die out—it might well engage in a struggle with that official ideology [and] ... if it is not merely the motive of a déclassé loner, then it has a chance for a future and perhaps even a victorious future."[25] Brave words indeed for one who himself was in great danger of becoming a déclassé loner.

CHAPTER 8

The Formalists

Bakhtin and the Formalists were made for each other. The history of ideas has provided few encounters in which the opponents were so well matched in their strengths, even if they were different strengths. Bakhtin was given to speculation and broad synthesis, the Formalists to methodological innovation and close interpretation. Rarely is the pattern of the opposing points of view when taken together so satisfyingly symmetrical. Bakhtin developed a theory of communication in which the author's personality, ethical values, and social context are the defining features of an utterance, including a literary text. At precisely the same time, the Formalists evolved powerful arguments for conceiving the literary text as a result of impersonal forces at work in the system of literary language itself. The text they defined as free of all values except those unique to literary discourse, a self-contained object independent of its extraliterary environment.

The group of young Leningrad literary critics, such as Viktor Shklovsky, Boris Eikhenbaum, and Yury Tynyanov, and of Moscow linguists, such as Roman Jakobson, who came to be known as the Formalists were enormously influential throughout the 1920s.[1] Although members continued long after to be active, and today Shklovsky still appears frequently on Soviet television, the Formalists' activity as a group was restricted almost entirely to that decade. There were three different periods of activity: the years of struggle from 1916 to 1920, of triumph from 1921 to 1926, and of rout from 1926 to 1930. During this time the Formalists made lasting contributions to literary study, mostly on the basis of positions that were diametrically opposed to those of Bakhtin. The Formalists were the yin demanded by Bakhtin's yang.

But this symmetry is apparent only in retrospect. In the 1920s, when both camps were at the height of their powers and the positions that now give clear-cut profiles to each were still emerging, Bakhtin did not appear to be a figure capable of offering any kind of definitive resistance to the Formalists. Bakhtin was something of an outcast in Russian intellectual life during these years. He was not associated with any academic institution, publishing house, or editorial board of any journal. And the old Bakhtin circle from Nevel and Vitebsk had only the loosest association. Bakhtin, for the most part, was alone. The Formalists, by contrast, were indeed a circle. Not only did they read and discuss each other's works, but they collaborated in joint publishing and teaching ventures. While Bakhtin was working alone at his desk in a one-room flat with barely enough to eat, the Formalists were actively and collectively exploiting the new opportunities for assuming prominence in Soviet intellectual life that had opened up after the Revolution. They proved remarkably astute and successful in finding a niche for themselves where, initially, they were able to teach and work as they liked, without interference. They succeeded in monopolizing one of the new academic centers in Leningrad, the Division for the History of the Language Arts in the State Institute for the History of the Arts. This was one of those rare opportunities, which take virtually a revolution to afford, when the young are able to run their own academy and train their own followers.

Despite the differences between Bakhtin's position at the periphery of events and the Formalists' position at the center, there was no lack of opportunities for exchange. Bakhtin sought to take advantage of some of these, as he was eager to debate the Formalists for a number of reasons. Much as he had earlier tried to take part in the ideological battles immediately following the October Revolution by engaging in public debate, in the 1920s he tried to debate the leading isms of the time in print. Formalism was even more important for him than either Freudianism or Marxism, the two other "interlocutors" that he took on in these years, because the Formalists were made to order for his strategy of dramatizing his own ideas through struggle with conflicting ideas of others.

From the beginning Bakhtin argued that language was important only because of its capacity to express values, in other words, to mean something. In order to have the potential to mean, an utterance must never be "finished"; a residue of meaning must be left over even after the most exhaustive analysis of an utterance. With this open-ended semantics as his base, Bakhtin maintained that literary texts are also utterances and therefore never finally completed. This proposition called for a very special sort of literary criticism, indeed a whole new poetics, for all previous work in poetics, with the exception of the German Romantics, assumed that the art object not only could be but had to be treated as if it were a completed whole. And no one had been quite so explicit or so radical in making this claim as the Formalists. In Bakhtin's literary criticism the dominant slogan was always that the text is not given, but conceived. The Formalists' principle was diametrically opposed: the text is the sum of its devices.

Bakhtin first spoke out on issues raised by the Formalists in his article "The Problem of Content, Material and Form in Verbal Artistic Creation," which he had worked on in Vitebsk and which was to be published in 1924 in *Russian Contemporary*.[2] This journal, though very much tied up with leading figures at the Institute for the History of the Arts in general and with the Formalists in particular, was nevertheless open to debating their ideas. The journal was suppressed before Bakhtin's article could appear, but even if the article had come out, it might well have been lost in the welter of other essays directed against the Formalists in those years. Everybody who had anything at all to do with literature, and many who did not, felt called upon to attack Formalism. It was where the action was, both intellectually and, insofar as its representatives presided over powerful academic and publishing institutions, politically.

The widespread reaction against Formalism broke down into a right wing and a left wing. The right wing was made up of all those who based their objections on one or another of the traditional schools of criticism, such as those biographical or historical approaches that had been taught in the university before the Revolution. The most powerful arguments from the right were mounted less by literary critics than by philosophers, such as Gustav Shpet or Alexander Smirnov, or by those who were thoroughly at home in philosophy. Bakhtin had a certain affinity with this camp, if only because he fully subscribed to its charge that the Formalists' ingenious interpretations of particular works lacked a theoretical base in a full-blown aesthetics. This was the characteristic charge of the Formalists' right-wing opponents. The attack from the left, chiefly mounted by such eminent Marxists as Trotsky and such representatives of sociological criticism as P. N. Sakulin, maintained that the Formalists ignored social and political factors in their work.[3]

Although Bakhtin shared many of these left-wing reservations as well about the Formalists, the philosophical poverty behind their methodological practice is chiefly what occupies him in "The Problem of Content." He agrees with the Formalists' drawing attention to the linguistic features of literary texts: literary study "must not ignore language as linguistics conceives it; rather, it must take advantage of all the work of linguistics to understand . . . the technical aspects of the poet's creation."[4] But he warns that such aspects are only part of a work of art. Technical features have mostly to do with the material out of which a work is crafted, and just as it is important to understand marble in order to analyze a statue, it is also necessary to understand language in order to analyze literature. But what is important about a Praxiteles statue is ultimately the human form, not the stone, and similarly the aesthetic aspect of a literary work of art goes beyond words, at least as they are treated by linguists. After all, Bakhtin explains, although the sculptor uses a chisel, that chisel does not go into the work of art.

Bakhtin here introduces an important concept, the aesthetic object, which according to him is the real subject of criticism.[5] The aesthetic object is not completely coincidental with the external, material form but is nevertheless inseparable from it, much as the self is defined in *The Architectonics* as never coincidental with itself and always a function of the other, which it is not but without which it could not be. The aesthetic object is present as a totality of the values conveyed by the material form when combined with the other values, such as political or religious, that come into play in any specific act of perceiving the object. The aesthetic object is roughly equivalent to the meaning of an utterance insofar as it is always slightly different for each perceiver, a feature that art exploits to give freshness to the world. The aesthetic object is never fully grasped but is rather an act of understanding that is not yet completely understood. Like other deeds, it lives by that which it is not yet. Any attempt to limit art to its brute form treats art as if it were over, as if it were a thing and not a deed.

In the years between the writing of this article and the publication of *The Formal Method in Literary Scholarship,* which came out under Medvedev's name in 1928, the give and take between the Formalists and their opponents became less theoretical and increasingly political and shrill. As the liberal period of the 1920s was coming to a close, the stakes in the dispute were raised to ominous levels. *The Formal Method* reflects these changes. It is more sharply polemical than the earlier article, a feature that was also required by the need to make the book jibe with Medvedev's other pronouncements on the Formalists. The language and many of the arguments are similar to other Marxist attacks, but the work is not simply another broadside from that camp. Bakhtin remarks that though the opposition between the Formalists and the Marxists appeared to be a debate, the dispute was not a true dialogue, for neither side was able to accommodate the other. The two sides did not really listen to each other; they talked past each other, not to each other. In order to succeed against the Formalists, a theory was needed capable of engaging specific texts and concrete problems of literary analysis as effectively as did the Formalist theory, and this the Marxists had not provided.

The Formal Method is thus unique in that it is not only a criticism of the Formalists but a critique as well of the Marxist critics of the Formalists. Bakhtin attacks the Marxists for being too vague in their own program and just as unprincipled in their attack on the theory of the Formalists. He distinguishes his own account of Formalist shortcomings from any thus far provided by the Marxists, who in his view had been hardly less mechanical than their adversaries. The majority of Marxist literary theoreticians were content to repeat the clichés of classical Marxist dogma that literature was no more than an ideological superstructure reflecting the economic base; how this process actually took place in concrete examples from literary history remained to be specified. Bakhtin charges that "Marxist criticism refuses to meet Formalism on the real territory of the problems they raise."[6]

The real problems raised by the Formalists in Bakhtin's view had to do with the nature of literary language as opposed to other uses of language, and this set of problems ultimately bore on how change comes about in history. An a-priori condition of all the Formalists' practice was the distinction they drew between poetic and practical language. Practical speech they defined by its desire to have an effect in the world outside words: it is aimed outside it-self toward extralinguistic action, as in "Close the door!" or "Please pass the salt!" Practical utterances should be transparent, since the more attention they draw to themselves, the less able they are to incite actions outside themselves. "Terminate the openness of yon portal" is less likely to get a door closed than to evoke a question about its status as an utterance: "What was that you said?" By contrast, poetry is "violence practiced on language" in order to draw attention to the utterance itself. Rhyme is an obvi-ous example of how verse insists on drawing attention to itself. Po-etic language is defined by its power to make readers perceive words afresh. It does so by slowing down the normal processes of perception, which without such intervention are directed at the message rather than the medium in which it is conveyed. When this impulse to hurry beyond the words is "braked," one begins to perceive the words themselves. Language in art becomes "de-automatized." The essence of "literariness" (*literaturnost'*), ac-cording to Formalist doctrine, is to be found precisely in this "deautomatization" (*ostranenie*), a term sometimes translated as "making it strange," which Shklovsky first introduced in 1914 when he argued that the goal of literature was the "Resurrection of the Word."

In *The Formal Method* Bakhtin is highly critical of the un-spoken assumptions behind the separation of language into poetic and practical divisions, especially as defined by the Formalists. For all their vaunted attention to "the text itself," their definition of literature in the end came down to an extratextual explanation based on assumptions about perception or, in other words, about human psychology. In effect, Bakhtin charges, they merely re-directed the old-fashioned critical concern for the psychological life of authors and characters to the psychology of readers.

Not only did the Formalists fail to purge "literary science" of traditional psychological concerns but they became more and more involved in traditional questions about literary history. Deautomatization, first invoked as a means for getting at the es-sence of literature, was named as the engine of literary evolution as well. This use of the concept draws Bakhtin's heaviest fire. Ac-cording to the Formalists, a new poetic text has to struggle with texts written in practical language by using devices that call at-tention to itself as a text. Thus, at any present moment there is a battle going on between poetic language and practical language. Such an account sufficed for explaining the differences between literary and nonliterary texts. But the Formalists sought as well to account for differences between texts that are within literary language by appealing to the same mechanism of deautomatization. The history of literature, they argued, is a constant struggle of the poetic text not merely to define itself by deautomatizing language as used in the world of practical speech but also to define itself by deautomatizing the language of other poetic texts. A poem or novel has to be perceived by readers as new not only in terms of the language used in their own generation but also against the background of language used in texts perceived as literary in previous generations. There is a constant struggle between old works that have lost their power to engage the public and newer works that are more able to challenge the awareness of readers, between old habits of reading and new procedures of writing. A work "travels down the inevitable path from birth to death; from seeing and sensory perception, when every detail in the object is savored and relished, to mere recognition, when the object or form becomes a dull epigone which our senses register mechanically," Shklovsky observed in 1923 in *The Knight's Move,* a title that is a metaphor for the Formalist conception of literary genealogy. That is, the line of succession is not direct, as in the linear move of a rook or a bishop. The line of succession is rather skewed, a dog's leg, a knight's move. As Shklovsky proclaimed elsewhere in the same year, "in the history of art the legacy is transmitted not from father to son, but from uncle to nephew." In another version of succession offered by Tynyanov in 1929 in his *Archaizers and Innovators,* the search of the younger generation for a different style from that of the preceding generation often results in a return to a style characteristic of an even older generation: "In the struggle with his father, the grandson turns out to resemble his grandfather."[7] In the Formalist system the tensions of the Oedipal conflict are very much present, but instead of sons seeking to displace their fathers, they attempt either to replace their uncles or to become their own grandfathers.

Bakhtin points out that these singular genealogical tables flout the logic both of Mendelian genetics and of Freud's "family romance" because they are based less on a principle of true movement from one generation to the other than on a theory of individual biography. Perception of the rudimentary kind invoked as the source of change in Formalist literary history is understood to happen within the individual perceiver. Automatization and deautomatization are processes that not only are psychological but also take place within the psyche of single individuals. The Formalists never explained how these individual reactions coalesce into normative patterns characteristic for whole generations. The only alternative would be to posit the even more problematical locus of a collective unconscious, which the Formalists did not do. They argued that only in the consciousness of a single perceiver can deautomatization work as an explanatory device of change in literary history. Bakhtin sums up the logical difficulties of such a position: "If Pushkin is automatized for one person, while another is in raptures over [the younger, but contemporaneous] Benediktov, there can be no connection between the automatization and the perceptibility of these two temporally successive objects, just as there can be no connection between one person's upset stomach and another's overeating."[8]

On top of his other arguments, Bakhtin charges that the Formalists failed to evolve a convincing account of literary dynamics because there was no place in their scheme for anything new in poetry itself. The distinction that they assumed between poetic and practical language, on which was based their theory of deautomatization, had the effect of making literature wait until the creative forces at work in practical language had developed something new before literature could begin its own work of deforming practical language to the point where it could be perceived as a medium and not as a message. For the Formalists, poetic speech is, as Shklovsky put it, "purposely created to deautomatize perception . . . thus, we arrive at the definition of poetry as speech that is braked (*zatormožennyj*), distorted."[9] In other words, poetry depends for its effects on nonpoetic language, much as a parasite depends on its host. Poetic novelty is a secondary, willed creation built on the primary, unwilled changes in practical language. Such a concept of the specificity of literature, argues Bakhtin, is impoverished. Surely there is more to the complexity of poetic language than sheer "difference from."

In *The Formal Method* Bakhtin points out some of the absurdities in Formalist ideas about literary dynamics when those ideas are taken to a logical extreme, but he does not put forward his own opposing theory of historical change. That theory is based on his vision of language not merely as the struggle between two types of discourse, which the Formalists maintained with their opposition of poetic versus practical speech, but as a battle between hundreds of discourses. Any national language, according to Bakhtin, is made up of manifold sublanguages, such as those peculiar to legal usage and to the practice of other professions, including thievery and politics, as well as languages unique to specific generations and social classes. In this constant exchange between intra- or sublanguages of Russian, for instance, literary usage is only one of a myriad of contending discursive practices, each of which seeks to be normative, privileged, more full of meaning than the others.

In two books published a year later, *Marxism and the Philosophy of Language* and *Problems of Dostoevsky's Creative Works,* Bakhtin would lay out the linguistic basis for a historical poetics to counter that of the Formalists, but it is already clear from his critique of deautomatization that he operates with a completely different time sense from that of the Formalists. Bakhtin sees literary language as part of and as subject to the same conditions as other divisions of natural language, unlike the Formalists, who saw poetic speech as different in its fundamentals from other forms of language. Since Bakhtin perceives literature as part of the normal processes of language, he sees literary evolution as occurring very slowly, for the history of linguistic changes is always very conservative and drawn out. Thus, instead of studying the kind of dramatic turnabouts in literary history so beloved of the Formalists, he turns, for instance, to the complex, centuries-long filiation between the ancient Greek romance and the modern European novel. He is constantly seeking unexpected strands connecting the present to a past that is often quite distant. The Formalist idea that the old generation's forms soon become habitual and need to be deformed in order that art may once again be perceived in the next generation is seen by Bakhtin as betraying a desire to negate the past. History becomes reduced to a constant present or a permanent contemporaneity. For the Formalists, "Everything must fit within the framework of the contemporary. If the following epoch continues the business of the preceding in a positive manner, does not destroy or hybridize it, then it is a fruitless epoch of epigonism."[10]

As the Formalists themselves were proud to admit, there was a close relation between the rise of their literary theory and the meteoric career of the Russian Futurist school of poetry. Not only were Futurists close personal friends of leading Formalists, but the triumph of the Futurists over the Symbolists who preceded them provided a textbook illustration of how a younger generation succeeds in overcoming an older. The very title of the Futurist movement implies a direction in time, although in fact the Futurists were utopians or millenarians who dreamt of a future too perfect to be realized in any actuality. According to Jakobson, Mayakovsky was "quite capable of giving full due to the creative missions of those kids of the collective . . . but at the same time he bristled whenever an actual 'kid' ran into the room. Mayakovsky never recognized his own myth of the future in any concrete child."[11] This cavalier, or utopian, attitude toward the real permeates Formalist historical theory as well, accounting for its impatience with any process slower than the lightning of revolution.

There were many opportunities for Bakhtin to confront the Formalists directly. He knew them, if "only very slightly," as he later described it. And the Formalists were at all times remarkably open to debate. During the years when they still had a base at the Institute for the History of the Arts, they provided a forum for many who were unsympathetic to their ideas, including several of Bakhtin's friends. Yet on no occasion was there ever a debate between these representatives of two of the most powerful bodies of literary theory in the modern period. Bakhtin preferred more indirect forms of engagement, such as the written word. At a personal level such indirection was very much in line with the general elusiveness of Bakhtin's character. But he had theoretical reasons for it as well. Primary among these was the subordinate role that his polemic with the Formalists played in the larger task he had set himself in these years of working out the implications of his own dialogism. Issues raised by the Formalists were of great relevance and interest only as local illustrations of the more comprehensive set of issues preoccupying him, the theory of values, which he referred to as the science of ideologies. This theory included all the issues first raised in *The Architectonics* bearing on the nature of the person, the relation of selves to others in patterns of social behavior, and the way those patterns are modeled in language practices. He was not simply being disingenuous, then, when he chose to open *The Formal Method* with the line, "Literary scholarship is only one branch of the study of ideologies."[12]

One of the recurring questions of Bakhtin's science of ideologies is how different belief systems can be in dialogue with one another, or how they can manage to sort themselves out into viable hierarchies of value and discourse in social structures in the present and over time in history. In other words, he always sought for connections between different people, texts, ideologies, and languages, not for cut-offs between their differences. This dialogic understanding of how different idea systems relate to each other underlies Bakhtin's critique of the Formalist theory of deautomatization. That theory was based on the principle of either/or, mutual exclusion rather than communication between different texts. Bakhtin's version of the history of ideologies seems more than justified in the particular clash between his own ideas and those of the Formalists, for subsequent generations have gone on to struggle with issues raised by each side. As a result, the exchange that was initiated in the 1920s, when the two sides appeared to be talking past each other, has since become a mutually interacting set of still living possibilities. As Bakhtin never tired of saying, the last word is never said. Subsequent history has shaped a relation between the two sides in which it is increasingly apparent that Bakhtin and the Formalists provide a particularly grateful "other" for each other.

CHAPTER 9

Discourse in Life
and Art

Bakhtin's thinking between 1919 and 1929 was devoted to a single project, a gradually developing philosophy of language grounded in the communicative aspect of speech. This new vision of language as rooted in the historical particularities of specific utterances had manifold consequences for the understanding of art, linguistics, psychology, and epistemology. All Bakhtin's works during this extraordinarily productive period, either under his own name or under the name of others, apply this general theory of language to specific problems or questions. *Freudianism* and *The Formal Method* are such applications, but two other works give the clearest and most sustained exposition of Bakhtin's philosophy of language at this point in his development: "Discourse in Life and Discourse in Art," published in 1926, and *Marxism and the Philosophy of Language*, published in 1929.

"Discourse in Life and Discourse in Art" is concerned with the difference between aesthetic verbal communication and speech in everyday life, while *Marxism and the Philosophy of Language* deals with linguistics as such. The article thus bears a relationship to the book roughly analogous to that of "Beyond the Social" to *Freudianism*. It is a kind of warm-up exercise, a preliminary sketch of a problem and its solution. The problem in this case is the absence of a viable sociological poetics. There were many candidates claiming to be such a poetics, but in Bakhtin's eyes they were all in one way or another flawed. He found himself in the position of Dostoevsky, who said that the atheists were so timid that he had to invent powerful arguments for them. Thus Bakhtin, as a non-Marxist, sought to establish a poetics more sophisticated in its sociology than any put forward by the Marxists. The Formalists had provided admirable interpretations of literary texts which did not require taking into account the social and historical context. Their work put the Marxists on the defensive, who insisted that literature was an ideological reflection of forces at work in the economic bases of social organization. But no one so far had been notably successful in showing precisely how a specific literary work was determined by the impersonal imperatives of the economic system in which it was created.

There was no lack of critics who were attempting to show such connections, both in the West and in the Soviet Union. The most sustained attempts were made in Russia, where the study of literature was tied to specifically Marxist ideas about the determining role of class struggle and economic base over ideological superstructure. At the turn of the century, Plekhanov had established a philosophical basis for such an approach by arguing that social being determined social consciousness. Consequently, to evaluate a work of art, critics had to elucidate the particular aspect of social or class consciousness it expressed. Debates soon developed over the degree to which social factors actually shaped a given work. Plekhanov, who represented one extreme, maintained that individual authors as such made little or no contribution to a work; what they did was fated by their class origins and the historical situations in which they worked. A counter to this view was offered by Alexander Bogdanov, who argued that individuals could in fact shape texts more or less to their intentions, depending on the particular historical circumstances in which they worked.

After the Revolution, Plekhanov's view, which came to be known as the "sociological method" of literary analysis, was taken up by a group that included P. N. Sakulin, V. M. Friche, and V. F. Pereverzev, all of whom were extremely powerful in the Soviet cultural hierarchy through the 1920s, largely because their careers as leftist intellectuals had been established before the Revolution. Sakulin, an expert on Russian Romanticism, attempted to create a balance between individual talent and the distinctive social features of a particular time and place. Friche, head of such party organizations as the literary section of the Red Professorate and the Communist Academy, institutions that the party established to rival the Academy of Sciences left over from czarist times and still prestigious enough to exclude Communist scholars, sought to show that the history of literature was a constant struggle among different styles, each of which represented a different

class. And Pereverzev, an expert on Gogol and Dostoevsky as well
as the most intransigent exponent of the absolute dominance of
economic determinism, maintained that the critic must pay exclusive attention to a writer's position in the history of production
techniques.

These sociological critics shared a belief in Freudianism that
was no more complex or sophisticated than their understanding of
Marx. They argued that a writer's subconscious was formed out of
images deriving from the place occupied by that writer in the class
struggle. Thus, if writers were proletarian, the images dominating
their work would be ineluctably proletarian. Gogol, born into a
family of small landowners in the Ukraine and then a bureaucrat
in czarist institutions, wrote, quite predictably in the view of these
critics, about small Ukrainian landowners and petty officials in
Petersburg. "Nobody has the power to change his style," was a
catchphrase of Pereverzev.

In "Discourse in Life and Discourse in Art" Bakhtin attacks
these representatives of the sociological method, even though they
were such a politically powerful group. Bakhtin's opposition to
these official types was in fact an exercise with potentially much
direr consequences than his opposition to the Formalists. His effort in this essay to initiate a new understanding of the role of social factors in literature was yet another of his moves to enter into
dialogue with one of the major intellectual currents of his day.

Bakhtin's article primarily attacks Sakulin, not only because
he was the most sophisticated of these sociological critics but also
because his *The Sociological Method in Literature* (1925) sought
to solve a problem that preoccupied Bakhtin as well, how to place
art into the historical and socioeconomic currents of life outside
books, while at the same time not losing sight of art's distinctively
aesthetic dimension. Sakulin's solution to the problem was to
posit a kind of split personality for art. Its history was in fact two
histories which were parallel but separate, one immanent and the
other causal. The immanent aspect of a text constituted the "artistic core" of literature. It was determined by features that were
peculiar to literature, such as normative plots in certain genres or
developments in rhyming techniques in verse. But the rules con-
trolling such factors were constantly being affected by other factors that were exterior to them, such as the laws governing
censorship or the literacy rate. These historical factors Sakulin la-

belled causal and argued that they were the proper subject for the sociology of literature.

Bakhtin rejects such a simple-minded dualism and sees "the work" rather as an interaction of both immanent and causal factors operating simultaneously. By 1919 he had already defined art as an event, the acting out of an exchange, the clash of values between a work and its audience. In "Discourse in Life and Discourse in Art" he once again argues for art as a special kind of relationship, an act of communication. But the encompassing rhetoric is now sociological. Specifically Marxist terminology is used as a means both for inserting the argument into the Soviet context and for suggesting a more radical and complex degree of analysis than was present in competing Marxist sociologies of literature.

Bakhtin takes issue with Sakulin's main argument that "Every item that becomes the object of supply and demand . . . is subject, as concerns its value and circulation within human society, to the governing socioeconomic laws." Bakhtin cautions that even if these laws were known, they would not shed any light on the physical and chemical structure of whatever object was in question, much less the internal composition of a work of art. Art as a social factor is located "within the overall system of sociological governance—but from that governance we shall never be able to derive art's aesthetic essence, just as we cannot divine the chemical formula for this or that commodity from its circulation within the economy."[1]

Bakhtin denies a correspondence between the material makeup of a thing and the aesthetic constitution of an art work. He implicitly draws on the distinction made in "The Problem of Content, Material, and Form in Verbal Artistic Creation" between the work as an object and as an aesthetic object, but he draws as well on the even more fundamental categories examined in *The Architectonics,* all based on the Kantian distinction between mind and world. The thing aspect of an art work, the ink and paper of a printed poem, the paint in a painting, all belong to the realm of "givenness," whereas the aesthetic aspect of the poem or painting belong to the "conceptual" realm of mind. And while there are significant differences between the material object and the aesthetic object, these differences are not absolute, as Bakhtin had shown in his prior analysis of how mind and world relate to each other as an active unity. The failure to perceive the relation between the thingness of a thing and the human use to which the thing is put results in an incomplete perception of any commodity, which was the fault with Sakulin's argument about the law of supply and demand. This failure is particularly egregious in the case of art works, which are more heavily charged with conceptual or, as Bakhtin now says, with "ideological" significance than are other commodities because they have no existence outside the uniquely human consumption of them as art works. For this reason "the aesthetic, just as the juridical and cognitive, is only a variety of the social. A theory of art, consequently, can only be a sociology of art."[2]

In order to clear a conceptual space for his own model, Bakhtin again divides his opponents into two camps, each of which represents an untenable extreme. The polarity is between those critics who make a fetish out of the material aspect of an artwork, such as the stone of a statue or the grammatical features of a poem, and those critics who restrict their study to mere impressions of an art work in the minds of artists or audience, completely ignoring a work's material and formal makeup. Bakhtin charges that the first concept of criticism, associated with the Formalists, isolates a poem from its social occurrence, because it has no way to conceive of language as a means of communication. Bakhtin brands the second concept of criticism, which concentrates on the individual psyche of those who either make or contemplate artworks, with the charge of "idealism." Idealism is a word that has had a particularly negative, even sinister, meaning in the Soviet Union. During the 1930s it meant not only an opposition to the materialist principles underlying most forms of Marxism but also a willful opposition to Soviet communism in particular. But in this essay Bakhtin wishes merely to convey that those he labels idealists emphasize the activity of the individual psyche in shaping reality at the expense of the exterior world. On the one hand, the Formalist extreme is too mechanical and misconstrues the constitutive role of social intercourse in defining the place and being of art. On the other hand, the idealist extreme, represented by most pre-Formalist schools, such as Potebnya's, is too individual in its assumptions and fails to recognize the necessarily collective nature of human communication: "To continue our economic analogy, we might say such a thing is similar to the attempt to analyze the individual psyche of a proletarian in order thereby to describe the objective production relations that determine a place in society."[3]

Any theory of art must take into account three elements: creators, artworks, and perceivers. Formalists overprivilege the second category, while idealists invest too much in the first and third categories. Both extremes get the subject wrong: "They attempt to discover the whole in the part . . . Meanwhile, the 'artistic' in its total integrity is not located in the artifact and is not located in the separately considered psyches of creator and contemplator; it encompasses all three of these factors. It is a special form of interrelationship between creator and contemplator fixed in a work of art."[4]

Art, then, is a form of communication, but of a distinctive kind: "To understand this special form of social communication realized and fixed in the material of a work of art—that precisely is the task of sociological poetics." Such a poetics must assume a Januslike gaze in two directions at once. It must never ignore the features that are unique to poetry and which set it off from other types of ideological communication, such as the political, juridical, and ethical. At the same time, such a poetics must never forget that this unique form of communication does not exist in isolation: "it participates in the unitary flow of social life, it reflects the common economic base, and it engages in interaction and exchange with other forms of communication."[5]

Bakhtin distinguishes artistic communication from the sort of communication that reigns in everyday life, much as the Formalists opposed poetic language to practical language. But while both Bakhtin and the Formalists sought to find the distinctive features of the literary, they looked for them in different directions. The Formalists tried to isolate a fixed catalogue of devices that belonged to one language but not to the other, which was comparable to trying to write astrological dictionaries for recurring symbols in dreams. Bakhtin, however, emphasizes communicative function rather than linguistic features as such. He assumes that there are no static items peculiar either to literature or to everyday life. There are only different functions of the same words and devices in both spheres.

The distinguishing feature of everyday discourse is not its vocabulary or syntactic pattern but its relative dependence on immediate context. Statements in everyday life depend for their meaning on two factors. One factor is the formal features of the utterance itself, which might be called the text of the statement. But this is never enough. In addition, such statements depend on the context, the situation in which they are uttered, not merely the verbalization of the utterance itself. Evaluative statements such as "that's true" or "that's a lie," be they ethical, cognitive, or political, "take in a good deal more than what is enclosed within the strictly verbal (linguistic) factors of the utterance. *Together with the verbal factors, they also take in the extraverbal situation of the utterance.* These judgments and evaluations refer to a certain whole where the verbal discourse directly engages an event in life and merges with that event, forming an indissoluble unit."[6]

Bakhtin illustrates this point with a Russian parable, which was written in the same cold and poverty that it portrays:

"Two people are sitting in a room. They are both silent. Then one of them says, 'Well!' The other does not respond.

"For us outsiders this entire 'conversation' is utterly incomprehensible . . . In order to disclose the sense and meaning of this colloquy, we must analyze it. But what is it exactly we can subject to analysis? Whatever pains we take with the purely verbal part of the utterance, however subtly we define the phonetic, morphological, and semantic factors of the word *well*, we still shall not come a single step closer to an understanding of the whole sense of the colloquy.

"Let us suppose that the intonation with which this word is pronounced is known to us: indignation and reproach moderated by a certain amount of humor. This intonation fills in the semantic void of the adverb *well* but still does not reveal the meaning of the whole.

"What is it we lack, then? We lack the 'extraverbal context' that made the word *well* a meaningful locution to the listener. This *extraverbal context* of the utterance is comprised of three factors: (1) the *common spatial purview* of the interlocutors (the unity of the visible), (2) the interlocutors' *common knowledge and understanding of the situation*, and (3) their *common evaluation* of that situation.

"At the time the colloquy took place, both interlocutors *looked up* at the window and *saw* that it had begun to snow; both *knew* that it was already May and that it was high time for spring to come; finally, *both* were *sick and tired* of the protracted winter, *were looking forward* to spring, and were *bitterly disappointed* by the late snowfall. On this 'jointly seen' (snowflakes outside the window), 'jointly known' (time of year) and 'unanimously evaluated' (winter wearied of, spring looked forward to)—on all this the utterance *directly depends,* all this is seized in its actual, living import—is its very sustenance. And yet all this remains without *verbal* specification or articulation. The snowflakes remain outside the window; the date, on the page of the calendar; the evaluation, in the psyche of the speaker; and nevertheless all this is *assumed* in the word *well.*"[7]

The meaning of the word *well* (*tak*) here, a word that in itself means virtually nothing, can be understood not only by analyzing the relationship between what is said and what is unsaid. Both constitute the whole utterance, not merely what is spoken. This is a radical definition of utterance that has momentous consequences.

The simplest consequence is that insofar as the utterance is not merely what is said, discourse is not merely specular. It does not reflect an extraverbal situation in the way that a mirror reflects an object. Rather, discourse, whether in life or in art, is active, productive. It resolves a situation, brings it to an evaluative conclusion or extends action into the future. Discourse does not reflect a situation; it *is* a situation.

As such, discourse, like any other situation, joins people: "The utterance depends on the actual material connection of [speaker and listener] to one and the same segment of being and gives to this material commonness both ideological expression and further ideological development."[8] This is yet another version of Bakhtin's preoccupation with simultaneous differences. What he here calls the "same segment of being" was in *The Architectonics* conceptualized as an "event/situation" (*sobytie*), or as the "co-being" (*so-bytie*) of "being" (*bytija*). An utterance joins self and other, forging between these two poles of all perception the very possibility of their being joined in a simultaneity.

Bakhtin invokes these different terms for what is essentially the same problem, the interdependence of elements quite different from each other and the complex whole that results from otherwise nonidentical parts. His conceptual models are taken over from the philosophy of language, such as the special meaning that he gives to utterance, and from classical logic. Both models have in common the simultaneity of what is said and what is not said. In the utterance, as in the reading of "Well," there is both a vocally realized text and an intonationally created bridge to context. Bakhtin similarly plays with the enthymeme, a form of syllogism in which one of three premises is assumed but not expressed. An example is "All men are mortal. Socrates will die," in which the unspoken middle portion is "Socrates is a man." The *tertium comparitionis* of classical metaphor, the unstated third term joining two otherwise dissimilar elements, is a rhetorical example of the same kind of simultaneity between what is expressed and what is unexpressed but at the same time necessary to the meaning of what actually gets articulated. We must supply the unspoken quantity "fierce strength" in order to comprehend the statement, "Hercules is a lion."

We literally enact cultural values in our speech through the process of scripting our place and that of our listener in a social scenario. We anthropomorphize values. In speech, "the aboriginal myth-making spirit seems to have remained alive. Intonation makes it sound as if the world surrounding the speaker were still full of inanimate forces—it threatens and rails against or adores and cherishes inanimate objects and phenomena."[9] In the dramaturgy of actual speech situations we concretize the Kantian categories by which mind organizes the world. Intonation is the way in which the general categories of space and time are turned into specific interpretations of reality. Just as the abstract rules of a game are translated into particular applications when a game is actually played, so categories of rank and degree of intimacy between speakers get transformed into specific configurations when they are particularized in the sound patterns of actual utterances.

The scenario of any utterance must contain the same three *dramatis personae*: the speaker, the listener, and the topic. All utterances are born, live, and die in the drama that is played out in the interaction between these participants. In order to emphasize the dramaturgical aspect of these forces, Bakhtin anthropomorphizes the topic, since it is the one element of the triad that might otherwise appear to be a nonhuman actor. He calls it "the hero" of the playlet which unfolds in any utterance. Like authors, speakers work on the topic of what they are saying. While literary authors shape the heroes who are their characters, speakers have to shape their topics, and in this sense topics are to speakers as characters are to authors.

The word *hero* also suggests that the utterance is a form of struggle, as Bakhtin clearly conceived speech situations to be. How we act in such dramas reveals who we are. An utterance is always between a self and an other and constitutes the primal workings of self-identification. Like Freud, on whom he was working at the same time, Bakhtin has a specific conception of identity formation. But there the similarity ends, for Bakhtin's model is the polar opposite of that on which classical psychoanalysis is based. In Freud, the movement is from the infant's complete ego, through increasing repression, to the socialized self of adults who can delay ego gratification. In Bakhtin, on the contrary, the movement is from a nonself, through the acquisition of different "languages," to a self that is the sum of its discursive practices. In *Freudianism* he argues that "any instance of self-awareness (for self-awareness is always verbal, always a matter of finding some specifically suitable verbal complex) is an act of gauging oneself against some social norm. Social evaluation is, so to speak, the socialization of oneself and one's behavior. In becoming aware of myself, I attempt to look at myself, as it were, through the eyes of another person."[10] In Freud, self is suppressed in the service of the social; in Bakhtin, self is precisely a function of the social. In Freud, the more of the other, the less of the self; in Bakhtin, the more of the other, the more of the self.

This emphasis accounts for Bakhtin's insistence on the dual nature not only of the sign (signifier/signified) but of the utterance, which is always a combination of what is actually verbalized and what is nonverbalized but assumed by both speaker and addressee: "Life does not effect an utterance from without, it penetrates and exerts an influence from within, as that unity and simultaneity of being surrounding the speakers and that unity and simultaneity of basic social value-judgments that arise from their being, and without which no intelligible utterance is possible."[11] This formulation continues Bakhtin's emphasis on simultaneity as "the unified and unitary event of being," but it also changes the nature of Bakhtin's own discourse, for his metaphysical language has taken on a more immediate and programmatic edge, in which the event of being is specified as the act of communication.

This re-emphasis is found in the new treatment of self/other relations as relations between what is said and what is unsaid in any actual utterance. The simultaneity of the said and unsaid is apparent in the effects of intonation (how a thing is said) on language (what is said). Intonation, more than any other aspect of utterance, stitches its repeatable, merely linguistic stuff to the unrepeatable social situation in which it is spoken. Intonation is the immediate interface between said and unsaid: "it, as it were, pumps energy from a life situation into verbal discourse—it endows everything linguistically stable with living historical momentum and uniqueness."[12]

The ligature joining experience and expression in everyday life, the site where life and speech articulate with each other, is thus utterance. Bakhtin defines utterance as the simultaneity of what is actually said and what is assumed but not spoken. In the utterance, unlike the enthymeme, what remains only assumed is not some mystical essence of self whose locus is in the heart or mind of the individual speaker, for the "individual and subjective are both grounded . . . by the social and objective. What I know, see, want, love, recognize, and so on, cannot be assumed. Only what all of us speakers know, see, love, recognize—only those points on which we are all united can become the assumed part of an utterance . . . Assumed value judgments are therefore not individual emotions but regular and essential social acts. Individual emotions can come into play only as overtones accompanying the basic tone of social evaluation. 'I' can realize itself verbally only on the basis of 'we.' "[13] These assumed values go so deep that they are virtually flesh of the flesh of utterances. They constitute an assumptive world whose contours represent the outside limit of reality for those within its sphere. When a value judgment ceases to be automatic, when it needs to be explained or rationalized, its basis in the society has already begun to crumble.

The purest expression of the values assumed in any utterance is found at the level of intonation, for the reason that intonation always lies on the border between the verbal and the nonverbal, the I and the other. Intonation clearly registers the other's presence, creating a kind of portrait in sound of the addressee to whom the speaker imagines she is speaking. A common illustration of this tendency is found when we hear someone talking on the telephone to another person whose identity we do not know, but whose relation to the speaker we can guess from the speaker's speech patterns. Intonation serves as the material means for stitching together the said, in the speech of the speaker, and the unsaid, in the context of the situation. The community of shared values gives the physically articulated acoustical shifts in pitch or loudness different semantic weight. Through intonation we express a judgment on what we are simultaneously conveying as information in an utterance: "The commonness of assumed basic value judgments constitutes the canvas upon which living human speech embroiders the designs of intonation."[14]

Verbal discourse, then, is the means by which actual life situations structure themselves. They do so as scenarios dramatizing specific events. Any account of utterance must "reproduce this event of the mutual [or simultaneous] relationships between speakers, must as it were restructure it, with the person wishing to understand taking upon himself the role of listener. But in order to carry out that role, he must distinctly understand the position of the other as well."[15] Bakhtin's insistence on the necessity of "understanding" the position not only of the other but of all others, by adding communication theory to theology, extends the meaning of Christ's biblical injunction to treat others as we would be treated ourselves, to take on, in other words, the role of others with the same depth of sympathy and understanding that we bring to our own perception of ourselves. In Bakhtin's system this is not merely a moral imperative but an epistemological requirement.

Bakhtin seeks the aesthetic where it was traditionally avoided, in the totality of the author/text/reader relationship. The inclusiveness of such a totality is greater than that of most other definitions of the aesthetic. Bakhtin exposes himself to the danger of appearing indiscriminate. But he does not batter down all of the walls traditionally assumed to separate aesthetic from nonaesthetic realms. This would fly in the face of his assumption that all cultures consist of different discursive functions, one of the most important of which is the aesthetic. Instead, Bakhtin defines the difference between art and nonart as one of degree, as relational rather than absolute.

This distinction differs from the Formalists' opposition between poetic and practical language. Their difference was in danger of being reduced to the merely arithmetical, because it consisted not only in tropes but in the sheer number of devices that poets were impelled to include in their discourse to achieve their aim of braking perception to the point where discourse itself would become the object of attention. For Bakhtin, aesthetic difference is found rather in the degree to which a text depends on the context in which it is perceived. The relative independence of aesthetic texts from the immediate contexts in which they are experienced, such as the mood of a single reader on a particular occasion, makes them more open to contexts of greater scope. They can continue to interact with a multitude of new historical and cultural environments because they are not, like other kinds of utterance, as locally dependent on any one context. Aesthetics is a special instance of communicating in which the text makes a minimal appeal to its environment for help in constructing its meaning.

In the opposite case of everyday life, an utterance presumes connections with its environment that supplement the information contained in the words alone. The simple word "Well!" was able to wring complex meanings and rich stores of information out of its immediate setting in Bakhtin's parable. But the gift of meaning that such an economy of purely verbal means extracts from the environment is not without its price, for once severed from its setting, such an utterance loses as much import as it had gained due to the particular conditions of that setting. People who do not know the circumstances in which such a statement was made do not then have access to the whole statement. They have only the verbal portion of the text, without its extraverbal context. As a result, the utterance is literally incomprehensible.

The verbal aspect of an utterance in everyday life is merely a small key that opens the treasure room of contextually provided meanings. When that wealth of particularity is exhausted, the key itself becomes merely a curiously shaped lump of matter. The Russian term for "password," *parol'*, is a calque from the French *parole*. Thus, Bakhtin intends a macaronic pun redolent with irony when he says of this situation, "Every utterance in the business of life is akin to a 'password' known only to those who belong to the same social purview."[16]

The feature that distinguishes art speech from everyday speech is first of all not absolute but relative. Both forms of utterance depend for their meaning on an ecological relationship between verbalized text and nonverbalized elements in their context. There is no such thing as "the text itself," that autotelic object dreamed up by Russian Formalists and American New Critics. There are only texts that are more or less implicated in their environments, much the same as there are no organisms in themselves but only animals that are more or less dependent on the conditions of a specific ecosystem. People live everywhere, but koalas live only in restricted areas of Australia because of their dependence on leaves from a limited number of species of gum tree.

This text/context relation parallels Bakhtin's self/other relation not only in ecological structure but also in the values attaching to each of its poles. A self, or a text, can never achieve complete autonomy, but the less determined each is by its local environment, the freer each is to live and have meaning in other contexts, life and meaning being equivalent in Bakhtin's thought.

The important role that this ecological model of semantics plays for Bakhtin is not restricted to aesthetics. It lies at the heart of his psychology, in the struggle between innerly persuasive discourse and authoritative discourse.[17] And it is central to his politics, in the struggle between official and nonofficial ideologies. Because of Bakhtin's constant meditation on the ways in which self/other relations play themselves out at these different levels of complexity, he conceives style much more broadly than most other theorists. Style is more than a catalogue of tropes and devices. When style is understood as how something gets expressed, as opposed simply to what is expressed, it is a means not only for enhancing meaning but also for adjusting and registering relations between the speaker or writer, their subject or "hero," and their audience. The number of such relations in any given utterance is potentially very high. Before a particular configuration among the three is worked out in what actually gets said, many different battles have to be fought, and many compromises have to be made among the speaker, "hero," and audience. Since style is a way to work out differences among conflicting parties, Bakhtin argues that it is a form of politics: "The internal politics of a style is determined by its external politics (its relation to alien discourse)."[18]

Style is a struggle, a politics, and the freer from specific alterities or the less subordinate to local conditions of expression a text becomes, the more aesthetic it becomes. Aesthetics, in other words, constitutes a version of liberty. The association of art with liberty is far from novel with Bakhtin. It goes back at least to Plato's recognition that poets were a threat to his closed society in the Republic, and in Bakhtin's time the same threat was perceived by Stalin. Insofar as the aesthetic is indeed a sphere in which local factors are least determining, it is always the world of greatest otherness, the biggest loophole through which the present may escape to a future undreamed of in worlds of less expansive discourse, such as politics or religion, where the future is a knowable outcome of the present. The most frequent witnesses to the proposition that art is tied to liberty have been the censors. More positive attempts to state an equation between aesthetics and freedom have something potentially sentimental about them, as in the lesser Romantics. Bakhtin avoids this danger in his conflation of the two by accounting for their inseparability in a full-fledged philosophy of language. That philosophy is founded on the rock of praxis, the immediacy of utterance, and the stern necessities of dialogue, which requires that the freedom to shape meaning constantly be won anew.

CHAPTER 10

Marxism and the Philosophy of Language

Bakhtin's dialogism is essentially a philosophy of language. It is a "translinguistics," which constitutes a master optic for perceiving all categories rooted in language, and Bakhtin assumes that all aspects of human life are so rooted. His formulation of the traditional claim for a humanist territorial imperative, *Homo sum; humani nihil a me alieanum puto,* which usually translates, "I am a man, nothing human is foreign to me," might well read, "My life is an utterance, therefore nothing in discourse is foreign to me." On the basis of this unifying theory of language, Bakhtin rethought a wide variety of topics that had previously been conceived as belonging to separate disciplines. Thus, while there are differences in what he has to say on such subjects as psychology, linguistics, and literary criticism, his probes in each of these areas exhibit recurring concerns, which include the importance of locating semantics in the specificity of actual utterances, the primacy of dialogue over monologue, and the inability of descriptive systems based on logical models to comprehend the variety and historicity of meaning. Like the Structuralists with whom he is often confused, Bakhtin uses a particular view of language as a conceptual philosopher's stone for turning the dross of previously atomized disciplines into the golden unity of a common science, although the view of language by which he accomplishes the feat is fundamentally at odds with Structuralist linguistics.

Marxism and the Philosophy of Language is the most comprehensive account of Bakhtin's translinguistics. It sets out the major presuppositions on which all his other works are based by addressing two topics: the role of signs in human thought and the role of utterance in language. Each of these topics is then linked to the way in which we report in our speech the speech of others.

The search for understanding on these issues oscillates between the broadest generality and the densest particularity because Bakhtin is trying to generalize about particularity. He wants to include in his description of language all the factors outside words that have a profound bearing on their meaning, such as differences in age or social rank, in whether the words are being spoken in an intimate conversation between close friends or publicly to an audience that includes many listeners unknown to the speaker, and in whether something is said on impulse or as part of an obligatory response in a ritual. The number of such factors is so high as to be inconceivable, and most linguists have carefully excluded such considerations from their accounts because they seemed to undermine any attempt to describe language as a system. In Bakhtin's view the conceptual power of the systems so developed is limited, for by concentrating on words outside the contexts in which they are used, linguists have bought their neat paradigms and dictionary definitions at the price of what is most important in language, the capacity of words to mean. The only way that words can mean is to be understood. And the only way that they are understood is by particular speakers and listeners, who are also speakers, in particular situations. Linguists have looked at language from the wrong end of the telescope in their attempts to gain a global view. Bakhtin, by contrast, focuses his attention on the individual speaker rather than on the chimera of "the words themselves."

Bakhtin argues that by conceiving words as if no one ever actually spoke them, linguists have turned dialogic signs into monologic signals: "The speaker's focus of attention is oriented by the particular, concrete utterance he is making . . . What is important for him is not that a word is a stable and always self-equivalent signal, but an always changeable and adaptable sign." The ability to use language is not defined by the mastery one acquires over the kind of knowledge of syntactic rules, word lists, or grammatical norms so beloved of linguists. Language mastery consists rather in being able to apply such fixed features in fluid situations, or in other words, in knowing not the rules but the usage of language. From the point of view of the speaker and not the grammarian, language's center of gravity "lies not in the identity of the form but in that new and concrete meaning it requires in the particular context . . . The task of understanding does not basically amount to recognizing the form used, but rather to understanding its meaning in a particular utterance, i. e., it amounts to understanding its novelty and not to recognizing its identity."[1]

Marxism and the Philosophy of Language concentrates on factors that cannot in the nature of things ever be reduced to a tidy system, because they are so various. But this does not mean that they cannot be dealt with in an orderly fashion. Bakhtin's strategy for doing so is to highlight the one universal feature present throughout the vast array of possible contexts. No matter how bewilderingly various are such contexts, their power to change the meaning of words is not unlimited, for they are able to do so only on one condition: they can have their effect only within the space where differences in a word's meaning can be registered, namely between two speakers. The one constant in the ceaselessly shifting, ever new conditions in which an utterance is pronounced is the unique locus where such conditions are able to have an effect, the locus constituted by the individual speaker and his addressee. For this reason Bakhtin concentrates on the relatively limited number of factors governing the practice of speakers as a way to order the unlimited number of contexts in which they speak. He resolves the old and apparently unbridgeable dichotomy between the obviously systematic features of language, such as syntax, grammar, or the relatively fixed meanings of words, and their unsystematizable contexts, which interact with such stable features in any actual conversation, by reducing the differences between them to another set of differences, those between specific speakers in particular situations.

Bakhtin makes this move by arguing that the word is always "oriented toward an addressee, toward who that addressee might be . . . each person's inner world and thought has its stabilized social audience that comprises the environment in which reasons, motives, values, and so on are fashioned . . . the word is a two-sided act. It is determined equally by whose word it is and for whom it is meant. As word, it is precisely the product of the reciprocal relationship between speaker and listener, addresser and addressee. Each and every word expresses the one in relation to the other. I give myself verbal shape from another's point of view, ultimately from the point of view of the community to which I belong. A word is a bridge thrown between myself and another . . . it is territory shared by both addresser and addressee."[2]

In this emphasis on the degree to which a word's meaning never coincides with the word itself, on the unsystematic, open aspects of language, and above all on the relation between speaker and addressee, Bakhtin refines his earlier preoccupation with given versus conceived worlds, with finished versus unfinished aspects of experience, and with relations between self and other being translated from a discourse appropriate to a philosophy of morals into a discourse appropriate to a philosophy of language. In the process, dialogism demonstrates a capacity to incorporate aspects of language that linguists had either completely ignored or treated cursorily. It recognizes, for instance, far better than do formal grammars in such crude registers as pronouns, the need to account for the presence of the other to whom a person is speaking. This is true even when the pronomial system is as sensitive to differences as it is in Palaung, a language spoken by a small tribe in the northern Shan states of Burma, which has eleven pronouns, eight of them plurals, whereas English has only three plural pronouns. In such a language it is possible to indicate precisely the borders between those included and those excluded from being implicated in the meaning of a statement. Complex rules govern the use of even such minimal pairs as "you"/"thou." And in a language such as American English, where the second person singular is no longer used except in prayer, the kinds of distinctions that such a pronominal option makes available in, say, French or German are nevertheless expressed in other ways, such as addressing one another by name (Bill versus William) or by title (Brown versus Mr. Brown).[3] In traditional societies it is nearly impossible to say anything without indicating the social relationship between the speaker and the listener in terms of status and familiarity, and the same is true closer to home. Although English lacks fully worked-out formal vocabularies of hierarchy, it is no more possible in spoken English to avoid recognizing rank than it is in Bindibu, Polish, or Japanese. For example, a recent invitation to an army social was addressed to "Officers with their ladies and enlisted men with their wives."

Bakhtin had little influence on sociolinguistics in his day, largely due to his long exile and the lack of translators. But his conviction that the "immediate social situation and the broader social milieu wholly determine—and determine from within, so to speak—the structure of an utterance" has since found confirmation. W. Labov showed that lower class Blacks and Puerto Ricans in New York are perfectly capable of interpreting sentences in standard English when they hear them but use only substandard English when speaking among themselves. E. M. Albert showed that among the Burundi of East Africa "a peasant may command the verbal abilities stressed and valued in the culture but he cannot display them in the presence of a leader or other superior. In such cases appropriate behavior is that in which their words are haltingly delivered or run on uncontrolled, their voices are loud, their gestures wild, their figures of speech ungainly, their emotions freely displayed, their words and sentences clumsy."[4]

Each of these examples dramatizes the enormous difference between naked words out of context and words as they are exploited in social situations. Isolated words constitute the language studied by linguists; social words are the more broadly conceived subject that Bakhtin takes as his own. For example, when words are conceived as mere words, the same words are known equally to both whites and blacks in New York City or to both lords and peasants among the Burundi, although only the upper classes actually use them in both cases. By going beyond the words as such, Bakhtin seeks to explain both the upper class use of certain words and the lower class avoidance of the same words. He wants to go outside the conception of language animating most linguistic descriptions in order to understand not only the words of the rulers but the expressive silence of the ruled. Thus his philosophy is a "meta-" or "trans"-linguistics insofar as it includes in language factors that are shunned by most linguists. One of the ways Bakhtin formulates this distinction is to say that linguists study language, whereas he is concerned with communication.

Bakhtin posits the utterance as the fundamental unit of investigation for anyone studying communication as opposed to just language. Utterances provide the building blocks of the logosphere, just as atoms do for the natural world. Utterance is Bakhtin's covering term for a situation whose duality had been obscured by the unitizing assumption that speaking and listening were exclusive and integral activities. People were thought to do either the one or the other. But Bakhtin's experience confirmed that people do both simultaneously.

Discourse is an action. This activity is more complicated than the action of machines, which owing to mechanical limitations must transmit and receive sequentially. When people use language, they do so not as machines sending and transmitting codes, but as consciousnesses engaging in simultaneous understanding: the speaker listens and the listener speaks. Any utterance is a link in a complex *chain* of communication.

Utterance is the awareness of what Bakhtin calls "addressivity" (*obraščënnost'*), the otherness of language in general and of given dialogic partners in particular. This awareness turns the general system of language to the needs of specific experiences: "language enters life through concrete utterances."[5] Consciousness is the medium and utterance is the means by which two otherwise disparate elements—the quickness of experience and the materiality of language—are harnessed in a volatile unity.

The stasis characterizing language is not completely obliterated in communication. For even from the point of view of individual speakers, the words that they use have at least the appearance of being "always already there," insofar as the vocabulary and grammar that they must use always preexist them: no one, no generation ever invested a fresh language all its own. But that obvious fact reveals only part of the story. From the point of view of the speaker, his words are not only "always already there"; they are also "never ever before" because those words must be spoken in contexts that are utterly unique and novel to the speaker. For instance, we know not only what "joy" signifies but also the meaning of locutions such as, "Any joy is now bitterness to me." Moreover, we can understand further dimensions of the word 'joy' as they come up in actual utterances, such as this sentence.

A dialogue in Bakhtin's system is a datum from experience that can serve as an economical paradigm for a theory encompassing more global dimensions. In an exchange between two speaking subjects, what each says to the other is difficult to describe in terms of language alone. The talk is segmented not only by words and sentences but also by protocols that determine who is talking. The different ways in which speakers indicate appropriate points for others to respond are enormously varied, depending on the topic, the speakers, and the context of the utterance. But the relations between utterances are always conditioned by the potential response of an other. Thus, these relations are part of communication and cannot be adequately dealt with in terms of the language system alone.

Bakhtin argues that the utterance is a more comprehensive

unit than the sentence. It constitutes the whole that underwrites the completedness of sentences which act its parts. The limits of an utterance are marked not by the sentence structure but rather by the ability of other speakers to respond to it. This guarantees its finalization, although such finalization is always partial, sufficient only to the moment.

The integrity of an utterance or its identity as a whole results from a configuration of three other factors: the semantic exhaustiveness of its theme, or essentially how much of its possible complexity can be expressed in a single utterance; the speech plan of the speaker as evaluated by his addressee, or what we feel the speaker is trying to express by speaking in the particular way in which he addresses us; and generic forms for indicating finalization, or the conversational equivalents of "And they all lived happily ever after," such as intonations indicating a question or a command. Semantic exhaustiveness refers to the form an utterance must have before it is adequate to expressing a complete meaning. For instance, certain themes are dealt with in highly standardized ways in which small amounts of information are usually delivered and the limits on interpretable meanings are rigidly set, as in military orders or other fixed exchanges. The majority of utterances have much more flexibility, and assessments of the speaker's speech plan are required to help us know when he has completed an utterance. In any utterance we perceive, posit, or imagine what the speaker wishes to say, and according to the judgment that we form of this intent we also measure whether the utterance is completed or not. There is an individual, subjective element in such judgments, which is why we are sometimes wrong in assessing the other's speech plan. But more often than not such judgments are also based on relatively objective criteria, for as competent speakers of a language, we know that most speech situations fall into certain patterns and that generic exchanges have developed to reflect such patterns. Two people waiting at a bus stop are very likely not only to discuss the topic of the weather but to do so in utterances shaped by conventions of the genre "talking about weather."

Although Bakhtin's concept of speech genre points to the cardinal fact that utterances are always in some degree formulaic, he does not catalogue the precise shapes that these formulas assume, in accord with his principle that meaning is context bound but that context is boundless. The name of this boundlessness is "heteroglossia." For Bakhtin, a rigorous poetics of speech genres would have roughly the same invidious status that a normative catalogue of dream symbols would have for Freud.

In effect, the will of the speakers can never be more than partially realized, and then only in their selection of this speech genre versus that one in any given instance. These typical forms of utterance come to us as we learn to speak and continue throughout our conscious lives. In fact, "to learn to speak means to learn to construct utterances . . . we learn to cast our speech in generic forms and, when we hear others' speech, we deduce its genre from the first words; we anticipate in advance a certain volume (that is, the approximate length of the speech whole) as well as a certain compositional structure. We foresee the end; that is, from the very beginning we have a sense of the speech whole."[6]

The speaker's evaluation of what he is talking about, even when he is attempting to be neutral, and his judgment as to whom he is addressing determine the choice of language units, whether lexical or grammatical, and the choice of communication units, such as the style of an utterance or the speech genres employed. This evaluative component of speech, though necessary and unavoidable, allows for the only possible freedom we have in speech, for it determines the expressive aspect of an utterance. Phonemes and syntax have in common with speech genres a tendency to limit the freedom of individual speakers. Not only are words and sentences "always already there," but so are the forms for their combination into utterances. Yet speech genres, the units of communication, are still far less normative and binding than are grammatical forms, the units of language, which allow no play.

The individual style of the utterance can be determined by its expressive side because the forms of communication are more open to play and intervention than are the forms of language. Intonation, word choice, and selection of speech genre are open to "assimilation" (osvoenie) by individual speakers as a means of shaping the values they cannot avoid registering. Some genres are more malleable than others: the give and take at the information counter of a railroad station are maximally codified, whereas the give and take between intimate friends present possibilities for minimal, but never absent, generic control. Jakobson, for example, argued that in the combination of linguistic units there is "an ascending scale of freedom" from distinctive features, moving from phonemes at the bottom, where the freedom of the individual speaker is zero since he has no choice but to use the available forms, up to words and sentences at the top, where freedom is greater because more combinations and substitutions are possible.[7]

Language invokes the political concept of freedom because language is struggle against the necessity of certain forms. Language is a unitizing noun developed for the action of what is a scattered and powerful array of social forces. Whether or not social interaction is conceived as class struggle, social forces are never conceived otherwise than as being in conflict, except in utopias, which is why the word *utopian* has come to mean "unreal." Bakhtin argues that language is where those struggles are engaged most comprehensively and at the same time most intimately and personally. It is in language, not in the nation-state, that social force finds its most realized expression: "Each word . . . is a little arena for the clash of and criss-crossing of differently oriented social accents. A word in the mouth of a particular individual is a product of the living interaction of social forces."[8] In Turgenev's *Fathers and Sons* the Nihilists all go on about principles, as do their parents. However, the young radicals pronounce the word *printsip*, whereas the older conservatives say *principe* "in the soft French way." Behind this small difference between consonants lie all the philosophical and political differences between a generation turning to German scientism and a generation still espousing French deism. This difference between two possible ways of pronouncing a word brought into the open the major political and intellectual conflicts of the 1860s in Russia.

As Bakhtin observes, "Within the arena of . . . every utterance an intense conflict between one's own and another's word is being fought out . . . The utterance so conceived is a considerably more complex and dynamic organism than it appears when construed simply as a thing that articulates the intention of the person uttering it." Speakers have only so much freedom of their own to exercise as they can win in battle with the other's word. This does not mean that all speech is an aspect of argument, although it does mean that all speech is willy-nilly rhetorical. One person must deal not merely with the other person's intention but with the resisting otherness of the whole situation in which they both find themselves: "The immediate social situation and the broader social milieu wholly determine—and determine from within, so to speak—the structure of an utterance."[9] No matter how basic the subject of the utterance, even if it is something so primitive and universal as hunger, its expression is determined by the participants in the speech event, by both explicit and implicit addressor and addressee, connected by a specific situation. These factors determine whether even so immediate a need as hunger is expressed as a demand or a request, in flowery or plain style, hesitantly or confidently.

In *Marxism and the Philosophy of Language* Bakhtin turns a previously reigning set of master categories on its head. When he attacks linguists, it is usually Saussure he has in mind. Saussure preferred the timelessness of system to time-bound performance. In applying this principle to linguistics, he privileged "synchronous language" or *langue,* the systematic aspect of a language as it exists in one moment of time without considering its past history, over "diachronous speech" or *parole,* the unsystematic use of language by actual speakers over time.

Bakhtin inverts the values of language and speech. Instead of possessing a Leibnizian timelessness and a Cartesian logic, Bakhtin insists, language always partakes of the messiness of history and the vagaries of individual performance. Language is found not in a Platonic dream of order but in the hurly-burly, the give and take of speech in everyday life: "The actual reality of language—speech—is not the abstract system of linguistic norms . . . and not the psychophysiological act of its implementation, but the social event of verbal interaction implemented in an utterance."[10]

Saussure cut off the abstraction and timelessness of system from the particularity of performance in language. The world of system and that of performance were seen merely as different levels for the functioning of the same phenomenon, but the "higher" level of system was all-determining. Speech was to system as an actual triangle to the Platonic idea of triangle.

Bakhtin argues, however, that the cutoff is not merely between linguistic system and speech performance but also between mind and matter. Each is so different from the other that categories and practices appropriate to the one do not suffice for the other. The systematic, repeatable aspects of language are very close to the things of the world: grammar, syntax, lexicon, and phonetics are all dead stuff to be put into the service of a living understanding in actual speech situations. A phoneme as such is just as dead as a grapheme as such. The systematic aspects of language are to speech as the material world is to mind. Thus they differ from each other but always operate together. The two sets of features interact in a dynamic unity and cannot without conceptual violence be separated from each other. The arena where they intermingle and the force that binds them are both what Bakhtin understands by "utterance."

What Bakhtin means by utterance is not the same as what Saussure intended by speech. Saussure still ascribed a degree of hegemony to individual speakers. In his diagram of the speech situation, which has two heads separated by arrows, an active speaker is sending a message to a passive listener. This diagram is a virtual icon for the age-old suppression of the communicative aspect of the word. For all its schematicism, this drawing models a view of language that still privileges the individual, subjective world of the speaker. The arrows in the space between the two talking heads in the drawing represent the intention of each, traveling in an unimpeded freedom to its unproblematic goal.

For Bakhtin, utterance is not speech conceived as a holiday from system, representing the individual ability to will language elements into freely chosen combinations. Besides forms of language, there exist as well forms of combinations of these forms. The determining role of the other in actual speech communication shows not only that there is a system in language outside of any particular articulation of language but also that there is a system governing any actual utterance.

To avoid the old dualism of system and performance, Bakhtin posits "communication," instead of "language," as the subject of his investigation. Language is usually conceived as including grammar, lexicon, syntax, and phonology; it knows no unit of word combinations more comprehensive than the sentence. All these features play a role as well in Bakhtin's translinguistics, but they are in constant dialogue with other features that come into play only in particular acts of communication.

Bakhtin locates the roots of Structuralist linguistics in the old European philological tradition of studying dead languages, such as ancient Greek, or phantom languages, such as proto-Indo-European. Linguistics was the child of philology, and as such, it had always taken "as its point of departure an utterance that was finished, monologic: the ancient written monument, considering it the ultimate realism . . . Despite the vast differences in cultural and historical characteristics, from the ancient Hindu priests to the modern European scholar of language, the philologist has always and everywhere been a decipherer of alien, 'secret' scripts and words . . . The first philologists and the first linguists were always and everywhere priests. History knows no nations whose sacred writings or oral tradition were not to some degree in a language foreign and incomprehensible to the profane. To decipher the mystery of sacred words was the task meant to be carried out by the priest-philologists."[11]

Because philology was so deeply implicated in the historical role of the alien word, it was blind to its own complicity in alien words. Philologists were thus unable to break out of their obsession with esoteric or dead languages and turn their attention to familiar speech, the living native language. Saussure, for example, privileged abstract, extrahistorical language over the vivid specificity of spoken speech. Linguistics not only treated a "living language as if it were a dead language" but even treated the "native language as if it were an alien tongue."[12]

The place where language resides, according to Bakhtin, is not elsewhere, other in space or past in time. Language is rather here and now; it lives in concrete utterance, where the traces of the past are re-presented. But Bakhtin admits the danger of going too far in this direction and locating the seat of language in the individual psyche of speakers. Linguists such as Wundt and Vossler in Germany, Croce in Italy, and Potebnya's followers in Russia conceived the basis of language to be the individual creative act of speech. The laws of language, according to this school, were the laws of individual psychology.[13]

For Bakhtin, the weakness of this position was its inability to assimilate the undeniably systematic aspects of language. Phonetics, grammar, and syntax are not merely phantoms in an obsessional fantasy but constitute the normative, given side of language, even when language is defined as utterance. Language, among other things, is systematic, standing before the individual user as a set of prior norms: "The individual acquires the system of language from his speech community completely ready-made. Any change within that system is beyond the range of his individual consciousness. *But the peculiar status this systematic aspect has in reality must be put to the question.*"[14]

Language does not exist as a set of rules chiseled into tablets by an academy, nor as a preinscription in some mysterious collective mind. The normativeness of language rules is similar rather to any other system of social norms, which is why linguistics can serve as a kind of *ars generalis* that has the capability of restructuring the social sciences. The systematic norms of language are analogous to a system of moral, judicial, or aesthetic norms in the sense that these systematic aspects of language exist only with respect to the subjective consciousness of individuals belonging to some particular community governed by such norms. These norms may vary, but the nature of their existence remains the same: they exist only with respect to the subjective consciousness of members of some particular community.

Because the logic of language rules is social, they can never be hypostatized into neo-Platonic forms generated by individuals out of the pure energy of their own subjectivity. Language is not a set of laws that is completely objective in the sense, say, that the laws of thermodynamics are objective. Nor is it a set of completely subjective phenomena that are distinctive to individual persons in the way, say, that fingerprints are uniquely one's own.

For Bakhtin, individual intention is a relative matter, inasmuch as the "I" is a function of "we." Thus, the amount of freedom available to the individual speaker in a given case depends on the constantly shifting ratio between inner speech, which is conscious thought, and outer speech. Similarly, society invests the individual through the medium common to both—signs, or language.

Bakhtin's term for the world of signs both in the psyche and in the world is "ideology." He never gives a full-scale definition of ideology, but according to contemporary theorists of ideology who were influenced by Bakhtin, "every historically given culture generates some special model of culture peculiar to itself . . . underlying all definitions is the notion that there are certain specific features to a culture . . . [it] is never a universal set, but always a subset organized in a specific manner. [It] never encompasses everything, but instead forms a marked off sphere." Members of different cultures have competence in the specific ways whereby their own systems assign order to the world. They know when something is "correct" or not in table manners, dress codes, and sexual relations, just as surely as they know when someone is or is not using the spoken language of the culture correctly. Culture's capacity to invest physical nature with significance for human beings, on the one hand, and of language, on the other, are intimately related: "The fundamental task of culture is in structurally organizing the world around man. Culture is the generator of structuredness, and in this way it creates a social sphere around man which, like the biosphere, makes life possible. But in order for it to fulfill [such a] role, culture must have within itself a structural 'diecasting mechanism.' It is natural language that gives the members of a social group their intuitive sense of structuredness that with its transformation of the 'open' world of 'realia' into a 'closed' world of names, forces people to treat as structures those phenomena whose structuredness, at best, is not apparent."[15]

When Bakhtin asserts that "everything ideological has semiotic value," he means that all products of the human mind, from the simplest tools to the most elaborate cosmologies, are born of thought, which at its higher levels can execute ordering and generative tasks only by means of signs: "The domain of ideology coincides with the domain of signs."[16] There are enormous differences among the signs that particular communities feel are appropriate at a given time and place to such different spheres as the law, religion, or gossip. But insofar as all these spheres are organized as different categories of signs, they all partake of a semiotic nature. Bakhtin thus feels empowered to seek a basis for all human behavior in a general philosophy of language.

Bakhtin's concept of the sign is similar to Saussure's in that a sign is always an inseparable unity composed of two parts: a mark that is simply an indicator, the signifier, and a concept that is so indicated, the signified. Bakhtin, however, concentrates on the worldly, sensory aspect of the sign: "Every phenomenon functioning as a . . . sign has some kind of material embodiment, whether in sound, physical mass, color, movements of the body, or the like. In this sense the reality of the sign is fully objective. This conviction that the sign has a body corresponds to Bakhtin's ontotheological view that the spirit has a Christ. The kenotic event that is reenacted in language is the mode of God's presence to human beings: "understanding itself can come about only within some kind of semiotic material (e.g. inner speech) . . . Sign bears upon sign . . . consciousness itself can arise and become a viable fact only in the material embodiment of signs." Bakhtin praises Neo-Kantianism for considering the dominant trait of consciousness "to be *representation*. Each element of consciousness represents something, bears a symbolic function."[17]

For Bakhtin, the theater where the sign functions and has meaning is not the individual mind alone but a vastly more comprehensive area, the sea of interpersonal relations called the "social." Just as no fish can live out of water, no individual human mind can exist outside the ocean of signs: "Signs can arise only on *interindividual territory* . . . [they] do not arise between any two members of the species *Homo sapiens*. It is essential that the two individuals be organized socially, that they compose a group (a social unit); only then can the medium of signs take shape between them."[18]

The comprehensiveness and power of signs is manifest primarily in spoken speech: "the existence of the sign is nothing but the materialization of communication. Such is the nature of all ideological signs. But nowhere does this semiotic quality . . . of social communication as conditioning factor appear so clearly and fully expressed as in language. *The word is the ideological phenomenon par excellence.*" There are three reasons for the primacy of the word among all other signs. The first is its semiotic intensity: "The entire reality of the word is wholly absorbed in its function of being a sign. A word contains nothing that is indifferent to this function, nothing that would not have been engendered by it."[19] A hammer and sickle, or a cross, can be signs, but they are also other things, having purposes other than sheer semiosis. By contrast, a word is only, and all, a sign.

The second reason for the primacy of the word is its ideological neutrality, which is inseparable from and makes possible its purity and intensity. Other kinds of signs are capable of being compromised by the uses to which they are put. In an American context a graphic representation of an elephant suggests the Republican Party, and depending on how people feel about the policies of that party, they perceive a positive or negative charge in assimilating the sign of the elephant. As a sign, the elephant has been infected with Republicanism. But the word *elephant* cannot be so easily restricted. It maintains its capacity to convey a myriad of meanings without ever being completely exhausted by any of them. A word is "neutral with respect to any specific ideological function. It can carry out ideological functions of any kind—scientific, aesthetic, ethical, religious, etc."[20]

This multivalence of the word is the third reason for its power, since people are themselves distinguished by the multifariousness of their natures. They are able to accommodate their bodies to great extremes of physical environment, for example. And this is so not merely because they are warm-blooded animals with the metabolic capacity to adjust to different temperatures, an ability that they share with other animals, but also because they have invented new skins for themselves that permit them to go into ever more improbable extremes of heat or cold and to adjust to environments, as on the moon, which lack the basic conditions required for life. Such self-contained ecosystems constitute a metaphor for the use of words, which are the vehicles that permit people to move from one meaning of the same word to another and from one stratum of the cultural system to another.

Bakhtin conceives differing social strata ecologically. The ocean's appearance of watery unity, for instance, is in fact traversed by innumerable layers of different kinds of water, each with its own temperature and salt content. Fish are not free to roam the land, but neither are they free to go everywhere in the sea. They are confined to the strata in which the temperature, light availability, and salinity accord with their biological constitution. As the sea is all water, so the logosphere is all words, but words are not all the same. Even when words give the appearance of sameness, they mean different things in different situations. Those who do not learn to exploit the capacity of words to mean different things in different epistemological layers of their culture system are condemned to exist unfreely, within a very small number of such layers. Language is not a prison house; it is an ecosystem.

The psychologist A. R. Luria found evidence of this ecosystem in the differences between literate and nonliterate subjects in Russia's central Asian republics. Subjects who had some exposure to literacy were able to make use of abstract categories, as opposed to subjects without such experience. When shown drawings of a hammer, a saw, a hatchet, and a log, literate Uzbeks arranged the first three items into one category, for tools, and the log into another category, whereas illiterate subjects typically said things such as, "They are all alike." When told that another subject had categorized the saw, hammer, and hatchet separately, one illiterate peasant responded that all four items must work together and thus the man who had separated the items "probably has a lot of firewood, but if we'll be left without firewood, we won't be able to do anything." When an exasperated Luria answered that this was no doubt true but a hammer, a saw, and a hatchet are all tools, the peasant replied, "Yes, but even if we have tools, we still need wood. Otherwise we can't build anything." This peasant could not get out of his environment. Freeing ourselves from the immediate situation depends in large measure on our ability to reflect on decontextualizing word meanings. The precise meaning of the word "tool" in a 1930s encounter between a Russian Jewish scientist and an Uzbek farmer is impossible to reconstruct, but whatever its meaning, it was a step out of the immediate situation of the utterance, a step denied to the Uzbeks who could not conceptualize the specificity of the hammer, saw, and hatchet into tool. Without what Luria called "the decontextualization of mediational means," reflective reasoning could not emerge.[21]

Bakhtin explains how such abstract generalized thought arises in particular individuals at specific times by reference to the mediating term for both, "society." Although a word is always part of a system existing in the interpersonal space between individuals, it has at the same time a capacity which makes it unique among signs, that of being produced by the individual organism's own means, without recourse to any other extracorporeal material: "This has determined the role of the word as the semiotic material of inner life, of consciousness (inner speech). Consciousness could have developed only by having at its disposal material that was pliable and expressible by bodily means. And word is exactly that kind of material. The word is available for . . . inner employment."[22]

Bakhtin subsumes psychological problems under the more comprehensive category of translinguistics, suggesting that "the reality of the inner psyche is the same reality as that of the sign." The locus of consciousness, the psyche, is found somewhere on the border between the individual organism of the body, conceived as sheer meat and chemicals, and the workings of the exterior world. But because the operations of mind and the operations of the world are so different, the encounter between them needs to be mediated. The sign is the means for translating between the two: "Psychic experience is the semiotic expression of the contact between the organism and the outside environment . . . what makes a word a word is its meaning. What makes an experience an experience is also its meaning."[23]

Bakhtin attacks the models of mental life provided by such thinkers as Heinrich Rickert and Edmund Husserl, because in one way or another they fail to conceive the unity of psychic operations. The most extreme form of such a disunified conception is Freud's account of the cutoff between the conscious and the unconscious. Bakhtin insists that there are no ontological differences between inner and outer speech, only relative degrees of sharedness between language at the deepest level, where mind borders mere brain, and at the highest level, where outer speech converges with the language of the encompassing social system: "Between the psyche and ideology no boundaries do or can exist . . . every outer ideological sign, of whatever kind, is engulfed in and washed over by inner signs—by the consciousness. The outer sign originates from this sea of inner signs and continues to abide there, since its life is a process of renewal as something to be understood, experienced, and assimilated, i.e., its life consists in its being engaged ever anew into the inner context."[24]

Bakhtin's opposition to overinvestment in the subject was reinforced by his contemporary, the psychologist Lev Vygotsky, who experimented with speech acquisition.[25] Vygotsky's model of how humans make the transition from babbling infants to language-using children, which is the greatest step that we make in our growth, parallels Bakhtin's model, particularly in its insistence that the self comes from the other: the "I" is a function of social forces. Vygotsky assumed that we have consciousness, or thought of a rudimentary sort, before we acquire language. But self-consciousness comes to us only after we enter the world of signs. The reason that children prior to the age of roughly three years seem so marvelously unselfconscious is that they as yet have no self of which to be conscious. Young humans are similar to chimpanzees in that they can manipulate their surroundings by indulging in a primitive use of "tools," such as cracking nuts with rocks. They also have a limited vocabulary of coded signals, such as warning cries ("Hot!"). But they do not at this stage have language signs, as opposed to mere signals.

Somewhere between the third and seventh year, most

humans go through a transitional stage during which they seem to "speak to themselves." In this stage in language acquisition, called by Piaget "egocentric speech," children speak only about themselves and never take on the point of view of a listener. The children are not interested in whether others listen to them, and they do not expect an answer. The essence of this behavior is expressed in Piaget's formula: "The child talks to himself/herself as though he/she were *thinking aloud.*" The next stage, termed by Piaget the acquisition of "socialized speech," is usually in full swing by age seven. In it children exchange thoughts with others, through such means as requests, threats, criticism, and questions. Vygotsky defined this period as a movement not merely from one stage of language capability to another but also from mere consciousness to real thought, when humans learn to think. It is thus a period of transition from external to internal speech. Vygotsky's view that "higher mental functions appear on the *inter*-psychological plane before they appear on the intra-psychological plane" was his way of expressing Bakhtin's fundamental principle that the self is not a completely internal but rather a boundary phenomenon, which enjoys "extraterritorial status" since it is "a social entity that penetrates inside the organism of the individual person."[26]

Development in thinking is thus not from the individual to the socialized or, as Bakhtin would say, from the self to the other, but rather from the social to the individual, or from the other to the self. Self and society are the two poles of ideology, the limits of language and the antipodes of meaning. Between the two there is no absolute gap, only a relative gap in communications. The more deeply woven a sign is into the psychic system, the less capable it is of being shared with others as an expression of the values of society. However, as the sign moves in the direction of fitting into available ideological formations, it casts off more and more of the uniqueness of the psychic context in which it had been held.

The units of inner speech are less discrete than those of outer speech, having a more diffuse quality. These entities of inner speech are what Bakhtin calls "total impressions of utterances," which he glosses as "the still undifferentiated impression of the totality of the object—the aroma of its totality, as it were, which precedes and underlies knowing the object distinctly. So, for example, we sometimes cannot remember a name or a word, though it is on the tip of our tongue, i.e., we already have a total impression of the name or word but the impression cannot develop into its concrete differentiated image."[27] These units of inner speech are organized more economically than is the syntax of outer speech. They are like lines in a dialogue insofar as they depend on conflict. The utterance is always a combination of the actual verbalization and of the nonverbalized elements assumed by addressor and addressee. The more familiar each person is with the other, the more material may be assumed and therefore left unsaid. Since inner speech is a dialogue within the psyche, its language is in a maximally intimate environment and therefore proceeds with the minimum of verbalization.

Any utterance, whether it be in outer or inner speech, has a meaning as a whole unit that guarantees the unitariness of the utterance as a distinctive unit. Bakhtin calls this global meaning the utterance's "theme" (smysl). Theme is characterized by transitoriness, since its significance is appropriate only to the moment of its utterance and to no other. It is unique and unreproducible. Theme has such exquisitely fine shades of significance that most of us do not countenance them in the rush of daily communication. Bakhtin argues that the utterance "What time is it?" has a different meaning each time it is used and hence a different theme, depending on the particular situation in which it is expressed and of which it is a part.[28] The theme of an utterance is thus a product as much of a real-life situation as of such conventional linguistic categories as syntax, grammar, and lexicon.

The other essential aspect of language, according to Bakhtin, is "meaning" (značenie). This is the fixed, repeatable aspect of any utterance, which is reproducible and self-identical: "The unreproducible theme of the utterance 'What time is it?' taken in its indissoluble connection with the concrete historical situation cannot be divided into elements. The meaning of the utterance 'What time is it?'—a meaning that of course remains the same in all historical instances of its enunciations—is made up of the meanings of the words, forms of morphological and syntactic union, interrogative intonations, etc., that form the construction of the utterance."[29]

Intonation is particularly important as a means for expanding the capacity of the same old words to meet new and unrepeatable situations. Bakhtin cites an encounter of Dostoevsky's with six drunken workmen who used the same obscenity with different intonations to express six different meanings, whereas if the word had appeared in print and thus out of the specific context, it would have seemed to be the same word simply repeated six times.[30] Intonation's power to create significances that are situationally particular recalls Bakhtin's thesis that values determine consciousness. Language is merely the most complex and at the same time the most paradigmatic form in which the play of values is expressed in human activity: "There is no such thing as word without evaluative accent." It follows that "each element in a living utterance not only had a meaning, but also a *value.*" Bakhtin specifically rejects the common terms "denotation," indicating a reference, and "connotation," indicating an attitude, because of the cutoff point between the two. This disjunction misses Bakhtin's point that referential meaning cannot be separated from the evaluating use to which it is put: "A change in meaning is, essentially, always a re-evaluation."[31]

The dialectical relationship between the two building blocks of utterance, theme and meaning, is also the basis of understanding. Understanding occurs primarily in the aspect of theme, where it is the activity of a living sign responding to a living sign: "To understand another person's utterance means to orient oneself with respect to it, to find the proper place for it in the corresponding context. *Any true understanding is dialogic in nature.* Understanding is to utterance as one line of dialogue is to the next . . . *Therefore there is no reason for saying that meaning belongs to the word as such.* In essence, meaning belongs to a word in its position between speakers . . . meaning is realized only in the process of active, responsive understanding . . . [it] is not in the word or in the soul of the speaker or in the soul of the listener. Meaning is the *effect of interaction between speaker and listener produced via the material of a particular sound complex.*" The Bakhtinian myth of significance is thus a story of a dying and reviving God: "meaning—an abstract, self-identical element—is subsumed under theme and torn apart by theme's living contradictions so as to return in the shape of a new meaning with a fixity and self-identity only for the while, just as it had before."[32] The Christological overtones here patently recall *The Architectonics.*

To conceive of language as essentially dialogic requires an explanation for the rules that separate one voice from the other in dialogue. Bakhtin's concern for the living context of meaning had the ironic effect of forcing him to take up problems in the area of traditional linguistics which had long been felt to be the most formal and most static. Syntax was much more the business of rhetoricians than of linguists. Its neglect among linguists resulted in the inadequacy and imprecision of the units of speech, such as "sentence" or, worse, "paragraph." Because linguistics had failed to recognize the living utterance as its proper subject, it had lost all sense of the whole. And lacking a sense of the whole, it could not generate a workable theory of the parts. Bakhtin cites the case of an utterance consisting of a single word, such as the word "Well": "If we apply to this word all the categories used by linguistics, it will immediately become apparent that these categories define the word exclusively in terms of a potential element of speech and that none encompasses the whole utterance. That extra something which converts this word into a whole utterance remains outside the scope of the entire set of linguistic categories and definitions."[33]

To enlarge and illuminate the study of syntax, Bakhtin turned to the area of "reported speech" (*čuzaja reč'*, literally "speech of the other"). Reported speech, or quoting, is a suitable subject for this crucial role because it is so simple and ubiquitous a phenomenon. Reported speech is "speech within speech, utterance within utterance, and at the same time also *speech about speech, utterance about utterance.*" The significant difference between reported speech and all other kinds of utterance is its intensely reflexive nature. Reported speech is the most self-conscious: "once it becomes a constructional unit in the author's speech . . . the reported utterance concurrently becomes a theme of that speech. It enters into the latter's thematic design precisely as reported, an utterance with *its own autonomous* theme: the autonomous theme thus becomes a theme of a theme."[34]

Whereas the strenuous effort of becoming conscious of consciousness can keep even philosophers from achieving such a state, everybody is always involved in the rigors of reported speech, if only because so much of what is said is composed of, or about, what others have already said. The problem in reported speech is how to handle the borders, how to demarcate the places where one person's speech ends and the other person's speech begins, and ends. The answers to such questions, the ways to control the traffic in voices, constitute the substance of whole disciplines and social institutions. Jurisprudence, for example, developed a set of procedures to try to overcome the notorious porousness of borders, producing such rebarbative categories as "parties of the first part" and "parties of the second part." The law's most important assumption about the borders between authorial and reported speech holds that the speech of those before the bench is prey to contingency and subjectivity. Law assumes a disparity between this subjective speech and the objectivity of the court's own apparatus of investigation and reporting. Religious wars have been fought over the borders between those who truly reported the word of God and those who, while claiming to report God's speech, were merely speaking in their own human voices. Literature has worked out not very satisfactory ways of distinguishing between influence and plagiarism. The problem in each case is to find the true author, the person answerable for the words in question.

But the commonest way in which people encounter the borders between their own speech and that of others' is in the rules of grammar that have been set up to mark such distinctions. English and most European languages have essentially three kinds of grammar: rules for pronomial usage ("I heard *him* say"), rules for subordinate clauses ("I heard him say *that*"), and rules for tense distinctions ("I heard him say that *he was going to do*"). Rules for subordinate clauses, which in Russia are a rich area of academicism, have limited usefulness in the West, are often highly artificial, and break down in actual practice, largely because they depend on grammatical meaning rather than on living theme. Depending on them alone conduces to missing the point of what is actually said. Meaning is the effect of an interaction between speaker and listener produced via the material of a particular sound complex. It is like an "electric spark," to use one of Bakhtin's rare nonorganic metaphors, which occurs "only when two terminals are hooked together. Those who ignore them. . . want in effect to turn on a light bulb after having turned off the current." Grammatical attempts to limit reported speech to subordinate clauses forget that "only the current of verbal intercourse endows a word with the light of significance."[35] The same is true for attempts to legislate the borders between authorial and reported speech on the basis of tense alone, such as explaining a passage by invoking the general necessity of keeping tense sequence in English in past and future constructions, or by appealing to the absence of such a rule in Russian as an explanatory principle. Such rules are important more for revealing prejudices about meaning in general or for indicating historical periods and national types than they are for pointing up the specific theme of a given utterance.

Bakhtin identifies two basic attitudes toward the boundary markers between authorial and reported speech. The first, which he calls "linear," attempts to maintain the integrity and authenticity of the speech being reported. Hard-edged boundaries are placed between one person's speech and the speech of another being quoted. These boundaries serve "to demarcate the reported speech as clearly as possible, to screen it from penetration by the author's intonations, and to condense and enhance its individual linguistic characteristics." This tendency is reflected in all societies in such areas as the law, but is more typical in some periods and places than in others, as in seventeenth century France and eighteenth century Russia.[36]

The linear tendency in speech demarcation is typified by the impulse to construct clear-cut, external contours for reported speech. The opposite tendency, which Bakhtin calls "pictorial," devises means for infiltrating reported speech with authorial retort and commentary. The reporting context "breaks down the self-contained compactness of the reported speech, to resolve it, to obliterate its boundaries."[37] Such an impulse characterized the end of the eighteenth century, especially in France, and virtually the entire nineteenth century, the two periods that were closest to Bakhtin's heart.

Applying his expositional device of dyadic organization, Bakhtin gives each of these two basic attitudes toward speech demarcation an answering analytical strategy. The strategy corresponding to the linear impulse, called "referent analyzing," dissects meaning into its constituent, ideational referential units: "a built-in tendency to thematicize another speaker's utterance ... preserves the cohesiveness and autonomy of the utterance, not so much in constructional terms as in terms of significance." The emphasis is on the meaning of the utterance, not its style, so there is a certain amount of depersonalization of the reported speech. This analytical attitude "occurs only within an authorial context that is somewhat rationalistic and dogmatic in nature," where the argument is intellectual, between ideas rather than persons. Tolstoy often uses this strategy in the polemical passages of his works.[38]

The opposite strategy, called "texture analyzing," is to put an utterance into quotation marks less to emphasize the distinction between authorial and reported speech than to underline the typicality of the set-off words themselves. An example from *The Brothers Karamazov* is the narrator's treatment of two Poles during Dimitry's interrogation: "they appeared with a show of pride and independence. They loudly testified that, in the first place, they were both 'in the service of the crown,' and that 'Pan Mitya' had offered to buy their favor for 3000 rubles." The Poles' words are here "made strange" in the sense that "they are particularized, their coloration is heightened, but at the same time they are made to accommodate shadings of the author's attitude—his irony, humor, and so on."[39] Dostoevsky is the best representative of the texture-analyzing approach, while Tolstoy is the best exponent of the referent-analyzing approach.

The differences between these two modes of expression and the analytical tendencies proper to each mark a master distinction between culture systems. The linear modality is in general characteristic of older societies, the pictorial of the modern age. Cultures are always given to one more than to the other. That is, the Russians are less linear and more pictorial, while the French are less pictorial and more linear. But beyond such gross distinctions, thin striations in the archeology of mind are traced along the lines marked by the movement from one modality to another. Bakhtin erects a whole cultural anthropology on the basis of the shifting relations among authorial and reported speech.

Bakhtin is able to move smoothly and coherently between a discussion of stylistics and a discussion of whole societies because the problem of reported speech has to do with the politics of quotations. The question of how much of the other's meaning I will permit to get through when I surround his words with my own is a question about the governance of meaning, about who presides over it, and about how much of it is shared. It has to do, in other words, with the relative degrees of freedom granted by speakers to those other speakers whose words they appropriate into their own.

How people characteristically treat the speech of others does not merely reflect literary stylistics or the rules of grammar or punctuation that apply when quoting but also reveals attitudes about the circulation of alien words typical of whole cultures. The way discourse is ordered in a given society is the most sensitive and comprehensive register of how all its other ideological practices are ordered, including its religion, education, state organization, and police. Cultures can be classified as open or closed according to the way in which they handle reported speech. Thus Bakhtin's study of the phenomenon is intended as a contribution not merely to poetics, but to politics: "In the vicissitudes of the word are to be found the vicissitudes of the society of word users."[40]

The fact that the book containing these words was published in the same year in which Bakhtin was arrested may give some idea of the urgency Bakhtin attached to the subject of respecting others' words. In this book the moral preoccupations of his early period are put to new purpose as they become a means for rethinking linguistics. But it is also clear that political and ethical concerns are still the main force animating his philosophy of language.

CHAPTER 11

Dostoevsky's Poetics

Dostoevsky was decisive in shaping Bakhtin's thought, and the fortunes of Bakhtin's book on Dostoevsky similarly affected Bakhtin's personal fate, intensifying Dostoevsky's status as a secret sharer in Bakhtin's existence. None of Bakhtin's other works ever directly affected his life in the way this book did. The appearance in 1929 of its first edition, titled *Problems of Dostoevsky's Creative Works,* was for Bakhtin both a hail and a farewell, a Janus-faced event that marked both his first successful attempt to break into publication under his own name, barring the ephemeral broadside that had appeared ten years earlier in Nevel, and yet also his last appearance in print before disappearing into exile and obscurity. The second edition of 1963 no less neatly brackets the period that Bakhtin spent in the wilderness, for its appearance heralded his re-emergence onto the Soviet publishing scene and his rise to international prominence. The book even saved Bakhtin's life on the occasion of its two appearances. Lunacharsky's favorable review of the first edition helped Bakhtin's friends in their efforts to have his sentence reduced from certain death in the labor camp to a relatively mild exile in Kazakhstan. Three decades later the Dostoevsky book inspired young scholars at the Gorky Institute to seek out the aging Bakhtin in his Mordovian retreat, which initiated the process that was to issue in the rescue of Bakhtin's other unpublished works from moldering away in a Saransk woodshed. The first edition saved Bakhtin from physical death in Solovki; the second saved him from the literary death of neglect.

The relations between Bakhtin and Dostoevsky went beyond the normal limits of critic to author and achieved the kind of intimacy that exists between doubles. Dostoevsky, the author who felt himself inadequate to the "great idea" of the double, and Bakhtin, the thinker who devoted his life to meditating the role of the other in the self, had much in common. Even at the level of personal experience there were affinities between them. Both were arrested for political crimes, and just as Bakhtin's sentence to certain death in Solovki was changed to exile in Kazakhstan, so was Dostoevsky's death by firing squad on Semyenovsky Square commuted to exile in Siberia. Both men wrestled with the more outré paradoxes of Russian orthodoxy. And each sought to reconcile a deep affection for European culture with a hatred for atomized, capitalist society.

The most significant monument to the double-voicedness of the two is *Problems of Dostoevsky's Creative Works,* which Bakhtin dedicated to Dostoevsky and which occupies a unique status among Bakhtin's other works. With the exception of *The Architectonics of Answerability,* this book absorbed Bakhtin's attention for a longer time than any other work. Since its major theme carries on from that portion of *The Architectonics* devoted to author/character relations, the book may have engaged him as early as 1919, but he at least began work on the book before leaving Nevel for Vitebsk in 1920. In a letter of January 18, 1922, to Kagan, Bakhtin reports, "I am now writing a work on Dostoevsky, which I hope to complete in no time at all."[1] By November of that year the work was far enough along for it to be announced as forthcoming in the Petrograd journal *The Life of Art,* but for unknown reasons the book did not appear. And it was not actually published until seven years later. Just as the Dostoevsky book had grown out of Bakhtin's earlier work, so it fed into the various essays and books on the novel that he later produced, especially in the 1930s. Its themes continued to preoccupy him until his death, for his very last essays and notebook jottings return again and again to the concerns of the Dostoevsky book. Of all the voices with which Bakhtin mingled his own, from Rabelais and Goethe to Voloshinov and Medvedev, the one that was most congenial to his own was the voice of Dostoevsky.

The second edition of the book, which bore the new title *Problems of Dostoevsky's Poetics,* was the variant Bakhtin himself preferred, and it is the fuller of the two versions. Although a small portion of the 1929 book dealing with the role of adventure-type plots in Dostoevsky was deleted from the second edition, major new material was added, consisting primarily of the history of menippean satire, its relation to other forms of literature, and its connection with such extraliterary phenomena as carnival and other discrowning rituals.[2] The book deals essentially with a problem of structure, the formal procedures by which Dostoevsky permits each of his characters to speak in their own voices with a minimum of interference from him as author, the effect of which is to create a new genre. Bakhtin calls this genre the "polyphonic novel" because it has many points of view, many voices, each of which is given its full due by Dostoevsky.

The book opens with a demonstration of on-the-job dialogism. Bakhtin does to other Dostoevsky critics what Dostoevsky does to his characters. Bakhtin lets all of the critics speak in their own voices, through long quotations from each, but in so doing, they make the very points that he, Bakhtin, wishes to make. While each critic differs from all the others, there is one point on which they agree: the typical Dostoevskian novel is organized as a conflict among enfleshed ideas. Critics are aware of the difficulty of opting for and sticking to one or the other of the swarming ideologies that collide with each other in Dostoevsky's world, and yet sooner or later they end up choosing one of the conflicting voices as "truly representing" Dostoevsky's "own" point of view, which is really their own point of view.

Bakhtin argues that this polyphony of Dostoevskian criticism is testimony to a polyphony in Dostoevsky himself. This polyphony constitutes not only the hallmark of his novels and his unique achievement in the history of literature, but also a breakthrough to a new understanding of how self-consciousness, or consciousness of the self, works in human interaction even outside literature. Dostoevsky establishes a unique relationship with his characters. He creates "not voiceless slaves . . . but *free* people, capable of standing *alongside* their creator, capable of not agreeing with him and even of rebelling against him."[3]

This essential feature of Dostoevsky's novels derives not from the ideational power, the argument, of any single character but from the relation of each character to the words of the others. Ivan Karamazov is distinguished not by his philosophy as such but by the way he shapes that philosophy in the face of all the objections and additions from the other characters in the novel, each of whom, such as Smerdyakov or the devil, is equally capable of mounting powerful arguments of his own. Ivan's so-called "monologues" are aquiver with consciousness of the other. Each of Ivan's speeches is a dialogue, not only with himself or Alyosha but with many other points of view as well, all of which are carried out simultaneously. Ivan's consciousness teems with the consciousness of others. His greatest and longest speech, containing the legend of the Grand Inquisitor, is a monologue about a dialogue that is shot through with other voices. None of these voices is louder than that of Christ, whose silence indicates the superficiality of the mechanical, phonic aspect of what we normally call "voice."

The dialogue of such characters is the essence of Dostoevsky's achievement. Dostoevsky creates a new kind of unity in his novels, not the familiar unity based on the pervasiveness of a single idea or theme, but the expressive unity inherent in the dialogic relations between several opposed ideas or voices. Thus, Dostoevsky's world is characterized by a very special kind of time and space. It consists of "the artistically organized coexistence and interaction of spiritual *diversity,* not stages of an evolving unified spirit." He concentrates in a single time and place, a single split second, the greatest possible diversity: "In every voice he could hear two contending voices, in every expression a crack, and the readiness to go over immediately to another contradictory expression . . . he perceived the profound ambiguity . . . of every phenomenon. But none of these contradictions and bifurcations ever became dialectical, they were never set in motion along a temporal path or in an evolving sequence: they were, rather, spread out in one plane, as standing alongside or opposite one another."[4]

Dostoevsky is able to create such simultaneity and diversity because he opens his characters to each other. Like the underground man, he is aware that there is no final truth about people as long as they are alive. The root desire of individuals to upset all finalizing definitions of their selfhood is what Dostoevsky calls "living life" or "the man in man," and he stresses this quality in each of his characters.

Bakhtin calls Dostoevsky "the creator of the polyphonic novel," the originator of "a fundamentally new novelistic genre," the first and only author to succeed in the "new artistic task . . . of constructing a polyphonic world and destroying the established forms of the fundamentally monologic (homophonic) European novel."[5] Later, however, Bakhtin came to regard the Dostoevskian novel less as an unprecedented event in the history of the novel than as the purest expression of what had always been implicit in the genre. He thereby established Dostoevsky's paradigmatic, rather than generative, importance for the novel.

Bakhtin was the first critic to perceive Dostoevsky's use of polyphony because he was the only Dostoevskian critic to have a fully worked-out theory of discourse that is as complex as Dostoevsky's own. Neither Dostoevsky as novelist nor Bakhtin as critic was first in devising such a theory; rather, the two together erected a translinguistics that can reveal the significance of authorship in a world where meaning can result only in dialogue. Dostoevsky is the other whom Bakhtin most needed to be himself: Bakhtin uses Dostoevsky as an originating figure, whose primacy flies in the face of all Bakhtin's other arguments against primacy. Dostoevsky thus serves as yet another mask for Bakhtin; the discoverer of heteroglossia stands behind the "discoverer" of polyphony.

The phenomenon that Bakhtin calls "polyphony" is simply another name for dialogism. As Bakhtin admits: "Every thought of Dostoevsky's heroes . . . senses itself to be from the very beginning a *rejoinder* in an unfinalized dialogue. Such thought is not impelled toward a well-rounded, finalized, systematically monologic whole. It lives a tense life on the borders of someone else's thought, someone else's consciousness."[6]

Dostoevsky's polyphony illustrates the concept of authorship that Bakhtin had proposed at a more abstract level in 1919 in *The Architectonics* and again in 1924 in "The Problem of Content, Material, and Form in the Verbal Work of Art." This concern for the relations between authors and their creations in turn specifies an even more complex aspect of Bakhtin's thinking, the grounding of all values in two different centers, the I and the other. There is one set of values that I apply by myself to myself and another that I apply to all the others who are not me. They in turn make the same distinction between themselves and others. In the gap between the two value systems is the space where dialogue is pursued at its deepest level.

Furthermore, such an arrangement is not only an architectonics of value but also a politics: I may relate as a despot to others, that is, completely monologically, or I may relate to them democratically, that is, polyphonically or dialogically. Bakhtin's concern for how authors relate to their characters, then, is not merely a concern for the formal properties of point of view but also a way to flesh out possibilities of self/other relations. *The Architectonics* treated such relations as a problem in the phenomenology of consciousness and described them in abstract philosophical language, whereas *Problems of Dostoevsky's Poetics* translates "all these structural aspects of the interdependency of consciousness into the language of social relations, into inter-individual relations in everyday life (i.e., into plot relations in the broad sense of the word)."[7]

Bakhtin conceives of literature as a special use of language, which permits readers to see things that are obscured by the restraints on expression in other applications of language. The novel as a genre, and in particular the Dostoevskian novel, is in effect another organ of perception. The Dostoevskian novel makes it possible to see paradigms of human interaction that are nowhere else so clearly drawn or perceptible. They can be seen because of the particular point of view that Dostoevsky adopts toward point of view, the articulation of which in his novels gives readers a point of view from which to see self/other relations in a new light. In the language of *The Architectonics,* which Bakhtin was still using in his notebooks while reworking the Dostoevsky book for its second edition, Dostoevsky shares his "surplus of vision" (*izbytok videnija*) with his characters, a surplus that then extends to his readers as well, but only to those readers who are able to discard conventional ideas about point of view.[8]

One conventional idea that must be discarded, which Bakhtin earlier attacked in "The Problem of Content," is the concept of the work of art as a finished thing, a hermetic unity. Insofar as the work continues to live, it must be engaged in dialogue, which is possible only when the work is still open and capable of interaction: the work of art is never finished. Characters in a novel are not like flies, immobilized in the objectlike amber of the text that surrounds them.

Another conventional idea which must be discarded holds that authors are able to manifest their intentions completely in their works, so that readers can know precisely "what they meant." A corollary view holds that if readers cannot articulate a single point of view that may be read back into the texts as the will of their authors, the authors had no point of view, or at least none powerful enough to structure their fictive world, and thus they failed. Dostoevsky's polyphony is often denied on the grounds that if his characters were indeed as independent as they often seem, it would mean that Dostoevsky had been somehow passive or irresponsible in his role as author. But Bakhtin does not assert "that there is any kind of passivity on the part of the author, who only assembles others' viewpoints, completely rejecting his own viewpoint. Not at all! It's rather a completely new and special interrelation between his truth and that of others."[9]

Bakhtin argues that the way Dostoevsky relates to his characters is more complex than traditional conceptions of authorship are capable of perceiving. Most theories of how authors shape meaning in literary texts have been extensions of ideas about how speakers in everyday situations shape meaning in their communication. That conception has always been essentially monologic: just as it was assumed that people can unequivocally convey an intention that is exclusively theirs to an addressee and thereby directly affect the response, so most theories of literature have taken it for granted that authors are able, in more or less mediated ways, to control their characters in such a way as to have predictable effects on readers. The sum total of the characters' collective interaction is a message whose meaning was that intended by their creator. This view of authorship has had such sophisticated defenders as Henry James and Wayne Booth. It is essentially the theory of authorship represented by Saussure's drawing of the two talking heads who send out messages to each other that monologically embody their intentions.

Because Bakhtin assumes a quite different scenario of how people communicate with each other in everyday life, his assumption of how authors shape meaning is also quite different: "The author is profoundly active, but his activity is of a . . . dialogical nature. It is one thing to be active in relation to an inanimate thing—voiceless stuff that can be molded at will; it is quite another thing to be active in relation to another living, equally privileged consciousness."[10]

To perceive the difference between the two versions of authorship requires more than adjusting certain attitudes about formal properties of literary texts. Monologism, as Bakhtin had argued since the beginning of his career, is an all-pervasive world view. To move from a monologic to a dialogic conception of the world is to make a move almost as great as that from a geocentric to a Copernican world view. Time and again Bakhtin returns to this cosmological shift: "Dostoevsky effected, as it were, a small Copernican revolution." Much as the sun was moved out of its central place to make room for the complex interaction of the Copernican universe, so authors are removed from the center of the textual world to assume their place in the give and take of narrative energy in which the characters exert their own forces. The unity of the text is less that of a "one and only" than that of a dialogic harmony of unmerged dyads and multiples, much as the unity of the self is conceived by Bakhtin as dyadic: "The unity of Einstein's world is more complex and profound than that of Newton, and it is a unity of a higher order."[11]

During the same period when Bakhtin was reworking the book on Dostoevsky, he also produced the essay "The Problem of the Text" (1959–1961). In this article the problem is precisely how to understand the text's unity in a universe that is dominated by relativity and in which "the experimenter (in microphysics) becomes an aspect of the system being experimented on."[12] There is no longer a privileged space for metaexperiment and no longer an authorial metalanguage independent of the language of characters.

The dialogic principle as applied to authorship does not mean that Dostoevsky has no point of view of his own. Rather, his point of view is established by a different means and with a different effect from those of most other authors. Instead of assigning a privilege to the author that is unique to fictive discourse, where the creator occupies an ontic status different from that of the created, Bakhtin defines Dostoevsky's relation to his characters as governed by the same set of conditions that obtain in all discourse. For this reason Bakhtin's views on Dostoevsky cannot be separated from Bakhtin's general theory of discourse, in which I am never free to impose my unobstructed intention but must always mediate that intention through the intentions of others, beginning with the otherness of the language itself in which I speak. I must enter a dialogue with others. This does not mean that I cannot make my own point of view understood; it simply implies that my point of view will only emerge through the interaction of my own and another's words as they contend with each other in particular situations.

The Dostoevskian author resides in a place Bakhtin calls "ex-

extralocality" (*vnenaxodimost'*). Extralocality describes a position which can be known only through the most complex triangulation of interpersonal relations. It is a relationship and an activity more than a place, a location that has no existence in physical space. Dostoevsky is not beside his characters, as is Thackeray, say, in *Vanity Fair*. Nor is Dostoevsky below his characters, as in Gogol, whose stance as author is to be continually impressed by his characters' trivial accomplishments and to dramatize his inadequacy to the task of simply conducting his narrative. Nor is Dostoevsky above his characters, as is Flaubert in relation to the victims of his relentless irony in *Madame Bovary*.

Dostoevsky and his characters are all equally compounded of language. They are words, combinations of their own and others' words, all selves constructed out of other selves. The subject of Dostoevsky's novels cannot be reduced to this or that theme or this or that life because his subject is "the other's I, not as object but as another subject."[13] And since the dialogue of self/other is prosecuted as an exchange of live meanings and not dead forms, Dostoevsky is among the words of his characters. The characteristic feature of his authority is less temporal and even less spatial than kinetic. It is an activity, a constantly performed deed, something in motion rather than a state or location. When Dostoevsky says that he wishes to study the "man in man," he means what is more usually called the "I-for-itself." He is emphasizing the degree to which his characters are perceived not as biographically complete units who experience birth, death, and all the intervening stages but rather as self-consciousnesses, who are conscious of the others out of whom they produce themselves. Dostoevsky has no interest in the aspects of life that are not the immediate constituents of consciousness. He is interested in children, for example, only at the border stage of adolescence, or at precisely that point where they are entering self-consciousness. And he is utterly uninterested in death, which is where we depart self-consciousness, insofar as we can never know completely all the factors of our own death, only a termination of the activity of our self-consciousness.

Dostoevsky and Bakhtin both kept notebooks on work in progress; indeed, the work in progress is often the notebooks. Any reading of a "finished" text by either must therefore be put into the context of the unfinished version provided by the notebooks.

Appropriately, the most interesting observations that Bakhtin makes on the unfinishable nature of consciousness in Dostoevsky's novels are contained not in the published versions of the book but in the working notebooks for the second edition. In these Bakhtin isolates a formal feature in Dostoevsky's novels that intensifies their focus on consciousness, once again using Tolstoy as a useful contrast. Above and beyond the greater number of deaths found in Tolstoy than in Dostoevsky, there is a qualitative difference in his formal handling of death scenes. Tolstoy is primarily interested in what it feels like to die inside the person who is dying. He is less interested in what such a death means for others. This requires a certain violation of logic in the point of view that must be adopted in such scenes. It is as if the person describes his own death, after he is dead. Such a contradiction is possible only in fiction, because only in fiction can the truth of the ineluctable difference between self and other be ignored. Consciousness is life, and therefore the self cannot know itself as dead. Its very existence is coterminous with consciousness, and consciousness is precisely what ceases with death. In the moment of death, two things occur simultaneously: consciousness ceases, and the self becomes totally other. The self dies; otherness goes on. There is nothing left to resist the multiple alterities in biology or society. To portray death from the inside, as does Tolstoy, is "to move from one consciousness to another, as if one were merely going from one room to another. Tolstoy does not recognize the absolute threshold that exists between them."[14]

Bakhtin's reading of the handling of death in Tolstoy and Dostoevsky provides insight into characteristic formal features of each. For instance, death is more often than not forced on characters in Tolstoy. Death is rarely willed, rarely intentioned. In Dostoevsky's world, in contrast, there is a great "interest in suicides as *conscious* deaths—links in the chain of consciousness in which a man finalizes himself from within."[15] Moreover, death is a useful heuristic device, a structural metaphor, for all the other ways in which Dostoevsky's preoccupation with "living life" works itself out as a concern for the unfinalizability of consciousness. The fact that consciousness is equated with life and that consciousness has no end which it knows itself as an end—inasmuch as consciousness cannot cognize its own nonbeing except in the imagination, in literature—parallels certain Christian ideas about the immortality of the soul, as Bakhtin recognizes. But he never-theless insists that the metaphysical and ontological conclusions drawn by Dostoevsky from the notion that death cannot be a fact of one's consciousness do not contradict materialism, a point of view that conforms with dialogism.

One of the closest bonds between Dostoevsky and Bakhtin is their distinctive idea of the nature of Christ. Dostoevsky observed that even if Christ were proved mistaken, he would still prefer to remain with Christ. Bakhtin explains this paradox in terms that describe as well his own sense of Christ, that is, not as a God in whom one has blind faith and with whom one seeks to merge com-pletely. What is important about Dostoevsky's Christ is the life model he provides, a kind of ideal other; to prefer to err while re-maining with Christ is to choose to be without truth in any abso-lute or even theoretical sense, to give up truth as a formula or truth as a proposition. Dostoevsky, and Bakhtin as well, conceive of Christ as the kind of figure about whom one can ask, "What would *he* do?" and receive answers that work in everyday experi-ence. As a kind of question, then, Christ is part of an ongoing inner dialogue.

It is from such an understanding of Christ that Dostoevsky's innovative novelistic techniques derive. To invoke Christ, or a ver-sion of Christ, as an explanation for formal experimentation in one of the most complex areas of narrative, namely point of view, is not an exotic Russianism. Bakhtin is simply realizing one of the most common metaphors for the formal structuring of point of view: the theological trope. According to this metaphor, the authors' rela-tions to their characters are akin to the relations of God to humans. This relation, after all, is one of creator to created, which is why it is so often described by terms taken over from religion. The fact that authors are relatively free to make what they will of the world in their texts seemed a blasphemy to Plato; in Flaubert it was a goal and a responsibility. The authors as gods of their fiction have not only the rights but the duties that theologies have tradi-tionally assigned to first causes. Flaubert still assumed that au-thors as Jehovahs could exercise a kind of Old Testament power over their characters. The characters in such works are a little like the protagonists in Kafka's story "Investigations of a Dog," where the canine hero, unlike his fellow animals, suspects there is an-other order, higher than that of dogs, from which food perpetually descends whenever the dogs stand on their hind legs to pray or perform other ritual acts. Authors are "everywhere felt but nowhere seen," being of a different order of reality from their creatures, just as gods are usually conceived as belonging to a higher order of existence than that of the creatures they have made.

Bakhtin, adopting a term first used by the German aesthetician Johannes Cohn, calls the position of the superior partner in such a relationship "transgredient." That is, the authors, being on a higher plane than their creations, are able to see into the complete existence, the deepest meanings, of their characters. The characters, on the other hand, not only do not know many of the things about themselves that the authors know but act as if they did not even suspect that the authors were there manipulating them. Transgredient authors are invisible to their characters because they occupy a higher plane. These creators parallel the omniscient, omnipotent deity of the Old Testament.

Bakhtin describes Dostoevsky's authorial preserve in similar religious terms. Dostoevsky's activity in the text is the activity of God in relation to man. But this is a God unlike the Old Testament Jehovah, who is the animating force behind most conceptions of the author. Dostoevsky is rather a Christ to his characters, like the Christ in *The Brothers Karamazov*: a loving deity, who is silent so that others may speak and, in speaking, enact their freedom. In the best kenotic tradition, Dostoevsky gives up the privilege of a distinct and higher being to descend into his text, to be among his creatures. Dostoevsky's distinctive image of Christ results in the central role of polyphony in his fiction.

Since such an image of Jesus may seem merely idiosyncratic, Bakhtin establishes historical connections between Dostoevsky and the earliest manifestations of Christian culture. Tracing the various strands that came together in the ancient genre of menippea, Bakhtin posits a link between the formal features of the menippea and the historical period in which it arose as a means for explaining the relationship between the formal features of Dostoevsky's novels and the times in which he lived. The menippea developed at a time when classical antiquity was in great crisis, national traditions were in decay, and ancient ideals of dignity and seemliness were breaking down. It was an epoch of intense rivalry among contending philosophical and religious systems, when ultimate questions were not confined to academies but were debated in marketplaces, inns, taverns, and baths. In other words, it was the formative period of Christianity, when there was nothing at all unusual in carpenters proclaiming a new order or fishermen preaching in harbors or along the highroads.

These turbulent times contrasted with the later period of the Middle Ages, when Christianity experienced its triumph as a religious system and a new stability reigned, greater even than that which had existed in Classical times. The opposition was between a polyphonous age of variety and conflict and a monologic period of calm and unity. The creative, founding figure of the prophet and miracle worker who preached outside the appointed, ritual times and places, who came from the folk and not the priestly class, who consorted with known prostitutes and was sympathetic to thieves, who preached in private homes or from the deck of a ship, was associated with the first period. The epigonic follower, the copier of old texts, the celebrator of stasis, the medieval monk, was typical of the second age. At the outset of Christianity, a vibrant, engaged man appeared, a voice alive and in dialogue with other persons and other voices. But in the following centuries there was a calcification of the founder's living word, a loss of his most engaged, fullest, and most present meaning.

The earlier, chaotic period, Bakhtin argues, witnessed not only the rise of Christianity but the rise as well of the new genre of the menippea, within which the characteristic narrative forms of the New Testament took shape. Bakhtin regards the account in the canonical Gospels of the "King of the Jews" entering the Jewish capital on a lowly donkey and the crown of thorns that is an anticrown, along with other details in the life of Christ that are similarly gestures of the most radical overturning of authority, as indications that Biblical narrative is permeated by menippean carnivalization. This juxtaposition of the Gospels and menippean tradition was also made by another philologist, Erich Auerbach, who, like Bakhtin, did some of his finest work in exile. Auerbach argued for the central role of Christ's life in the breakdown of Classical rhetoric and in the new hybrid of high and low styles that characterized the works not only of a satirist like Lucian but also of the apostles: "The true heart of the Christian doctrine—Incarnation and Passion—was . . . totally incompatible with the principle of the separation of styles. Christ had not come as a hero and king but as a human being of the lowest social station . . . That the King of Kings was treated as a low criminal . . . that story no sooner comes to dominate the consciousness of the people than it completely destroys the aesthetics of the separation of styles."[16]

The living phenomena of carnival and dialogue found their positive significance, Bakhtin argues, in the person of Christ, and their highest textual expression in the Christian Gospels. A long decline then set in until the medieval world gave way to the Renaissance world and carnival again celebrated the freedom that comes from inversions in social hierarchy, suspension of sexual restraints, and the possibility of playing new and different roles. These phenomena, which unfold in the lived experience of carnival itself, are also powerfully present in the Rabelaisian novel. The otherwise paradoxical relation between the Gospels, on the one hand, and *Gargantua,* on the other, is thus established through the common element of carnival. This interpretation, which Christians may find as offensive as certain Marxists find Bakhtin's equally unorthodox version of Marx, grows directly out of the twin Russian traditions of venerating Christ as a human being and venerating holy fools (*jurodovye*) who perform disgusting and frequently obscene acts as Christlike.

Bakhtin actually maintains that Dostoevsky presents truth in the spirit of Christian ideology as embodied in the person of Christ. The formal principle that Bakhtin deduces from this essentially ethical world-view is the primacy of dialogue in Dostoevsky's novels, for which polyphony is only a locally applied variant. Dostoevsky's polyphony must be conceived against the larger meaning of dialogue in human existence. To be is to communicate. When the dialogue is finished, everything is finished. Such a reading of Dostoevsky is typical of Bakhtin's own philosophy, as is much of the book's terminology. The emphasis on mutuality and communication gives rise to coinages that feature the prefix 'co-' (*so-*), as in *The Architectonics.*

Bakhtin's unchanging emphasis on flux, his single-minded advocacy of heterodoxy, presents something of a paradox. Yet his own concern for openness and dialogue is not the same thing as the monologism that he deplored in others. His various redactions of the Dostoevsky books, covering a period of over forty tumultuous years, make clear that Bakhtin learned well the polyphonic lessons of the figure he chose as his authority: Dostoevsky occupies for Bakhtin the same position that Bakhtin ascribes to Christ in relation to Dostoevsky. Bakhtin pleads for the superiority of a dialogic approach to literature and life over a monologic approach, but he does so in different voices and by different arguments. When he closes the Dostoevsky book by exhorting his readers to renounce their old monologic habits, his gesture is a commentary on a political situation which increasingly permitted only a single authoritative voice to be heard and which sent those such as Bakhtin himself, who could not be monologized, into exile. It is also a manifesto for the heteroglossia to which Bakhtin would next devote himself.

CHAPTER 12

Kustanai, Saransk, and Savelovo
1930-1945

In 1930 Bakhtin arrived with his wife at his place of exile. Kustanai is located in northwestern Kazakhstan, south of Siberia and just east of the Urals. Most of Kazakhstan is arid steppe or desert and high flat plateau, but Kustanai occupies the edge of the black soil region, which is the most fertile band of soil in the Soviet Union. In consequence, the area in those days was largely agricultural, the principal occupation being pig breeding. A rail link had been constructed to Kustanai during 1912–1913, and the town functioned as a regional center where agricultural produce was processed or shipped. The population of the city of Kustanai doubled between 1926 and 1939, when it reached 34,000.[1]

Thus Bakhtin's place of exile was by no means the frozen wastes of Siberia. The climate was nevertheless "severe," as promised by the Leningrad secret police. The average temperature was -18.2° C in winter and 19.3° C in summer, which would have been reasonable for a Russian except for the poor snow cover and the winds. In summer the town was prey to the hot, dry *suxovej,* and in winter, to the infamous *buran.* These winds were so strong that when walking outdoors one had to hold on to cables in order not to be blown off one's feet.[2]

The cultural life of Kustanai during Bakhtin's stay was minimal. It is nevertheless possible that he found people to talk to among the other exiles there. The Menshevik leader Sukhanov, whose real name was Nikolai Nikolaevich Gimmer, was one of the exiles, and his wife typed the manuscript for Bakhtin's "Discourse in the Novel." Probably few of Bakhtin's friends visited him in

Kustanai, both because it was not acceptable to visit exiles and because Kustanai was so far from Moscow and Leningrad. Kanaev made the trip, however.

Conditions were no doubt hard, but Bakhtin was a survivor. Despite his impracticality, he somehow managed to get through even the most adverse circumstances. His ability to survive was due in part to his equanimity, his sense of humor, and his capacity for accepting gracefully any interlocutor. These qualities explain why he came out of exile so well, whereas Mandelshtam, who spent his exile in the relatively easier conditions of Voronezh, was devastated by the experience.

The only requirement placed on Bakhtin in exile was that he report once a week to the security police. Because of the charge against him of corrupting the young, he was not allowed to work in the schools, but he could choose any other suitable work and was even allowed to publish. At first he was unable to find a job, and Elena Aleksandrovna undertook odd jobs instead. She worked from April 15 to September 25, 1930, as a bookkeeper and cashier in an office overseeing compulsory grain deliveries from the newly formed kolkhozes, until December in the local library, and from January 1 to February 18, 1931, as a salesperson in the local government bookstore. Then on April 23, 1931, Bakhtin began work in the District Consumers' Cooperative, on computations to do with fulfilling the government's economic plan. In this job, which paid him 500 rubles a month, he capitalized on the accountancy skills learned from his father. In 1933 he also started work at the District Council as a consultant on planning questions.

Bakhtin got on quite well with what he called the "red partisans," the former Civil War fighters who ran the town. They were rough and uneducated but honest. They also needed the skills that Bakhtin had to offer, as they found it hard to do their own bookkeeping. In return, they made life more pleasant for him by supplying him with food and cigarettes that he might not otherwise have been able to get, and they periodically awarded him a bonus for his labors. He was also allowed to give public lectures. He did not lecture on his former subjects of literature and philosophy but on more practical and pedestrian topics. For instance, the title of a series of lectures that he offered at the Interregional Supply Base to help prepare managers of village stores was "The Organization and Techniques of Commerce and the Annual Financial Plan."

When Bakhtin arrived in Kustanai, he had just been involved, albeit in a minor way, in one of the major phenomena of the First Five-Year Plan in Leningrad, the purges of bourgeois professionals and the semirelated trials of intelligentsia religious groups. In Kustanai, he encountered another, more cataclysmic development of the Five-Year Plan, collectivization. The upheavals and losses caused by collectivization were proportionately greater in Kazakhstan than in any other part of the Soviet Union. Prior to collectivization, Kazakhstan had had a largely rural economy. In the central and southern regions were nomadic and seminomadic Kazakhs who were involved mostly in livestock rearing. In the north, with its more fertile soil, were Russian and Ukrainian settlers and non-nomadic Kazakhs who cultivated the lands for crops.[3]

The aims of collectivization in Kazakhstan included not just the founding of collectives and other types of agricultural communes but also a radical restructuring of the patterns of agricul-

Bakhtin (seated on stool at far right) with the former Red Guards who governed Kustanai in the early 1930s

ture and ethnic life. On the one hand, the acreage under culti-
vation was to be increased dramatically, necessitating a considerable northern migration on the part of the Kazakhs, since most
of their southern lands were not arable. On the other hand, the
Kazakhs were to be permanently settled, necessitating a change
in their nomadic or seminomadic way of life. Thus, collectivization in Kazakhstan had an added aspect of ethnic homogenization.

In executing this plan, the Soviets encountered a series of
setbacks and failures. Many Kazakhs actively resisted collectivization and resettlement; others simply migrated. Owing to the severe shortage of trained personnel and the low level of literacy, in
some collective farms the plan could not be fulfilled because no
one on the farm could read the instructions. When the Kazakhs
were resettled on collectives, often they were not supplied with
such essentials as tools, seed grain, and livestock.

The result was a disaster. Over 1.5 million Kazakhs lost their
lives in the course of the decade, and nearly 80 percent of their
herd was destroyed. As early as the end of 1932 the Kazakh economy was practically at a standstill, and 2 million pounds of grain
had to be shipped to Kazakhstan as relief aid. Even at the end of
the Second Five-Year Plan in 1937 the Kazakhs were still net im-
porters of grain. The Soviet response to these setbacks was to
mount frequent purges of officials, so that administrative offices
tended to have a revolving door.

Kustanai, which had a largely Russian population, did not
suffer as much as other parts of the Republic of Kazakhstan during this period. Conditions there also tended to improve more rapidly for Russians than for Kazakhs. Nevertheless, Bakhtin
experienced enough of the shortages, repressions, and disloca-
tions of collectivization to become profoundly upset. He felt that
collectivization had wreaked havoc with the traditional Russian
way of life. And when his red partisans were purged in the mid-
1930s, the atmosphere in the town deteriorated even further as far
as he was concerned.

Ironically, however, Bakhtin himself made a contribution to
the collectivization effort. Among the various kinds of necessary
trained personnel who were in short supply were bookkeepers,
and their shortage was keenly felt. In some areas, for instance, the
Soviets averaged only one bookkeeper for every twelve collective

farms. Moreover, the farms tended to be huge, often 200 square kilometers in area. Thus Bakhtin, who had been banned from teaching in exile because he might corrupt the young with his bourgeois ideas, suddenly found himself in demand as an instructor to teach pig farmers and others the very skills he had learned from his bourgeois-capitalist banker father. Bakhtin was, for instance, engaged to teach three-month courses in bookkeeping to workers from the local state and collective farms. In graduation photos from those days, Bakhtin sits amid an assortment of rough-looking Russians, Red Army guerrillas in their old uniforms, and Kazakhs wearing native headgear.

Bakhtin's only publication from this period stems from his bookkeeping work for the collectivization effort. In 1934 the central journal *Soviet Trade* published his article "Experience Based on a Study of Demand among Kolkhoz Workers." This article draws on findings from eight kolkhozes in the Kustanai area and is full of figures on all manner of economic indicators, right down to how many galoshes were ordered by the kolkhozes. But Bakhtin closes by warning his readers that the Kustanai region is not typical and cautioning them not to apply his findings elsewhere.[4] The fact that this journal sometimes gave exiles the opportunity to publish when they were unable to do so elsewhere might explain this odd caveat with which the article ends, for the whole piece may represent a nonserious venture into print for the sake of a fee but without much substance.

On August 4, 1934, Bakhtin's term of exile officially came to an end. But he stayed on in Kustanai because of the difficulty in those years of returning to Leningrad with the stigma of exile and no residence permit. He made only a brief trip back to Leningrad on September 14 for consultations about his illness. A medical examination in 1932 had found osteomyelitis in both legs; it was still plaguing him. Bakhtin may have used this occasion to see his old friends and ask for their help in finding work, although Voloshinov had lost contact with him while he was in Kustanai, partly because Bakhtin never wrote letters.[5]

In 1936 Bakhtin was granted permission to take a two-month summer holiday in Leningrad. While there, he asked Medvedev for his help in getting an academic job. On his way back to Kustanai in early August, he and his wife called in at Moscow for a few days. They stayed with the Zalesskys and had reunions with old friends from the Bakhtin circle, such as Yudina, who now lived in Moscow. The most emotional reunion was with Kagan, whom they had not seen for about ten years. Kagan was surprised at how well Bakhtin looked, better than his wife, despite his years of exile. The old friends hoped that Yudina could use her contacts to get Bakhtin some work in or near Moscow and secure him a residence permit so that they could be together again and continue their talks. Kagan was at a crossroads in his own life. He had been working on an encyclopedic atlas of the energy resources of the Soviet Union, a long-term project that was coming to an end, and he was looking for a new direction in his life. Bakhtin tried to persuade him to return to the humanities and gave him the text of his almost completed "Discourse in the Novel," which Bakhtin was trying to place with a publisher.[6]

Although nothing came of Kagan's dream that he and Bakhtin might be near each other once more, the trip did lead Bakhtin to find work more in line with his abilities than teaching pig farmers in Kustanai. On September 9, on Medvedev's recommendation, Bakhtin was invited to teach at the Mordovia Pedagogical Institute in Saransk. Accordingly, on September 26 he resigned his job at the Consumers' Cooperative and moved to Saransk.

Even with Medvedev's recommendation, Bakhtin was lucky to get such a job at this time. The most intense period of purges in Soviet history, often referred to as the Great Purge, had begun in Moscow in August with a show trial of the most senior party officials ever tried, the Zinoviev-Trotsky group. Now the purges were at their height. Yet Merkushin, the Second Secretary of the local soviet in Saransk, was extremely ambitious for Mordovian education and was prepared to take political risks in order to build up a high-caliber tertiary institution there. Bakhtin was not the only person with a dubious political record whom Merkushin cleared to be hired. The entire Physics Department at the Pedagogical Institute was a distinguished one thanks to Merkushin's zeal and courage.

Saransk is the capital of the Mordovian Autonomous Republic. It is situated on the River Insar on the western flank of the Volga River uplands, about 400 miles east of Moscow. The town is an important rail center, with lines running not only to Moscow but to Ryazan, Gorky, Kazan, Kuybyshev, and Penza. When Bakhtin first went there in 1936, Saransk was still a typical old

Russian provincial town with mostly one-storied, wooden houses, and plank pavements. Mordovia itself is located in the black soil belt and has traditionally been agricultural, with grains and tobacco the main crops. The climate is dry, however, and the agriculture is often plagued by drought. Saransk was fairly industrial by the time Bakhtin moved there, with factories for light industrial and consumer goods.[7]

In comparison to Kazakhstan, Mordovia was considerably less on the periphery and better supplied, though there still were food shortages, and Bakhtin had food parcels sent to him by friends. Geographically, Mordovia was situated within the borders of European Russia, but it could not offer the Bakhtins the sort of cultural milieu that they had enjoyed in other parts of Russia. Despite a considerable number of Russians in the towns, the majority of the population was Mordovian. The Mordovian people speak a language from the Finno-Ugric family. Prior to the Revolution, they had no alphabet for their native tongue, and only 13 percent of the population were literate.[8] Although great strides had since been made in education, the standard of preparation of Bakhtin's students was not on the same level as that of students in the major Russian cities. Mordovia also had the dubious reputation of being an area where many prison camps were concentrated. Since there was no law faculty in the area, prison officers took courses in Bakhtin's faculty in order to enhance their promotion prospects.

When Bakhtin started teaching at the Mordovia Pedagogical Institute in 1936, it was still in its pioneering phase. Founded only in 1931 with a mere 10 teachers, one of whom did not even have a degree, the Pedagogical Institute had expanded gradually. The year before Bakhtin arrived, the institute acquired a building of its own, and the number of teachers rose to 74, but it had to wait a few more years before a library was added. By 1957, when the institute was made a university, a third of its faculty still had no graduate degree and over half of its four thousand students were correspondence students.[9]

Bakhtin became virtually a one-man world literature department. His course load was incredible. During his first semester he gave three required courses—on literature, Russian literature and folklore, and modern Russian literature. He taught a fourth elective course on the novel of education, a subject about which he was then writing a book. In the second semester he taught third- and fourth-year modern Western literature, contemporary Western literature, medieval literature, classical literature, and the methodology of literature. He was also expected to lecture to official bodies in the town. For instance, at the invitation of the Saransk City Party Committee he gave a lecture to their Evening University of Marxism-Leninism on "Lenin and Stalin on Party-Mindedness in Literature and Art."

Bakhtin seemed finally to have found a place to teach and write, but his good fortune did not last long. The effects of the Great Purge were soon felt in the Pedagogical Institute in Saransk. In 1937 most of the party members of the faculty were purged, and Bakhtin was not entirely spared. He had what he called a "big scrape," from which he apparently emerged untouched. Indeed, in the end his accusers were purged. Nevertheless, he decided that he was at risk of being purged if he stayed there much longer, so on July 20, 1937, he resigned his position in Saransk and began trying to find comparable work in some other town.[10]

In August the Bakhtins visited Moscow, staying with the Zalesskys once more. By this time Kagan was in even lower spirits, having completed his work on the Soviet Union's energy resources. Bakhtin persuaded him to write a piece to commemorate the anniversary of Pushkin's death, which was being prominently celebrated in the Soviet Union that year, but the resulting article, "On Pushkin's Long Poems," was not published until 1974.[11] Even Bakhtin's moral support was of little avail to Kagan, who was in a nervous state and fearful of arrest. On December 26, 1937, he died prematurely, at age forty-eight, from angina pectoris.

Bakhtin also visited Leningrad at this time, where he hoped to find work. But friends warned him that the secret police had started rearresting people who were formerly sentenced to exile or camp. In hopes of avoiding rearrest, the Bakhtins decided to return to Kustanai in late August to straighten out their affairs and then move to some new place where they would be less conspicuous. In the fall of 1937 they moved to the town of Savelovo in the environs of Moscow, where they could stay in the dacha of a friend.

People such as Bakhtin with a political record were not permitted to reside any closer than 100 kilometers from Moscow. As a result, most of the towns, such as Savelovo, lying just beyond 100 kilometers and within reach of a railroad to Moscow were crammed with former prisoners and exiles. A.A. Meier, the former leader of the Voskresenie group whom Bakhtin had known for some time, was living nearby in Kalyazin, and Bakhtin visited him there for talks. Meier was in failing health and soon returned to Leningrad, where he died of cancer in 1939.

Savelovo is a small railway center on the Volga about four and a half hours by train from Moscow and just across the river from Kimry, a large manufacturing town noted for its shoes. Mandelshtam, a former political exile in the same category as Bakhtin, and his wife, Nadezhda, also found shelter in Savelovo from June 1937 until the fall, although they did not meet the Bakhtins, for Nadezhda claimed in her memoirs that no other political exiles were there. Presumably the Bakhtins arrived after the Mandelshtams had left. Nadezhda described Savelovo as "set in sparse woodland, and in the market peasants sold berries, as well as milk and buckwheat for making kasha . . . Savelovo is a village with two or three streets. All the houses looked well-built and were made of wood with old-fashioned fretwork window frames and gates . . . The inhabitants of Savelovo worked mainly at the nearby factory, but they got their livelihood from the river by catching fish and selling it on the black market. It also provided them with fuel for winter—on summer nights they used boat hooks to pull in logs as they floated in from lumber camps on the upper reaches of the river."[12]

Savelovo sounds almost idyllic by comparison with other options open to Bakhtin, such as Kustanai or points even farther east, but his first months there were very hard. Having no job, Bakhtin did not have enough money to live on, and he would have starved if his friends and family had not helped out by sending money. Also, his right leg caused him a lot of pain. It became so bad that the decision was made to remove it. The amputation took place on February 13, 1938, and Bakhtin stayed in the regional hospital until April 14 recovering from the operation. He had to use crutches or a stick for the rest of his life and became even less mobile than before.

The Great Purge reached its climax at this time with the second great show trial, that of Bukharin and his supporters. By the second half of 1938, however, the purge had begun to lose momentum, and in December of that year it ended when the head of the secret police, Yezhov, was dismissed and replaced by Beria. The political situation gradually eased. Many of those arrested and awaiting trial were released, and the number of arrests diminished considerably.

From now until the entry of Russia into World War II in June 1941 was a more liberal time for the intelligentsia. Bakhtin's own situation improved considerably, giving him hope that he might be able to make some sort of reentry into the intellectual life of Moscow or Leningrad. On October 26, 1938, he was invited to contribute an entry on satire to the *Literary Encyclopedia,* although the volume never appeared because his entry fell in the same volume as the entry on Stalin, which was too sensitive to be passed. Bakhtin was probably paid for his article, however. By 1940 he had begun to do internal reviewing for publishing houses to bring in some revenue.

Despite his dubious political status, Bakhtin was very much in circulation at this time and was invited to participate in scholarly functions, such as a conference on Shakespeare held at the House of Literati in Moscow on April 25–28, 1940. In addition, he began an association with the Gorky Institute of World Literature in Moscow, which was part of the Soviet Academy of Sciences. Although the institute was interested in giving him work, it was unthinkable to hire him outright because of his political record. The suggestion to offer him some sort of adjunct status that would enable him to work there also came to nought. Bakhtin finally was invited to give some lectures. On October 14, 1940, he lectured to the institute's Department of Literary Theory and Aesthetics on "Discourse in the Novel," and on March 24, 1941, he lectured on "The Novel as Literary Genre."[13]

Bakhtin's prewar years in Savelovo were one of those highly productive periods that he had at different points in his life. Because he had no employment, there was more time to write. He was also spurred on to write by the hope of obtaining some sort of work in Moscow or Leningrad that better befitted his abilities than the work he had done to date. But the most important factor of all was that in Savelovo he was well supplied with books. Bakhtin liked best to work with all the necessary books available simultaneously. At this time he was fortunate to have a friend, presumably Kanaev, with borrowing rights at the Leningrad library, who procured most of the books Bakhtin needed there. To have borrowed from the Lenin Library in Moscow would have attracted too much attention. As it was, the books were brought to the dacha in secret.

In Savelovo, Bakhtin finished his book *The Novel of Education and Its Significance in the History of Realism* written between 1936 and 1938.[14] He also worked on the essay "Forms of Time and the Chronotope in the Novel" and another piece "On the Philosophical Bases of the Humanities."[15] He reworked one of his lecture series into two long essays, "From the Prehistory of Novelistic Discourse" in 1940 and "Epic and Novel" in 1941. Finally, he wrote a doctoral dissertation for the Gorky Institute on "Rabelais in the History of Realism," a reworked version of which was published in 1965 as *The Work of François Rabelais and Folk Culture of the Middle Ages and Renaissance*. Bakhtin was never formally a graduate student at the institute, but he took advantage of the right that one had to present a work for a postgraduate degree without going through formal graduate studies.

The war put a stop to the progress of Bakhtin's dissertation and to the progress of his scholarly career generally. Materially, however, Bakhtin's situation was improved by the war. He was given exemption from military service on account of his ill health and amputated leg. With so many adults in the army, there was a shortage of trained manpower, so the authorities became more lenient about political records and began to give jobs to former exiles. On September 27, 1941, Bakhtin was appointed to teach German in the local schools. As soon as the Germans advanced to the vicinity of Savelovo, which they never actually occupied, Bakhtin, in a somewhat pointed exercise in heteroglossia, began using as texts in his German classes the propaganda leaflets that they had dropped on the town. From January 19, 1942, until September 22, 1945, he was allowed to teach Russian in the schools. This was considered a step up, as Bakhtin had not initially been passed for the honor of teaching the language of the motherland; he had only been allowed to teach the language of the enemy.

Employment was a mixed blessing for Bakhtin because it left him with little free time to work on potential publications. However, it helped rehabilitate him in the eyes of the authorities. For instance, the local party committee asked Bakhtin in 1944 to lecture to it on a certain I. A. Kirillov. When the war was over, Bakhtin was even able to resume his post at the Pedagogical Institute in Saransk.

The 1930s and the war had not been as kind to most former

members of Bakhtin's circle. Most of them were now dead; some had died from natural causes, others perished in the camps. In all cases they had been better situated both professionally and geographically than was Bakhtin, until misfortune struck.

The disparity between the fortunes of Bakhtin and the members of his circle was strikingly illustrated in the case of Medvedev. Medvedev had advanced in all areas of his multifaceted literary career. He became a full professor at the Leningrad Historical Philological Institute, the Herzen Pedagogical Institute, and the Tolmachev Military Academy. At the last he was made head of the Department of Literature and wore "a general's uniform with three rhomboids." He added Gorky's *Literary Study* to the list of journals to which he was a regular contributor. He published on such acceptable topics as Gorky and Lenin and wrote textbooks on literary history.[16] Medvedev's work of the 1930s has the mark of someone anxious to please, and he does not appear to have been set back by the Great Purge at first. Indeed, in March 1937 he took on the less than laudable role of being one of the chief speakers at a meeting of Leningrad writers called to attack the Leningrad Board of the Writers' Union. In March 1938, however, his career came to an unexpected halt when he was arrested, perhaps in a purge of faculty from the Tolmachev Military Academy. Many people wrote letters of protest to the security police on his behalf, but to no avail. He was apparently shot shortly after his arrest, although when he was posthumously rehabilitated in 1956, the official document stated that he had died in 1941 at a location which could not be ascertained.

Pumpiansky, like Medvedev, enjoyed a successful career as a Leningrad professor of literature, from 1934 at the conservatory and from 1936 at Leningrad State University as well. He died of cancer of the liver in 1940. Another member of the Bakhtin circle, the scholar Tubyansky, had a more dramatic career. In 1927 he was sent to work in the Soviet Embassy in Mongolia, where he largely did research for the Tibetan Study Group of the Mongolian State Scholarly Research Committee. While there, he collected materials for a dissertation on "Ancient Indian Materialism as Found in Tibetan Sources." He also worked on a Tibeto-Mongolian dictionary, a reference dictionary of Indian and Tibetan medicine, and studies of Tibetan Lamaism and Buddhism in India, Tibet, and Mongolia. He returned to the Soviet Union in April

1937, where he rejoined the Institute of Eastern Studies as a senior research fellow. Tubyansky had many plans for future research, and most of his proposals were approved by the institute and included in its scholarly plan for the period 1938–1949, but as one Soviet source put it cryptically, "these plans were not destined to be realized." In other words, Tubyansky was soon arrested, possibly in the aftermath of the arrest of the Soviet ambassador to Mongolia in June 1937. He may have been accused of involvement with Mongolian cults that used cannibalism in their rituals. He died in camp in 1943.[17]

The other orientalist in the circle, though only an occasional attender at the philosophical nights, was Konrad. He too was arrested and held in prison from 1938 until 1941, but he returned to resume a successful academic career, including membership in the Academy of Sciences. The other occasional attenders of the circle were less lucky. Vaginov died a natural death in 1934; Engelhardt and Frankovsky perished in 1942 in the blockade of Leningrad.

The period also saw the demise of the three old schoolfriends Voloshinov, Zubakin, and Rugevich. At the beginning of the 1930s, Voloshinov was doing well in his academic career as a docent at the Herzen Pedagogical Institute and a senior research worker at the State Institute for Speech Culture. However, the tuberculosis from which he had suffered since 1914 had come out of its brief remission in 1927, and his health deteriorated rapidly. By 1934 he was already in a sanatorium and no longer able to work. He died in 1936 without being able to finish his dissertation and leaving an unfinished translation of the first volume of Cassirer's *Philosophy of Symbolic Forms* (1923), to which Bakhtin referred frequently in his writings. Zubakin was arrested as early as 1929 and exiled to Arkhangelsk. Enterprising as ever, while there he made statues of Lomonosov and other famous scientists, published a book about the northern craft of bonecarving, and married Tatyana Stepanovna Romanova, a teacher of English. He was arrested for visiting Leningrad illegally for the funeral of Voloshinov, his best friend. He and his wife were sent to a camp in the northeast, where he died in 1937 or 1938. Rugevich was also arrested in 1936, on grounds that his father had returned to Poland after the Revolution and held a high post there. Rugevich perished in the camps.[18]

The members of the old circle who worked in music fared better than the others. Even though Yudina and Sollertinsky had their scrapes with the conservative forces in Soviet music, their professional status continued to improve. Yudina gained a position at the Moscow Conservatory in 1936, even though it was a black year for Soviet lovers of modernist music like herself. Sollertinsky suffered in that year too, for his support of modernist music, yet he went on to become a full professor at the Leningrad Conservatory in 1939, and in 1943 he added the post of lecturer at the Leningrad Theatrical Institute to his long list of jobs. When in May 1941 he addressed the Soviet Composers' Union in Leningrad, he did not offer predictable paeans but echoed the discourse of the Bakhtin circle in the 1920s by describing a Beethoven symphony as "polypersonalist," a type of symphony based on the dialogical principle rather than the monological, on the principle that a multiplicity of consciousnesses, competing ideas and wills should be involved, on the affirmation—in contradistinction to the monologic principle——of the "other I." The pressure of his wartime work load was too great even for Sollertinsky, however, and in 1944 while in evacuation with the conservatory in Novosibirsk, he died of a heart attack.[19]

Thus, by the end of the war only Kanaev, Yudina, Zalessky, and Bakhtin remained from among his old circle. The infamous 1930s had not, after all, been as bad for him as for many of his peers. Fate sent him to some unexpected places and assigned him a variety of jobs, none of them entirely suitable for a person of his intellectual stature. But at the same time these were years of great productivity for him, in which he managed to produce two book-length manuscripts and at least five long essays. And he survived.

Certain patterns emerge in Bakhtin's work of the 1930s and early 1940s that set it off from his earlier writing. The most striking characteristic is a narrowing of his interests to literary questions, specifically the theory of the novel. He thus found a way to concentrate his wide-ranging interests into a single subsuming obsession. In the 1920s he had written on separate topics that are not ordinarily conjoined. In this period he continued to meditate and develop his ideas on broad philosophical, mythological, and linguistic issues, but he did so in the service of a single subsuming category, the novel.

In the Soviet Union in those years the novel was the central topic of literary scholarship, as shown in the pages of *The Literary Critic* (*Literaturnyj kritik*), the main theoretical journal. Moreover, in 1934–1935 a debate on the nature of the novel was organized at the Communist Academy in Moscow, with Lukacs as the main speaker.[20] Thus Bakhtin's turning to the novel evinced the same pattern as had his choice in the 1920s of Freud, the Formalists, Dostoevsky, and the philosophy of language, which had then been modish topics among intellectuals but could also be used as vehicles for exploring his own concerns. In the later instance, however, his own concerns played an even greater role in the choice of topic.

In the 1929 Dostoevksy book Bakhtin's conception of the novel had already been so idiosyncratic that it could contain almost any topic. This potential became more important for him under the more restricted and repressive conditions of intellectual life in the 1930s. Soviet society was passing several milestones on the route of progressive Stalinization, including the centralization of all cultural institutions, the cult of personality, the heightened power of the secret police, the chauvinism, and the purges. Such trends necessarily alarmed someone of Bakhtin's basic assumptions and principles. But the institutions of Stalinism were by no means all that troubled him. He was most disturbed by what was happening to that key element in his philosophy, language. The official language had become homogenized and dominated all aspects of public life. Most literature and literary scholarship were mere subfunctions of the official rhetoric and myths. Official pronouncements were absolutely authoritative and final.

Bakhtin had always opposed language's becoming automatic, mechanical, or authoritative. He decried monologue and extolled open-endedness and incompleteness. The great oppositions that he had adduced in *The Architectonics* and then invoked in virtually all of his subsequent writings—such as being/becoming, given/created, and finished/unfinished—capsulate the basic incompatibility between Stalinist culture and Bakhtin's views. In each instance Stalinist culture stands for the first, closed, and completed term of the opposition, whereas Bakhtin stands for the second, open-ended one.

Bakhtin did not respond to the challenge of Stalinism with silence. Most of his works thus far had read as manifestos disguised as academic inquiries, to which his current works were no exception. But the vogues and debates of the intelligentsia occupied a lesser position. The major contemporary implicitly addressed in these writings was not one of his peers among the intelligentsia but Stalinist culture itself. Bakhtin used his ostensible subject matter as a medium to convey his critique of Stalinist ideology.

Bakhtin's writings of this period constitute a recognizable whole, dealing with much the same concerns and ideas. There are two landmarks among them, however, his first known work of the period, "Discourse in the Novel," and his last, the dissertation on Rabelais. "Discourse in the Novel" sets up all the broad topics and themes that would absorb Bakhtin throughout this period. Written in 1934–1935, it is his first major work produced in exile. Although his pen had probably not been inactive in the previous four years, there were special reasons that now moved him to write. Periods of productivity in his career correlated with times when he had some hope of advancement or publication, and this was such a time. Bakhtin's term of exile had officially ended, making it thinkable for him to resume an academic or publishing career, as had several former exiles in his category. His friends in Moscow and Leningrad were trying to help him find work. Additionally, in Leningrad he was able to obtain the books that he needed for his work, for his writings of this period show too much erudition to have been written totally from memory.

Thus, in "Discourse in the Novel" Bakhtin resumed the scholarly career broken off by his forced exile. In some respects the essay takes up his ideas at the very point he had left off when he was arrested in 1929. For example, the discussion of heteroglossia as the natural condition of any society's language returns to his interest in novelistic polyphony of the Dostoevsky book, though broadened in its frame of reference.[21] The essay recognizes the primacy of the social in language, as does *Marxism and the Philosophy of Language*. It repeats Bakhtin's old distinction between dead and living languages. Indeed, "Discourse in the Novel" seems almost to have melded the ideas of Bakhtin's two earlier books, taking the discussion of polyphony out of its narrow focus on the novel and art. Polyphony, like heteroglossia, is now both the keystone of his philosophy of language and a function of life itself. The essay resolves any doubt that the Dostoevsky book and *Marxism and the Philosophy of Language* were written by the same man.

Both "Discourse in the Novel" and "From the Prehistory of Novelistic Discourse," written in 1940, address the old themes and ideas of the Formalists and of people close to them, such as Vinogradov. Like Tynyanov, Bakhtin gives a central role to parody in his evolution of the novel. He commends the Formalist notion of "laying bare the device." Like Shklovsky, Bakhtin argues that we can lose our sense of language when language becomes too "automatic." The pool of works that Bakhtin uses as examples in both of these essays overlaps with the old favorites of the Formalists. In particular, the Western sources cited, other than Rabelais, seem almost entirely Formalist. These include Sterne, Don Quixote, and the one Dickens novel that Shklovsky dwelt on, *Little Dorritt*.[22]

Inasmuch as by 1934 the Formalists and Vinogradov were no longer publishing works written in this vein, "Discourse in the Novel" might seem to have been written before Bakhtin's arrest, when he would have been in dialogue with their current position, but evidence in the text itself indicates that it was written, at least in the sense of being put together, in 1934. In particular, the essay addresses the burning questions of that day. Indeed, the essay first presents a sort of Janus face that appears in all of Bakhtin's works of this period. One of its faces is turned backward toward the intellectual debates of the 1920s, and the other is turned forward toward contemporary events.

"Discourse in the Novel" marks a change in Bakhtin's writing. There is a new vehemence, a new terminology, and a new frame of reference. In a characteristic preamble Bakhtin points out the errors in two major opposing approaches to discourse in the novel, the idealist and the Formalist. But he soon focuses on the opposition between the illusion that there is in society or literature a "single, unified language" (*edinyj jazyk*) and the reality that heteroglossia abounds in any society and that language itself is multiplanar and has a proclivity for "breaking down into separate discourses" (*rassloenie jazyka*). Bakhtin distinguishes between the language of the novel and of what he calls the "official genres." In another one of his huge historical surveys, he maps the various points in history where persons or institutions, such as the church, have tried to impose a "single language of truth" or "correct language," despite language's natural variegation and flux. He charts an epic struggle over time between the forces of "centralization," which he also calls "the centripetal forces of sociolinguistic life," and the "centrifugal" forces of heteroglossia. The struggle has at times been won by the forces of centralization, as when a particular language or dialect is able to dominate a given society's culture or a particular "ideological system" is "canonized," but this is an unnatural situation. At other times, the "decentralizing" centrifugal forces have dominated, and these times favor the development of the novel.[23]

Such terms as "unified language," "centralization," "official genres," "canonization of the ideological system," and "correct language" could not in 1934 have been innocently or randomly chosen. They were invoked by Bakhtin at a time when the memory of collectivization was yet green, of that attempt by "one people united" (*edinyj narod*) to homogenize the rural economy and, in Kazakhstan, to homogenize ethnic diversity as well. These terms were also invoked in conjunction with a more recent event, the First Writers' Congress sponsored by the Writers' Union in August 1934.

The formation of a single Writers' Union in 1932 had meant the centralization of Soviet literature, but as yet only on an institutional level. Shortly thereafter, however, all writers were required to follow the one literary "method" of "socialist realism," a newly coined term for the stipulation that all literature be "party-minded" (*partijnyj*). Official pronouncements over the next few years by people like Gorky further defined the term, and the First Writers' Congress, attended by prominent foreign writers, functioned as an elaborate ritual to endorse the concept of socialist realism.

Actually, socialist realism is a somewhat elusive concept, which has been defined in practice rather than in theory. It is essentially a canonical system which rests on exemplars. Even in these first years of its history, authoritative sources indicated to the writers which works they should use as models in their writing. In consequence, socialist realist literature became so conventionalized that its production was comparable to icon painting in that writers copied tropes, gestures, and standardized epithets from the offical models. Nowhere was socialist realism more conventionalized than in the novel, which was also the genre from which authorities drew most of the canonical exemplars. Gradually elements from these exemplars congealed into a de-facto formulaic masterplot which could be used to produce socialist realist novels on any acceptable topic, in the manner of an imperative poetics.[24]

It is surely no accident that Bakhtin during this period offered a somewhat idiosyncratic notion of the novel, whereby the novel is the product of the "centrifugal" forces that undermine the "single language" imposed on a culture with a playful celebration of society's natural heteroglossia. Bakhtin does not actually mention socialist realism in "Discourse in the Novel," but it is the implied referent as he discusses the use of "smooth and pure univocal language" in novels to purge them of all traces of language's natural pluralism and relativism. He concludes that such a folly can only be the product of arrogance or stupidity.[25]

Bakhtin did not develop this elaborate historical model merely to disguise his attack on the direction that Soviet literature was taking. He had long been interested in the evolution of the novel as a case study in the sociology of knowledge, having started to translate Lukacs' *Theory of the Novel* in the early 1920s. Moreover, the centrifugal/centripetal model that he sets up in this essay is only a variant of those earlier binaries he had advanced in *The Architectonics*. But that other plane or referent, a commentary on contemporary events, is unmistakably present in this multiplanar utterance.

Most of the guidelines for socialist realism are discussed by Bakhtin in this indirect way. For instance, his concept of heteroglossia, which seems to have grown out of the monologue/dialogue opposition in his earlier writings, is also related to the charge laid down by spokesmen for socialist realism in 1932–1934 that Soviet literature should be accessible to the masses and that writers should not jeopardize accessibility by using vocabulary which was abstruse or used only by a particular group in society, such as dialects. Similarly, Bakhtin's stress on the central role played by parody and verbal play in fiction and his insistence that these elements do not lead to empty aestheticism or rob fiction of meaning, while reflecting his interest in Formalism, also serves as a response to another stricture in the official guidelines for socialist realism, that authors not indulge in such "formalist" techniques of writing as parody, experimentalism, and self-conscious stylization.[26]

The official demand that socialist realist writing be accessible to the masses was accompanied by the stipulation that it draw on folklore for some of its models, for folklore is "the unwritten compositions of the toiling man." This had long been Gorky's pet idea for what should happen in Soviet literature. In a speech to the First Writers' Congress he elaborated the idea, tracing the influence of folklore on literature itself: "The moment came when the 'simpletons' of folklore, now turned into Sancho Panza, Simplicissimus and Eulenspiegel, became smarter than their feudal masters and had courage enough to mock their masters . . . oral folklore most definitely exercised a constant influence on the creation of such major works of literature as *Faust, Baron Münchhausen's Adventures, Gargantua and Pantagruel,* and *Till Eulenspiegel.*"[27]

Bakhtin deliberately gives an account similar to Gorky's of the role of these "unwritten" or "folk" sources in the development of the novel, but with some all-important differences. Whereas Gorky identified the folk hero who mocks his masters as a simpleton (*durak*), Bakhtin cites a troika of such heroes, which includes as well the fool and the "rogue" (*plut*), a category that Gorky identified with the bourgeoisie. Moreover, although both writers stress the role of the folk as debunkers of those in power, Gorky recommended the use of folk models in socialist realism primarily as a source for fantastic heroes to inspire the populace. Whereas in the past the folk hero's function in literature had been iconoclastic, in the modern day his function was to affirm the status quo and impress the public with his monumentalness.[28] For Bakhtin, by contrast, the folk provides a healthy antidote to that which is overweighty, official, or artificially monologic. It is a force which brings reality back to its life size. Folk culture is the culture of the lower orders, of the fair tent and the marketplace from which come his three heroes, the rogue, the fool, and the simpleton. That is where nonreceived language, scatology, and dialect are heard. According to Bakhtin's scenario, in the marketplace and square the high language of the "poet, scholar, monk, knight" is parodied in irreverent play, farce, and repartee. Hierarchy and the "single language of truth" are put to rout by the folk, and thanks to them, heteroglossia prevails. There, in short, are found the beginnings of a movement that culminated in the development of the novel as a bastion of heteroglossia.

Although Bakhtin never mentions socialist realism by name in these publications, he does deal with the subject in *The Novel of Education and Its Significance in the History of Realism,* of which only fragments survive. The main focus of this book was apparently Goethe, one of Bakhtin's favorite authors, who played an enormous role in his thought throughout his life.[29] In this instance Bakhtin concentrated on Goethe's *Dichtung und Wahrheit* and his Wilhelm Meister books. But he took his coverage of the novel of education as far as Gorky and socialist realism, and the account he gave of them could not have been unfavorable, since the book was accepted by the publishing house Soviet Writer. Publication was never carried through, however, because the war intervened, and the manuscript was destroyed. Bakhtin used much of his remaining copy for tobacco paper, which was then in short supply, and the fragments that have survived do not include his coverage of Gorky or socialist realism. Although circumstances explain the disappearance of most of the manuscript, the question as to why Bakhtin destroyed his one overt critique of socialist realism is one of the many enigmas left by him.

Even if Bakhtin had not written on socialist realism specifically, the general subject of this book, the novel of education, is highly relevant to socialist realism. The cornerstone of the socialist realist tradition is the positive hero, a figure who stands at the novel's end as an emblem of Bolshevik virtue. The education or "formation" (*stanovlenie*) of the positive hero, specifically the growth of the hero's political consciousness, structures the de facto masterplot according to which most socialist realist novels are written. Elsewhere in his writings of the 1930s Bakhtin raises doubts about whether such emblematic figures are appropriate in a novel. For instance, in "Discourse in the Novel" he asserts that in the modern day literature cannot achieve univocal, mythic language with its absolute norms of thought. Myth could have this kind of hold only in prehistoric times or at the beginning of history. Consequently, in literature a "hero without faults" can no longer achieve the sought-after unity between the inner and outer person, between the person and his world.[30]

Such remarks, made en passant, are presumably intended as critiques of socialist realism. By the time of Bakhtin's essay "Epic and Novel" in 1941, the absence of overt references to socialist realism seems odd, for in this piece he systematizes the doubts about the socialist realist novel merely alluded to earlier and evolves a comprehensive account of the true essence of the novel, to which he counterposes what he labels the "epic." Although Bakhtin maintains that the spirit of the novel is irreconcilable with the spirit of the epic, he describes the epic in terms that are patently applicable to the socialist realist novel.

Epic and novel, Bakhtin maintains, are not merely two different genres with their own formal characteristics but also two diametrically opposed expressions of reality. The epic depicts a completed, perfected world, one that is separated from the world of the author and the audience by an absolute and unbridgeable past. An epic past does not mean merely a past age, for its actual location in time is not as important as its valorization of a time, its closedness and "perfectedness." The epic is told as legend; it is sacred and incontrovertible. Thus, the epic is comparable to what both the official Soviet rhetoric and socialist realism were trying to achieve.

Bakhtin sees the novel, by contrast, as the genre of an imperfect, incomplete world. It is constantly generating new forms and, unlike other major genres, cannot be pinned down to any set of formal characteristics. In other words, it is formally as incomplete as the world it depicts. The rise of the novel was a product of the breakdown of the epic world view, which came about when writers began to parody and mock the styles, heroes, and world view of the old forms. The genre thus generated, the novel—or rather the new sensibility, "novelness"—is by its very nature forever iconoclastic, forever questing.

Thus, Bakhtin identifies three categories—novel, folk, and heteroglossia—as the triumvirate which prosecutes the cause of a sort of permanent revolution in human consciousness. Using the scenarios of struggle that were so characteristic of the official culture of his day, he turns his erudite essays of these years into agons of cultural change. Relegated to the periphery of society as he was, Bakhtin was able to critique his own society while others were being obliged to monologize.

Bakhtin's writings of the period do not reduce to mere Aesopean language, or to mere commentary on his times. He was deeply interested in the theory and evolution of the novel, as well as in the general, philosophical issues that may be raised in this context, such as the nature of space and time and the nature of language. Indeed, his works of this period show the same sort of double-voicedness of which he so often spoke. On the one hand, they are addressed to his times, but on the other, their main addressee is theory in general, both literary and philosophical.

CHAPTER 13

The Theory
of the Novel

In the 1930s and early 1940s Bakhtin devoted four essays to a common theme, the nature and evolution of the novel. In addition to "Discourse in the Novel," these include "Forms of Time and the Chronotope in the Novel: An Essay on Historical Poetics" (1937–1938, to which a conclusion was added in 1973), "From the Prehistory of Novelistic Discourse" (1940), and "Epic and Novel: On a Methodology for the Study of the Novel" (1941).[1] Together they cover Bakhtin's ideas about the nature of the novel, his notions about space and time in the history of the novel, and his views about the changing perception of language in the evolution of the novel.

Bakhtin's account of the nature of the novel is highly singular and in some ways perverse and personal. He implicitly takes issue with the main points made by Lukacs at a conference on the theory of the novel held at the Communist Academy in 1934–1935, as well as with most of the leading theories of the novel of the day. Bakhtin conceives poetics in general, and the novel in particular, in a very broad framework. He looks at genres not just in their narrow literary context but as icons that fix the world view of the ages from which they spring. Genre is to him an X-ray of a specific world view, a crystallization of the concepts particular to a given time and to a given social stratum in a specific society. A genre, therefore, embodies a historically specific idea of what it means to be human. Bakhtin does not see poetics as a normative category, *à la* Aristotle or Boileau, where there are "high" and "low" genres piled up in a fixed hierarchy organized by some timeless essence, such as "good taste." In fact, Bakhtin plays around with these suppositions by inventing generic hierarchies in order to upend them in pursuit of his own "antipoetics."

Genres traditionally despised or dismissed are elevated to the place of honor, and the formerly exalted genres are "discrowned." Despite Bakhtin's polemicism and even contentiousness, which sometimes blurs the outlines of his thought, he devises an extremely plastic and historically sensitive conception of genres and their interactions.

Among the various genres, Bakhtin singles out the novel as his personal hero. The novel is for him not just another literary genre but a special kind of force, which he calls "novelness." In 1929 he had made extravagant claims for Dostoevsky's uniqueness, but in the following period Bakhtin came to regard the Dostoevskian novel not as an absolutely unprecedented event in the history of the genre so much as the purest expression of what had always been implicitly present in it. Viewing the history of the novel in the light of Dostoevsky's example had revolutionary consequences. The novel became not only "the leading hero in the drama of literary development in our time" but the most significant force at work in the history of consciousness, even in periods when it had been thought that no novels were being written, as in Plato's Athens or the Middle Ages. Traditionally, the novel was said to have "risen" with Cervantes, Defoe, or Richardson. Their works and the nineteenth-century psychological novel that evolved from them had become canonical for the novel conceived as a genre like any other. Even in the Soviet Union a class-oriented version of this view of the evolution of the novel prevailed. Bakhtin disagreed with this generally accepted account, which led him to make statements such as "the utter inadequacy of literary theory is exposed when it is forced to deal with the novel" or "faced with the problem of the novel, genre theory must submit to a radical restructuring."[2]

Instead, Bakhtin assigns the term "novel" to whatever form of expression within a given literary system reveals the limits of that system as inadequate, imposed, or arbitrary. Literary systems are composed of canons, and the novel is fundamentally anticanonical. It does not permit generic monologue. It insists on a dialogue between texts that a given system admits as literature and those texts that are excluded from such a definition. The novel is a kind of epistemological outlaw, a Robin Hood of texts. Because the fundamental features of any culture are inscribed in its texts, not only in its literary texts but in its legal and religious ones as well, "novelness" can work to undermine the official or high culture of any society.

The novel conceived in this way has a long history which exists outside the bounds of traditional literary history. Bakhtin charts this history through the attacks made on a given culture's higher literary forms by its lower forms, as in Cervantes' parody of knightly romances, or Sterne and Fielding's sentimental fiction. But these are merely late examples of a tendency that has been abroad at least since ancient Greece. Bakhtin comes near to naming Socrates as the first novelist, because his gadfly role, which was tied up with a belief in the importance of self-consciousness ("Know thyself!") and was played out in the drama of a dialogue, corresponds closely to the role of the novel. That role has also assumed such unexpected forms as the confession, the utopia, or the menippean satire. During the nineteenth century even the drama, as in Ibsen or other naturalists, the long poem, such as *Childe Harold* or *Don Juan,* and the lyric, as in Heine, were masks for novelness. As formerly distinct literary genres are subjected to the novel's antinormative power, their systematic purity is infected, and they become "novelized."

The history of the novel is for Bakhtin a grid that provides different reference points from which to chart a history of consciousness. Two major variables are fundamental in the evolution of the novel and thus of consciousness as well: attitudes to space and time, and attitudes to language. Bakhtin was obsessed with the interconnection of space and time. In the 1920s this interest had been widely shared by Soviet intellectuals. Einstein and Bergson were particularly in vogue. But in Bakhtin's exploration of this question he initially relied not on these thinkers but on others, especially Kant and the Neo-Kantians. It was Kant, after all, who had placed cognition at the center of his philosophy, which gave a fundamental new importance to the mechanisms by which the mind organizes experiences. And preeminent among these mechanisms are the categories of space and time.

Kant in a lecture on "Anthropology" posed the question "What is man?" This question, combined with the emphasis placed on perceptual categories in his *Critique of Pure Reason,* led to the creation of philosophical anthropology, a discipline that seeks to understand the historic specificity of what it means to be human in different ages by establishing the differing world views held by people at various times. Over the centuries people have had widely divergent ideas about what it means to be human. Philosophical anthropology is an attempt to recover those ideas by studying the way, say, Byzantine Greeks organized the world in their conception of it, or how the world was conceived by ancient Egyptians or Renaissance Italians. In each place and period a different set of time/space categories obtained, and what it meant to be human was in large measure determined by these categories. The Greeks saw time as cyclical, for example, while the Hebrews assigned greatest value to the future.

In the 1920s Bakhtin's concern for space and time was reflected in a theory of value that had a double base: the different perceptual categories that are grounded in the self and all the other categories that are perceived as nonself. In the 1930s his interest in time and space assumed a differing shape and direction, increasingly emphasizing the immediacy with which these categories are felt in actual experience. The study of such experience he translated into a historical poetics of the novel. To this end, he introduced the term "chronotope." The word literally means time/space, and in Bakhtin's use it is a unit for studying texts according to the ratio and nature of the temporal and spatial categories represented.

Unamuno said that anyone who invents a concept takes leave of reality. But chronotope is a way not to take leave of reality; it is precisely the opposite, a concept for engaging reality. Over the centuries people have organized the world of their immediate experience into a number of different world pictures. The fundamental categories for creating these images are time and space, which philosophers have always speculated upon but Kant came closest to demonstrating. Bakhtin, taking his cue from Minkowski's suggestion of a fourth dimension, insists on the inseparability of these categories.[3] He insists as well on the historical nature of such concepts, the fact that at different times, differing combinations of space and time have been used to model exterior reality. The most paradigmatic expression of past chronotopes is to be found in literary texts. Since authors model whole worlds, they are ineluctably forced to employ the organizing categories of the worlds that they themselves inhabit.

The chronotope plays a central role in all Bakhtin's essays of this period, but nowhere more so than in "Forms of Time and the

Chronotope in the Novel." Although Bakhtin was at times rather casual about indicating the precise links in the dialogic chain of his ideas, this particular essay opens with two footnotes that indicate the twin sources of his inspiration. One is Kant, whom Bakhtin praises for having shown him the importance of space and time as the primary categories of perception, although Bakhtin differs from Kant in regarding these categories "not as transcendental, but as forms of the most immediate reality." The other source is the physiologist Ukhtomsky, to whom Bakhtin owes his insistence on the immediacy of space and time in human experience.[4]

Ukhtomsky's vision of the body led Bakhtin to emphasize its central role in the representation of the world. When Ukhtomsky stated, "our dominants stand *between* us and reality," he was using the term "dominant" in the sense of the total integration of neurological and psychological forces into a characteristic pattern that shapes our perception of the world. Analogously, according to Bakhtin, our particular totally integrated sense of space and time shapes our sense of reality. We are constantly engaged in the activity of *re*-presenting the signals we get from our exterior environment, shaping those signals into a pattern by means of particular chronotopes. Bakhtin argues that particular chronotopes are the defining or dominant features of persons, periods, and works of art: "Within the limits of a single work and within the total output of a single author we may notice a number of different chronotopes and complex interactions among them, specific to the given work or author; it is common, moreover, for one of these chronotopes to envelop or dominate others."[5]

In the 1973 conclusion to Bakhtin's chronotope essay, which was one of his last pieces of sustained work before his death, he again stresses the split between mind and world with which he began his career more than fifty years earlier in "Art and Answerability": "There is a sharp and categorical boundary line between the actual world as source of representation and the world represented." The chronotope is a bridge, not a wall, between the two worlds. Language is not a static prison house but a constantly activated conveyor belt: "Out of the actual chronotopes of our world . . . emerge the reflected and created chronotopes of the world represented." The old distinction between "given" and "conceived" is reconceptualized here in terms directly taken from physiology, which again owes much to Ukhtomsky: "However forcefully the real and represented world resist fusion . . . they are nevertheless indissolubly tied up with each other and find themselves in continual mutual interaction; uninterrupted exchange goes on between them, similar to the uninterrupted exchange of matter between living organisms and the environment that surrounds them." The organism needs its surroundings, just as the text needs its context, for "if it is thrown out of its environment, it dies."[6]

Time and space are always intertwined, but some of the ways they combine are more significant than others for revealing the specific world views from which they spring. This is especially true in literature, "where spatial and temporal indicators are fused into one carefully thought-out, concrete whole. Time thickens, as it were, takes on flesh, becomes . . . visible; likewise, space become charged and responsive." Time assuming flesh is something more than a trope here, for those who enflesh the categories are people. It is precisely the differing ways people are represented that determine the differences between chronotopes: "the chronotope as a formally constitutive category determines . . . the image of man in literature . . . the image of man is always intrinsically chronotopic." Chronotopic features also serve to distinguish particular authors. In Dostoevsky, time is "essentially instantaneous," whereas Tolstoy loves "duration, the stretching out of time." Primarily, however, the chronotope distinguishes broader categories within the history of literature. The chronotope both defines genre and generic distinction and establishes the boundaries between the various intrageneric subcategories of the major literary types.[7]

By focusing on the way a particular chronotope defines a particular genre or subgenre, Bakhtin traces the rise of the novel back to Hellenistic Greece. He pinpoints three literary developments in classical times which show that the long process culminating in the appearance of true novels was then already underway. All three developments were characterized by their own chronotope. Moreover, each of these chronotopes was fundamentally important to the subsequent history of literature and lived on in various guises long after the conditions that brought it forth had passed away.

The first of these chronotopes, "adventure time," is most fully developed in the Greek romances, such as *Leucippe and Cli-*

tiphon by Achilles Tatius, *Daphnis and Chloe* by Longus, and *Aethiopica* and *Anthia and Habracomes* by Heliodorus. These texts are associated with the second Sophistic movement and thus date anywhere from the second to the sixth century A.D. The stories are all very much of a piece. In ancient times they were called neither romances nor novels but *erotika pathemata,* because they tell about the sufferings of young lovers.

According to their typical narrative formula, a young boy and girl of marriageable age, beautiful and chaste, meet and fall in love suddenly and unexpectedly. But their marriage cannot take place because they are parted. There are shipwrecks, pirates, slavery, prison, miraculous rescues, recognition scenes, court trials, and sleeping potions. The story ends happily, with the marriage of the two lovers. This plot is, in other words, the original of the boy meets girl, loses girl, gets girl stereotype.

In this formula Bakhtin sees the essence of adventure time. There are only two major events, falling in love and getting married: "All action in the novel unfolds between these points. These points—the poles of the plot's movement—are themselves crucial events in the heroes' lives; in and of themselves they have a biographical significance. But it is not around these that the novel is structured; rather, it is around that . . . which takes place *between* them. But, in essence, nothing need lie between them." Because the love and chastity of the hero and heroine remain unchanged, "it is as if nothing had happened between these two moments, as if the marriage had been consummated on the day after their meeting . . . It is precisely an extratemporal hiatus between two moments of biographical time . . . All the events of the novel that fill this hiatus are a pure digression from the normal course of life; they are excluded from the kind of real duration in which additions to a normal biography are made."[8]

The important feature of adventure time is that it is completely abstract. There are no identifying traces of the historical period. It is a time outside of other temporal series, such as everyday, biographical time. There is even an absence of biological or maturational change. Time is composed of short, unrelated segments, set off by words emphasizing their alienation from developmental time, such as "suddenly" or "at just that moment." Adventure time has its own logic of random contingency. If something happened a moment earlier or later, there would be no plot at all. The individual adventures are strung together in what is effectively a nontemporal sequence, so that their number is potentially infinite: "These hours and days leave no trace, [so] one may have as many of them as one likes."[9] The initiative in such time is handed over to change; the human heroes are mere pawns in the game of fate.

Since each adventure in works with adventure time leaves no trace either on the protagonists or on the plot's ultimate resolution, it can virtually occur in any geographical space or historical time. For a shipwreck, one must have a sea, but which particular sea in the geographical and historical sense makes no difference at all. Likewise, what happens in Egypt can happen in Byzantium, and vice versa, and what happens on day one can equally well happen on day six. Thus both time and space are essentially abstract and nonspecific. The adventure chronotope is "characterized by a technical, abstract connection between space and time, by the reversibility of moments in a temporal sequence, and by this interchangeability of space."[10]

The adventure chronotope, which is still recognizably alive in the great bulk of popular culture in modern times, contrasts with the second literary chronotope from ancient times, "adventure time of everyday life." *The Golden Ass* of Apuleius and the *Satyricon* of Petronius are the original exemplars of this everyday life chronotope, which represents a great leap forward from the type found in Greek romances. This fact accounts for the greater influence of these two texts on subsequent literary history. Two basic features distinguish the everyday life chronotope. In terms of time, the particular adventure is now some kind of metamorphosis. And in terms of space, some kind of social space replaces a physical landscape. Whereas in the strict adventure chronotope one found abstract seas and continents, in the everyday life chronotope one finds social hierarchies.

The Golden Ass differs from Greek romance in that the adventure defining its narrative leaves traces on the chief character. In *Aetheopica,* for example, the "suddenly's" can be transposed, for they mark no more than the transition to yet another adventure. But the "suddenly" that turns Lucius into an ass marks a difference that is registered in the biographical progression of the hero. The passivity of the hero and the tyranny of chance which characterizes the adventure chronotope pass gradually into a form

in the everyday life chronotope where the hero himself begins to
show initiative. He has individual responsibility, experiences guilt,
and can therefore be punished and ultimately redeemed. Metamorphosis "is a mythological sheath for the idea of development—but one that unfolds not so much in a straight line as
spasmodically, a line with 'knots' in it, one, therefore, that constitutes a distinctive type of temporal sequence."[11]

Two seemingly contradictory aspects of metamorphosis account for the distinctiveness of the everyday life chronotope: dramatic change and continuity. In such ancient celebrations of
change as Hesiod's *Works and Days* or *Theogony,* there is a
change from spring to winter or from the Bronze Age to the Gold
Age. But amid all this diversity the unity of the theogonic process,
the historical process, nature, and agricultural life is preserved.
The various series of changes that are bonded into a single over-
reaching unity in Hesiod become unraveled in later works, such
as Ovid's *Metamorphosis.* Changes there are no longer isometric:
they are isolated and lack wholeness. The general idea of transformation is now conceived as the private metamorphosis of isolated
beings. Metamorphosis becomes a vehicle for conceptualizing and
portraying an individual, personal fate that is cut off from both
cosmic and historical sequences. Mankind is torn out of the sky.

The emphasis on change becomes an emphasis on personal
crisis, while the emphasis on continuity now concentrates on the
continuity of individual identity. The progression of Lucius the
man to Lucius the ass and finally to Lucius the priest of Isis hints
at the cultic origins of the everyday life chronotope. It is clearly a
rite of passage, which Bakhtin insists has its origins in the unme-
diated, oral tradition of folklore. Its pattern resembles that pointed
out by anthropologists such as Van Gennep and Victor Turner,
who showed the importance of the middle or betwixt-and-between
stage called "liminality" which in a rite of passage separates the
initial state of identity from the identity achieved at the conclusion
of the rite. This cultic aspect of the chronotope is present in
Christian hagiography as well, where metamorphosis is encountered as conversion experience.[12]

The time aspect of this chronotope is thus characterized by a
sudden change that leaves its trace in the further life of the individual. It is a time of biographical crisis, threshold moments. The
corresponding space of this chronotope is characterized by the fu-

sion of "the course of an individual's life (at its major turning points) with his actual progress through space or his road—i.e., with his wanderings. Thus is realized the metaphor 'the path of life' . . . An individual's movement through space . . . loses that abstract and technical character it had in the Greek romance, where it was merely a mannered enchaining of coordinates both spatial (near/far) and temporal (at the same time/at different times). Space becomes more concrete and saturated with a time that is more substantial."[13]

This new concreteness makes possible the incorporation of everyday life into literature. The road of the hero's life passes through the valleys as well as over the heights of experience. In the case of Apuleius, Lucius is a beast of burden in the very depths of common life—living among muleteers, working for a miller, serving gardeners, soldiers, and a host of shrewish or lascivious wives.

The transformation of Lucius has significance for the subsequent history of character portrayal. The guilt-redemption cycle makes possible the complete personal identity. The transformation in Lucius is also important for the development of another formal feature, point of view. The positioning of Lucius as an animal, a creature who intelligently observes those he watches while they pay him no heed, implies a whole new philosophy, the philosophy of the third person in private life. The third person is intensely interested in private life but has no place in it. This is a variation on Bakhtin's concept of extralocality, for the third person sees everything in sharp focus, as a whole, in all its nakedness. He plays out the roles but fuses his identity with none of them.

Although the *Satyricon* offers no redemptive pattern, it belongs to this chronotope. In fact, it provides an even closer fusion of adventure and everyday time than does *The Golden Ass*. Scenes such as Trimalchio's feast bring out the socially heterogeneous elements of the time. They also provide some sort of temporal whole that encompasses and unifies the separate periods of everyday life.[14]

The third major chronotope from ancient times is "biographical time." It is the most complex chronotope, of which there are a number of different forms. Although in classical times there were no biographical novels as such, these autobiographical and biographical forms had a profound effect not only on the development of later European biography but on the European novel as a whole.

Bakhtin identifies two basic types of biographical time. The first, "Platonic time," is the life course of one who seeks true knowledge. It is close to folkloric sources insofar as the subject's passage from one stage of development to the next is charted as an actual road. Space is symbolic, and features such as height and length are indicators not only of distance but also of conceptual difficulty and progress toward the truth. Such texts usually contain something like a conversion experience, as in Plato's *The Apology,* where the words of the oracle form a turning point in Socrates' life and are thus related to ancient Greek cults and Christian hagiography. The other basic type of biographical time is "family time," which is found in rhetorical or autobiographical works that are derived from the public lament, such as *trenos* or *encomium.*[15] In Roman times this kind of biographical time was also found in histories of clans and families.

The distinctive feature of works informed by these two major types of biographical time is the presentation of the protagonist and point of view as entirely exterior, and the course of the life in question as entirely determined by events. The identity of the protagonist, even in the case of Socrates, is overwhelmingly public. In consequence, there is no difference between the approaches that the narrator takes to his own life or to the life of another, between the biographical and autobiographical points of view. Thus the most characteristic space for this chronotope is the agora, the public square in Athens where important issues were decided and reputations were made, defended, or destroyed.[16]

An utter exteriority determines all aspects of works defined by the biographical chronotope. When, for instance, Plato conceives of thought as a conversation that people carry on with themselves, the self that he has in mind is not a private, inner *pour-moi.* Rather, such "conversation turns into conversation with someone else, without a hint of any boundaries between the two."[17]

This marked exteriority characterizes two other forms of ancient biographical time, "energetic time" and "analytical time," both of which are heavily influenced by Aristotle's concept of entelechy. Energetic time is based on the Aristotelian idea of *energia.* Plutarch is the master of this biographical model, which assumes that identity is a function of action: "energy" manifests itself as the unfolding of character in deeds. People have no inner essence independent of what they do, and historical reality is nothing more than "an arena for the disclosing and unfolding of human character."[18] Character itself is conceived as an unchanging essence that time merely fills in: at birth character is imperfectly known; only at death, as the sum of its achievements, is it fully revealed. There is no becoming, only fulfillment.

Analytical time tends to organize a life according to nontemporal schemata. The analytical biography chops up the narrative progression of a life and slots the pieces into pigeon holes with rubrics such as family life, conduct in war, physical appearance, and memorable sayings. Once again, the character is from the first a whole, and everything coming later falls into preexisting categories. The major representative of this type of biography is Suetonius, whose influence on narrowly biographical genres, especially during the Middle Ages, was enormous.

Bakhtin traces the development of yet three more variations on the biographical chronotope, all of which are more open to the expression of self-consciousness and a unique individuality. The first of these, the "satirical-ironic time," is found in satirical or parodic forms of ancient biography, above all in Propertius and Ovid, where personal topics, lacking a vocabulary for their expression, begin to emerge in irony. The second variation, "epistolary time," emerged in the rise of the personal letter as a genre, as in the messages of Cicero to Atticus, where a new tone of intimacy becomes the norm. This tone is so pervasive that even the physical setting is changed from something dramatic or idyllic, as in earlier variants, to a "landscape" in the sense that nature is presented only in terms of what a single person can see and is treated as an environment for a completely private, singular individual who does not interact with it.[19]

The third and most important new variant on the biographical chronotope is "Stoic autobiographical time." It is exemplified in Cicero, Marcus Aurelius, and *The Confessions* of Saint Augustine. In such works, as opposed to Platonic conversation, there are solitary talks with oneself that cannot, without damage to the integrity of the discourse, be immediately translated into dialogue with others. These works give the first inklings of the authentically solitary individual who first makes an appearance in the

Middle Ages. They are also the necessary harbingers for that complex self which is the subject of full-fledged novels in the modern period. Bakhtin does not specify the distinctive features of the modern novel as such, but he sets up a pattern that remains in force through the nineteenth and twentieth centuries with only minor changes in emphasis.

In the 1973 conclusion to the chronotope essay Bakhtin provides two new and influential time/space nodes. One of these is the castle in Gothic fiction, where the complex time relations present in the struggle of different generations can be seen spatially in the different kinds of architecture, furnishings, and portraits. The other node is the salon of Balzac, where political intrigues, financial deals, and erotic maneuverings turn into markers for the whole epoch, which thereby becomes not only "graphically visible" in space but also "narratively visible" in time.[20]

The chronotope emerges as the crucial factor determining what the genre is. Bakhtin ignores the usual generic divisions, such as epic, lyric, and drama, and proposes instead one master division within all genres, between "epic" and "novel." In "Epic and Novel," the last and least complex of his four essays on novel theory, he relates the fundamental distinction between these two master genres to two different ways of incorporating time into language structures, each presuming a different image of mankind. The time of epic is not chronological; it is rather a world of beginnings and peak times in the national history, a world of firsts and bests. Epics are not simply set in a time that has receded, for epic time is best perceived as a value. What was in the past is automatically considered to be better, bigger, stronger, or more beautiful. In epic, someone is speaking about a past that is to him inaccessible, and he adopts the reverent point of view of a descendant. In its style, tone, and manner of expression, epic discourse is far removed from the discourse of a contemporary addressed to other contemporaries. Even though both its singer and its implied listener are located in the same time and value system, the represented world stands on an utterly different and inaccessible time and value plane, separated by epic distance. It is impossible to change, to rethink, or to reevaluate anything in epic time, for it is finished, conclusive, and immutable. It exists in a world without relativity or any gradual, purely temporal progressions that might connect it with the present where people constantly rethink, change, and reevaluate.[21]

Many of the features that Bakhtin ascribes to the epic have been noted by others. The theorist who comes closest to Bakhtin's analysis is Lukacs, though he draws diametrically opposed conclusions. Whereas Lukacs mourns the death of the epic and the rise of the novel, Bakhtin, who sees epic tendencies as still living in non-novelistic genres, takes delight in their erosion in the novel. Epic tendencies are also still found in texts that aspire to monologue, because this tendency essentially determined the history of high literature until at least the nineteenth century. What holds for the epic thus holds more or less for the rest of literature as well. The hierarchy of times ascribed to epic, epic past versus the living present, permeated the high genres of antiquity, which in their turn so permeated the foundation of subsequent literature that the epic sensibility continued to live in them up to the nineteenth century and even further.[22]

In ancient times, attempts were made to render life in the present in literary texts. But these treatments of the present were always consigned to the low places in the hierarchy of genres, such as comedy and satire, or else they went unrecorded in the oral traditions of the folk, while the idealization of the past in high genres had something of an official air.[23] Thus Bakhtin characterizes the epic as a genre cut off from the present, a textual museum of antiquated speech, and a simulacrum of official values. He does so not only to contrast it with the novel but also to pinpoint the features that set off all other genres from the novel. Each non-novelistic form in its own way perpetuates the epic chronotope.

Bakhtin's account of the chronotope and literary evolution is bound up with his analysis of the different ways people use and perceive language, which for him are related to the different stages in literary evolution. Though he explores this relationship in all his essays of the period, it is especially prominent in the chronotope essay and "From the Prehistory of Novelistic Discourse." In both these essays he argues that the history of the novel is ineluctably tied to another history whose movements precede and enable it. This other history is the changing attitudes that people have demonstrated toward their own language. At times they were unconscious of the cutoff between the order of things and the order of the signs that nominate those things.

In such a period in Homeric Greece the great triad of genres that has determined European literary history first came into being. Epic, lyric, and tragedy spring from a world of direct words. It is a world in which poets are convinced that they can create in their own language, a language "that is perceived as the sole and fully adequate tool for realizing the word's direct, objectivized meaning. This meaning is inseparable from the straightforward language of the person who creates it. Likewise, objects and themes are born and grow to maturity in this language, as well as in the national myths and traditions."[24]

The myth of a single language, the Greek idea about the unitary nature of language, is based on two assumptions. First, it assumes that one's own language is the only complete, "real" language. The Greeks knew that there were many other national languages in the world, but they made a distinction between their own tongue and all other languages. Those other languages were all the same insofar as they were barbarian, or inferior to Greek. Second, the myth of monoglossia assumes that one's own language is homogeneous, one, free from the play of differences among the various discourses, patois, and dialects which in fact are the constituent features of any national language. The first assumption is deaf to polyglossia, or interlanguage differences; the second refuses to hear heteroglossia, or intralanguage differences.

The dual assumptions behind a mythic unified language were gradually eroded both by the power of laughter and the interaction with other national languages, each of which assumed its own unity and uniqueness. Laughter, through the instrument of satire and parody, called the sanctity of the unified language into question. And as contact with other languages became more common and sustained, the illusion of the absolute privilege of any single language was worn away. The role of polyglossia in this slow death of the myth of a unitary language was enormous: "Where languages and cultures interanimated each other, language became something entirely different, its very nature changed: in place of a simple . . . sealed off Ptolemaic world of language, there appeared the open Galilean world of many languages, mutually animating each other."[25]

Even in the Homeric age there were tremors of otherness, a dawning suspicion that there is no direct connection between word and meaning. Each serious form was accompanied by a parodying twin, "a laughing double." Tragedy was presented in units of four plays: a trilogy of tragic dramas followed by an obligatory fourth drama that was always a ribald farce. Even epic had its comic alter ego in such works as *The War Between the Mice and the Frogs* or *The Margites*. These parodies were parasites on the genres they mocked, constituting not a full-fledged, independent form in their own right but a "special extra- or intergeneric world." Yet this world was unified by a common purpose: "to provide the corrective of laughter and criticism to all existing straightforward genres, languages, styles, voices; to force men to experience beneath these categories a different and contradictory reality that is otherwise not captured in them."[26]

These parodying forms lacked the power to coalesce into a genre of their own, although they prepared the ground for the later appearance of the supergenre of the novel. At this point their major achievement was not the creation of new ways to conceptualize the world, which would have been a positive contribution. Rather, their role was negative, iconoclastic, taboo destroying: "They liberated the object from the power of the language in which it had become entangled, as in a net; they destroyed the homogenizing power of myth over language; they freed consciousness from the power of the direct word, destroyed the thick walls that had imprisoned conciousness in its own discourse, within its own language."[27]

Bakhtin proposes ancient Rome as the first time and place in European literary tradition when a full-fledged consciousness of the relativity of language was first experienced. Roman authors were never permitted the monologic luxury of their Greek precursors to assume that their words were actually their own words. Latin was always perceived against a Greek background, and in southern Italy, where Oscan was still very much alive, not only a bi- but a trilingual environment reigned. With the spread of the Roman empire, which was "merely the concluding phase of Hellenism," the Latin sense of other-languagedness "infected" the monologic barbarian tongues of its subject peoples.[28]

At this time a sense of the differences between specific languages first made itself felt with so much urgency that it created a whole new attitude toward the activity of language itself. This polyglot condition was accompanied by a new sense of the difference between the various discursive strata within a national language, the condition that Bakhtin calls "heteroglossia." This term is most fully explored in "Discourse in the Novel," where he looks at language as the heart of any culture and focuses on the nature of the utterance, conceived as the place where struggles between centrifugal and centripetal forces are fought out in miniature. An utterance takes shape in an environment of dialogized heteroglossia. The utterance articulates extrapersonal forces. But at the same time, it is concrete: as the expression of particular persons in nonrecurring situations, it is always filled with specific content.[29]

The utterance, understood in this way, serves Bakhtin as a touchstone for separating individual authors, schools, genres, and even the worlds of poetry and prose. All these can be categorized according to which side they support in the struggle in language between centripetal and centrifugal forces. For instance, Dostoevsky emphasizes variety, Tolstoy unity; Romanticism favors experiment and fragment, Classicism normative rules and whole texts; the novel is a vehicle that uses heteroglossia for its effect, the sonnet strives to focus and unify meaning; prose is in general decentralizing, poetry pursues the ideal of oneness. Having set up these categories and demonstrated a bias in favor of the first, unruly element in each pair, Bakhtin shows how they work within the history of a single genre, where at a less abstract level distinctions between forces supporting one or the other side of the struggle in language become subtler and less clear-cut. The novel is the great instrument for exploiting and simultaneously strengthening heteroglossia.

Bakhtin does not define the history of the novel as a mere expression of heteroglossia. In his system that definition pertains to the ideal novel, the expression of novelness. He rather sees the history of the novel as a long contest between two stylistic lines of development. Bakhtin himself never names these two lines, but they might be called the "monoglot" (meaning a single language as distinct from "monologic," a single voice) and the "heteroglot." The monoglot line of development not only preceded the heteroglot but also has had a much longer history and contains by far the largest number of examples. Initially, monoglot novels were typified by such ancient Sophistic forms as the Greek romance, but the line continued through the chivalric romance to all genres that privilege respectable language, such as the idyll, the pastoral, the Baroque *Prüfungsroman,* and the eighteenth century novel of sentimental pathos. All these forms presume heteroglossia as a background and interact dialogically with various aspects of this heteroglossia. Even the abstract, idealizing quality of this stylization "involves a sideways glance at others' languages, at other points of view and other conceptual systems, each with its own set of objects and meanings." This stylistic line knows only a single language and single style, which is more or less rigidly consistent: "heteroglossia remains outside this novel, although it has an effect on the novel as a dialogizing background in which the language and the world of the novel are polemically and forensically implicated."[30]

The characteristic tactic for ordering flux is to impose a unitary, "literary" language throughout a work. Like a discursive Midas, everything the monoglot novel touches, no matter how base in itself, is ennobled and turned to gold. There are a lot of slaves and pirates in Sophistic novels, many peasants in the chivalric romance, many rough soldiers in Baroque and sentimental novels—but they all speak in the dignified accents of a stylized literary language.

The heteroglot novel developed much later. Like the monoglot novel, it knows that the world and the language it speaks are profoundly heteroglot. But instead of seeking to conceal the fact in an apparently monoglot style, it revels in variety and conflict. It constitutes itself out of the very stratification of discourse that the monoglot novel wishes to cover over.

The heteroglot novel uses as one of its primary techniques for displaying this heterogeneity an attack on literary and other monologizing, "refined" languages. Rabelais and Cervantes are the classic examples. But the heteroglot novel's impulse to dramatize and intensify heteroglossia is not limited to parodies of the reigning literary language and the respectable genres which it inhabits. This novel shows the partiality and poverty of all discourses of pathos. It is skeptical of all languages that assume they are the only voice of truth, a claim to exclusive privilege that Bakhtin calls the "lie of pathos." The heteroglot novel opposes to this lie the "joyful deception" of another kind of lie, "a gay and intelligent deception, a *lie* justified because it is directed precisely to *liars*. Opposed to the language of priests and monks, kings and seigneurs, knights and wealthy urban types, scholars and priests—to the languages of all who hold power and are well set up in life—there is the language of the merry rogue, wherever necessary parodically reprocessing any pathos, always in such a way as to rob it of its power to harm, to 'distance it from the mouth,' as it were, by means of a smile of deception, mock its falsity, and thus turn what was a lie into joyful deception."[31]

The heteroglot line of novels includes the texts that are the most authentic exemplars of novelness. In these works the novel finds its fullest range of voices. The development of the heteroglot novel runs from Rabelais in the sixteenth century to the picaresques of the seventeenth century and through virtually all the great novels of the modern period, including many Bakhtin does not list, such as Joyce and Proust.

The rise of this kind of novel gives a radically new tone to discourse about human beings. In picaresque novels a fresh image of humanity begins to emerge, but in the sixteenth century this new concept of personality is still groping for a discourse of its own. Such texts as *Lazarillo de Tormes* prepare the way for the great exemplars of the heteroglot line, such as *Don Quixote,* in which "the novelistic genre realizes its fullest potential."[32]

The two lines, monoglot and heteroglot, come together and merge at the beginning of the nineteenth century. Although the major representatives of the novel are from that point on mixed, features of the heteroglot line tend to dominate. Because the heteroglot novel is more open to difference, it could more easily absorb the increasing tide of self-consciousness. In other words, the heteroglot novel was able to accommodate more of the self because it is more sensitive to otherness.

Bakhtin's views on the history of changing attitudes toward language have much in common with the controversial idea of such American linguists as Edward Sapir and B. L. Whorf that the shape of a culture system is determined by the "shape" of that culture's language. There is no such thing as an objective, unchanging world, unencumbered by the integrative layers with which language sediments it. In Sapir's formulation, "the 'real world' is to a large extent built up on the language habits of the group . . . The world in which different societies live are distinct worlds, not merely the same world with different labels attached . . . We see and hear and otherwise experience very largely as we do because the language habits of our community dictate certain choices of interpretation."[33] Thus, different societies carve up reality differently, and the most sensitive indicator of the coordinates that give shape to any culture's world picture is to be found in the characteristic arrangements of time and space in the texts that each society nominates as art.

The novel is a particularly sensitive indicator of society's deeply held assumptions about the nature of space and time precisely because it, as opposed to other literary and nonliterary genres, is conscious of the relativity of its own architectonic prejudices. There is no "language of the novel," because it can assimilate all languages, including those characteristic of other genres. Other genres do change, even though they court stasis and are drawn to formal features, such as meter and rhyme, that permit the maximum possible degree of repetition. No matter how strenuously they resist otherness, the monologic purity of their defining discourses is "infected" by the heteroglot world out of which they spring. Moreover, as literary texts, they show change more rapidly and comprehensively than other kinds of texts, such as codes of laws or religious doxies. But among literary texts, the novel, as the genre which is constituted by openness to change and which seeks variety, indicates shifts in the coordinates governing perception more precisely and comprehensively than all other art forms. All these factors make the novel Bakhtin's preferred means for dramatizing his ideas about language, social theory, and the history of perception. For Bakhtin, the novel is the great book of life.

CHAPTER 14

Rabelais and His World

It would be difficult to imagine two figures more different from each other than Rabelais and Bakhtin. The one is an epic poet of sheer physicality, whose name conjures up mountains of sausages and oceans of wine. Rabelais sings the joys of endless food and the delights of tireless sex. A familiar at the court of the quintessential Renaissance prince, Francis I, he was close to the centers of power during an age that has become synonymous with cultural achievement. Bakhtin would appear in all these respects to be the polar opposite: an ascetic scholar who spent most of his time sipping tea while working at his desk, citizen of a dark time and a place notorious for its cold and hunger. The precise period during which he wrote about Rabelais was not one of humanist experiment, but of socialist realist canonization, an era best metaphorized not in its carnivals and public squares but in its purges and prison camps. Instead of being at the center of power, Bakhtin was its victim, cast away as an exile in the remote reaches of his vast country. A sufferer from chronic bone disease with its searing fevers and an amputee, he seems hardly comparable to Rabelais, who was not a patient but a doctor and also celebrator of the human body.

Yet Rabelais belongs with Goethe, Dostoevsky, and Dante as one of the four most significant figures in Bakhtin's private pantheon, and *Rabelais and His World*, a study of *Gargantua* and *Pantagruel,* is one of Bakhtin's most important works, which quickly became a classic of Renaissance studies. Although the confrontation between the French novelist and his Russian critic might easily be dismissed as the attraction of opposites, even more significant are the similarities between the two. They resemble each other in their breadth of knowledge, their stylistic tic of long catalogues, their love of jokes, and their deep tolerance. Each was born with a gift for laughter and a sense of the world as slightly mad. But more important than their personal affinities is the distinctive way in which each through his writing inscribed himself into his times. The early Renaissance and the Russian Revolution were threshold ages, border situations on the map of history. Each created in the inhabitants of its moment an urgent awareness of radical change. Each was a rip in the fabric of time. As such, those who lived in these periods were willy-nilly thrown into the work of history. The commonest man was denied the luxury of believing that he could be a passive spectator in history's theater, able to sit back and watch the kings and prophets who enacted the drama. Each age was, to use Bakhtin's expression, a "theater without footlights."

This breakdown of the border between stage and gallery, between actors and audience, in their respective ages is a key to the obsessive concern in the work of both writers for the breakdown of borders of all kinds. Each is fascinated by unusual combinations, mixings, the interpenetration of elements regarded at other times or by less heterodox contemporaries as mutually exclusive. Rabelais' work is infamous for its breaches of "good taste," its weird confluence of learned allusion and scatological detail, the willful intermingling of medical, technological, and highbrow, self-consciously literary vocabularies with the crudest billingsgate. Such discourses rarely rub shoulders with each other in periods less scandalous than the 1530s of Rabelais or the 1930s of Bakhtin. This feature of Rabelais' work is the one that most excites Bakhtin and that he, of all Rabelais' readers, understands best.

Bakhtin grasps so well the meaning of Rabelais' readiness to mingle discourses because of the parallels between their two periods. Bakhtin, like Rabelais, knew he was living in an age such as the world has rarely experienced. Unlike Dickens in the opening of *A Tale of Two Cities,* Bakhtin did not feel that all historical epochs are essentially the same. There are periods, such as his own, when generations are presented with unusual dangers and unique opportunities. He responded so deeply to the Renaissance because it was an age similar to his own in revolutionary consequences and in the acute sense it engendered of one world's death and another world's birth. Such ages, whatever the consequences for those who live through them, create particularly favorable conditions for study of the relativity of cultural systems, of the holes in the discursive walls erected by cultures to order their religions, laws, and genres.

In these ages the concept of text is both problematicized and expanded—problematicized because the usual idea of the text as a closed, hermetic structure that is always adequate to itself is brought into question. In Rabelais' age medical or military manuals "leaked" the styles and topics that were regarded as proper to these texts into other texts, such as literary ones, where the specialized languages clashed with each other. In Bakhtin's age, newspapers blended into novels and novels into political pamphlets. Problematicized in this way, the texts in these ages overflowed the bounds of what had been conceived in more settled times to be the proper textual limits. Moreover, the idea of text was no longer limited to written documents once the old ways of interpreting events had broken down and new strategies for reading the world had become necessary.

This pathos of the open text accounts for Rabelais' experiments with unusual discursive, not merely lexical, combinations. *Gargantua* is a happy Frankenstein's laboratory, and Rabelais is a madcap scientist stitching together catalogues of body parts and functions that subsequent generations of scholars would call monstrous. Critics have rarely shared Rabelais' almost malicious joy in demonstrating the incompleteness and corresponding plenitude of texts. This is why Bakhtin declares in *Rabelais and His World* that, of all the great writers of world literature in the four hundred years since *Gargantua* appeared, "Rabelais is the least popular, the least understood and appreciated."[1]

Bakhtin claims that after all these centuries of incomprehension his own book finally explains Rabelais' book. Bakhtin feels justified in making this extravagant advertisement for the intertextuality of the two books because they are both born out of a similar uniqueness. Each springs from an age of revolution, and each enacts a particularly open sense of the text. Bakhtin can hear Rabelais' laughter because he knows how to read Rabelais' book, and he demonstrates this capability in the act of writing his own book.

Bakhtin's *Rabelais* might well have had as its subtitle the title of one of Bakhtin's later essays, "The Problem of the Text." The book is not only about the openness of Rabelais' novel but is itself an example of that kind of text. In Book IV of *Gargantua,* Master Villon wishes to organize a passion play that will involve a good deal of devilry. All that is needed is a costume for God the Father. The local sacristan, shocked by what Villon intends, refuses to lend any church vestments for the occasion. Villon takes revenge by staging a dress rehearsal just as the sacristan rides by; the players create enough commotion to frighten the horse of the churchman, who is dragged along the ground until only a stump of his foot is left in the right stirrup. Bakhtin makes of this tale a metaphor for what Rabelais himself is doing throughout his novel. Just as Villon through his diablerie makes fun of and seeks to destroy the agelasts, those who hate laughter and are the serious forces of stasis and official ideology, so does Rabelais through his *Gargantua:* "In his novel, and by means of his novel, Rabelais behaves exactly as did Villon . . . he acts according to Villon's methods. He uses the popular festive system of images with its charter of freedom consecrated by many centuries; and he uses them to inflict severe punishment on his foe, the Gothic age . . . In this setting of consecrated rights, Rabelais attacks the fundamental dogmas and sacraments, the holy of holies of medieval ideology."[2]

This passage is one of the loopholes that Bakhtin always leaves open in his own work. In describing Rabelais' strategy, he reveals his own. The relation of Rabelais to Villon mirrors the relation of Bakhtin himself to Rabelais. Bakhtin has written a book about another book that constantly plays with the categories and transgresses the limits set by the forces of official ideology. Like Rabelais, Bakhtin throughout this book is exploring the interface between a stasis imposed from above and a desire for change from below, between old and new, official and unofficial. In treating the specific ways in which Rabelais sought to find gaps in the walls between what was punishable and what was unpunishable in the 1530s, Bakhtin is looking for similar loopholes at those borders in the 1930s. His examination of Rabelaisian license is a dialogic meditation on freedom.

Bakhtin, who is so self-conscious of his own text's status as text, also employs textology as its basic strategy. Bakhtin knows that there is much left unsaid in his own text, and thus his major key for opening up *Gargantua* is to seek the unsaid in Rabelais' text. This approach assumes that a text is recognizable as such, an entity with distinct borders, because it is a manifestation of a system. A legal text is codified by the legal system, a literary text by the literary. The systems that texts manifest may also be thought of as ideologies. Ideology in this sense is locatable in all that texts take for granted, the preconditions held to be so certain by their authors that they need not be stated. The pillars supporting a text's assumptive world are thus invisible insofar as they need not be expressed. Ideology must be seen in a text's holes, in what it has felt it could leave unuttered. Insofar as ideology is the stuff out of which a culture manufactures its greatest certainties, ideology is always extremely conservative in its effect. Great effort is required even to see it, since so much of its function is to ensure that it never becomes an issue independent of the material it organizes. As Bakhtin notes, "Every age has its own norms of official speech and propriety. And every age has its own type of words and expressions that are given as a signal to speak freely, to call things by their own names, without any mental restrictions and euphemisms . . . All peoples . . . have enormous spheres of speech that have not been made public and are nonexistent from the point of view of literary, written language."[3] The history of Rabelais scholarship is the tale of how successive generations of experts have suppressed those aspects of Rabelais which they considered, in light of their own prejudices, to be improper or unliterary.

Thus, when Bakhtin seeks to hear what is unsaid in *Gargantua,* he does two things. First, he literally recovers those portions of Rabelais' texts that, insofar as they were ignored or repressed in previous ages, have gone "unsaid." Second, he charts the parameters of the Renaissance social system which enabled a more balanced ratio of permitted versus unpermitted language than has since then obtained. Bakhtin treats the spheres of permitted and unpermitted language as texts in their own right, each with its own characteristic gaps and holes. He identifies two subtexts: carnival, which is a social institution, and grotesque realism, which is a literary mode. *Rabelais and His World* is a study of how the social and the literary interact. In addition, it is a study of the semantics of the body, the different meanings of the body's limbs, apertures, and functions.

Bakhtin approaches the general division between official and unofficial as a particular distinction between high and low cultures, a distinction that can be charted in the attitude of each level of culture toward laughter: "A boundless world of humorous

forms . . . opposed the official and serious tone of medieval and ecclesiastical and feudal culture."[4] Three such humorous forms are
open-air spectacles, such as were shown on market days or celebrated during carnivals; parodies, especially of church ritual; and
various genres of billingsgate, curses, and oaths. The most important of these forms by far, and the one that most clearly reveals the
underlying meaning of them all, is carnival.

Although carnival has become impoverished in modern
times, as both an event and a concept, it played a central role in
the life of all classes in the Renaissance, when cities devoted as
much as three months a year to such festivals. The importance of
carnival, however, lay not in the great chunks of time given over to
it but rather in the unique sense of the world it embodied. First of
all, carnival was one of the few areas that the hegemony of the
Roman Catholic Church did not reach. Carnivals are ritually devoid of mysticism and piety. They are without prayer or magic:
"They do not command nor do they ask for anything . . . All these
forms are systematically placed outside the church and religiosity.
They belong to a completely different sphere." Not only do such
forms fail to belong to official religiosity, but they also fail to follow
the rules of official aesthetic norms: "The basic carnival nucleus
of this culture is a purely artistic form . . . and does not, generally
speaking, even belong to the sphere of art at all . . . In reality, it is
life itself . . . shaped according to a certain pattern of play."[5]

Unlike ritual, carnival is not organized by a separate caste of
specialists who create it according to their exclusive dictates,
whether religious or aesthetic. Everybody makes carnival, everyone is carnival: "Carnival is not a spectacle seen by the people;
they live in it, and everyone participates because its very idea em-
braces all the people." Carnival extends a kind of general hegemony not only over everyone but also everywhere: "While carnival
lasts, there is no other life outside it. During carnival time life is
subject only to its laws . . . the laws of its own freedom."[6] Carnival
is a minimally ritualized antiritual, a festive celebration of the
other, the gaps and holes in all the mappings of the world laid out
in systematic theologies, legal codes, normative poetics, and class
hierarchies.

Carnival must not be confused with mere holiday play. The
ability to revel in the world's variety, to celebrate its openness and
its ever-renewed capacity to surprise, is a "special form of life

(*osobaja žiznennaja forma*)," a kind of existential heteroglossia.[7] Carnival is a gap in the fabric of society. And since the dominant ideology seeks to author the social order as a unified text, fixed, complete, and forever, carnival is a threat.

The festive laughter engendered by carnival keeps alive a sense of variety and change. Such laughter has an intimate connection to changing seasons, "to the phases of sun and moon, to the death and renewal of vegetation, and to the succession of agricultural seasons. In this succession all that is new or renews . . . is emphasized as a positive element expressing the people's hopes of a happier future." Such an emphasis on change and becoming is directly opposed to the official emphasis on the past, to a stasis so complete that it becomes eternity. Through carnival, the folk are "freed from the oppression of such gloomy categories as 'eternal,' 'immovable,' 'absolute,' 'unchangeable,' and instead are exposed to the gay and free laughing aspect of the world, with its unfinished and open character, with the joy of change and renewal."[8]

With its crowds and abundance of food, the feast is a carnivalesque form insofar as it is a "temporary transfer to the utopian world." Like other forms of carnival, the feast is an "island" in the sea of history. It is not just a consuming of enormous quantities of food, a mere physical excess. It is rather "a primary indestructible ingredient of human civilization; it may become sterile and even degenerate, but it cannot vanish," because it is "a liberation from all that is utilitarian, practical."[9]

Bakhtin traces the phenomenological significance of food back to its primitive roots, the joy of primitive men at the conclusion of the hunt: "Man's awakening consciousness could not but concentrate on this moment, could not help borrowing from it a number of . . . images determining the feast's relation to the world. Man's encounter with the world in the act of eating is joyful, triumphant; he triumphs over the world, devours it without being devoured himself."[10]

Like other aspects of carnival, the feast is a victory over fear. As in carnival dramas in the late medieval marketplace, which concluded with the burning of the scenery depicting "hell," the feast celebrates the destruction of what was formerly threatening. Here is the key to the relation of food to work: the struggle of people against a hostile nature is crowned with food, whether at the end of the hunt or at the conclusion of the harvest. People "swal-

low that which they have defeated." A special pathos characterizes the frequently hungry Bakhtin's statement that "no meal can
be sad." But banquets are especially festive. At their core is always
the celebration of life over death: "The victorious body receives
the defeated world and is renewed." Bakhtin hypothesizes that
the origins of language itself may lie in the sharing of food as a
primal expression of culture over nature, establishing a connection between digestion and dialogue: "Even for authors of the an-
tique symposium, for Plato, Xenophon, Plutarch, Athenaeus,
Macrobius, and others, the link between eating and speaking was
not an obsolete remnant of the past but had a living meaning."[11]

The sharing of food is an extremely important aspect of the
feast. In general, all features of carnival serve to bring people
together in a communality. Just as the feast is not merely another meal, the carnivalesque throng is not merely another crowd:
"It is the people as a whole, but organized *in their own way* . . . it
is outside of all socioeconomic and political organization, which is
suspended for the time of the festivity." This heightened sense of
collectivity is made possible by the unique sense of time and space
that reigns in carnival: "The unofficial folk culture of the Middle
Ages and even of the Renaissance had its own territory and its
own particular time." Just as the space and time of the official
world enforce restraints, the coordinates of the carnival world
conduce to freedom and fearlessness: "The individual feels he is
an indissoluble part of the collectivity, a member of the people's
mass body. In this whole the individual body ceases to a certain
extent to be itself; it is possible, so to say, to exchange bodies, to be
renewed (through changing costume and mask). At the same
time the people become aware of their sensual, material, bodily
unity and community."[12]

Bakhtin here connects carnival with two key elements in his
scheme, time and the body. The kind of time peculiar to carnival is
the release from time, a respite from the relatively closed and rigid
historical patterns that dominant ideologies impose on time's flux.
But this freedom cannot be understood merely as playing hooky
from the norms of noncarnivalized life at any particular point in
history. The physical experience of carnival expresses not just a
negative escapism but has a positive aspect as well. Carnival is not
time wasted but time filled with profound and rich experience.
The unity experienced by the folk in carnival has a specifically his-

torical character: "The body of the people on a market square during carnival is first of all aware of its unity in time." The festive crowd is not merely experiencing a mindless plunge into unconscious license, a kind of nothing. On the contrary, it is highly aware, extremely conscious of something unique to it: "It is conscious of its uninterrupted continuity in time, of its relative historic immortality . . . the people do not perceive a static image of their unity (*eine Gestalt*) but instead the uninterrupted continuity of their becoming and the ceaseless metamorphoses of death and renewal."[13]

In this experience a specific carnivalesque time is connected with a specific carnivalesque body. This fusion is symbolized in the Roman terra-cotta figurines found at Kerch depicting ancient hags, their faces contorted by laughter, their stomachs swollen in pregnancy: "It is pregnant death, a death that gives birth . . . Life is shown in its twofold contradictory process: it is the epitome of incompleteness."[14]

If the body is to tell this distinctive kind of timeless time, it must be conceived as a special kind of clock. Bakhtin's covering term for the vision of the body that emphasizes changes in its nature through eating, evacuation, or sex, as opposed to the static ideal represented in classical Greek marbles, is "grotesque." The grotesque body is flesh as the site of becoming. As such, the key elements of the body are precisely those points at which it "outgrows its own self, transgresses its own limits . . . conceives a new, second body, the bowels and the phallus . . . Next to the bowels and the genital organs is the mouth through which enters the world to be swallowed up . . . All these convexities and orifices have a common characteristic; it is with them that the borders between one's own and other bodies and between the body and the world are breached . . . the grotesque image ignores the closed, smooth, and impenetrable surface of the body and retains only its excrescences (sprouts, buds) and orifices, only that which leads beyond the body's limited space or into the body's depths."[15]

This image of the body is related to carnival time, which is free and becoming, because it shares the carnival's set toward space as something free, unconfined, constantly overcoming limits. Once again, the pregnant old hags of the Kerch ornaments capture this striving to break through borders typical of the grotesque body. Plant, animal, and human forms are fancifully interwoven in them, "as if giving birth to each other. The borderlines that divide the kingdoms of nature in the visual picture of the world were boldly infringed. Neither was there the usual static representation of reality. There was no longer the movement of finished forms, vegetable or animal, in a finished and stable world; instead the inner movement of being itself was expressed in the passing of one form into the other, in the ever incompleted character of being."[16] Just as the carnival enacts the intertextuality of ideologies, official and unofficial, so the grotesque body foregrounds the intertextuality of nature. The grotesque is intertextually perceived at the level of biology. Bakhtin's concern with rampantly physical aspects of the body dates back to his interest in *corpus Christi,* the actual body of the living man Jesus, and to his interest in the science of physiology.

Carnival and the grotesque both have the effect of plunging certainty into ambivalence and uncertainty, as a result of their emphasis on contradictions and the relativity of all classificatory systems. This is why the mask is so important to both forms. The medieval feast, like the ancient carnival, has two faces. The mask of carnival is the aspect of Janus: "Its official, ecclesiastical face was turned to the past and sanctioned the existing order, but the face of the people of the marketplace looked to the future and laughed, conscious it was attending the funeral of the past and present." The mask, which is "the most complex theme of folk culture . . . is connected with the joy of change and reincarnation, with joyful relativity and the happy negation of uniformity and similarity; it rejects conformity to one's own self. The mask is related to transition, metamorphoses, the violation of natural boundaries."[17] The mask is the very image of ambiguity, the variety and flux of identities that otherwise, unmasked, are conceived as single and fixed.

Ambiguity allows Bakhtin to chart the relation between bodily expression and speech expression. Carnival has not only its own space and time but also its own language practices. Carnival language appears in medieval dialogues, such as *Cyprian's Supper,* and in the parodies of the fifteenth and sixteenth centuries where "the images of banqueting liberate speech." These parodies often relate to the Last Supper: "The grotesque symposium travesties and debases the purely idealistic, mystic, and ascetic victory over the world, the victory of the abstract." But such travesty is not merely a destructive satire and not exclusively an attack on spiritual things. A narrowly focused satire, intended to injure a specific target, is not part of the culture of laughter. A travesty is carnivalesque precisely in its duality and ambiguity: it parodies the spirit in order to praise the body. Free play with the sacred is the basic content of the grotesque symposium of the Middle Ages. In this playing with the most rigid ideological categories, unofficial elements begin to seep into language: The power of food and drink to liberate human speech can be seen in the manner in which "the schoolmen and clerics' talks were invaded by a wide range of 'colloquial' parodies and travesties of sacred texts related to defecation and foods." This is the essence of Rabelais' novel, and thus the reason that it was violently opposed by Calvin and other contemporary churchmen, who related the atheistic and materialistic trends of their time directly to the banquet atmosphere which they characterized as "prandial libertinism."[18]

The extraliterary significance of Bakhtin's *Rabelais* extends beyond the banquet table or public square in carnival. When a work written in the Soviet Union in the late 1930s and early 1940s makes so much of freedom and the unofficial/official distinction, it cannot fail to be in part a comment on its times. Although these concepts were previously invoked by Bakhtin, in *Rabelais* they are given their most powerful airing. The book thus marks a distinct shift in Bakhtin's writing. It is more passionately argued, more visionary, and more obviously ideological. Although on the surface it is less Russocentric than his earlier writings, it represents Bakhtin's most comprehensive critique to date of Stalinist culture, that singular system which had just reached its height in the purges of 1936–1938.

Rabelais must be seen in the context of its times. In the original dissertation on which *Rabelais* is based Bakhtin, who peppered his earlier texts with references to Russian writers such as Pushkin, Lermontov, Dostoevsky, and Tolstoy, makes little mention of Russia or Russian writers. But this near absence of Russia in the text makes it all the more present as a referent. Indeed, the most cryptic of Bakhtin's rare references to things Russian are Aesopean hints of the political dimension of the work.

At only five places in the text does Bakhtin mention Russia. Two of these passages are not particularly significant. One is a review of Rabelais scholarship in Russia to date, the sort of thing that was a standard exercise in all Bakhtin's longer writings and was required as well by Soviet dissertation conventions. The other is an analysis of the Rabelaisian aspects of Gogol, which is the weakest part of the text and gave Bakhtin particular trouble in trying to get his dissertation passed. This section was cut out of the published book in 1965 but was later included as a separate item in the 1975 collection of his essays.

The three shorter references to things Russian all refer to rulers. The first passage, also not included in the 1965 book, invokes Lenin's metaphor for revolution, a woman in labor. The second passage, slipped into the middle of the book, commends Peter the Great and Ivan the Terrible as czars who "carnivalized Russia," although Peter's effort was the lesser of the two because he introduced Western rather than native rituals.[19] This reference seems to be a gesture toward official thinking, since both Peter and Ivan were used in 1930s rhetoric as symbols for the model ruler whom Stalin was purported to represent, and by the time Bakhtin began his dissertation, Ivan had superseded Peter as the chief model. Yet the reference is also ambiguous, as Bakhtin would have it anyway, because the very names of these czars are synonymous with autocratic rule and repression.

This passage about Peter and Ivan draws attention to itself by being introduced as a non sequitur, and Bakhtin's final reference to things Russian, which concludes the book, likewise draws attention to itself by the abrupt manner of its presentation. This reference includes a well-known quotation from Pushkin's *Boris Godunov,* although neither the author nor the title is identified in the text: "In every historical epoch there has always been a square filled with the laughter of the folk, the very same as appeared before the pretender in a nightmare: 'Below the people swarmed on the square / And laughingly pointed at me; / I felt ashamed and was filled with fear.' " The fact that the "pretender" is the false Dmitri becomes clear only indirectly, through the introduction of the quotation, from which Bakhtin also omits the crucial but equally well-known line, "The people fell silent." Bakhtin then ends the book with the remark that every historical act has been accompanied by the laughter of the chorus, but that not in every epoch has the chorus been able to find a coryphaeus like Rabelais.

The reference to a "pretender" may be a hint at Stalin's worthiness to lead Russia, and the remark about the lack of a coryphaeus may be a reproach of contemporary writers for their cowardice. Yet overall this work cannot be reduced to the status of a mere political tract *à clef.* Although Bakhtin doubtless intends both of these cryptic references to Russian rulers to suggest the fact of Stalin's authoritarian rule, he usually criticizes his times from a higher, more general plane.

Rabelais presents, *inter alia,* a critique of contemporary Soviet ideology. It offers a counterideology to the values and practices that dominated public life in the 1930s. This counterideology is itself a particular and somewhat singular articulation of ideas commonly found among the intelligentsia of the 1920s, primarily among the avant-garde and Bakhtin's friends. Bakhtin presents his counterideology not through a frontal attack on Stalinism but rather through a dialogue with it.

By 1935 Stalinism, the ideology to which Bakhtin's text addresses itself, had become crystallized. It entailed not just the hierarchization and centralization of all Soviet institutions and the increase of state control and repression, but also the very distinctive ethos and cultural myths that accompanied these trends. Stalinist rhetoric singled out entire groups of "remarkable people," such as Stakhanovites, aviation heroes, and mountain climbers, as official harbingers of a revolution in human anthropology soon to affect every Soviet person. These "new men" were said to be superior to all previous heroes. They represented a new order of humanity, unlike the old Ivans, and strikingly like their role models in the Stalinist leadership.

These superheroes functioned as mythic figures justifying the de facto division within society between the powerful and privileged, on the one hand, and the masses, on the other. Representing categories outside the power structure as they did, they presaged the day when the masses themselves would attain such an exalted status. The division that they celebrated between the elect and the nonelect was only one instance of the fundamental division in Stalinist ontology between the ordinary and the extraordinary, the mythic, the great.

Corresponding to this dualism were two orders of time and two orders of place. The two times formed a pattern analogous to that of sacred and profane time, the "sacred" time of Stalinism being associated with the life of a Soviet leader or a significant moment of Bolshevik history, and the "profane" time being identified with a mundane, unmarked historical event.[20] Similarly, the "sacred" places of Stalinism were those illumined by the presence of leaders, such as the Kremlin, while the rest of Soviet space was as yet merely "profane." Thus, the rhetoric of Stalinism established a vertical ordering of reality, which was simplified to a binary contrast between everything ordinary and "low," on the one hand, and, on the other, everything different, extraordinary, and "high." Stalinist epistemology was a crude form of Neo-Platonism in which only the elect, specifically the leaders, had access to the higher order of reality.[21]

Bakhtin's response to Stalinism is organized around the dichotomy common to all his earlier writings, the distinction between official culture and the culture of the folk. In the case of Rabelais' world, the official culture was that of the Roman Catholic Church and the Holy Roman Empire, while the folk culture was that of the lower orders in the carnival and marketplace. The function of folk culture is not just to debunk authority figures and received notions, as a healthy antidote to the dullness and dryness of official culture. Folk humor amounts to considerably more than mere playful irreverence, for the folk assume willy-nilly the role of a bulwark against repression. The peculiarity of carnival laughter is its "indissoluble and essential relation to freedom." The serious element in class culture and the "monolithic seriousness of the Christian cult and world view" go hand in hand with fear and repression, while "power, repression and authority never speak in the language of laughter."[22]

The give and take between the medieval church-and-state nexus, on the one hand, and the carnival, on the other, was a real power struggle. The state had its own temporal and spatial borders, and so did the carnival. These two ideological countries were in conflict. Carnival laughter "builds its own world in opposition to the official world, its own church versus the official church, its own state versus the official state."[23]

Bakhtin's critique of Stalinism does not stop at its repressiveness but tackles its fundamental epistemological principle, the vertical ordering of all reality. In the Middle Ages, the dominant, high culture was invested in church teachings and involved a "vertical world" of absolute values.[24] There was a fixed hierarchy of social and political status, as of moral and philosophical value. The church wanted to organize everything, to fill conceptual

space completely. But the carnival ethos undermined this epistemological megalomania. It undermined or debunked absolute
ideas and introduced instead a spirit of "joyful relativity," a phrase
found in all Bakhtin's works of this period.

The two principal weapons used in this onslaught by carnival
were "reverse hierarchy," which is a humbling, debunking, or de-
basing of whatever is lofty by the lowly, as when beggars insulted
kings or lay brothers mocked the manners of the abbot of a monastery, and the lowering of all forms of expression in language or
art.[25] Attempts were made by Stalinists to coopt these carnival
techniques of inversion for their own purposes. In the Stakhanovite movement, for instance, workers on the lowest level were elevated to the highest status in society. A. Stakhanov, after whom
this movement was named, provided an irresistible metaphor, a
miner who was brought up from the depths to become a Hero of
the Soviet Union. The Stakhanovites were generally unskilled or
semiskilled workers and nonparty members who were singled out
for their spectacular achievement in overfulfilling production
norms, although their feats were mostly choreographed and
staged by local party officials. At public rituals celebrating these
workers' successes, their superiors in the local government hierarchy, as opposed to the party hierarchy, were humiliated, or
lowered, by being brought to task for hindering the workers' efforts.

Although under Stalin the various ceremonials associated
with the ritual elevation of the inferior included standard pieces
debunking authority figures and were thus comparable to the reverse hierarchy that Bakhtin identifies as a basic element in carnival, the impulses in carnival and in Stalinism were diametrically
opposed. The function of carnival was to provide a general lowering and democratization of language or classes, whereby the august air of official ceremonial would be undermined. In contrast,
the function of Stalinist ritual was to affirm and strengthen the
status quo and hierarchical structure. The Stakhanovite workers'
superiors were chided in order to assert the power of *their* superiors, the Soviet leadership itself. In other words, there was a general elevation, even if only tokenly and symbolically, rather than a
lowering of tone, language, and individuals.

In the customs of other societies, such as the children dressing up as monsters to frighten the adults at Halloween, reverse hi-

erarchy serves as a sort of safety valve whereby the inferior are elevated above their superiors temporally and ritually as a way of securing the status quo and making it possible for hierarchy to prevail over the potentially anarchic lower orders. Bakhtin, however, postulates the carnival spirit and carnival world as models for a superior world order that is organized horizontally rather than vertically.[26] In the carnival, he contends, all are considered equal and brotherhood is universal. Moreover, the carnival spirit is fundamentally opposed to all hierarchies in epistemology, all canons and dogmas, for in carnival everything is constantly moving and changing. Its essential qualities are incompleteness, becoming, and ambiguity.

The question raised by Bakhtin's carnival, with its emphasis on brotherhood, universalism, and antidogmatism, is whether such a horizontally ordered world can be maintained for any length of time without introducing some kind of hierarchy, be it epistemological or political. There is, in other words, a strong element of idealization, even utopian visionariness, in Bakhtin's analysis of carnival. This is particularly apparent in his characterization of the folk. At this very time the official platform, both literary and political, was assigning the folk a major role in its own scheme of things. For instance, Gorky in 1934 urged writers to model their heroes on folklore. With official encouragement, folklore was collected and published in great quantity. Folk bards were set to writing epic songs and ditties glorifying the new age, its leaders, and their "struggles." The folk assumed a larger role in political rhetoric and ceremony. The leadership slotted folk proverbs into speeches, folk bands and dance groups became a standard feature at official ceremonies, and selected individuals from the folk, such as the Stakhanovites, were singled out for public acclaim.

Bakhtin decries the narrow conception of the folk prevailing at his time, which excludes the culture of laughter and the marketplace with all its subversiveness, blasphemy, and blatant physicality. The result of this exclusion is a prettified, emasculated version of the folk, with no bite. But while opposing one idealized conception of the folk, Bakhtin's own counterimage is no less idealized, dripping with urine and feces though it be. Like other intellectuals such as Blok and the Scythians, Bakhtin consistently idealizes the folk as an untamable, rebellious, and regenerative force that will destroy the status quo, but from the ashes will rise newer and finer worlds. For instance, the folk are held to be instinctively anti-absolutist, pro-universalist, and anti-war. They are even the repository of "the second truth about the world." Amid the hurly-burly of political life, Bakhtin maintains, only the folk are able to maintain their healthy stance of joyful relativity.[27]

Bakhtin attacks yet another unacknowledged idealism that had crept into Stalinism, the underlying assumption of all official rhetoric that there is a higher order of reality to which ordinary citizens do not have access. This assumption is expressed, for instance, in the main slogan of the decade, "Higher! (*Vyše!*)." Bakhtin stresses the value of whatever is this-worldly and praises the folk for their function of debunking and unmasking pretensions of representing something more august and elevated. Whereas Bakhtin earlier manifested his antimetaphysical bias in such ways as opposing the Vosslerian notion of an inner source for the word, he now gives the bias a new twist by emphasizing that least metaphysical and most unethereal of all carnival's aspects, the body and its functions.

A primary element in carnival, Bakhtin maintains, is the "free intermingling of bodies," the unabashed display of bodily functions, including defecation, copulation, and even labor and birth, and the free interplay between the body and the outside world, in such acts as the ingestion and expulsion of food. Official culture regards such bodily functions as unseemly and tries to deny the body its wonderful orifices and protrusions, to put a stop to the joyous celebration of the body and life. It would have the body reduced instead to an "unresponsive surface, a flat plane (*gluxaja poverxnost', ravnina*)."[28]

Bakhtin's refusal to homogenize the surface of the body or to deny its lust to mingle with other bodies is more than a defiant stand against the prevailing idealism of his day or a sally against the puritanism of Stalinist society. The body is a common metaphor for the state, and xenophobic societies which are trying to control the behavior of their citizens and keep them from outside contacts often stress the idea of keeping the body pure. It certainly was stressed under Stalin, as in that Soviet institution of the "purge." Mary Douglas has described the general dynamic of this idea: "if a man recognizes a very strong allegiance to a social group . . . then the group is likened to the human body: the orifices are to be carefully guarded to prevent unlawful intrusions, dangers from poisoning or loss of physical strength . . . inside becomes good and outside evil." According to Bakhtin, the carnival tries to overcome this sort of thing through its celebration of the bodily.[29]

Bakhtin's delight in Rabelais' celebration of bodily processes is an affront as well to the principles and practices of socialist realism. In 1932–1934, when the guidelines for socialist realism were being formulated, official spokesmen cautioned writers against the literary practice of showing sex and the bodily functions, which was euphemistically called "naturalism" or "zoologism." In consequence, explicit sex relations were virtually taboo in Stalinist novels. Bakhtin prudently tries to cover himself against charges of "zoologism" by claiming that Rabelais' particular use of the bodily is something higher than "crude materialism or physiologism."[30] Bakhtin's reaction against the Soviet emphasis on transcending the physical body is consistent with his former rejection of Pauline ideas about the need to cast off physicality as expressed by theologians such as Florensky or the followers of Saint Seraphim of Sarov.

Bakhtin's stress on the body is far from his only affront to socialist realism in *Rabelais*. He goes far beyond his previous attacks by positing a countervailing ideal, which he calls "grotesque realism." To Bakhtin, the grotesque is the expression in literature of the carnival spirit. It incorporates what for him are the primary values: incompleteness, becoming, ambiguity, indefinability, noncanonicalism—indeed, all that jolts us out of our normal expectations and epistemological complacency.

Thus, in a time of increasing regimentation, Bakhtin wrote of freedom. In a time of authoritarianism, dogmatism, and official heroes, he wrote of the masses as ebullient, variegated, and irreverent. At a time when literature was composed of mandated canons, he wrote of smashing all norms and canons and ridiculed the pundits who upheld them.[31] At a time when everyone was told to look "higher" and to deny the body and its dictates, he extolled the virtues of the everyday and advocated reveling in the basic functions of what he called the "lower bodily stratum."

Bakhtin made all these points palatable by an adroit use of Aesopean language and allegory in the Russian intellectual tradition. He exploited the device of ambiguity that he himself admired in others, especially in Rabelais. He was also canny enough to draft his thesis in the form of an amplification of views already expressed by such relatively authoritative voices as Gorky and Lunacharsky. He made several points that they had made and adopted some of their terminology, though disagreeing with their conclusions in fundamental respects.

The references to Gorky could not have gone amiss with the doctoral committee, since the dissertation was presented in the Gorky Institute of World Literature and Gorky was still the official founding father of socialist realism. In 1934 Gorky had cited Gargantua and Pantagruel as examples of the influence of "oral folk literature" on written literature, an influence that he wanted to see more of in socialist realism. Moreover, he found exemplified in Gargantua and Pantagruel the sort of folk tradition where the lower orders "have acquired the courage to ridicule their masters."[32] But these remarks by Gorky were not intended to be taken much further than the context of class antagonism and certainly not to the general stance of Bakhtin against all received authorities.

At the same time that Gorky was making his claims for the folk, Lunacharsky, the former Commissar of Education, set up a Commission for the Study of Satiric Genres and himself planned to write a book entitled "The Social Role of Laughter." In January 1931 he spoke to the Academy of Sciences on the importance to the history of satire of the old institution of the carnival which allowed "free raillery." This speech was not published until 1935, when a version of it appeared in the leading theoretical journal, *Literary Critic*. Bakhtin presumably read the article at about that time, which could account for the appearance of the word "carnival" in his own work. Bakhtin and Lunacharsky account similarly for what happens in carnival but explain its basic dynamic in diametrically opposed ways. Whereas Bakhtin maintains that in carnival the lower orders deal a blow to the epistemological megalomania of the official culture, Lunacharsky concludes that institutions like the carnival are merely "safety valves" which the ruling classes use as a way of allowing the lower orders to let off steam in a harmless, temporary event.[33]

Rabelais typifies the sort of thing Bakhtin also did elsewhere, as in *Marxism and the Philosophy of Language*. He coopts the ideas and rhetoric of his age and uses them to his own ends. Moreover, he coopts only those elements that can in some way be made to approximate his own views; *Rabelais* is no capitulation. According to Bakhtin, the novel is that genre which executes its own intention by bending the discourses of other ideologies. *Rabelais* is a scholarly variant on this appropriation of other discourses for one's own purposes.

Bakhtin, for instance, uses a striking number of catch phrases of Stalinism, such as "the people are immortal," "the progressive movement forward," and "the new and better future," which might seem a lapse on the part of someone who decried the standardization of language. But the contexts in which these catch phrases are used suggest meanings other than those they ordinarily represent. "The people are immortal," for instance, is invoked in one place to validate Bakhtin's notion that the "people" are always growing and developing into something new, and in another place to describe an idea of human immortality like that formulated by Nikolai Fyodorov, an eccentric thinker whose ideas about the ethical imperative of sons to band together in order to raise their fathers physically from the grave influenced the late Dostoevsky. In other cases Bakhtin introduces Bolshevik catch phrases only to reveal the simplistic assumptions behind them.[34]

When Bakhtin coopts the actual official ideas of his time, the levels of meaning are even more multiple. For example, he isolates three political villains that at the time of Rabelais were threatening the cultural climate and which Rabelais, armed with folk humor, vanquished. The first villain is the bourgeoisie, who in the best Marxist-Leninist tradition are described as fostering "isolationism," "elitism" (*kamernost'*), "atomization," and "alienation." Bakhtin, who places great value on the intermingling of voices from all possible levels of discourse, shares the Marxist-Leninist distrust for bourgeois culture as thus described, but he also extends his attack on the bourgeoisie to include qualities not normally ascribed to them in Marxist-Leninist writings and very much present in Stalinism, namely antagonism toward imagination and fantasy in literature and overattachment to dreary common sense and practicality.[35]

The second villain among the nexus of political forces in sixteenth century France is the Holy Roman Empire. Bakhtin takes pains to point out that Rabelais sided with the "progressive" nationalist movements, such as those headed by the French kings who struggled against the hegemony of the Holy Roman Empire. This can be read as a commentary on Stalin's attempts to stifle nationalist movements in the Soviet sphere.[36]

The third and major villain is the Roman Catholic Church, which Bakhtin argues is the enemy of all that Rabelais espoused. Bakhtin's representation of the church's role in Rabelais' achievement serves four different intentions simultaneously. First, to illustrate his general theses about folk humor and the development of the novel, Bakhtin describes the actual phenomenon of anticlerical humor in the carnival and allied folk institutions which sought to undermine the church's claim of universal authority. Second, he intones standard pieces from official Soviet ideology about the church's oppression of the lower classes and its "dry scholasticism," "mysticism," cult of the priests, and "obscurantism." Indeed, a chief butt of folk humor is precisely these qualities of the church. Third, he uses the church, the self-proclaimed "sole possessor of truth," to stand for the party in his attacks against all claims to the possession of an absolute truth and against all sources of monologism. Finally, he expresses a view of the Roman Catholic Church that has long been popular among the Russian intelligentsia. In Dostoevsky, for instance, the church stands for dry scholasticism, authoritarianism, and inquisition. The Bolsheviks were in fact able to draw on a rich local tradition in formulating their own attacks on Roman Catholicism. In the circles in which Bakhtin once moved, both the Roman Church and the Orthodox Church were felt by many to represent a travesty of true spirituality because of their dogmatism, obtuseness, and power mongering. For instance, Blok distinguished between a "true clergy" and that "caste of morally obtuse people who claim the title priest."[37] Thus, Bakhtin's anticlerical remarks should not be regarded entirely as Aesopean language but should be taken in part at face value.

Although there is undoubtedly an element of political allegory in *Rabelais*, the work cannot be written off as an anti-Bolshevik or anti-Stalinist tract. Nor can it be reduced to a mere commentary on Bakhtin's times. Bakhtin suggests as much himself when describing Rabelais' own use of political allegory. It was customary in Rabelais' day to identify characters in a book with contemporary political figures. But, Bakhtin argues, in Rabelais each image is greater than its political allusions. As a result, "It would be vain to look for a definite . . . key to every image."[38] What comes through most forcefully in *Rabelais* is in fact not the negative aspect of Bakhtin's dialogue with his times, but rather the positive. Bakhtin does not so much attack Stalinism as advance his own vision of the kingdom of "joyful relativity."

Bakhtin describes Rabelais as a "deeply revolutionary spirit." This remark is not a cynical manipulation of Bolshevik rhetoric on Bakhtin's part, for he shared with other leading nonparty intellectuals of his day the Bolshevik enthusiasm for revolution, though he understood it in a different, more idealized, and more idiosyncratic sense. This group of intellectuals included several of Bakhtin's friends in the Symbolist movement or the Religious-Philosophical Society. They welcomed the Revolution and sought some sort of permanent revolution in society or culture as well, although nothing like the sort of permanent political revolution advocated by people like Trotsky. For instance, many of them, including Bakhtin, opposed violence and bloodshed. They looked rather to the end of bourgeois society with its hypocritical morality, its conventionality, its fuddy-duddy cultural and intellectual establishment, its love of material comfort, and its complacency.

Ultimately, however, they reacted not so much against the bourgeoisie per se as against any kind of intellectual or moral stasis, fixity, and neatly ordered "logical" systems. Their concept of revolution was a dramatic thrust for perpetual renewal, for confounding canons, for randomness and diversity. One of them, Evgeny Zamyatin, a shipbuilding engineer, utopian, and the author of *We*, used the scientific metaphor of energy and entropy in his definition of revolution: "Revolution is everywhere, in everything. It is infinite. There is no final revolution, no final number . . . It is a cosmic, universal law, like the laws of conservation of energy and of the dissipation of energy (entropy) . . . When the flaming, seething sphere (in science, religion, social life, art) cools, the fiery magma becomes coated with dogma—a rigid, ossified, motionless crust. Dogmatization in science, religion, social life, or art is the entropy of thought. What has become dogma no longer burns; it only gives off warmth—it is tepid, it is cool."[39]

Bakhtin uses metaphors from language and literature rather than from the natural sciences to express his own sense of revolution. Instead of Zamyatin's "There is . . . no final number," Bakhtin observes, "There is no last word." He speaks of "the *renewal* of old objects by a new use or new and unexpected juxtapositions," of the importance of destroying the old images of things and looking at them anew, and of the need to get "a new sense of all old words, things and concepts . . . by freeing them temporarily of all semantic links, and freely recreating them." Bakhtin singles out this characteristic in the various genres of carnival humor, as in the lengthy exchanges of elaborate insults or the obscene versions of solemn church ritual. He identifies such genres as alogical celebrations in which words are released "from the shackles of sense in order to enjoy a period of play and complete freedom and to establish unusual relationships among themselves."[40]

Another paradox in Bakhtin is the contradiction between his desire for new forms and experimentation in theory and his conservative aesthetic tastes in practice. Though Bakhtin expresses ideas close to those of the avant-garde and though he preaches verbal and compositional innovation, at no point does he either appreciate or advocate the sort of avant-garde writing being produced all around him. Moreover, his favorite authors—Goethe, Dostoevsky, Dante, Rabelais—are all conventional choices, typical of the highly educated in Russia at this time.

One of the many enigmas about Bakhtin is that he makes no mention in *Rabelais* of James Joyce's *Ulysses,* a book that might be described as a celebration of heteroglossia and of the body as well. This is especially surprising since Joyce was known to several of Bakhtin's associates. Pumpiansky was at work on a book on Joyce in 1932, and V.O. Stenich, who was close to members of the Bakhtin circle in Leningrad and was depicted in Vaginov's *The Satyr's Song,* translated Joyce. Once again, Bakhtin's choosing not to include Joyce could have been motivated politically. As of at least the First Writers' Congress in 1934, *Ulysses* could no longer be praised in print, and this was still true in 1965 when the dissertation was published as a book.[41] Thus, Bakhtin effectively had two choices as regards Joyce, to attack him or not to mention him.

Rabelais is important to Bakhtin not because Rabelais adopts linguistic innovations per se but because he turns away from the stultified and artificial language of the official culture of his day and makes extensive use of the more vital, variegated, and changeable kinds of language to be found in carnival. Bakhtin admires Rabelais primarily for the number of new words he press-gangs from the strictly oral areas of society, like the marketplace and the tradesman's patois, and brings into the French literary language for the first time. With Calvin, ironically, Rabelais was the founder of the modern French language. Rabelais puts these new words into contiguity with old words that had become sclerotic through continued use by the law, the court, the church. He creates a relativity of languages. And as Bakhtin remarks in *Marxism and the Philosophy of Language*, "Languages are philosophies—not abstract but concrete social philosophies, penetrated by a system of values inseparable from living practice and class struggle.[42]

In creating a relativity of speech practices, Rabelais relativizes world views, all of which seek hegemony and claim unique privilege. He carnivalizes language itself and, in so doing, "discrowns" the authority that official ideologies seek to claim for themselves within the isolation of their own characteristic discourses: "In the world of carnival . . . established authority and truth are relative." For this reason, Rabelais' importance lies not in his own particular ideology but in his awareness of the limits, the incompleteness, of any ideology. No matter how serious Rabelais appears to be at any point in a text, he makes sure to leave a gap, to provide what Bakhtin calls a "merry loophole—a loophole that opens on the distant future and that lends an aspect of ridicule to the present or to the immediate future. Rabelais never exhausts his resources in direct statements."[43]

Rabelais lived at a special moment in the history of language. The official versus unofficial struggle could then be seen with particular clarity because the conflict between the two forces "was drawn along the line dividing Latin from the vernacular which invaded all spheres of ideology and expelled Latin." The battle was in fact a three-way struggle, since the vernacular was opposed not by one but by two versions of Latin: the spoken *lingua franca* of medieval Europe and the Latin of the schoolmen which was closer to ancient classical norms. Macaronic poems were written that brought these languages together: "In this process of mutual clarification, an exceptional self-awareness was developed by living reality, that is, by all that was new and had not existed formerly: new objects, new concepts, new points of view."[44]

Bakhtin's sensitivity to this breakdown of old languages and birth of new languages is underwritten by his own experience of the same "pregnant death of the past" in his age. The generation that lived on both sides of 1917 saw a particularly violent discrowning of one authority system and the accession of another with a completely opposed ideology. This political event was marked by enormous changes in the language as well. The distinctive patois of the formerly suppressed Bolsheviks now became the discourse of authority, as "comrade" replaced "mister" or "madame" as a term of polite address. The very orthography was changed, so that one could actually see the difference, when the frequently used old diacritical mark indicating the "hard" pronunciation of consonants fell away in the new Bolshevik alphabet. The years immediately following the Revolution constituted a linguistic as well as political "theater without footlights," in that "The boundaries between periods and between philosophies were acutely realized. The flow of time could never have been so sharply and clearly felt within the confines of a single, gradually evolving language system."[45]

Rabelais is important not only because he lets Bakhtin speak about language evolution and the interrelation between the literary language and the vernacular, but also because he permits Bakhtin to return once again to the major topic of his career, the dialogic nature of language and its relation to the dialogic nature of the world. The parodical litanies which play so important a role in *Gargantua* epitomize the distinctive features of carnival language. Insofar as they both praise and abuse simultaneously, they speak to the "dual-bodied world of becoming." The borders that separate the different strata of discourse outside the carnival world are broken down: "The more unofficial and familiar the speech, the more often and substantially are those tones combined, the less distinct is the line dividing praise and abuse. Indeed, the two coincide in one person or object as representing the world of becoming. The hard, official dividing lines between objects, phenomena, and values begin to fade. There is an awakening of the ancient ambivalence of all words and expressions, combining the wish of life and death, of sowing and rebirth. The unofficial aspect of the world of becoming and of the grotesque body is disclosed."[46]

Rabelais is the last expression of a complete harmony between the popular, carnivalesque impulse and its possible expression in literature: "The grotesque tradition peculiar to the marketplace and the academic literary tradition have parted ways and can no longer be brought together . . . The link with the essential aspects of being, with the organic system of popular festive images has been broken. Obscenity has become narrowly sexual, isolated, individual, and has no place in the new official system of philosophy and imagery." The sense of the body that is celebrated in carnival is now restricted, too: "Anything that protrudes, bulges, sprouts, or branches off . . . is eliminated, hidden, moderated." This restricted sense of the body is accompanied by restraints on speech: "The verbal forms of official and literary language, determined by the canon, prohibit all that is linked with fecundation, pregnancy, childbirth. There is a sharp dividing line between familiar speech and 'correct' language."[47]

For Bakhtin, then, Rabelais participates not only in political history, which has a relatively high velocity of change, but also in the history of language, which has a much slower rate of change. The intersection between these two velocities in *Gargantua* marks Rabelais' ultimate importance. He is significant not for his opposition to any particular political force. He has a key place in the history of freedom rather because he uses language in a way that can always be recouped as a weapon in the struggle against tyrannical ideologies.

CHAPTER 15

Saransk to Moscow
1945-1975

The Second World War, which wrought so much destruction in Russia, was at the personal level a setback in Bakhtin's career. On the eve of the war he had seemed about to find a place for himself in mainstream Soviet intellectual life. His book on the novel of education was about to be brought out by the publisher Soviet Writer (Sovetskij pisatel'), and he had submitted his Rabelais dissertation to the Gorky Institute, which was asking him to give lectures there. But when the war came, both the publication of the book and the defense of the dissertation were put off, and Bakhtin's contacts with the Gorky Institute petered out as scholars were drafted or evacuated from the capital. Worse still, the building which housed the Soviet Writer archive was bombed, and Bakhtin's manuscript was destroyed. This might not have been such a tragedy except for the fact that during the war years, when paper was scarce, the insouciant Bakhtin used most of his own copy of the manuscript as tobacco paper.

Although the war meant the end of any thought of a career in the capital, it was not a total disaster for Bakhtin, as it was for so many others in the Soviet Union. Probably his wartime teaching helped compensate for his political record, for immediately after the war he was able to return to Saransk and resume his old position at the Pedagogical Institute. Soon he was even promoted, for on July 6, 1945, he was appointed chairman of the Department of General Literature, and on September 18 he was raised to the rank of docent.

In 1945 conditions in Saransk were primitive even by provincial standards, as they would remain throughout the period of postwar reconstruction. The town was very poorly supplied with food; not even sausage was available. Heavy investment was put into the further industrialization of the town, however, and new factories were built for manufacturing light bulbs, cable, and machine tools and for overhauling equipment.[1]

The town had an acute shortage of accommodations, and the only place that could be found to house Bakhtin was a disused jail. Even this jail was in such a bad state of repair that it was considered unfit for use, but Bakhtin, who had a soft spot for rogues, not only moved in but made friends with a thief who lived in the basement. As a former jail, the building was constructed with long corridors and rooms along either side. The Bakhtins' room was divided into two sections. The first part was his wife's territory where all the domestic matters were attended to. One had to pass through this section in order to reach Bakhtin's domain, which was dominated by his large desk.[2]

Despite his politically dubious past, Bakhtin was popular with the authorities in the town, who did all they could to help him. For instance, it was hard for him to get about on his one leg. The authorities decided to provide him with transportation, and since there was a shortage of vehicles, they at first sent a horse to take him to lectures. Later, when the city's postwar transportation problem eased, they sent a chauffeured car. In October 1947 the Supreme Soviet of Mordovia also awarded Bakhtin a certificate of commendation for long service, although he had actually worked only the two previous years and the year of 1936–1937. This fact was overlooked in order to give him the benefit of the certificate, which entitled him to a larger pension.

In Saransk Bakhtin turned again to his dissertation "Rabelais in the History of Realism." In 1946 the wheels were set in motion for its examination, and a defense date was set for November 15. The timing proved unfortunate, for before the defense could take place, the party passed measures signaling an end to the relative cultural liberalism of the war years. On August 14 the Central Committee issued a directive criticizing the journals *Zvezda* and *Leningrad* for printing works deemed unacceptable in Soviet literature. The chief party spokesman on ideological questions, A. A. Zhdanov, also called for stricter adherence to the socialist realist canon in literature and warned against works that were too critical of "Soviet reality." Thus was born a new dark age of Soviet culture, which became known as the Zhdanov period. In addition, Zhdanov sounded an end to the idolization of folk forms in literature and criticism and condemned works that made Soviet people and Soviet reality seem "primitive": "The time has come to raise the level of sophistication in literature. The reading public is better educated and simply will not tolerate poor or simplistic literature." Taking their cue from these remarks, critics came out in strength and with alacrity to declare the excessive veneration of folk forms "misconceived."[3] Thus, one of the major strategies used by Bakhtin in his dissertation and elsewhere to advance his philosophy of freedom in a politically acceptable way, by identifying his theory with the notion of Gorky and other authorities that folk forms and folk humor had played a major role in the evolution of literature, was no longer viable.

The postwar years were also the high point of the Cold War. Within the Soviet Union national chauvinist sentiment colored official rhetoric, and most things foreign or Western were looked at askance. A so-called anticosmopolitan campaign was launched, which was partly a disguised form of anti-Semitism but also manifested such rabid anti-Westernism that those working in literary theory or criticism found it hard to write about Western literature or even to cite Western authorities. Thus the topic of Rabelais was converted from a common one for those interested in literary theory, as it had been when Bakhtin wrote his dissertation at the end of the 1930s, to a politically tricky subject. The problem was compounded by the fact that in the Zhdanov era Soviet society became even more puritanical than it had been in the 1930s. Special legislation was passed making divorce more difficult to obtain and stressing the responsibility of all parents to be procreators and educators of the new socialist generation. Schools were even segregated by sex. This trend made the subject of Rabelais' *Gargantua,* with its explicit eroticism, an area to be avoided.

Because of these circumstances, Bakhtin's defense of his thesis turned into an epic event. First to speak were his three examiners, A. A. Smirnov and I. M. Nusinov, both doctors of philology, and A. K. Dzhivelogov, a doctor of fine arts. They not only praised the dissertation but also recommended that it be considered for a doctor's degree, even though it had only been submitted for a candidate's (the doctor's degree is roughly equivalent to a D.Litt. in the West, the candidate's to a Ph.D.). Moreover, when the thesis was thrown open for discussion, several people supported Bakhtin from the floor. However, Bakhtin encountered vehement

opposition on ideological grounds, particularly from N. K. Pik-
sanov, an expert on Russian classics and Gorky, N. L. Brodsky, a
scholar of the nineteenth century, and V. Ja. Kirpotin, an old party
member who as head of the Literary Section of the Central Committee from 1932 to 1936 had played a central role in the institution-
alization and formulation of socialist realism. All three scholars
had been zealous in uncovering the ideological content of literary
works, and they found the Rabelais dissertation objectionable for
its blasphemy and scorn of dogma. Their criticisms obliged the
official examiners to argue for the dissertation a second time,
after which a stormy discussion continued for seven hours. In
closing, Bakhtin gave his own spirited defense of the work. The
dissertation was passed unanimously for a candidate's degree but
was recommended for a doctorate by a vote of only seven to six.
This was so close that the decision on both degrees was turned
over to a reviewing body, the Higher Attestation Committee.[4]

The committee members resolved to hold a hearing on the
matter. On May 9, 1947, they invited Bakhtin to appear on May 21
or 28 and cited their misgivings about the dissertation, such as:
"You completely ignore the conception [of Rabelais' novel] and
its ideological side and this gives your work a formalistic character
[a term of abuse]. You concentrate almost exclusively on the so-
called folklore realism of Rabelais, on scenes and images involving
the fool, and, moreover, show a proclivity for looking at images of a
crudely physiological character ... with such an approach you
have diminished Rabelais' realistic style quite insupportably."
They objected to the way Bakhtin drew parallels between Rabelais
and Gogol, ignoring the ideological content and national significance of Gogol's work by focusing on his "images and scenes involving the fool."[5]

What took place at this defense is not known, but meanwhile
the worsening of the political climate was making a positive decision less likely. In November 1947, the article "We Must Not Lag
Behind in Working Out Current Problems in Literary Scholarship," by V. Nikolaev, appeared in the journal *Culture and Life*
(*Kul'tura i žizn'*), which marked a milestone in the anticosmopolitan campaign. The article attacked the Gorky Institute for its
lack of a "militant Bolshevik spirit" and for the "fear and cowardice" in its work. In the resulting shakeup at the institute, all the
directors, including Kirpotin, were replaced by officials from the

Cultural Section of the Central Committee, and several scholars were fired. The article also castigated the institute's Academic Council for its "irresponsible, antigovernment attitude" in reviewing recent dissertations and singled out Bakhtin's dissertation as an example, calling it "Freudian" (by then a term of abuse) and "antiscientific" with its "grotesque bodily images."[6]

After this article appeared, the Higher Attestation Committee decided to postpone consideration of Bakhtin's dissertation, and they did not make a ruling until June 1951. The committee then decided against awarding Bakhtin a doctor's degree for the dissertation, although it granted him a candidate's degree. This verdict was not made official until September 12, and Bakhtin was not actually awarded the degree until June 2, 1952. In other words, it took almost twelve years after finishing the dissertation for Bakhtin to receive the degree. Bakhtin passed off the stupidity of granting him only the lesser degree with a shrug.[7] The decision meant, however, that the Rabelais work would remain unpublished for a full twenty-five years.

The anticosmopolitan campaign had not only put Bakhtin's dissertation in jeopardy but had threatened his career as well. In the late 1940s Bakhtin was in danger of dismissal or arrest both as a former political prisoner and as a faculty member at the Pedagogical Institute who lectured primarily on Western literature, teaching courses on European literature of the classical and medieval periods, the Renaissance, and the nineteenth and twentieth centuries.[8] In this instance, however, fortune favored him. The enlightened Merkushin invited Bakhtin and his wife home on New Year's Eve of 1950 to drink champagne with him. This public gesture was interpreted as a signal, and Bakhtin was never touched.

Despite being lucky, Bakhtin remained circumspect. During his postwar years at Saransk he played the role of model Soviet departmental head. He went to teachers' conferences, kept up a correspondence with his counterparts at other provincial pedagogical institutes, and made many official speeches. In fact, he was such a superb public speaker that for years he was called on to make the graduation address for the whole university. Bakhtin tailored his speeches to the style and language required in that day. He did not think ill of those who adapted to Stalinism, and he himself tried to be diplomatic in responding to even the most extreme

Bakhtin (third row center) with his students in the second-year
world literature course at the Mordovia State University,
Saransk, late 1950s

rhetoric of the Zhdanov era. As a last resort, he would always say,
"That's very interesting." Although unworldly in other ways,
Bakhtin was attuned to political nuances. For instance, for a
speech about Stalin's Seventeenth Party Congress address he
made underlinings and marginal jottings on the Stalin text which
indicate that Bakhtin was reading between the lines. Bakhtin was
presumably circumspect in his undergraduate lectures as well,
especially since he lectured on such sensitive subjects as "Stalin
and the English Bourgeoisie" and "Marx and Engels on Byron."
But he was also able to lecture on subjects closer to his heart, such
as Dante, Shakespeare, Cervantes, and Sophocles.

Bakhtin was an enormously popular teacher. His classes attracted such a wide audience that the officially enrolled students
often found it hard to find a seat unless they went to the lecture
hall well beforehand; otherwise the hall would be packed with
students from all the other faculties of the Pedagogical Institute.
Bakhtin enhanced his lectures by dramatic renditions of poetry
delivered from memory. He recited classical Greek or Latin poetry

in the original, and although the audiences could not necessarily understand it, they were captivated by the sounds.[9] Bakhtin himself was often carried away by the pathos of the poetry. In one lecture on the composer Dargomyzhsky he got so worked up while singing old Russian folk epics that he threw away his crutches and hopped around on one leg.

Regardless of his disparaging comments about poetry as compared to prose forms, Bakhtin essentially lived with poetry. When he spoke to groups of people or to individuals, both formally and informally, he frequently broke out into a spontaneous recital of a poem that he particularly loved and which seemed apropos at that moment.[10] Russians have a remarkable capacity for memorizing great chunks of poetry, but Bakhtin's memory for verse was prodigious even by Russian standards. Nevertheless, while lecturing often on poetry and writing periodically on topics like Pushkin and the lyric, Bakhtin kept his main focus definitely on prose.

Bakhtin's lecturing in Saransk was by no means confined to the Pedagogical Institute. For years he also ran a seminar on aesthetics and the history of the theater at the Mordovia Theater for Music and Drama, as he had in Nevel and Vitebsk. In addition, he lectured to the Mordovia Writers' Union and gave hundreds of lectures to employees of various kinds in Saransk, primarily to factory workers but also to schoolteachers and civil servants.[11] Bakhtin proved enormously popular even among the workers in area foundries. He was able to pitch his lectures to any level. A series of lectures on aesthetics that he gave in the late 1950s at a light bulb factory were always packed, with as many as 700 electrical workers attending, despite the abstruseness of the subject. Bakhtin interested his audience in a subject by using an approach somewhat in the tradition of Florensky; that is, he started with an example from everyday life and moved from there to more abstract or difficult ideas. He opened one lecture, for instance, by talking of binocular vision, the reason people have two eyes instead of one, and what happens when they lose one eye. He moved from there to the fact that Pushkin's characters sometimes have crossed eyes, and then he went on to discuss the adage "The eyes are the mirror of the soul." At this point he broached his main topic: What is aesthetics? Bakhtin also gave private lessons, as he had done in Vitebsk and Leningrad.

All this lecturing and administration left Bakhtin little time for his own work. Moreover, he was extraordinarily generous in helping students with their reading and writing, which took time away from his own. Little has survived from all the years he worked in Saransk, from 1945 to 1961, although this fact alone is no guarantee that he did not write, because he was notoriously cavalier about preserving manuscripts. He may have contributed periodically to the local newspaper *Soviet Mordovia* (*Sovetskaja Mordovija*), for he is known to have published one article there in 1954 on Maria Stuart.[12] The only known work from these years is "The Problem of Speech Genres," written in 1952–1953. Bakhtin was emboldened to try to get into print again by Stalin's own article "On Linguistics," published in 1950. In this article Stalin attacked the regnant account of language put forward by Marr, which held that language is a function of the economic base and hence that there are different languages for different classes. Bakhtin agrees with Stalin that language is more a product of the base than of the superstructure, and he specifies the way the same words can be used by different classes. In order to help the article's publishability, Bakhtin also wrote a preamble to it containing a series of quotations from Stalin. But the preamble was to no avail, for the article was not then accepted for publication, and the preamble was omitted when the article was included posthumously in Bakhtin's *The Aesthetics of Verbal Creation* (1979).

Despite his heavy load of responsibilities and notwithstanding the political limitations on him, Bakhtin's position in Saransk was probably the best he had known in his adult life. Not only was he secure materially for the first time, but he also gained local recognition. He was a Saransk celebrity. The town itself was not a complete cultural desert, having acquired a theater. More important, it was sufficiently close to Moscow and Leningrad for Bakhtin to be able to get to those towns more often than he had from Kustanai. Despite his bad legs, he managed to make the trip occasionally. In 1948, for instance, he attended a jubilee evening in Moscow for the Jewish actor Mikhoels, who had been a near contemporary of his at Petrograd University but was killed shortly thereafter, presumably because of the continuing anticosmopolitan campaign. In the late 1940s Bakhtin also gave a lecture on the ballad to Yudina's students at the Gnesin Institute of Music in Moscow, and he attended a reading by Pasternak of his new translation of Faust in Yudina's home in Moscow. Bakhtin also visited Leningrad at least once, around 1951, for a reunion of what remained of the old group, including Kanaev, Nina Arkadievna Voloshinova, and Anna Sergeevna Rugevich. Various of Bakhtin's old friends were also able to visit him in Saransk. Yudina, for instance, visited him in 1951 or 1952. Since it had been a long time since Bakhtin last heard her play, she decided to give an impromptu local concert. This created problems, since there was no concert hall in the town, and no piano worthy of a concert pianist. The best piano was at the local radio station, and so she gave her concert there. Word quickly spread around the town that she was to play, and people crammed into the small studio to hear her.[13]

After Stalin's death in March 1953 and especially after Nikita Khruschev's rise to power in the mid-1950s, many of the wrongs done to intellectuals under Stalin were reversed. Thousands of political prisoners were released, and many of those who had been imprisoned or exiled were rehabilitated by having their sentences revoked and, when possible, their former rank and honors returned to them, often posthumously. Most of those who had long been forbidden to reside in the major cities of Russia were allowed to return, and many who had been blacklisted for years could finally be employed in positions more appropriate to their abilities and qualifications and could even be published.

For Bakhtin, however, the Khruschev era did not initially bring with it any redress of the years of obscurity that he had endured on the national scene, nor any promotion to a position more appropriate for a man of his achievements, such as a professorship at the Gorky Institute of World Literature in Moscow. Strictly speaking, Bakhtin could not even be rehabilitated, because he had never been formally charged. But the main reason that his position was not ameliorated was that he was insufficiently aggressive and did not actively seek redress. An aging and infirm man with one leg who resided far from Moscow could not conduct the sort of relentless campaign it would have taken to get his books republished. Bakhtin might nevertheless have achieved more if he had not been so phlegmatic and singularly lacking in ambition, as shown by his aversion to writing letters.

Bakhtin's situation improved in other ways, however, and without his efforts. On October 1, 1957, the Polezhaev Pedagogical Institute of Mordovia where he taught was elevated in status and renamed the Ogarev University of Mordovia. On March 14, 1958, Bakhtin himself was elevated to Chairman of the Department of Russian and Foreign Literature in the new university. One tangible benefit from this promotion was that he received better accommodations. For the remainder of his stay in Saransk he lived in a two-room apartment on the second floor of a prestigious building on the central square of the town. The poet of carnival delighted in being able to watch the parades from his own apartment.[14]

In this new apartment the Bakhtins lived in relative peace and comfort. In Bakhtin's study were large bookcases crammed with books. He also had a desk made specially to his order, as well as a large armchair with wooden armrests convenient for resting books or papers. Bakhtin's habit was to sit in this armchair reading or chatting with students or friends while his wife worked in the kitchen making food or one of his eternal cups of tea. Toward the end of Bakhtin's stay in Saransk he and his wife also spent one or two months every summer on vacation at a Writers' Union sanatorium near Moscow, as guests of their friends the Shakespeare scholar L. E. Pinsky and his wife. On the way home the Bakhtins would stay with Zalessky in Moscow and visit other old friends.[15]

This quiet life away from the limelight was what Bakhtin preferred. He was not personally ambitious, and he always refused in Saransk to be promoted to a full professor or to become a member of the Writers' Union. He felt that if he joined the Writers' Union, all the local writers would keep wanting to come to his apartment to drink. Some opportunities arose for him to move to positions at more central institutions, but he did not take them up. For instance, in 1958 he was invited to take a job in the Novzybkovsky Pedagogical Institute near Bryansk. This idea appealed to the Bakhtins because the institute was in the same general area as Nevel and Vitebsk, but they turned it down nevertheless. Bakhtin also corresponded with an institute near Moscow about a job, but he failed to follow through on the idea. Neither he nor his wife was in good health. His years of heavy smoking had taken their toll, and he had severe emphysema, in addition to osteomyelitis in his remaining leg, while she had heart problems. They did not want to go through all the bother of moving, so they stayed in Saransk.

Gradually, however, the world once more became aware of Bakhtin's existence. He had never actually been blacklisted, and

Bakhtin in Moscow, late 1960s

thus his Dostoevsky book had not been withdrawn. It was merely unwise politically to refer to him. In consequence, outside Saransk, he was known primarily to those few people who had been aware of his work in the 1920s. Apparently the first person to mention him in print after this long hiatus was an American, Vladimir Seduro, who in 1955 discussed Bakhtin's Dostoevsky book in a study of his own. Ironically, the first known Soviet mention of Bakhtin for more than twenty-five years was made by the former Formalist, Victor Shklovsky, who in 1957 resumed their dialogue of the 1920s by making respectful criticisms of Bakhtin's Dostoevsky book in his *Pro and Contra: Notes on Dostoevsky*. Another former Formalist, Roman Jakobson, played a major role in bringing Bakhtin back to scholarly attention when in May 1956, as a member of the International Committee of Slavists meeting in Moscow to organize an international conference, he spoke on numerous occasions not only of Bakhtin but also of Vygotsky, who was likewise all but forgotten. Jakobson also referred to Bakhtin in a review of Shklovsky's *Pro and Contra,* which was published in 1959 in the inaugural issue of the *International Journal of Slavic Linguistics and Poetics.* Jakobson took preview copies of this article with him to the International Congress of Slavists in Moscow in September 1958, where he distributed them widely. The article attracted considerable attention, since Soviet scholars were then caught up in a controversy over *Pro and Contra.* Between Shklovsky and Jakobson, Bakhtin became widely known for the first time; his Dostoevsky book had actually attracted little attention when it appeared in 1929 because he was already in exile. By the late 1950s students in senior seminars at Moscow University were discussing Bakhtin's book on Dostoevsky, which had never been mentioned in class before.[16]

The people who did most to propel Bakhtin out of obscurity and establish him as a major figure with an international reputation were not those of his own generation, however, but ambitious young literary scholars who had never heard of him until now. The young were his loophole. The most zealous among them was Vadim Valerianovich Kozhinov, who has since published widely on Russian poetry and literary theory. Kozhinov came across Bakhtin's Dostoevsky book while still a graduate student at the Gorky Institute. To his surprise, he learned that Bakhtin had actually had some association with the institute; some of the fellows there could even recall the lectures Bakhtin had given just before the Second World War. Eventually Kozhinov learned of the Rabelais dissertation in the archives of the institute, and he gained permission to have it brought out and read.

Believing that Bakhtin was dead, Kozhinov set about trying to get his books into print. In 1960, together with two fellow graduate students, Sergey Georgievich Bocharov and Georgi Dmitrievich Gachev, Kozhinov wrote to the director of the institute recommending that the Dostoevsky book be republished. There was no response. On December 20 Kozhinov again wrote to the director, suggesting that something be done about the brilliant manuscript by Bakhtin on Rabelais that was languishing in the archives of the institute. This request was rejected.

In the meantime, Kozhinov had discovered that Bakhtin was alive, and he entered into correspondence with him. On June 6,

1961, he received a letter from Bakhtin's wife urging him to visit, and soon thereafter the three friends, Kozhinov, Bocharov, and Gachev, set off by train to see their idol in Saransk. They were to make many more such trips but by then they were not alone, as Moscow had finally begun to take notice, and Bakhtin received many young disciples in Saransk. In 1962, for instance, the literary scholar Vladimir Nikolaevich Turbin made the trip. Turbin led an extremely popular literature seminar at Moscow University, and one of his pupils there, Leontina Sergeevna Melikhova, also began to visit Bakhtin.

Bakhtin's visitors were not destined to sit passively at the feet of their master. Something about the man inspired others who came into contact with him to rally around and help. Wherever he lived he found people to save him from the worst that fate had to offer. And now these energetic young people undertook to take him back to Moscow, first figuratively and then literally. Toward this end, they worked out a division of labor. Kozhinov and Bocharov looked to Bakhtin's publications and literary archives, Turbin to the problems of resettling him, and Melikhova to the medical needs of the couple.

Kozhinov discussed with Bakhtin quite early the possibility of republishing the Dostoevsky book. Although Bakhtin was ambivalent on this question, he agreed to rework the book in the hope of publication. On July 24, 1961, he asked to retire from his university post on the grounds of ill health, but he was doubtless motivated in part by a desire to have more time for reworking his manuscripts. Bakhtin's problem in publishing, however, continued to be his phlegmatic nature and his inability to bring any text to completion.

As early as December 9, 1961, Bakhtin also raised with Kozhinov the possibility of publishing his Rabelais dissertation and offered to revise it. Kozhinov realized that it would be extremely difficult to get the Rabelais published, so he adopted a strategy of pressing for publication of the Dostoevsky book first and then trying for the Rabelais. But even the revised version of the Dostoevsky book languished in the publishing house Soviet Writer for some time without any sign that it would be accepted.

As a last resort, Kozhinov used a ruse to move the publishers. He knew the Italian Slavist Vittorio Strada, who had become familiar with Bakhtin's Dostoevsky book while a graduate student at

Moscow University in the late 1950s. Strada had entered into correspondence with Bakhtin and contracted to publish a reworked version of the Dostoevsky book in translation as part of a multivolume edition of Dostoevsky's works which Strada arranged to publish with the Italian publishing house Einaudi. According to the contract, the work was to be finished by September 1961. Kozhinov showed a copy of the Einaudi contract offer to officials at Soviet Writer, in order to frighten them with the suggestion that they might have "another *Dr. Zhivago*" on their hands. The reference was to the scandal in the Soviet Union in 1958 when Pasternak's novel, which had been withdrawn from publication there, appeared in Italy; ritual denunciations of the poet were made by officials, critics, and writers, and he was stripped of his Writers' Union membership. Kozhinov also managed by various ruses to get an interview with the Deputy Minister of Trade, whom he persuaded, with his *Dr. Zhivago* analogy, to sign a document that urged Soviet Writer not only to publish the Dostoevsky book but also to rush it through to publication immediately.

Kozhinov delivered this letter to the publishing house personally, but still the publication of the Dostoevsky book dragged on, so he pulled more strings. First he drafted a letter to Soviet Writer declaring that the Dostoevsky book was a major work which should be published without fail. He prevailed upon a group of writers and literary scholars to sign the letter, including the Dostoevsky scholar L. Grossman, the leading Soviet writer and establishment intellectual K. Fedin, the conservative literary specialist M. Khrapchenko, the historian of Stalinist literature L. Timofeev, the party literary functionary B. Riurikov, Vinogradov, Shklovsky, and Kirpotin. When the publishing house claimed to have lost this letter, Kozhinov mounted a press campaign.[17] Finally the book was accepted, and on September 26, 1963, Bakhtin wrote to Kozhinov to tell him that "a miracle" had occurred: he had received advance copies of the new edition. Only someone with the energy, determination, resourcefulness, and guile of a Kozhinov could conceivably have brought the thing off. In other words, even in the liberalized post-Stalin climate of the Khrushchev years, the Dostoevsky book, and therefore most of Bakhtin's other publications as well, might never have seen publication—a sobering thought.

The Dostoevsky book was generally received favorably, and in

1964 a special evening was devoted to it at Moscow University. There were detractors, however. For instance, the old party literary theoretician A. Dymshits attacked Bakhtin in an article "Ideology and Monopoly" in the *Literary Gazette* of July 1964.[18]

Even before the appearance of the Dostoevsky book, Kozhinov had begun to work toward publication of the Rabelais dissertation. Bakhtin, who was always quite fastidious about sources, said that he could not rework the dissertation unless Kozhinov obtained for him all of the major criticism on Rabelais that had come out in the West since Bakhtin had originally written the work in 1940. Bakhtin himself knew of about seventy books and articles, and Kozhinov was able to bring them to Saransk in stages, about ten at a time. Bakhtin was nevertheless even more reluctant to part with this manuscript than he had been with the Dostoevsky, and in the end his wife told Kozhinov simply to wrest it from Bakhtin on one of his visits, which Kozhinov did. This book proved easier to get published because the Dostoevsky had already been accepted. It nevertheless took a press campaign. Kozhinov arranged, for instance, for the writer Fedin, the philologist Vinogradov, and the French translator Liubimov to publish a letter urging publication, under the title "A Book the People Need," in the *Literary Gazette* of June 1962. By December 7 Bakhtin had received word that the book had been accepted.[19]

Some delicate matters remained to be ironed out. The book contained a good deal of scatology, which to a cultural establishment as puritanical as the Soviet could in no way be passed for publication. Some sections had to be excised, but Kozhinov tried to salvage what he could by suggesting that some of the more offensive words be kept in the original French, such as *baton de mariage* for "penis." In his usual diplomatic style, Bakhtin on November 4, 1965, congratulated Kozhinov on the corrections, which he claimed even he could not detect. The main difference between Bakhtin's dissertation and the published version is the omission of a chapter on Gogol. Also omitted from the published version is an analysis of a speech of Lenin's in which he compared revolution to a woman in labor and some passages inserted originally to appease the Stalinists.

Although Bakhtin was now in retirement in Saransk, he did not lose contact with the university. Generous as ever with his time, he received a stream of former students and colleagues whom he helped with their own work and publications. He also continued to take an interest in the world around him. He was an avid listener to the radio news and followed the newspapers for intimations of political developments, underlining significant passages whenever he came across them. While staying at the Writers' Union sanatorium on his annual holiday, Bakhtin loved to go to the movies shown there, which included foreign films not shown to the general public, even though this meant climbing the stairs to the cinema hall on his one leg.

As the years progressed, however, the Bakhtins' situation became more and more difficult because of their declining health. In their last few years at Saransk they almost never went out, and their friends shopped for them. Around 1966 the situation became critical. Bakhtin's other leg had gone completely, and both he and his wife had several bouts in the hospital. Their Moscow disciples realized that they could no longer live by themselves and that they needed medical treatment. It was not easy to find a solution, however, for they had well-defined needs which were not easily met.

On the one hand, the Bakhtins had always led a simple, ascetic life, but on the other, their habits were so fixed at this point that there was very little flexibility. Elena, for instance, refused to take a housekeeper or to lighten her load in any way. Bakhtin drank tea all day, which she insisted on both making and serving herself. She would not agree to using an electrical kettle, so that whatever new accommodations were found would have to provide a stove on which she could boil water. She would not even let friends carry out the trash for her, although in her last years she could only hobble and shuffle. The two were so attached to each other that they insisted on not being separated, which was another difficulty because most institutions did not allow both sexes in the same room or ward.

By a lucky stroke, the daughter of Andropov, the head of the KGB, was in Turbin's seminar. She persuaded her father to set up Bakhtin and his wife in the prestigious Kremlin hospital, reserved for highly placed people, in Moscow.[20] Turbin organized the move in October 1969. The Bakhtins traveled by train, but since Bakhtin had only one leg, Turbin got permission from the station master in Moscow to drive his car onto the platform where the Bakhtins would be arriving. Apparently Bakhtin was so impractical that he did not even realize he needed to have his documents with him to register with the police in Moscow, and so he left his internal passport behind.

The Bakhtins were put in a wing of the Kremlin hospital for patients from the third world. Bakhtin, with his command of languages, interpreted for other patients so that they could communicate with one another. He was otherwise generally frustrated during his stay at the hospital, because all the medical procedures made it hard to work there. The area around his bed was piled high with folders of notes on which he was anxious to work. Elena, who had always believed in paying no attention to appearances or worrying about one's conduct, became quite conspicuous as she moved around the hospital dressed in an old nightgown. She resisted all suggestions that she buy a dressing gown, and the couple were so disheveled that they were assumed to be Old Bolsheviks.

Eventually Andropov told his daughter that even he could not keep the Bakhtins in the Kremlin hospital any longer, and again the problem arose of where to place them. At a nurse's suggestion, they moved to an old people's home in Grivno, near Podolsk and not far from Moscow, on May 15, 1970. There they were given an apartment intended for personnel rather than one of the rooms usually assigned to patients, so that they were able to live in relative independence while also receiving help. Although this arrangement seemed a good one at the time, they soon regretted the move. For a start, the location was inconvenient for their friends, who had to travel some distance to ferry them medical supplies and specialists. Above all, the atmosphere was very depressing in the home, where deaths were frequent and the residents, who had given up their pensions to live there, mostly had no money and often asked the Bakhtins for some.

In Grivno Bakhtin nevertheless had more peace than in the hospital and was able to write. He added material to the Rabelais chapter of his dissertation and wrote shorter pieces on various topics, most of which were published posthumously. Sometime in 1970 Bakhtin also prepared an "Answer to Questions from the Editorial Board of *Novy mir*," which once again treats his topics of extralocality, self versus other, and the semiotics of culture systems, but only in the most general and disengaged way.

In 1970 Bakhtin celebrated his seventy-fifth birthday. He received so many telegrams that the personnel at the old people's home inquired who he was. When they found out, the local teachers asked him to give a lecture, which he did in August, showing that he had not lost his ability to hold an audience under his spell with long recitations of poetry. This was probably his last public lecture.

In Grivno Elena's heart condition deteriorated to the point where she had to be hospitalized. As the Kremlin hospital was now closed to them, in late November 1971 she was placed in a hospital in nearby Podolsk, where she was put in the surgical wing because it was the only section that could offer the couple a double room. She died on the night of December 13, her last thoughts, as ever, being how to get tea for Bakhtin. Friends later organized a religious memorial service for her, conducted by Father Dmitri Dudko, a favorite among the Moscow intelligentsia, in his house in Moscow, which had all the minimum canonical requirements for a church. Bakhtin was not then in Moscow and did not attend.

Bakhtin suffered terribly after his wife died. They had been unusually close throughout their marriage, and now he lost much of his zest for life. People who had visited him in Saransk during the 1960s had been surprised to discover that Bakhtin did not look his age at all, but now he aged rapidly and lost weight, becoming untypically thin. His one consolation was a Persian cat called Kissing, who appeared soon after Elena's death.

Once again the problem arose of where to accommodate him. He wanted to live alone and did not want to go to any place that had associations with his wife, and this eliminated many possibilities. He finally agreed to become a member of the Writers' Union because of the housing and medical clinic that it offered, and forthwith his friends arranged for him to stay at the House of Creativity in Peredelkino, a hotel where writers can live without charge for "creative stays." Bakhtin moved there on New Year's Eve, 1971. The summer of 1972 was a bad one for Muscovites because of extreme heat. Fires broke out in the environs, destroying much of the forest, and smoke from the fires hung over Moscow. For Bakhtin, however, with his emphysema it was a good summer because the air was drier than usual. He was even able to go for walks.

In the meantime, a campaign was afoot to get Bakhtin an apartment in Moscow. He did not have the right to live in Moscow because of a system that limits the population of major Russian towns to people already registered there and to their immediate relatives. However, some extremely prominent members of the Writers' Union petitioned on his behalf, and Bakhtin was finally granted permission to register as a resident of Moscow. Technically, he ceased being a resident of Saransk and gained Moscow residency on July 31, 1972.

Bakhtin was mistrustful of state-owned apartments and wanted to buy himself a cooperative apartment. He had no shortage of money, for Elena, who had always thought that she would die before him, had been a notorious penny pincher, saving for the dark tomorrow, and there was now royalty money as well. Bakhtin bought a flat from the Writers' Union, which he paid for outright in cash and moved into during September. It was on Krasnoarmeyskaya Street, no. 21, flat 42. The numbers pleased Bakhtin, for he liked both three and seven, of which the address and flat number are multiples. Also, 21 was the number of his wife's grave plot.

So began Bakhtin's final phase. He lived alone in relative

Bakhtin's study, with his crutches, the armchair he designed for his own use, and an engraving of Dostoevsky, in his last apartment at 21 Krasnoarmeyskaya Street, Moscow, 1972–1975

comfort in a two-bedroom apartment, with a housekeeper occupying one bedroom and, from late 1974, nurses coming to the home as well. His own bedroom was sparsely furnished, as always, but it had the special writing desk and spacious chair for reading that had been made to his order in Saransk. A keen bibliophile in the past, he now no longer bothered to collect books for himself, and the shelves and walls were filled largely with books and objects given by visitors.

At last Bakhtin was enjoying the fame and respect he deserved. He was lionized by literary theoreticians, both by the structuralists and Tartu semioticians on the left, particularly Uspensky and Ivanov, and on the right by their archrivals, a group associated largely with *Kontekst,* a journal published annually by the theoretical sector of the Gorky Institute, and including several Russian Orthodox figures and Russian nationalists. All these people were of the younger generation, but Bakhtin's own generation did not neglect him either. Shklovsky, who lived in an apartment in the same Writers' Union complex, frequently came to visit. At one point the two apparently exchanged notes in which each professed that he was not in fundamental disagreement with the ideas of the other. Bakhtin often spent his days lying on a couch, in just a robe, and receiving the callers. He pointed out his resemblance to Oblomov in this habit, remarking ruefully that Russia only produced Oblomovs.

Bakhtin was not entirely the man of leisure, however. He kept up with the Soviet journals *Questions of Literature, Foreign Literature, Science and Life,* and *Pravda,* as well as with new books that appeared in a field of interest to him. He also did some writing. After his wife's death he had sent Kozhinov to Saransk to search out his manuscripts. Kozhinov was horrified to find them in poor condition, stored in a lumber room. The manuscripts included "Author and Hero" and other pieces from 1918–1920, as well as several long essays from the 1930s and early 1940s. Later, when it became apparent that Bakhtin's home medical care was going to eat into his finances, his friends decided to publish a selection of these essays and other earlier writings in order to secure royalties for Bakhtin. He reworked the texts a little, deleting in particular the religious passages. In the summer of 1973, for instance, he wrote a conclusion to "Forms of Time and the Chronotope," and in 1974 he worked on "The Methodology of Literary

Scholarship," a shortened version of "Toward a Methodology of the Human Sciences," which was published in 1974 in *Kontekst*. This article was the last piece that Bakhtin saw through to publication.

Bakhtin began work on a new project, a book on Gogol, and also took up an old project, a study of Dostoevsky and Sentimentalism. Neither project got very far, though he left a large number of notes on Gogol's *Selected Passages from Correspondence with Friends* and Dostoevsky's *Diary of a Writer*. Bakhtin's output from these years was not great, partly because his deteriorating health was sapping his energy, but also because there was no longer a pressing need to write. Melikhova, in an effort to encourage him, offered to take dictation from him, but he declined, explaining that he was not used to the practice and could not write that way. He also felt that he needed to be able to write for at least five or six hours at a stretch, because only then did his best ideas come to him, but he simply did not have the energy to work that long any more.

The fragments remaining from these last years are nevertheless among the most impressive of Bakhtin's achievements. There are greater wisdom and tolerance in the notebook entries and a ripeness of thought that qualifies them as a summa, although not in the sense of a final word, the impossibility of which is one of their recurring themes. Rather, these works serve as the most economical statement of positions that had earlier required whole books for their elaboration. Some of the jottings from the 1971 notebooks are so highly concentrated that they convey a sense of being koans.

By August 1974 Bakhtin's health had deteriorated to the point where he could work no longer. His emphysema made breathing difficult, and he was in considerable pain from suppurations in his leg and chest from the osteomyelitis. For years he had taken analgin for the pain, but it was no longer enough, and he began receiving pain killers in the form of injections. In anyone else this constant dose of pain killers would have damaged the heart, but Bakhtin's heart was so strong that it was unaffected. In fact, according to his doctors, had it not been for his lungs, Bakhtin might have lived for many more years.

The regimen of injections necessitated the hiring of nurses. At first there was only a night nurse and then two nurses, but

Bakhtin at work in his armchair, with characteristic cigarette
and cup of strong tea, spring 1974

Bakhtin became so panicked during the one and a half hours between his nurses' shifts that it was decided to hire a third. To alle-
viate Bakhtin's breathing problems, oxygen cylinders were
installed. Thus he effectively had hospital care within the home,
an arrangement that was extremely rare in the Soviet Union and
would otherwise have been found only among the elite. But the

expense of all this care consumed virtually all of Bakhtin's savings and royalties.

Bakhtin finally died at 2 A.M. on the morning of March 7, 1975. The only person in attendance was his night nurse, who copied down his final words, "I go to thee." These words are ambiguous, since they can mean either that he was hoping to rejoin his wife or that he was going to God. In any case, he was doing as he expired exactly what he had done throughout his long life, going out to meet the other. It was a good death for one who had never tired of saying that the great dialogue never ends.

Thus, even in his final utterance, Bakhtin was enigmatic about his religious position. The enigma was compounded by the fact that as he lay dying, a priest appeared in the doorway to give the last rites, and Bakhtin waved him away. But Bakhtin's refusal of the last rites was not in itself significant, since there is an established Orthodox tradition of refusing them and Bakhtin himself had always been skeptical about formal religious ritual, believing in the greater importance of inner spirituality and human communion.

Whatever Bakhtin meant by his last words and actions, once he had died his fate was taken over by the more religious among those who surrounded him. Yury Seliverstov, an artist of Russophile and Orthodox orientation, went to Bakhtin's apartment the night after he died and made a death mask. Then Seliverstov and other friends arranged to have Bakhtin's body laid out according to the ritual for a monk's burial because they considered him a religious figure.[21]

The funeral itself was a civil ceremony, however, and Bakhtin was buried in Vvedenskoe cemetery, sometimes called the German Cemetery, beside his wife. The grave of Yudina, who had died in 1970 of diabetes, was nearby. The pallbearers for Bakhtin were the old troika, Bocharov, Gachev, and Kozhinov, together with A. P. Chudakov, Vinogradov's literary executor; L. Shubin, Bakhtin's editor for the second edition of his Dostoevsky book; and B. A. Uspensky. A large crowd attended, for Bakhtin had by then become a veritable guru for the young intelligentsia. Shklovsky came too, the last major survivor of the original debates in the 1920s on the function of language in literature.

At a memorial meeting in the Fine Arts Museum later that year there were readings from Bakhtin's writings and solemn speeches, but it was Pinsky, a specialist on fools in Shakespeare, who sounded an appropriately Bakhtinian note. In a talk laced with irony, he characterized Bakhtin as a man who had "led a more peaceful life than ours . . . for thirty-five years nothing of his came out." Pinsky stressed the maverick role of Bakhtin in confounding the clichés of literary scholarship. He talked of the paradoxes and contradictions to be found not only in Bakhtin's life but in his work as well. For instance, Bakhtin showed the importance of individualism in Dostoevsky, who belonged to the quintessentially Russian tradition of communality, and Bakhtin used Rabelais, who came from the Renaissance with its new stress on the individual, to establish an extrapersonal dimension to existence. Pinsky concluded that Bakhtin's work is exciting precisely because of its contradictoriness and ability to spark different and unexpected interpretations, and that one should thus be careful not to assign his writings any single, authoritative interpretation.

As yet, however, most people in Pinsky's audience had only a

Bakhtin's body in an open casket, being carried out of 21 Krasno-armyskaya Street, March 9, 1975. From left: Gachev, Kozhinov, Shubin, and Uspensky. Hidden on the other side of the casket are Bocharov and Chudakov.

limited sense of what Bakhtin's writings were. Even with the post-humous appearance of Bakhtin's *Questions of Literature and Aesthetics* in that same year, Bakhtin was still seen as a literary theorist and historian, albeit with a philosophical bent. Kozhinov and Bocharov, to whom Bakhtin had left most of his literary and professional archives, set about correcting this image of Bakhtin by placing as many of the philosophical works as they could in journals and books. This aim was largely achieved with the publication in 1979 of *The Aesthetics of Verbal Creation,* edited by Bocharov. Little of the surviving material remains unpublished. Most of the materials yet to appear in print are notes taken by others on Bakhtin's lectures, such as those by Mirkina not already in print, and Bakhtin's notebook jottings.

As Bakhtin lay dying, he asked to be told again his favorite story, the tale in the *Decameron* where miracles are performed at the tomb of a man regarded as a saint, but who had in fact been a dreadful rogue. Among the morals to be drawn from so complex a story, the most significant one for an understanding of Bakhtin is that there is always a loophole: "Life is full of surprises," or "God works in strange ways, his wonders to perform." Such apparently banal conclusions recognize a condition which at another level has always bedeviled metaphysics: nothing is ever completed, no word is final, there are no ultimate explanations that everyone, without exception, will accept as exhausting all possibilities.

Bakhtin is not alone in recognizing the heterogeneity and contradiction that dominate human life and the consequent speciousness of all claims to the absolute. Unlike many others, he does not find the absence of certainty a matter to deplore. His uniqueness resides in the manifold ways he celebrates and specifies the world's unpredictability. Dialogism is founded on the ineluctability of our ignorance, the necessary presence of gaps in all our fondest schemes and most elaborate systems. Bakhtin rejoices in the fatedness of uncertainty, which he reads as the constant availability of a way out, with no dead end. Dialogism is a metaphysics of the loophole. And although the loophole is the source of the frustration, pain, and danger we must confront in a world so dominated by the unknowable, it is also the necessary precondition for any freedom we may know.

The ability, highly circumscribed though it is, of people to shape fleeting meanings in dialogue gave rise very early to the illusion that meaning is fixed. Those who held this view could forgo the messiness and uncertainty of a world that is in ceaseless flux.

But the price paid for such certainty was high: the superstition which said that absolute truth is possible gave rise to oppressive political and religious systems, from which we have never succeeded in liberating ourselves; and we will never do so as long as we accept the prior condition that enabled all of them, the possibility of any truth that is absolute. Monologic belief systems invariably hold that a single truth is contained in a single institution, such as the state, or in a single object, such as an idol or text, or in a single identity, such as God, the ego conceived as an absolute subject, or the artist-genius who produces unique texts. Monologism is the conceptual glue which holds together the complex mosaic of religious, political, psychological, and aesthetic attitudes that were typical of most cultures in the past.

Dialogism is Bakhtin's attempt to think his way out of such an all-pervasive monologism. Dialogism is not intended to be merely another theory of literature or even another philosophy of language, but is an account of relations between people and between persons and things that cuts across religious, political, and aesthetic boundaries. Despite the enormous range of topics to which it is relevant, dialogism is not the usual abstract system of thought. Unlike other systems that claim such comprehensiveness, Bakhtin's system never loses sight of the nitty-gritty of everyday life, with all the awkwardness, confusion, and pain peculiar to the *hic et nunc,* but also with all the joy that only the immediacy of the here and now can bring.

And unlike other philosophies that oppose radical individuality in the name of the greater primacy of socially organized groups, Bakhtin's philosophy never undercuts the dignity of persons. In fact, dialogism liberates precisely because it insists that we are all necessarily involved in the making of meaning. Insofar as we are all involved in the architectonics of answerability for ourselves and thus for each other, we are all authors, creators of whatever order and sense our world can have.

Since we have tried in this book to understand Bakhtin by using his own categories, it should come as no surprise that we cannot end it. The best we can do is to ask others to read Bakhtin. In that spirit, we pay homage to the generic expectation of closure by quoting Bakhtin's final words on the impossibility of endings, with which he closed the last article he ever wrote: "There is neither a first word nor a last word. The contexts of dialogue are

Bakhtin's death mask, prepared by Seliverstov,
March 8, 1975

without limit. They extend into the deepest past and the most distant future. Even meanings born in dialogues of the remotest past will never be finally grasped once and for all, for they will always be renewed in later dialogue. At any present moment of the dialogue there are great masses of forgotten meanings, but these will be recalled again at a given moment in the dialogue's later course when it will be given new life. For nothing is absolutely dead: every meaning will someday have its homecoming festival."[1]

SELECT BIBLIOGRAPHY
NOTES
INDEX

SELECT BIBLIOGRAPHY

For French translations of Bakhtin and scholarship on him in English and French, see Mary Sadowski, John Sadowski, and Clive Thompson, "Appendices and Bibliography of English and French Translations of Works by the Bakhtin Circle," and Mary Sadowski and Clive Thompson, "Analytical Bibliography of Recent Criticism in English and French on the Bakhtin Circle," *University of Ottawa Quarterly* 53.1 (Jan.–Mar. 1983): 125–131.

WORKS BY BAKHTIN

1919. "Iskusstvo i otvetstvennost' [Art and answerability]." *Den' iskusstva*, Nevel (Sept. 3, 1919): 3–4. Reprinted in *Voprosy literatury* 6 (1977): 307–308; M. M. Baxtin, *Èstetika slovesnogo tvorčestva* (Moscow: Iskusstvo, 1979), pp. 5–6.

c.1920–1924. "Avtor i geroj v èstetičeskoj dejatel'nosti [Author and hero in aesthetic activity]." In *Èstetika slovesnogo tvorčestva*. Extracted in "Problema avtora [The question of the author]," *Voprosy filosofii* 7 (1977): 148–160; "Problema otnošenija avtora k geroju [The problem of the relationship of author to hero]" and "Prostranstvennaja forma geroja [The spatial form of the hero], "*Voprosy literatury* 12 (1978): 260–310. Trans. in *The Architectonics of Answerability*, ed. Michael Holquist, trans. Vadim Liapunov and Kenneth R. Brostrom (Austin: University of Texas Press, forthcoming).

1924. "Problema soderžnija, materiala i formy v slovesnom xudožestvennom tvorčestve [The problem of content, material, and form in verbal artistic creation]." In *Voprosy literatury i èstetiki*. Moscow: Xudožestvennaja literatura, 1975, pp. 6–71. Trans. in *The Architectonics of Answerability*. Extracted in "K èstetike slova [Toward the aesthetics of the word]," *Kontekst, 1973* (Moscow: Nauka, 1974), pp. 258–280. Extract trans. by Kenneth R. Brostrom in *Dispositio* 4.11–12 (1977): 299–315.

1929a. *Problemy tvorčestva Dostoevskogo* [Problems of Dostoevsky's creative works]. Leningrad: Priboj.

1929b. "Predislovie [Preface]" to L. N. Tolstoj. *Polnoe sobranie xudožestvennyx proizvedenij*, ed. K. Xalabaev and B. Ejxenbaum. Moscow-Leningrad: Gosizdat, vol. 11, pp. iii–x.

1930. "Predislovie [Preface]" to L. N. Tolstoj, *Voskresenie.* In *Polnoe sobranie xudožestvennyx proizvedenij*, vol. 13, pp. iii–xx.

1934. "Opyt izučenija sprosa kolxoznikov [Findings based on a study of the requirements of collective farmers]." *Sovetskaja torgovlja* 3 (May–June 1934): 107–118.

1934–1935. "Slovo v romane [Discourse in the novel]." In *Voprosy literatury i èstetiki*, pp. 72–233. Trans. in *The Dialogic Imagination*, ed. Michael Holquist, trans. Caryl Emerson and Michael Holquist (Austin: University of Texas Press, 1981), pp. 259–422. Extract trans. in "The Word in the Novel," *Comparative Criticism Yearbook* 2 (1980): 84–95. Extracted in "Slovo v poèzii i v proze [Discourse in poetry and in prose]," *Voprosy literatury* 6 (1972): 54–83.

1936–1938. "Roman vospitanija i ego značenie v istorii realizma [The novel of development and its significance in the history of realism]." Extant portions in *Èstetika slovesnogo tvorčestva*, pp. 188–236. Trans. in *Speech Genres and Other Late Essays*, ed. Michael Holquist, trans. Vern McGee (Austin: University of Texas Press, forthcoming).

1937–1938. "Formy vremeni i xronotopa v romane [Forms of time and the chronotope in the novel]." In *Voprosy literatury i èstetiki*, pp. 234–407. Trans. in *The Dialogic Imagination*, pp. 84–258. Extracted in "Vremja i prostranstvo v romane [Time and space in the novel], *Voprosy literatury* 3 (1974): 133–179.

1930s–1940s. "K filosofskim osnovam gumanitarnyx nauk [On the philosophical bases of the human sciences]." Revised and shortened by Baxtin in 1974 as "K metodologii gumanitarnyx nauk." In *Èstetika slovesnogo tvorčestva*, pp. 361–373. Trans. in *Speech Genres and Other Late Essays*. Extracted in "K metodologii literaturovedenija [On the methodology of literary studies]," *Kontekst, 1974*, pp. 202–212.

1940a. "Iz predistorii romannogo slova [From the prehistory of novelistic discourse]." *Russkaja i zarubežnaja literatura.* Učenye zapiski saranskogo universiteta, no. 61. Saransk: Saransk University, 1967, pp. 3–23. Expanded in *Voprosy literatury i èstetiki*, pp. 408–446. Trans. in *The Dialogic Imagination*, pp. 408–446.

1940b. "F. Rable v istorii realizma [F. Rabelais in the history of realism]." Diss. in Gorky Institute of World Literature, Moscow.

1941. "Èpos i roman (k metodologii issledovanija romana) [Epic and novel (toward a methodology for the study of the novel)]." *Voprosy literatury* 1 (1970): 95–122. Expanded in *Voprosy literatury i èstetiki*, pp. 447–483. Trans. in *The Dialogic Imagination*, pp. 3–40.

1952–1953. "Problema rečevyx žanrov [The problem of speech genres]. In *Èstetika slovesnogo tvorčestva*, pp. 237–280. Trans. in *Speech Genres and Other Late Essays*. Extracted in *Literaturnaja učeba* 6.1 (1978): 200–219.

1954. "Marija Stjuart [Maria Stuart]." *Sovetskaja Mordovija* 245 (Dec. 12): 2.

1959–1961. "Problema teksta v lingvistike, filologii i drugix gumanitarnyx naukax: Opyt filosofskogo analiza [The problem of the text in linguistics, philology, and other human sciences: An attempt at a philosophical analysis]." In *Èstetika slovesnogo tvorčestva*, pp. 281–307. Trans. in *Speech Genres and Other Late Essays*. Shortened and altered as "Problema teksta: opyt filosofskogo analiza," *Voprosy literatury* 10 (1976): 122–151.

1960–1962. Letters to I. I. Kanaev on Goethe. In *Èstetika slovesnogo tvorčestva*, pp. 396–397.

1961. "K pererabotke knigi o Dostoevskom [On the revision of the book on Dostoevsky]." *Kontekst, 1976*, pp. 296–316. Also in *Èstetika slovesnogo tvorčestva*, pp. 308–327. Trans. in *Problems of Dostoevsky's Poetics*, trans. Caryl Emerson. Minneapolis: University of Minnesota Press, 1984.

1963. *Problemy poètiki Dostoevskogo* [Problems of Dostoevsky's poetics], revised and expanded version of *Problemy tvorčestva Dostoevskogo* (1929). Moscow: Sovetskij pisatel', 1963, also 1972, 1979. Trans. R. W. Rotsel (Ann Arbor: Ardis, 1973). Trans. Caryl Emerson (Minneapolis: University of Minnesota Press, 1984); extracted as "The Dismantled Consciousness: An Analysis of *The Double*," in *Dosteovsky* (*New Perspectives*), ed. Robert Louis Jackson, Twentieth Century Views (Englewood Cliffs, N.J.: Prentice-Hall, 1984), pp. 19–34.

1965. *Tvorčestvo Fransua Rable i narodnaja kul'tura srednevekov'ja* [The work of Francois Rabelais and popular culture of the Middle Ages], revised and expanded version of "F. Rable v istorii realizma" (1940). Moscow, 1965. Trans. in *Rabelais and His World*, trans. Helene Iswolsky (Cambridge: MIT Press, 1968, also 1971).

1970a. "Rable i Gogol' [Rabelais and Gogol]," expanded version of a chapter from "F. Rable v istorii realizma" omitted in *Tvorčestvo Fransua Rable*. In *Voprosy literatury i èstetiki*, pp. 484–495. Also published as "Iskusstvo slova i narodnaja smexovaja kul'tura (Rable i Gogol') [The art of discourse and folk humor (Rabelais and Gogol)]," *Kontekst, 1972*, pp. 248–259.

1970b. "Otvet na vopros redakcii 'Novogo mira' [Response to a question put by the editorial board of 'Novy mir']." Published as "Smelee pol'zovat'sja vozmožnostjami [Make bolder use of potential]." *Novyj mir* 11 (1970): 237–240. Republished under original title in *Èstetika slovesnogo tvorčestva*, pp. 328–335.

1970c. Internal review of L. E. Pinsky's *Šekspir* [Shakespeare]. In *Èstetika slovesnogo tvorčestva*, pp. 411–412.

1970–1971a. "O polifoničnosti romanov Dostoevskogo [On the polyphonic nature of Dostoevsky's novels]." *Rossija/Russia* 2 (Turin, 1975): 189–198.

1970–1971b. "Iz zapisej 1970–1971 godov [From the notebooks of 1970–1971]." In *Èstetika slovesnogo tvorčestva*, pp. 336–360. Trans. in *Speech Genres and Other Late Essays*.

1975. *Voprosy literatury i èstetiki* [Questions of literature and aesthetics]. Moscow: Xudožestvennaja literatura. Contains works of 1924, 1934–1935, 1937–1938, 1940a, 1941, 1970a. Trans. of 1934–1935, 1937–1938, 1940a, 1941 in *The Dialogic Imagination*.

1979. *Èstetika slovesnogo tvorčestva* [The aesthetics of verbal creation]. Moscow: Iskusstvo. Contains works of c.1920–1924, 1936–1938, 1952–1953, 1959–1961, 1960–1962, 1961, 1970b, 1970c. Trans. in *The Architectonics of Answerability; Speech Genres and Other Late Essays*.

WORKS BY "I. I. KANAEV"

1926. "Sovremennyj vitalizm [Contemporary vitalism]." *Čelovek i priroda* 1: 33–42; 2: 9–23.

DISPUTED WORKS BY "P. N. MEDVEDEV"

1925. "Učënyj sal'erizm [Scholarly salierism]." *Zvezda* 3: 264–276.

1926a. "Sociologizm bez sociologii (o metodologičeskix rabotax P. N. Sakulina) [Sociologism without sociology (on P. N. Sakulin's methodological works)]." *Zvezda* 2: 267–271.

1926b. Review of V. M. Žirmunskij, *Vvedenie v metriku*. *Zvezda* 4: 301–302.

1928. *Formal'nyj metod v literaturovedenii: Kritičeskoe vvedenie v sociologičeskuju poètiku* [The formal method in literary study: A critical introduction to sociological poetics]. Leningrad: Priboj. Reprinted Hildesheim: G. Olm, 1974. Extracted as "Problema žanra," in *Iz istorii sovetskoj èstetičeskoj mysli, 1917–1932: Sbornik materialov*, ed. G. A. Belaja. (Moscow: Iskusstvo, 1980), pp. 418–424. Trans. in *The Formal Method in Literary Scholarship*, trans. Albert J. Wehrle (Baltimore: The John Hopkins University Press, 1978).

DISPUTED WORKS BY "V. N. VOLOŠINOV"

1925. "Po tu storonu social'nogo [Beyond the social]." *Zvezda* 5: 186–214.

1926. "Slovo v žizni i slovo v iskusstve [Discourse in life and discourse in art]." *Zvezda* 6: 244–267. Reprinted as "Slovo v žizni i slovo v poèzii" in Belaja, *Iz istorii sovetskoj estetičeskoj mysli*, pp. 383–396. Trans. in *Freudianism: A Marxist Critique*, trans. I. R. Titunik (New York: Academic Press, 1973), pp. 93–106.

1927. *Frejdizm: Kritičeskij očerk* [Freudianism: A critical sketch]. Moscow-Leningrad: Gosizdat. Repr. "Les Editeurs Reunis," Paris, 1982. Trans. in *Freudianism*.

1928. "Novejšie tečenija lingvističeskoj mysli na zapade [The latest trends in linguistic thought in the west]." *Literatura i marksizm* 5: 115–149.

1929. *Marksizm i filosofija jazyka: Osnovnye problemy sociologičeskogo metoda v nauke o jazyke* [Marxism and the philosophy of language: Basic problems in sociolinguistics]. Leningrad: Priboj. 2nd ed. 1930. Reprinted The Hague: Mouton, 1972. Trans. in *Marxism and the Philosophy of Language*, trans. Ladislav Matejka and I. R. Titunik (New York: Seminar Press, 1973).

1930a. "Stilistika xudožestvennoj reči [The stylistics of speech in art]." *Literaturnaja učёba* 2, 3, 5.

1930b. "O granicax poètiki i lingvistiki [On the borders of poetics and linguistics]." In *V bor'be za Marksizm v literaturnoj nauke*, ed. V. A. Desnickij. Leningrad: Priboj.

STUDENT NOTES ON BAKHTIN'S LECTURES

Mirkina, R. M. "Iz lekcii po istorii russkoj literatury: Vjačeslav Ivanov [From the lectures on the history of Russian literature: Vyacheslav Ivanov]." In *Èstetika slovesnogo tvorčestva*, pp. 374–383.

———. "Konspekty lekcij M. M. Baxtina [Notes from M. M. Bakhtin's lectures]" (on Tolstoy). *Prometej: Istoriko-biografičeskij al'manax* 12 (Moscow, 1980): 257–268.

———. Lectures on A. Bely and F. Sollogub. In *Studia Slavica*. Budapest, forthcoming.

———. Lecture on A. Blok. In *Aleksandr Blok: Novye materialy i issledovanija*, book 4, vol. 92 of *Literaturnoe nasledstvo*. Moscow: Nauka, forthcoming.

MEMOIRS

Basixin, Jurij. "O Mixaile Mixajloviče Baxtine [On Mikhail Mikhailovich Bakhtin]." In *Rodnye prostory: Literaturno-xudožestvennyj sbornik*. Saransk: Mordovskoe knižnoe izdatel'stvo, 1978, pp. 203–209.

Nevel'skaja, K. (pseud.), ed. "M. M. Baxtin i M. I. Kagan." In *Pamjat':*
Istoričeskij sbornik, no. 4. Paris: YMCA Press, 1981, pp. 249–281.

WORKS ON BAKHTIN

Anon. "Pamjati M. M. Baxtina [M. M. Bakhtin, in memoriam]." *Sin-*
taksis 7 (Paris, 1980): 102–105.
Ivanov, V. V. "Značenie idej M. M. Baxtina o znake, vyskazyvanija i dialoge dlja sovremennoj semiotiki [The significance of M. M. Bakhtin's
ideas on the sign, utterance and dialogue for contemporary semio-
tics]." *Trudy po znakovym sistemam,* vol. 6 of *Učenye zapiski Tartus-*
kogo gosudarstvennogo universiteta. Tartu: Tartu University, 1973,
pp. 5–45. Trans. in *Semiotics and Structuralism: Readings from the*
Soviet Union, ed. Henryk Baran (White Plains, N.Y.: International
Arts and Sciences Press, 1974).
Konkin, S. S., ed. *Problemy poètiki i istorii literatury: Sbornik v čest' M.*
M. Baxtina [Problems of poetics and history of literature: Festschrift
to M. M. Bakhtin]. Saransk: University of Mordovia, 1973.
Morson, Gary Saul, ed. "Forum on Mikhail Bakhtin," with articles by
Morson, Caryl Emerson, Susan Stewart, Michael André Bernstein, and
Michael Holquist. *Critical Inquiry* 10.2 (Dec. 1983): 225–319.
Todorov, Tzvetan. *M. M. Bakhtine: Le principe dialogique.* Paris: Editions
du Seuil, 1981.

NOTES

INTRODUCTION

1. Roman Jakobson and Pyotr Bogatyrev, "Die Folklore als ein besondere Form des Schaffens," *Selected Writings,* vol. 1 (The Hague: Mouton, 1966), pp. 4–13.

2. Baxtin, "Slovo v romane," *Voprosy literatury i èstetiki* (Moscow: Xudožestvennaja literatura, 1975), p. 85, trans. in *The Dialogic Imagination: Four Essays by M. M. Bakhtin,* ed. Michael Holquist, trans. Caryl Emerson and Michael Holquist (Austin: University of Texas Press, 1981), p. 272.

3. Baxtin, "Slovo v romane," p. 272.

4. Sergej Kartsevsky, "Du dualisme asymetrique de signe linguistique," *Travaux du cercle linguistique de Prague* (Prague, 1929), p. 188.

5. V. N. Vološinov (M. M. Bakhtin), *Marxism and the Philosophy of Language,* trans. Ladislav Matejka and I. R. Titunik (New York: Seminar Press, 1973), pp. 85–86.

1. THE CORSICAN TWINS, 1895–1917

1. Another version of Bakhtin's birth date, which he himself sometimes used, is Nov. 17, but one of his literary executors, Sergei Bocharov, is convinced that Nov. 16 is correct.

2. A less glamorous version has it that his father was merely an employee in a bank.

3. Mother in Nevel to Nikolai in Paris, June 16, 1924, in the possession of R. F. Christian, Saint Andrews University.

4. Nicholas Bachtin, "Odnomu iz ostavšixsja," in R. F. Christian, "Some Unpublished Poems of Nicholas Bachtin," *Oxford Slavonic Papers* 10 (1977): 115.

5. Andrew Boyle, *The Climate of Treason* (London: Hutchinson, 1979), p. 63.

6. E. R. Dodds, *Missing Persons: An Autobiography* (Oxford: Clarendon Press, 1977), p. 113.

7. Roy Pascal to authors, Oct. 10, 1979.

8. Nicholas Bachtin Archive, University of Birmingham Library, Box 8, Envelope 16.

9. This is the view of Fanya Pascal, Roy Pascal's wife. See also Terry Eagleton, "Wittgenstein's Friends," *New Left Review* 135 (Sept./Oct. 1982): 64–90.

10. Francesca M. Wilson *et al.*, "Biographical Introduction," in *Nicholas Bachtin: Lectures and Essays*, ed. A. E. Duncan-Jones (Birmingham: University of Birmingham Press, 1963), p. 2.

11. Czeslaw Milosz, *Native Realm: A Search for Self-Definition*, trans. Catherine S. Leach (New York: Doubleday, 1968), p. 55.

12. M. V. Dobužinskij, *Vospominanija*, vol. 1 (New York: Put' žizni, 1976), p. 55.

13. Bakhtin, "From the Prehistory of Novelistic Discourse," *The Dialogic Imagination: Four Essays by M. M. Bakhtin*, ed. Michael Holquist, trans. Caryl Emerson and Michael Holquist (Austin: University of Texas Press, 1981), p. 64. See also Milosz, *Native Realm*.

14. Nicholas Bachtin, "The Russian Revolution as Seen by a White Guard," *Nicholas Bachtin*, p. 47.

15. Vjačeslav Ivanov, *Po zvezdam: Opyty filosifskie, èstetičeskie i kritičeskie,* repr. (Letchworth, Herts.: Bradda Books, 1971), p. 248.

16. Wilson *et al.*, "Biographical Introduction," in *Nicholas Bachtin,* pp. 2–3.

17. Ivanov, *Po zvezdam,* p. 427. See also Baxtin, "Iz lekcii po istorii russkoj literatury: Vjačeslav Ivanov," *Èstetika slovesnogo tvorčestva* (Moscow: Iskusstvo, 1979), pp. 374–383.

18. For these remarks by A. A. Meier, a member of the society who was close to Bakhtin, see George F. Putnam, *Russian Alternatives to Marxism: Christian Socialism and Idealistic Liberalism in Twentieth-Century Russia* (Knoxville: University of Tennessee Press, 1977), p. 96.

19. See Jutta Scherrer, *Die Petersburger Religios-Philosophischen Vereinungen: Die Entwicklung der Religiosen Selbstverständnisses ihrer Intelligencija-Mitglieder* (1901–1917) (Berlin: Osteuropa-Institut an der Freien Universität, Historische Veröffentlichungen, 1973), vol. 19; Putnam, *Russian Alternatives to Marxism,* pp. 74–76; Bernice Glatzer Rosenthal, *D. S. Merezhkovsky and the Silver Age: The Development of the Silver Age* (The Hague: Martinus Nijhoff, 1975), pp. 133–139.

20. Scherrer, *Die Petersburger Religios-Philosophischen Vereinungen,* pp. 329–330.

21. Vsevolod Roždestvenskij, *Stranicy žizni: Iz literaturnyx vospominanij,* 2nd enl. ed. (Moscow: Sovremennik, 1974), pp. 119–120.

22. Konstantin Močul'skij, *Aleksandr Blok* (Paris: YMCA Press, 1948), p. 135.

23. Fadej Zelinskij, *Drevnyj mir i my* (St. Petersburg, 1903), pp. 70–77; Zelinskij, *Religija èllenizma* (Petrograd: Academija, 1922), p. 13; Thaddeus Zielinski, *Die Märchenkomödie in Athen* (St. Petersburg, 1885); Roždestvenskij, *Stranicy žizni*, p. 175.

24. Viktor Šklovskij, *Žili-byli: Vospominanija, memuarnye zapisi, povesti o vremeni konca xix v. po 1964 g.* (Moscow: Sovetskij pisatel', 1966), p. 93.

25. W. S. Ferguson, "The Leading Ideas of the New Period," *The Cambridge Ancient History*, vol. 7 (Cambridge: Cambridge University Press, 1954), p. 36.

26. Zelinskij, *Drevnyj mir i my*, p. 64; *Nicholas Bachtin*, pp. 122–132.

27. See G. P. Fedotov, *I est' i budet: Razmyšlenie o Rossii i o revoljucii* (Paris: Novyj grad, 1932), pp. 202–203.

28. See F. Zelinskij, "Vjačeslav Ivanov," in *Russkaja literatura xx veka (1890–1901)*, ed. S. A. Vengerov, vol. 1 (Moscow: Mir, 1922), pp. 112–113.

29. For this and subsequent quotations in this chapter, see *Nicholas Bachtin*, pp. 43–44.

2. NEVEL AND VITEBSK, 1918–1924

1. D. P. Končalovskij, *Vospominanija i pis'ma (ot gumanizma k Xristu)* (Paris: Libraire du cinq continents, 1971), pp. 158–161; Veniamin Kaverin, *Sobesednik: Vospominanija i portrety* (Moscow: Sovetskij pisatel', 1973), p. 9.

2. Konstantin Močul'skij, *Aleksandr Blok* (Paris: YMCA Press, 1948), p. 397; Victor Shklovsky, *A Sentimental Journey: Memoirs, 1917–1922*, trans. Richard Sheldon (Ithaca: Cornell University Press, 1970), pp. 114–115, 175, 235.

3. Clarence Brown, *Mandelshtam* (Cambridge: Cambridge University Press, 1973), p. 85; Vsevolod Roždestvenskij, *Stranicy žizni: Iz literaturnyx vospominanij* (Moscow-Leningrad: Sovetskij pisatel', 1962), pp. 192–193; O. Dešart, "Vvedenie," in Vjačeslav Ivanov, *Sobranie sočinenij*, vol. 1 (Brussels: Foyer Oriental Chretien, 1971), p. 160.

4. See e.g. Brown, *Mandelshtam*, pp. 72–101.

5. Shklovsky, *A Sentimental Journey*, p. 156.

6. Bakhtin, *Trudovoj spisok* (Work Book, an official document). According to the Work Book, Bakhtin started work as a secondary school teacher on January 1, 1918, and began work in the gymnasium only in August, which would have meant that he moved to Nevel and started work there before graduating from Petrograd University in mid-1918.

This was quite possible in those chaotic times, and by early 1918 Bakhtin probably had to complete only his long essays in order to graduate. However, according to most accounts, Bakhtin moved to Nevel in the spring of 1918.

7. *Nevel'skij uezd pskovskoj gubernii: Istoriko-èkonomičeskij očerk* (Nevel': Krasnyj pečatnik, 1925), pp. 7, 27.

8. *Marija Veniaminovna Judina,* ed. A. M. Kuznecov (Moscow: Sovetskij kompositor, 1978), pp. 32, 308; "Pis'ma M. M. Baxtina M. I. Kaganu," *Pamjat': Istoričeskij sbornik,* no. 4 (Paris: YMCA Press, 1981), p. 266.

9. Interviews of Nina Arkadievna Voloshinova in Leningrad by Susan Layton, May 6, 1980, and by Katerina Clark, Nov. 19, 1983.

10. Both Nikolai and Pumpiansky cited Lopatto and Kobeko as two of their closest friends at the gymnasium.

11. Information on Kagan's life comes from oral sources and "Avtobiografičeskie zametki M. I. Kagana," *Pamjat',* no. 4, pp. 253–256, 276.

12. M. I. Kagan, "O vozmožnosti istorii," *Zapiski orlovskogo universiteta,* Social Science Series, no. 1 (Orel: Giz, 1922); "German Kogen," *Naučnye izvestija Akademičeskogo centra Narkomprosa,* vol. 2 (Moscow, 1922).

13. Entries in *Den' iskusstva,* no. 1 (1919): 8; *Molot,* no. 101 (June 13, 1919): 3; no. 96 (May 27, 1919): 1; no. 101 (June 13, 1919): 3; no. 81 (Apr. 1, 1919): 1; no. 128 (Aug. 18, 1919): 1.

14. *Molot,* no. 101 (June 13, 1919): 3; no. 81 (Apr. 1, 1919): 1; no. 128 (Aug. 18, 1919): 1.

15. *Molot,* no. 47 (Dec. 3, 1918): 3. For reports on the other three debates, see *Molot,* no. 47 (Dec. 3, 1918): 3; no. 93 (May 16, 1919): 3; no. 96 (May 27, 1919): 1; no. 136 (Sept. 9, 1919): 1.

16. *Molot,* no. 122 (Aug. 4, 1919): 2.

17. S. M., "Muzyka v derevne," *Den' iskusstva,* no. 1 (1919): 6; *Molot,* no. 162 (Nov. 19, 1919): 2.

18. See *Molot,* no. 80 (Mar. 28, 1919): 2; no. 178 (Dec. 22, 1919): 2; no. 63 (June 9, 1920): 2; no. 63 (June 9, 1920): 2; no. 65 (June 14, 1920): 2.

19. Entries in *Den'iskusstva,* no. 1 (1919): 2–3, 5, 7.

20. Entries in *Izvestija vitebskogo soveta,* nos. 188, 195, 196, 199, 211, 228, 230, 236, 276, 294 (Aug.–Dec. 1919).

21. *Al'bom "Vitebsk"* (Minsk: Zvezda, 1966); A. Sapunov, "Očerk vitebskoj gubernii v estestvenno-istoričeskom i geografičeskom otnošenijax," *Bjulleten' official'nyx rasporjaženij i soobščenij vitebskogo gub ONO,* no. 7 (Feb. 15, 1924): 30; Franz Meyer, *Marc Chagall: Life and Work,* trans. Robert Allen (New York: Harry N. Abrams, 1963), p. 21.

22. *Kratkij otčet vitebskogo gorodskogo soveta rabočix krestjanskix i*

krasnoarmejskix deputatov 3-go sozyva (*s 15–20 dekabrja, 1920 goda po 15–oe aprelja 1921 goda*) (Vitebsk, 1921), pp. 1–2; Nikolaj Andreevič Mal'ko in *Pamjati I. I. Sollertinskogo: Vospominanija, materialy, issledovanija* (Leningrad: Sovetskij kompozitor, 1974), p. 94; Pavel Medvedev, "K postanovke 'Danton' Romen Rolana (v mesto recensii)," *Iskusstvo*, no. 2–3 (Apr.–May, 1921): 25.

23. M. Pustynin, "Teatr-zverinec: Paradoksy o scene," *Iskusstvo*, no. 1 (Mar. 1921): 6.

24. Mark Šagal', "O vitebskom narodnom xudožestvennom učilišče (k pervoj otčetnoj vystavke učašixsja)," *Škola i revoljucija* (Vitebsk), no. 22 (June 30, 1919): 7.

25. Meyer, *Marc Chagall*, pp. 265–277. Chagall later returned to Vitebsk and then left the town for good in May 1920.

26. K. Malevič, "Unovis," *Iskusstvo*, no. 1 (Mar. 1921): 9; Jean-Claude Marcadé, "K.S. Malevich: From *Black Quadrilateral* (1913) to *White on White* (1917): From the Eclipse of Objects to the Liberation of Space," trans. Sherry Goodman, in *The Avant-Garde in Russia, 1910–1930: New Perspectives*, ed. Stephanie Barron and Maurice Tuchman (Cambridge: MIT Press, 1980), pp. 20–23; Eugen F. Kowtun, "Wera Michailowna Ermolaewa," in *Künstlerinnen der Russischen Avantgarde, 1910–1930: Ausstellung Dec. 1979–Mar. 1980*, Galerie Gmurzynska (Cologne, 1979), pp. 104–105.

27. S. M. Ejzenštejn, "Zametki o Majakovskom," *Iskusstvo kino*, no. 1 (1958): 73.

28. John E. Bowlt, "Some Very Elegant Ladies," in *Künstlerinnen der Russischen Avantgarde*, p. 39; Kowtun, "Wera Michailowna Ermolaewa," p. 105.

29. Ju. Vajnkop, in *Pamjati I. I. Sollertinskogo*, p. 138.

30. *Pamjati I. I. Sollertinskogo*, p. 262.

31. See P. Medvedev, "Vneškol'naja rabota v Vitebskoj gubernii: Bibliotečnoe delo v Vitebske," and P. M., "Proletkul't v Vitebske," *Vneškol'noe obrazovanie* (Petrograd), no. 4–6 (Feb.–Mar. 1919): 81–83; Pavel Medvedev, "Vitebskij gubernskij s"ezd po vneškol'nomu obrazovaniju," *Vneškol'noe obrazovanie* (Petrograd), no. 6–8 (1919): 100–102; Report on a program of lectures by Medvedev on the history of Russian literature and society, *Zapiski Vitebskogo proletarskogo universiteta*, no. 1 (Jan. 1919).

32. "Literaturnaja studija Sorabisa," *Iskusstvo*, no. 4–6 (1921): 48. Bakhtin's work in the Women's Department took on special poignancy in light of the charge that *Rabelais and His World* supports the antifeminist bias of *Gargantua*. Wayne Booth, "Freedom of Interpretation: Bakhtin and the Challenge of Feminist Criticism," *Critical Inquiry* 9.1 (Sept. 1982): 63.

33. R. M. Mirkina, "Baxtin kakim ja ego znala: Molodoj Baxtin," privately held, pp. 2–3.

34. "Zdes' žili poet i filosof / V surovye zimnie dni / I mnogo prokljatyx voprosov / Rešali v to vremja oni." Cited in Mirkina, "Baxtin kakim ja ego znala," p. 2.

35. M. M. Baxtin, "V narodnyj komissariat zdravoxranenija po delu o naznačenii vračebnoj komissii dlja osvidetel'stvovanija sostojanija zdorov'ja M. M. Baxtina: Zajavlenije," *Pamjat'*, no. 4, p. 267; Bakhtin to Kagan, *Pamjat'*, no. 4, p. 257; Bakhtin to Kagan, Mar. 1921, *Pamjat'*, no. 4, p. 260.

36. A. Romm, "Vystavka v Vitebske, 1921," *Iskusstvo*, no. 4–6 (1921): 41–42; *Von der Flache zum Raum*, Ausstellung vom 18 September bis Ende November, 1974, Galerie Gmurzynska (Cologne, 1974), p. 84.

37. *Pamjat'*, no. 4, p. 257; *Iskusstvo*, no. 1 (Mar. 1921): 23; Bakhtin to Kagan, Jan. 18, 1922, *Pamjat'*, no. 4, p. 263; S. G. Bočarov, note on "the Subject in Moral Life and the Subject in the Law," in M. M. Baxtin, *Èstetika slovesnogo tvorčestva*, ed. S. G. Bočarov and S. S. Averincev (Moscow: Iskusstvo, 1979), p. 363; "Teatral'no-literaturnaja xronika," *Žizn' iskusstva*, no. 33 (Aug. 22–28, 1922): 4.

38. M. M. Baxtin, "Avtor i geroj v èsteticeskoj dejatel'nosti," *Èstetika slovesnogo tvorčestva*, pp. 7–180.

39. Bakhtin to Kagan, Mar. 1921, *Pamjat'*, no. 4, pp. 260–261.

40. Pumpjanskij to Kagan, c.1926, *Pamjat'*, no. 4, p. 266.

41. M. M. Baxtin, "Iskusstvo i otvetstvennost'," *Èstetika slovesnogo tvorčestva*, p. 5.

42. M. M. Baxtin, *Èstetika*, p. 6.

43. See Katerina Clark and Michael Holquist, "Neo-Kantianism in the Thought of M. M. Bakhtin," in *Aspects of Literary Scholarship* (Festschrift for René Wellek), ed. Joseph P. Strelka, forthcoming.

44. V. I. Lenin, "Materializm i empirokriticizm," *Polnoe sobranie sočinenij*, vol. 18 (Moscow: Nauka, 1947), pp. 326–327; Lenin to A. N. Potresov, vol. 46, p. 30.

45. Konstantin Vaginov, *Kozlinaja pesn'* (Leningrad: Priboj, 1928), passim; Hermann Cohen, *Logik der reinen Erkenntnis* (Berlin, 1902), p. 379; M. M. Bakhtin, *The Dialogic Imagination*, ed. Michael Holquist, trans. Caryl Emerson and Michael Holquist (Austin: University of Texas Press, 1981), p. 85.

46. Exodus 3:15.

47. Quoted in Martin Buber, *The Writings of Martin Buber*, ed. Will Herberg (New York: World, 1956) p. 106.

48. Gustav Otto, *The Idea of the Holy*, trans. John W. Harvey (New York: Oxford University Press, 1958); Hermann Cohen, *The Religion of*

Reason out of the Sources of Judaism, trans. Simon Kaplan (New York: Ungar, 1972), p. 35.

49. Cohen, *The Religion of Reason,* p. 96.

3. THE ARCHITECTONICS OF ANSWERABILITY

1. Included under this title are the works published as "Art and Answerability" and "Author and Hero in Aesthetic Activity," lost or unpublished works such as "The Aesthetics of Verbal Creativity" (not the 1979 book with that title, edited by Bočarov and Averincev) and an untitled text on moral philosophy, and other work Bakhtin was doing on the philosophy of religion during 1918–1924.

2. Baxtin, *Èstetika,* p. 175.

3. Kant, *Critique of Pure Reason,* trans. N. Kemp Smith (London: Macmillan, 1929), p. 157; Baxtin, *Èstetika,* p. 8.

4. Baxtin, *Èstetika,* p. 27.

5. Baxtin, *Èstetika,* p. 112.

6. See Roman Jakobson, *Brain and Language* (Columbus, O.: Slavica, 1981), pp. 19–21.

7. Baxtin, *Èstetika,* p. 115.

8. Baxtin, *Èstetika,* p. 119.

9. Tzvetan Todorov, *Mikhail Bakhtine: Le principe dialogique* (Paris: Editions du Seuil, 1981), p. 151; *Reason and Hope: Selections from Hermann Cohen's Jewish Writings,* trans. Ewa Jospe (New York: Norton, 1971), p. 218.

10. Kenneth Burke, *The Rhetoric of Religion: Studies in Logology* (Berkeley: University of California Press, 1970), pp. 1–2, 13–14.

11. Nicholas Zernov, *The Russian Religious Renaissance of the Twentieth Century* (London: Darton, Longman, and Todd, 1963), p. 285.

12. George P. Fedotov, *The Russian Religious Mind* (Cambridge: Harvard University Press, 1946), I, 104.

13. Fedotov, *The Russian Religious Mind,* p. 129.

14. Anthony Ugolnik, "Tradition as Freedom from the Past: Contemporary Eastern Orthodoxy and Ecumenism," *Institute for Ecumenical and Cultural Research, Occasional Papers,* no. 17 (Nov. 1982): 2; "V. N. Vološinov," *Marxism and the Philosophy of Language,* trans. Ladislav Matejka and I. P. Titunik (New York and London: Seminar Press, 1973), p. 88; Baxtin, *Èstetika,* p. 51.

15. Baxtin, *Èstetika,* p. 52.

16. "Vološinov," *Marxism,* p. 11; Ugolnik, "Tradition as Freedom from the Past," p. 6.

17. Baxtin, *Èstetika,* p. 52.

18. See Bernice Glatzer Rosenthal, *Merezhkovsky and the Silver Age* (The Hague: Martinus Nijhoff, 1975), p. 99; Zernov, *Russian Religious Renaissance,* pp. 165–186, 283–308.

19. Baxtin, *Èstetika,* p. 8.

20. Baxtin, *Èstetika,* p. 9.

21. Baxtin, *Èstetika,* p. 9.

22. Emile Benveniste, *Problems in General Linguistics,* trans. Mary Elizabeth Meek (Coral Gables: University of Miami Press, 1971), p. 218.

23. Benveniste, *Problems,* pp. 218, 226.

24. Benveniste, *Problems,* p. 226.

25. Benveniste, *Problems,* p. 219.

26. Benveniste, *Problems,* p. 225.

4. THE LENINGRAD CIRCLE, 1924–1929

1. Cf. Gasparov, "M. M. Baxtin v russkoj literature xx v.," *Vtoričnye modelirujuščie sistemy* (Tartu: Tartu University, 1979), pp. 111–114.

2. The city was renamed Leningrad after Lenin's death in January 1924. Although Bakhtin's official registration for Leningrad is dated Sept. 27, 1924, he must have moved there before September, because a document calling him to jury duty there is dated Aug. 24, 1924. The concensus among those who knew him is that he moved there in the spring.

3. Irina Odoevceva, *Na beregax Nevy* (Washington: Victor Kamkin, 1967), p. 373.

4. See *Gosudarstvennyj institut istorii iskusstv, 1912–1927* (Leningrad: Gosudarstvennyj institut istorii iskusstv, 1927), p. 35; "Spisok dokladov začitannyx v gosudarstvennom institute istorii iskusstv s 1 janvarja 1919 g. do 1 janvarja 1927 g.," in *Gosudarstvennyj institut istorii iskusstv,* pp. 42–62; V. Zubov, *Stradnye gody Rossii, 1917–1925* (Munich: W. Fink Verlag, 1968); N. Stepanov in *Jurij Tynyanov: Pisatel' i učenyj: Vospominanija, razmyšlenija, vstrěci,* unnumbered vol. in *Žizn' zamečatel'nyx ljudej* (Moscow: Molodaja gvardija, 1966), pp. 126–127; V. Kaverin, "Vstreči v krasnoj gostinoj," in *Sobesednik: Vospominanija i portrety* (Moscow: Sovetskij pisatel', 1973), pp. 66–80; Rossiskij institut istorii iskusstv, *Zadači i metody izučenija iskusstv* (Petrograd: Academija, 1924), p. 220; A. G., "Diskussija o sovremennoj literature," *Russkij sovremennik,* no. 2 (1924): 273–278.

5. "Spisok dokladov," pp. 46–48, 55, 57, 61–62; "Otčet o naučnoj dejatel'nosti otdela istorii slovesnyx iskusstv GIII," in *Poètika: Sbornik statej* (Leningrad, 1926), pp. 155–162.

6. Mother to Nikolai in Paris, Sept. 19, 1924; Maria to Nikolai, Sept. 19, 1924.

7. Maria to Nikolai in Paris, Sept. 19, 1924.

8. No. 17 Znamenskaya Street.

9. No. 38 Preobrazhenskaya Street, apt. 5, now renamed Radischev Street and near Vosstanie Street.

10. Konstantin Vaginov, "Dva pestryx odejala. . . ," *Opyty soedinenija slov posredstvom ritma* (Leningrad: Izd. pisatelej v Leningrade, 1931), pp. 43–44.

11. No. 16 Saperny Lane, at the corner of Znamenskaya Street.

12. *Naučnye rabotniki Moskvy,* vol. 4 of *Nauka i naučnye rabotniki SSSR* (Leningrad: Akademija nauk, 1930), pp. 118, 108, 35, 188–189.

In 1927 Zubakin published a collection of poetry, *The Bear in the Boulevard,* one of whose poems, "Improvisation," is dedicated to Voloshinov. Zubakin, who had been living with Anastasia Ivanovna Tsvetaeva, sister of Marina Tsvetaeva, the poet, made a journey with her to Sorrento in 1927 at the invitation of Gorky, who had apparently been pleased when Zubakin improvised some mock Gorky poems. However, Gorky was taken aback at Zubakin when he actually appeared and apparently threw him out. A. M. Gor'kij, "Pis'ma k A. N. Tixonovu," in *Gor'kovskie čtenija, 1953–1957* (Moscow: Akademija nauk, 1959), pp. 53–54, 55, 57; A. I. Cvetaeva, *Vospominanija* (Moscow: Sovetskij pisatel', 1971), pp. 476, 480, 490, 517; Anastasija Cvetaeva, "Skaz o zvonare moskovskom: Povest'—Vospominanija, 1917–1976," *Moskva,* no. 7 (1977): 144–146. Zubakin's stated mission to Italy was to see the pope and attempt to reconcile Catholicism and Freemasonry. This may have been said in jest, though some say that Zubakin was the last Russian Mason and used the trip to evacuate the archive.

13. Baxtin, "Sovremennyj vitalizm," *Čelovek i priroda,* no. 1 (1926): 33–42; no. 2 (1926): 9–22. Nos. 2 and 3 of this periodical announced another "Kanaev" article in the next issue, but none appeared. Kanaev concentrated on the topic of Goethe as a naturalist but also wrote on morphological questions and the history of evolutionary theory, multiple births, hydras, and Leclerc de Buffon.

14. *Aziatskij muzej: Leningradskoe otdelenie instituta vostokovedenija AN SSSR* (Moscow: Nauka, 1972), pp. 35, 42, 90, 160–165, 227; S. I. Miliband, *Bibliografičeskij slovar' sovetskix vostokovedov* (Moscow: Glavnaja redakcija vostočnoj literatury, 1975), p. 557; I. Voznesenskij, "Tol'ko vostokovedy," *Pamjat': Istoričeskij sbornik,* no. 3 (Paris: YMCA Press, 1980), pp. 429–465.

15. *Pamjati I. I. Sollertinskogo,* 2nd ed. (Leningrad: Sovetskij kompozitor, 1978), p. 30. Pumpiansky also lectured on Proust at the Peterhof Institute for the Natural Sciences in the summer of 1926 and worked on Bergson, as did Zubakin, who lectured on Bergson in Minsk in 1920. Several footnotes to Bergson appear in P. N. Medvedev, *V laboratorii pisatelja* (Leningrad: Izd. pisatelej v. Leningrade, 1933), pp. 78, 82.

Bakhtin's "Contemporary Vitalism" also devotes a good deal of attention to Bergson.

16. *Testimony: The Memoirs of Shostakovich,* ed. Solomon Volkov, trans. Antonia W. Bouis (London: Hamish Hamilton, 1979), pp. 27–28. The authenticity of these memoirs has been questioned. Laurel E. Fay, "Sholokhov Versus Volkov: Whose Testimony?" *Russian Review* 39.4 (Oct. 1980): 484–493; D. Šostakovič, "I. I. Sollertinskij" in I. I. Sollertinskij, *Muzykal'no-istoričeskie ètjudy* (Leningrad: Gos. muzykal'noe izdatel'stvo, 1956), pp. 3–6; *Pamjati I. I. Sollertinskogo,* pp. 45, 57, 59, 89–90, 109, 250, 389; Boris Schwartz, *Music and Musical Life in Soviet Russia, 1917–1970* (New York: W. W. Norton, 1973), p. 126.

17. *Marija Veniaminovna Judina,* ed. A. M. Kuznecov (Moscow: Sovetskij kompozitor, 1978), pp. 49, 126, 135, 218–219.

18. N. Mandelshtam, *Hope Against Hope: A Memoir,* trans. Max Hayward (London: Collins and Hamill Press, 1971), p. 142; *Testimony,* p. 144; "Pis'ma B. L. Pasternaka k M. V. Judinoj," in *Zapiski otdela rukopisej gosudarstvennogo ordena Lenina Biblioteki SSSR imeni V. I. Lenina* (Moscow: Kniga, 1967), pp. 254–257; Olga Ivinskaya, *A Captive of Time,* trans. Max Hayward (New York: Doubleday, 1978), pp. 181–182.

19. No. 30 Palace Embankment, apt. 7.

20. Boris Fillipov, "Nikolai Kljuev: Materialy k biografii," in Nikolai Kljuev, *Polnoe sobranie sočinenij,* vol. 1 (New York: Chekhov Publishing House, 1954), pp. 86–89, 102.

21. This lecture differed from the simplified lecture on Ivanov that Bakhtin gave the Mirkina sisters, published in Baxtin, *Èstetika slovesnogo tvorčestva* (Moscow: Iskusstvo, 1979); R. M. Mirkina, "Baxtin kakim ja ego znala: Molodoj Baxtin," privately held.

22. *Testimony,* pp. 148–149.

23. *Maria Veniaminovna Judina,* pp. 18, 62, 139, 311, 356; *Testimony,* p. 41.

24. *Maria Veniaminovna Judina,* pp. 25, 51, 64.

25. Pumpiansky's other major publication of the period was an article on Tiutchev in the almanac *Uranija* (1928). See N. I. Nikolaev, "O teoretičeskom nasledii L. V. Pumpjanskogo," introducing L. V. Pumpjanskij, "K istorii russkogo klassicizma (Poètika Lomonosova)," in *Kontekst, 1982* (Moscow: Nauka, 1983), pp. 289–303; L. V. Pumpjanskij, "Lomonosov i nemeckaja škola razuma," in *XVIII vek,* vol. 14 (Leningrad: Nauka, 1983), pp. 3–44; N. Nikolaev, Introduction to L. Pumpjanskij, "Ob ode A. Puškina 'Pamjatnik': Nad strokami odnogo proizvedenija," *Voprosy literatury,* no. 8 (1977): 135.

26. "Ot redakcii," *V bor'be za marksizm v literaturnoj nauke,* ed. V. Desnickij *et al.* (Leningrad: Priboj, 1930); "Jazykoved," "Osnovnye na-

pravlenija v jazykovedenii," *Na literaturnom postu,* no. 20 (1929): 57; "Leningradskij institut sravnitel'noj istorii literatur i jazykov zapada i vostoka Rossijskoj associacii naučno-issledovatel'skix institutov obščestvennyx nauk (RANION)," *Literatura i marksizm,* no. 2 (1928): 149.

27. "Pavel Nikolaevič Medvedev," in *Nauka i naučnye rabotniki v Leningrade,* vol. 6 of *Nauka i naučnye rabotniki SSSR* (Leningrad: Akademija nauk, 1934); "Medvedev, Pavel Nikolaevič," *Kratkaja literaturnaja ènciklopedija,* vol. 4 (Moscow: Sovetskij pisatel', 1967), p. 723; E. Dobin, "Pavel Nikolaevič Medvedev," in P. N. Medvedev, *V laboratorii pisatelja* (Leningrad: Sovetskij pisatel', 1971), pp. 3–7.

28. For Medvedev's publications, including the disputed texts, see "Bibliografija izbrannyx trudov P. N. Medvedeva," in Medvedev, *V laboratorii pisatelja,* pp. 387–390.

29. P. Medvedev, "O 'Sodružestve' (k 4-letiju gruppy)," in *Sodružestvo: Literaturnyj al'manax* (Leningrad: Priboj, 1927), pp. 286–296; Boris Pasternak to Pavel Medvedev, in "Boris Pasternak: Iz perepiski s pisateljami," in *Iz istorii sovetskoj literatury 1920–1930-x godov: Novye materialy i issledovanija.* ed. E. B. and E. V. Pasternak, vol. 93 of *Literaturnoe nasledstvo* (Moscow: Nauka, 1983), p. 702.

30. Review of *Sovremennaja literatura: Sb. statej, Zvezda,* no. 2 (1925): 287; Review of Ioland Nejfel'd, *Dostoevskij: Psixolingvistićeskij očerk, Zvezda,* no. 3 (1925): 301.

31. Interview of Nina Arkadievna Voloshinova by Katerina Clark in Leningrad, Nov. 19, 1983; Interview of Yury Pavlovich Medvedev by Katerina Clark in Leningrad, Nov. 21, 1983; P. P. Gajdeburov, *Literaturnoe nasledie: Vospominanija, stat'i, režisserskie eksplikacii, vstuplenija* (Moscow: Vserossijskoe teatral'noe obščestvo, 1977), pp. 13, 29, 35, 40, 52, 205, 221; A. Krasnov-Levitin, *Lixie gody, 1925–41: Vospominanija* (Paris: YMCA Press, 1977), pp. 43–48.

32. Pavel Medvedev, "O 'vetre,' " *Zapiski peredvižnogo obščedostupnogo teatra Gajdeburova i Skarskoj,* no. 65 (Nov. 20, 1923): 1; Pavel Medvedev, "K dvenadcatoj godovščine smerti L. N. Tolstogo," *Zapiski peredvižnogo,* no. 39 (Nov. 20, 1922): 1.

33. Pavel Medvedev, "Točki nad i," *Zapiski peredvižnogo,* no. 44 (Dec. 26, 1922): 1–2.

34. V. N. Vološinov, (poem), *Zapiski peredvižnogo,* no. 37 (Nov. 6, 1922): 3; V. N. Vološinov, "Problema tvorčestva Betxovena," *Zapiski peredvižnogo,* no. 46 (Jan. 16, 1923): 4.

35. N. Skarskaja and P. P. Gajdeburov, *Na scene i v žizni,* pp. 63–64; P. N. Medvedev, "Put'ja i pereput'ja Sergeja Esenina," in Nikolaj Kljuev and P. N. Medvedev, *Sergej Esenin* (Leningrad: Priboj, 1927), pp. 19–86. Incidentally, Medvedev, an acquaintance of Esenin's, was an official police witness for his suicide.

36. Konstantin Vaginov, *Kozlinaja pesn'* (Leningrad: Priboj, 1928; repr. New York: Silver Age, 1978), p. 9. The novel distorts characteristics of group members, and the correspondence between protagonists and their purported real-life counterparts is far from absolute. See Katerina Clark, "How Konstantin Vaginov's Intellectual Milieu Is Refracted in His *Kozlinaja pesn'*," in *Russian History*, forthcoming.

37. S. Belomorcev, "Bol'ševizacija Akademii nauk," *Posev*, no. 46 (1951): 11.

38. Vaginov, *Kozlinaja pesn'*, pp. 95–96, 152–153.

39. Interview of Nina Arkadievna Voloshinova by Katerina Clark in Leningrad, Nov. 19, 1983.

40. P. N. Medvedev, Review of *Proletarij: Xudožestvenno-literaturnyj al'manax, Zvezda*, no. 6 (1926): 274–275; "Ot redakcii," *Zvezda*, no. 2 (1927); P. N. Medvedev, Review of *Zemlja i fabrika: al'manax*, no. 1 (1928): 150–152.

41. Naučno-issledovatel'skij institut kommunističeskoj akademii, *Literaturnaja ènciklopedija*, vol. 7 (Moscow: Sovetskaja ènciklopedija, 1934), p. 79. Even in 1930 Medvedev was cited in a list of contributors to *Literatura i marksizm* who were considered too "Formalist and sociologically eclectic." "Xronika," *Literatura i marksizm*, no. 6 (1930): 94.

42. See e.g. Vaginov, *Kozlinaja pesn'*, p. 80. The recurrent motif of Philostratus and his biography of Appollonius of Tyana is also a metaphor for this predicament.

5. RELIGIOUS ACTIVITIES AND THE ARREST

1. Interview of Victor Shklovsky by Michael Holquist and Katerina Clark, Mar. 25, 1978. Shklovsky may have exaggerated Bakhtin's involvement in the church, since he himself was far from those circles. But as late as April 19, 1925, Bakhtin's mother and sisters opened their Easter letters to Nikolai in Paris with the Russian Orthodox Easter greeting "Christ is risen!"

2. See e.g. P. A. Florenskij, "Pifagorovy čisla," in *Trudy po znakovym sistemam*, vol. 5 of *Učenye zapiski tartuskogo gosudarstvennogo universiteta* (Tartu: Tartu University, 1971); entry on "Florensky" in *Filosofskaja ènciklopedija*, vol. 5 (Moscow: Akademija nauk, 1970), pp. 373–379; E. Modestov, "P. A. Florenskij i ego sovetskie gody," *Mosty*, no. 2 (1959): 419–434; "Florenskij, Pavel Aleksandrovič," in *Naučnye rabotniki Moskvy*, part 4 of *Nauka i naučnye rabotniki SSSR* (Leningrad: Akademija nauk, 1930).

3. M. Pol'skij, *Novye mučeniki rossijskie*, part 2 (Jordanville, N.Y.: Holy Trinity Monastery, 1957), pp. 132, 134; M. V. Judina, "Nemnogo o ljudjax Leningrada," in *Maria Veniaminovna Judina*, ed. A. M. Kuzne-

cov (Moscow: Sovetskij kompozitor, 1978), p. 219; Z. V. Trifunovič, "I. M. Andreevskij," *Russkoe vozroždenie,* no. 4 (1978): 213; Nicholas Zernov, *The Russian Religious Renaissance of the Twentieth Century* (London: Darton, Longman and Todd, 1963), p. 206; Bishop Cassian, "Rodoslovie duxa (Pamjati Konstantina Vasil'eviča Močul'skogo)," *Pravoslavnaja mysl',* vol. 7 (Paris: YMCA Press, 1949), pp. 11–15; N. F. Platonov, "Pravoslavnaja cerkov' v 1917–1935 gg.," *Ežegodnik muzeja istorii religii i ateizma,* vol. 5 of *O preodolenii religii v SSSR* (Moscow-Leningrad: Akademija nauk, 1961), p. 258.

4. Based on documents in the possession of the Kagan family.

5. "Vol'naja filosofskaja associacija," *Kniga i revoljucija,* no. 2 (Aug. 1920): 91–92; A. V. Lavrov, "Vstupitel'naja stat'ja" to "Perepiska s R. V. Ivanovym-Razumnikom," in *Aleksandr Blok: Novye materialy i issledovanija* book 2, vol. 92 of *Literaturnoe nasledstvo* (Moscow: Nauka, 1981), p. 380; "Vol'naja filosofskaja associacija," *Zapiski peredvižnogo teatra Gajdeburova i Skarskoj,* no. 59 (1923): 5–6; "K stoletiju so dnja roždenija Dostoevskogo," *Letopis' doma literatorov,* no. 1 (Nov. 1921): 7.

6. "Vol'naja filosofskaja associacija," *Zapiski peredvižnogo teatra Gajdeburova i Skarskoj,* no. 59 (1923): 5.

7. "Vol'naja filosofskaja associacija," *Kniga i revoljucija,* no. 2 (Aug. 1920): 92. See also A. A. Meier, *Filosofskie sočinenija* (Paris: La Presse Libre, 1982).

8. There is doubt as to how long they continued their association with the group. S. Elenin and Ju. Ovčinnikov, Notes to N. P. Anciferov, "Tri glavy iz vospominanij," *Pamjat': istoričeskij sbornik,* no. 4 (Paris: YMCA Press, 1981), pp. 117–118nn12–13.

9. See Anciferov, "Tri glavy iz vospominanij"; Bibliography of Anciferov's works, *Pamjat',* no. 4, pp. 55–152; Anonymous (believed to be Fedotov's wife, E. N. Fedotova-Ivask), "Georgij Petrovič Fedotov (1886–1951)," in G. P. Fedotov, *Lico Rossii: Sbornik stat'ej* (Paris: YMCA Press, 1967), pp. ii–xix.

10. The group included at times Alexander Petrovich Smirnov, the icon curator of the Russian Museum; Tatiana Nikolaevna Gippius, Zinaida Gippius' sister; Kuzma Sergeevich Petrov-Vodkin, a writer and artist; Leon Abgarovich Orbelli, a physiologist; Lev Aleksandrovich Bruni, an artist; and Ivan Andreevich, a worker. Elenin and Ovčinnikov, *Pamjat',* pp. 117–120, 122, 125nn. N. Šemetov, "Pravoslavnye bratstva (1917–1945 gg.)," *Žurnal RSXD (Russkogo studenčeskogo Xristianskogo dviženija),* no. 131 (1980): 166–167.

11. V. Varšavskij, "Perečityvaja 'Novyj grad'," *Mosty,* no. 2 (1965): 275.

12. Anciferov, "Tri glavy iz vospominanij," p. 60.

13. Anciferov, "Tri glavy iz vospominanij," p. 67; G. P. Fedotov, "Dve stat'i," *Novyj žurnal*, no. 43 (1955). For the Voskresenie group, see anon., "Georgij Petrovič Fedotov (1886–1951)," pp. ii–xix; Jurij Ivask, "Esxatologija i kul'tura: Pamjati Georija Petroviča Fedotova (1886–1951)," *Vestnik RSXD*, no. 103 (1972): 100–110; N. Šemetov, "Pravoslavnye bratstva 1917–1945 gg.," pp. 147–181; O. E. Jasevič, "Iz vospominanij," *Pamjat': Istoričeskij sbornik*, no. 3 (New York: Khronika Press, 1978), pp. 93–158; N. P. Anciferov, "Voskresenie," *Pamjat'*, no. 4, pp. 57–60; A. A. Meier, unpub. memoirs.

14. S. Averincev, "Ličnost' i talant učenogo," *Literaturnoe obozrenie*, no. 10 (1976): 60.

15. M. Karpovič, "G. P. Fedotov" (obituary), *Novyj žurnal*, no. 27 (1951): 270–271; Ivask, "Esxatologija i kul'tura," p. 108; F. Stepun, "G. P. Fedotov," *Novyj žurnal*, no. 49 (1957): 222–223.

16. Stepun, "G. P. Fedotov," p. 237.

17. Anciferov, "Voskresenie," p. 58.

18. M. M. Baxtin, *Problemy tvorčestva Dostoevskogo* (Leningrad: Priboj, 1929), p. 241. This section was omitted from the second edition but reprinted in *Èstetika*, p. 187.

19. M. Osharov, "To Alien Shores: The 1922 Expulsion of Intellectuals from the Soviet Union," *Russian Review* 32 (July 1973): 294–298; Pol'skij, *Novye mučeniki rossijskie*, p. 135.

20. Anonymous, "Georgij Petrovič Fedotov," p. xvii; Ivask, "Esxatologija i kul'tura," p. 105.

21. "Iz pisem M. I. Kagana S. I. Kagan," *Pamjat'*, no. 4, p. 266. Pumpiansky himself converted to Christianity and was baptized in 1911, and Yudina in 1919.

22. Z. V. Trifunovič, "I. M. Andreevskij," *Russkoe vozroždenie*, no. 4 (1978): 128, 211–222.

23. V. Il'in, *Prepodobnyj Serafim Sarovskij*, 2nd rev. ed. (Paris: YMCA Press, 1930), p. 150.

24. Valentin Zander, "Saint Seraphim de Sarov et le saint curé d'ars," *Le Messager Orthodoxe*, no. 54 (1971): 61.

25. D. I. Andreev, *Prepodobnyj Serafim Sarovskij* (Munich: Izd. Pravoslavnogo detskogo doma "Miloserdnyj Samarjanin," 1947), pp. 7, 14.

26. Andreev, *Prepodobnyj Serafim Sarovskij*, p. 14; Svjašč. I. Efimov, "Prepodobnyj Serafim," *Žurnal moskovskoj patriarxii*, no. 8 (1954): 26, 27, 30, 32; Il'in, *Prepodobnyj Serafim Sarovskij*, p. 150.

27. George F. Putnam, *Russian Alternatives to Marxism: Christian Socialism and Idealistic Liberalism in Twentieth Century Russia* (Knoxville: University of Tennessee Press, 1977), p. 72; Pavel Florenskij, *Stolp i utverždenie istiny: Opyt pravoslavnoj teodicii v dvenadcati pis'max* (Berlin: Rossica, 1929), pp. 7, 419, 421; Pavel Florenskij, "Troice-Ser-

gieva Lavra i Rossija," in *Troice Sergieva Lavra* (Petrograd, 1919), repr. in *Kontinent*, no. 7 (1976): 260, 265, 275, 276.

28. Florenskij, *Stolp i utverždenie istiny*, pp. 92, 421, 434.

29. Florenskij, *Stolp i utverždenie istiny*, pp. 111–112, 127, 394, 434, 489; Pavel Florenskij, "Ikonostasis," *Bogoslovskie trudy*, no. 9 (1972): 83–88.

30. Florenskij, "Ikonostasis," pp. 96, 100, 102–105, 109, 111, 123, 134, 142, 148, 259; A. A. Dorogov, Vjač. Vs. Ivanov, and B. A. Uspenskij, "P. A. Florenskij i ego stat'ja 'Obratnaja perspektiva,' " *Trudy po znakovym sistemam*, vol. 198 of *Učenye zapiski tartuskogo universiteta* (1967): 378–380.

31. M. M. Bakhtin, "Discourse in the Novel," *The Dialogic Imagination*, trans. Caryl Emerson and Michael Holquist (Austin: University of Texas Press, 1981), p. 346.

32. Nikita Struve, *Christians in Contemporary Russia*, 2nd. rev. ed., trans. Lancelot Sheppard and A. Manson (London: Harvill Press, 1967); A. Krasnov-Levitin, *Lixie gody 1925–41: Vospominanija* (Paris: YMCA Press, 1971), pp. 98–105; I. Andreev, *Zametki o katakombnoj cerkvi v SSSR* (Jordanville, N.Y.: Holy Trinity Monastery, 1947), p. 6; Zernov, *The Russian Religious Renaissance of the Twentieth Century*, p. 206; Trifunovič, "I. M. Andreevskij," p. 213. One problem in accepting the idea that Bakhtin was associated with this church is Krasnov-Levitin's assertion about the church in Leningrad in the 1920s: "What repelled me from the outset about the Josephite movement was its obvious ideology of the Black Hundreds . . . a zoological anti-Semitism, references to the Protocols of the Elders of Zion, and even to the Beilis affair (not to mention its monarchist ideas)." *Lixie gody*, p. 108. Although there was anti-Semitism among some adherents to the Josephite schism, this was not characteristic of the schism and was certainly not a trait of Bakhtin's.

33. Protoerej D. B. Konstantinov, "Pravoslavnaja molodëž' v bor'be za cerkov' v SSSR," in *Issledovanija i materialy*, ser. 2, no. 45 (Munich: Institute for the Study of the USSR, 1956), p. 23; N. F. Platonov, "Pravoslavnaja cerkov' v 1917–1935 gg.," *Ežegodnik muzeja istorii religii i ateizma*, vol. 5 of *O preodolenii religii v SSSR* (Moscow-Leningrad: Akademija nauk, 1961), p. 206.

34. N. D. Uspenskij, "K istorii bogoslovskogo obrazovanija v Leningrade," *Žurnal moskovskoj patriarxii*, no. 4 (1977): 7–9; Metropolitan Gregory, "Toržestvo otkrytija Leningradskoj duxovnoj akademii i duxovnoj seminarii," *Žurnal moskovskoj patriarxii*, no. 10 (1946): 10–11; Pol'skij, *Novye mučeniki rossijskie*, II, 136.

35. "Xronika," *Literatura i marksizm*, no. 6 (1930): 86–87.

36. N. S. Timasheff, "Urbanization, Operation Anti-Religion and the Decline of Religion in the USSR," *Slavic and East European Review* 14.2

(Apr. 1955): 226; Adolf Keller, *Church and State on the European Continent* (London: Epworth Press, 1936), p. 285; William Fletcher, *The Russian Orthodox Church Underground 1917–1970* (London: OKUP, 1971), pp. 74–76; Andreev, *Zametki o katakombnoj cerkvi v SSSR,* pp. 6–7.

37. Andreev, *Zametki o katakombnoj cerkvi v SSSR,* p. 6; Konstantinov, "Pravoslavnaja molodež' v bor'be za cerkov' v SSSR," pp. 20–21.

38. Loren R. Graham, *The Soviet Academy of Sciences and the Communist Party, 1927–1932* (Princeton: Princeton University Press, 1967), pp. 120–129; Sergej Belomorcev, "Bol'ševizacija Akademii nauk," *Posev,* no. 46 (1951): 11–12; "Žertvy dela Akademii nauk: Martirologičeskij spisok," *Volja,* no. 10 (1952): 24–28; O. I. Jaševic, "Iz vospominanij," *Pamjat': Istoričeskij sbornik,* no. 1 (New York: Khronika Press, 1976), p. 100; Anon., "Georgij Petrovic Fedotov (1886–1951)," p. xix.

39. Anciferov, "Voskresenie," p. 62; "Čistka apparata Akademii nauk," *Izvestia* (Aug. 30, 1929): 4; S. Romanov, "Nekotorye vyvody iz čistki v Akademii nauk," *Izvestia* (Sept. 10, 1929): 2; G. Zajdel' and M. Cvibak, *Klassovyj vrag na istoričeskom fronte: Tarle i Platonov i ix školy* (Moscow-Leningrad: Gos. Social'no-ekonomičeskoe izd-vo, 1931), p. 47.

40. N. P. Anciferov, "Šaxtinskoe delo naučnoj intelligencii," in "Tri glavy iz vospominanij," pp. 85–110.

41. M. Šmejman, "Vtoroj internacional i 'krestovoj poxod' cerkovnikov," in *Men'ševistskaja kontrrevoljucija: Podgotovka intervencii cerkovnikov. sb. statej* (Moscow: Moskovskij rabočij, 1931), p. 30; D. Dalin, "Socialističeskij zakaz," *Socialističeskij vestnik,* no. 18 (Sept. 27, 1929): 4–5. Voskresenie was officially viewed as a "counterrevolutionary organization" which had "links to the White emigration in Paris and whose ultimate aim was to overthrow the Soviet government," but which also tried to influence the young and organized terrorist circles. *Leningradskaja Pravda,* Sept. 15, 1929.

42. Bakhtin may also have been involved in the so-called "Cosmic Academy of Sciences," an unofficial group organized by Andreevskij whose members were arrested at about the same time. One of its members provided a list of members of a future anti-Soviet government, but he drew it up under pressure from his interrogators. Elenin and Ovčinnikov, *Pamjat',* pp. 128–129nn.

43. V. Aleksandr (Al'bert) Robertovič Stromin had been made head of the Saratov NKVD, as the OGPU had by then been renamed, in 1936. He was arrested in 1938 and shot in 1939. I. Mdivani, Notes in *Pamjat': Istoričeskij sbornik,* no. 2, p. 371; Anciferov, "Šaxtinskoe delo naučnoj intelligencii," pp. 85–110; V. Cherniavin (Vladimir Vyacheslavovich), "Prison Life in the USSR (1930–31)," *Slavonic and East European Review* 12.34 (July 1933): 67–78; Anton Ciliga, *The Russian Enigma* (London: The Labour Book Service, 1940), p. 173.

44. O. Markova, "Ekaterina Pavlovna Peškova i ee pomošč' politzaključennym," *Pamjat'*, no. 1, pp. 313–324.

45. A. V. Lunačarskij, "O mnogogolososti Dostoevskogo (po povodu knigi M. M. Baxtina 'Problemy tvorčestva Dostoevskogo')," trans. in Anatoly Lunacharsky, *On Literature and Art* (Moscow: Progress Publishers, 1973), pp. 79–106; A. V. Lunačarskij, *Neizdannye materialy*, vol. 82 of *Literaturnoe nasledstvo* (Moscow: Nauka, 1970), pp. 162–163.

46. M. M. Baxtin, "V narodnyj Komissariat zdravoxranenija po delu o naznačenii vračebnoj Komissii dlja osvidetel'stvovanija sostojanija zdorov'ja M. M. Baxtina: Zajavlenije," *Pamjat'*, no. 4, p. 267.

6. THE DISPUTED TEXTS

1. For arguments against Bakhtin's authorship of the disputed texts, see I. R. Titunik, Preface to his translation of V. N. Vološinov, *Freudianism: A Marxist Critique* (New York: Academic Press, 1973). For a possible collaboration, see Tzvetan Todorov, *Mikhail Bakhtine: Le principe dialogique* suivi de *Écrits du cercle de Bakhtine* (Paris: Editions du Seuil, 1981), p. 20.

2. A. A. Leont'ev, *Psixolingvistika* (Leningrad: Nauka, 1967), pp. 86–88; Leont'ev, *Jazyk, reč' i rečevaja dejatel'nost'* (Moscow, 1969), p. 79; V. V. Ivanov, Report of a meeting at Moscow University to mark Bakhtin's seventy-fifth birthday, *Voprosy jazykoznanija*, no. 2 (1971): 160–162; Ivanov, "Značenie idej M. M. Baxtina o znake, vyskazyvanii i dialoge dlja sovremennoj semiotiki," in *Trudy po znakovym sistemam*, no. 6 of *Učenye zapiski tartuskogo gosudarstvennogo universiteta* (Tartu, Tartu University, 1973): 44.

3. For example, Bakhtin claimed authorship in a conversation with the American Slavist Thomas Winner in 1973. Thomas G. Winner, "The Beginnings of Structural and Semiotic Aesthetics," in L. Matejka, ed., *Sound, Sign, and Meaning*, Michigan Slavic Contributions #6 (Ann Arbor, 1976), p. 451n2. Bakhtin made the same claim to his literary executor, Sergei Bocharov. In Ivanov's presence Bakhtin's wife once reminded Bakhtin that he had dictated the Freud book to her. Interview with V. V. Ivanov, Mar. 20, 1978. The American Slavist A. J. Wehrle observed that when a copy of the "Medvedev" book was produced in front of Bakhtin and his wife, Bakhtin said nothing, but his wife exclaimed, "Oh, how many times I copied that!" Albert J. Wehrle, "Introduction," in M. M. Bakhtin/P. N. Medvedev, *The Formal Method in Literary Scholarship*, trans. Albert J. Wehrle (Baltimore: Johns Hopkins University Press, 1978). Victor Shklovsky knew as early as the 1920s that Bakhtin was the sole author of the Medvedev book about his own group, the Formalists. Interview of Victor Shklovsky by Holquist and Clark, Mar. 25, 1978.

4. Interview of Nina Arkadievna Voloshinova by Susan Layton, May 5, 1980; interview of Yury Pavlovich Medvedev in Leningrad by Clark, Oct. 21, 1983; interview of Natasha Pavlovna Medvedeva in Moscow by Clark, Dec. 15, 1983.

5. "Teatral'no-literaturnaja xronika,"*Žizn' iskusstva*, no. 33 (Aug. 22–28, 1922): 4. An announcement at the end of Pumpiansky's *Dostoevsky and Antiquity*, published in 1922, promised a forthcoming book by him entitled *Protiv formal'nogo metoda izučenija literatury*, which never appeared. Since Bakhtin and Pumpiansky were very close at this time, and both completed books on Dostoevsky at about the same time, Bakhtin was likely working on a book on the Formalists then, too. Like Dostoevsky, the Formalists were a modish topic in Bakhtin's circles.

6. M. M. Baxtin, "Iz zapisej 1970–71 godov," in *Èstetika slovesnogo tvorčestva* (Moscow: Iskusstvo, 1979), p. 360.

7. Preface by E. B. and E. V. Pasternak to "Boris Pasternak: Iz perepiski s pisateljami," *Iz istorii sovetskoj literatury 1920–1930-x godov: Novye materialy i issledovanija*, vol. 93 of *Literaturnoe nasledstvo* (Moscow: Nauka, 1983), p. 707.

8. M. M. Baxtin, "Problema teksta v lingvistike, filologii i drugix gumanitarnyx naukax: Opyt filosofskogo analiza," in *Èstetika*, p. 304.

9. Shklovsky claimed that Medvedev actually bought the book from Bakhtin, but as a former Formalist, Shklovsky had reason for putting a negative construction on the affair. Interview of Shklovsky by Clark and Holquist, Mar. 25, 1978.

10. E. B. and E. V. Pasternak, Preface to "Boris Pasternak: Iz perepiski s pisateljami," p. 707.

11. M. M. Bakhtin, *Rabelais and His World*, trans. Helene Iswolsky (Cambridge: MIT Press, 1968), pp. 7–8.

12. M. M. Baxtin, *Problemy poètiki Dostoevskogo*, 3rd ed. (Moscow: Xudožestvennaja literatura, 1972), p. 4.

13. Baxtin, *Èstetika*, p. 360.

14. Bakhtin, *Rabelais and His World*, pp. 268, 269.

15. Titunik, Preface to *Freudianism*, p. xiii.

16. M. M. Bakhtin, *Problems of Dostoevsky's Poetics*, trans. Caryl Emerson (Minneapolis: University of Minnesota Press, 1984), pp. 19–20. Lunacharsky himself noted in the margin beside this remark of Bakhtin's, "All this is very good and quite true." A. V. Lunačarskij, *Sobranie sočinenij v 8-i tomax*, vol. 1 (Moscow: Xudožestvennaja literatura, 1963), p. 161.

17. M. M. Baxtin, "Predislovie," in L. Tolstoj, *Polnoe sobranie xudožestvennyx proizvedenij*, vol. 11, ed. K. Xalabaev and B. Ejxenbaum (Moscow-Leningrad: Gosizdat, 1929), p. viii.

18. M. M. Baxtin, "Predislovie," to L. Tolstoj, *Polnoe sobranie*

xudožestvennyx proizvedenij, vol. 13 (Moscow-Leningrad: Gosizdat, 1930), p. xii.

19. At a Bakhtin conference in Toronto, July 1982, Ann Shukman advanced the thesis that the essay on *Resurrection* was a double-voiced parody.

20. F. Stepun, "G. P. Fedotov," *Novyj žurnal,* no. 49 (1957): 222.

21. Quoted in a memoir by Zellig Harris, *Language* 17 (1951): 297.

22. For example, after Pasternak had read *The Formal Method,* he wrote to Medvedev on Aug. 20, 1929, in surprise, "I did not know that you had such a philosopher in you." "Boris Pasternak—Pavel Medvedev," in "Boris Pasternak: Iz perepiski s pisateljami," p. 708.

23. Medvedev/Bakhtin, *The Formal Method,* pp. 6, 26.

24. Medvedev/Bakhtin, *The Formal Method,* pp. 18, 21, 28, 33–34, 67, 76.

25. "V. N. Vološinov," "Slovo v žizni i slovo v iskusstve," *Zvezda,* no. 6 (1926): 249, 250, 258, 259, 262; "V. N. Vološinov," "O granicax poètiki i lingvistiki," in *Voprosy metodologii jazyka i literatury,* ed. V. Desnickij *et al.* (Leningrad: Priboj, 1930), pp. 225, 226, 227; "V. N. Vološinov," "Konstrukcija vyskazyvanija," part 2 of "Stilistika xudožestvennoj reči," *Literaturnaja učeba,* no. 3 (1930): 68; Baxtin *Èstetika,* p. 299.

26. "V. N. Vološinov," "Po tu storonu social'nogo," *Zvezda,* no. 2 (1925): 198; "V. N. Vološinov," *Frejdizm: Kritičeskij očerk* (Moscow-Leningrad: Gosizdat, 1927), p. 89.

27. "Vološinov," *Frejdizm,* pp. 63, 104.

28. "Vološinov," *Frejdizm,* pp. 22, 202.

29. "Vološinov," *Frejdizm,* pp. 35, 110.

30. "Vološinov," *Frejdizm,* p. 125.

31. "Vološinov," *Frejdizm,* p. 24.

32. *Vestnik Kommunističeskoj akademii,* no. 12 (1935); "Vološinov," *Frejdizm,* p. 33.

33. "V. N. Vološinov," *Marxism and the Philosophy of Language,* trans. Ladislav Matejka and I. R. Titunik (New York: Seminar Press, 1973), pp. 18, 19, 21, 23.

34. Ivanov maintained that only the second part of this article is Bakhtin's. Vyacheslav Ivanov, "The Significance of M. M. Bakhtin's Ideas on Sign, Utterance and Dialog," in *Semiotics and Structuralism: Readings from the Soviet Union,* ed. Henryk Baran (White Plains: International Arts and Sciences Press, 1974), pp. 51, 342; "V. N. Vološinov," "Stilistika xudožestvennoj reči," *Literaturnaja učeba,* no. 3 (1930): 50, 66, 81.

35. "Vološinov," "O granicax poètiki i lingvistiki," pp. 220–221, 237–238.

36. "Vološinov," "O granicax poètiki i lingvistiki," p. 225.

37. Baxtin, *Èstetika*, pp. 354, 357.

38. Baxtin, "Problema teksta v lingvistike, filologii i drugix gumani-tarnyx naukax," p. 283.

39. Baxtin, "Iz zapisej 1970–1971 godov," in *Èstetika*, p. 357.

7. FREUDIANISM

1. R. M. Mirkina, Bakhtin's old student from Nevel, heard Sollertinsky read lectures on Freud at the Institute for the History of the Arts in 1926 and found that most of the ideas presented were already familiar to her from her work with Bakhtin. Interview.

2. A. F. Petrovskij, *Istorija sovetskoj psixologii* (Moscow: Nauka, 1967), pp. 79–94; M. G. Jaroševskij, *Istorija psixologii* (Moscow: Mysl', 1976), pp. 444–445; "V. N. Vološinov," "Po tu storonu social'nogo," *Zvezda*, no. 5 (1925): 186–214; "I. I. Kanaev," "Sovremennyj vitalizm," *Čelovek i priroda*, no. 1 (1926): 33–42; no. 2 (1926): 9–23; "V. N. Vološinov," *Frejdizm: Kritičeskij očerk* (Moscow-Leningrad: Gosizdat, 1927). Ironically, one of the best indicators of Freud's importance in the Soviet Union during these years is the advertisement on the back cover of this last volume for "The Library of Psychology and Psychoanalysis," comprising twenty-three volumes, including books by Freudians such as Melanie Klein and Ernest Jones, and translations of books about Freud such as the one by F. Wittel. The lion's share of this series is taken up by eight volumes of works by Freud himself, all published by the State Publishing House.

3. Quoted in Ernest Jones, *The Life and Work of Sigmund Freud*, ed. Lionel Trilling and Steven Marcus (Harmondsworth: Penguin, 1974), pp. 62–63.

4. A. B. Zalkind, "Frejdizm i Marksizm," *Krasnaja nov'*, no. 4 (1924); Zalkind, *Žizn' organizma i vnušenie* (Moscow-Leningrad, Gosizdat, 1927); "Vološinov," *Frejdizm*, pp. 16, 162.

5. *Čelovek i priroda*, no. 2 (1926), p. 17.

6. Cohen was so strongly moved by the Kant-versus-Hegel issue that he claimed "it was not only a question of the further intellectual health of German philosophy, but a vital question for the integrity of the German spirit as to whether in future it would be Kant or Hegel." Quoted in Karl Löwith, "Philosophie der Vernunft und Religion der Offenbarung in H. Cohens Religionsphilosophie," *Sonderdruck der Heidelberger Akademie* (Heidelberg: Carl Winter Verlag, 1968), p. 8.

7. See M. G. Jaroševskij, *Sečenov i mirovaja psixologičeskaja mysl'* (Moscow: Nauka, 1981), esp. pp. 9–14.

8. See Michael Holquist, "Answering as Authoring: Mikhail Bakhtin's Trans-Linguistics," *Critical Inquiry*, Dec. 1983; V. L. Merkulov, *Aleksej*

Alekseevič Uxtomskij: Očerk žizni i naučnoj dejatel'nosti (1875–1942) (Moscow-Leningrad: Izdatel'stvo Akademii Nauk S.S.S.R., 1960).

9. "Vološinov," *Freudianism,* pp. 24.
10. "Vološinov," *Freudianism,* p. 14.
11. "Vološinov," *Freudianism,* p. 68, 69.
12. "Vološinov," *Freudianism,* pp. 70, 73.
13. "Vološinov," *Freudianism,* pp. 75–76.
14. "Vološinov," *Freudianism,* p. 76.
15. "Vološinov," *Freudianism,* p. 77.
16. "Vološinov," *Freudianism,* p. 78.
17. "Vološinov," *Freudianism,* pp. 78–80, 83.
18. "Vološinov," *Freudianism,* p. 85.
19. "Vološinov," *Freudianism,* p. 83.
20. "Vološinov," *Freudianism,* pp. 87, 88.
21. "Vološinov," *Freudianism,* p. 88.
22. "Vološinov," *Freudianism,* p. 88.
23. "Vološinov," *Freudianism,* pp. 88, 89.
24. "Vološinov," *Freudianism,* p. 89.
25. "Vološinov," *Freudianism,* p. 90.

8. THE FORMALISTS

1. See Victor Erlich, *Russian Formalism: History—Doctrine* (The Hague: Mouton, 1965), 2nd rev. ed.; Peter Steiner, *Russian Formalism: A Metapoetics* (Ithaca: Cornell University Press, 1984).

2. M. M. Baxtin, "Problema soderžanija, materiala i formy v slovesnom tvorčestve," *Voprosy literatury i èstetiki* (Moscow: Xudožestvennaja Literatura, 1975), pp. 6–71.

3. Review of Eikhenbaum, *Theory of the Formal Method,* by V. I. Xarciev, *Červonyj šljax,* nos. 7–8 (Xar'kov, 1926): 184–187; Gustav Špet, *Vnutrennaja forma slova* (Moscow: GAXN, 1927); *Èstetičeskie fragmenty* (Moscow: GAXN, 1922–1923), 3 vols.; A. Smirnov, "Puti i zadači nauki o literature," *Literaturnaja mysl'* no. 11 (1923): 91–109; L. Trockij, "Formal'naja škola i marksizm," in *Literatura i revoljucija* (Moscow: Gosizdat, 1923), pp. 125–139; P. N. Sakulin, *Russkaja literatura i socializm* (Moscow: Gosizdat, 1922, 1924). Špet, an eccentric and brilliant phenomenologist, was associated with the State Academy of the Artistic Sciences, as was Bakhtin's old friend M. I. Kagan in these years. Kagan also wrote a critique of the Formalists, but it was published only after his death. M. I. Kagan, "O Puškinskix poèmax," in *V mire Puškina* (Moscow: Russkaja literatura, 1974), esp. p. 87. See also S. Ju. Baluxatyj, *Teorija literatury, annotirovannaja bibliografija* (Leningrad: Priboj, 1929).

4. Baxtin, "Problema soderžanija," p. 15.

5. Baxtin, "Problema soderžanija," pp. 17–18.

6. M. M. Bakhtin/P. N. Medvedev, *The Formal Method in Literary Scholarship: A Critical Introduction to Sociological Poetics*, trans. Albert J. Wehrle (Baltimore: Johns Hopkins University Press, 1978), p. 146.

7. Viktor Šklovskij, *Xod konja* (Moscow, 1923), p. 88; V. Šklovskij, *Literatura i kinematograf* (Moscow, 1923), p. 27; Ju. Tynjanov, *Arxaisty i novatory* (Moscow, 1929), p. 562.

8. Bakhtin/Medvedev, *The Formal Method*, p. 151.

9. V. Šklovskij, *Teorija prozy* (Moscow, 1925), p. 22.

10. Bakhtin/Medvedev, *The Formal Method*, p. 171.

11. Roman Jakobson, "On a Generation That Squandered Its Poets," trans. E. J. Brown, in *Major Soviet Writers: Essays in Criticism*, ed. E. J. Brown (New York: Oxford University Press, 1973), p. 21.

12. Bakhtin/Medvedev, *The Formal Method*, p. 3.

9. DISCOURSE IN LIFE AND ART

1. "V. N. Vološinov," "Discourse in Life and Discourse in Art," in *Freudianism: A Marxist Critique*," trans. I. R. Titunik (New York: Academic Press, 1976), pp. 95–96.

2. "Vološinov," "Discourse in Life," p. 96.

3. "Vološinov," "Discourse in Life," p. 97. This is aimed at Pereverzev.

4. "Vološinov," "Discourse in Life," p. 97.

5. "Vološinov," "Discourse in Life," pp. 97–98.

6. "Vološinov," "Discourse in Life," p. 98.

7. "Vološinov," "Discourse in Life," p. 99.

8. "Vološinov," "Discourse in Life," p. 100.

9. "Vološinov," "Discourse in Life," p. 105.

10. "Vološinov," *Freudianism*, pp. 76–77.

11. "Vološinov," "Discourse in Life," p. 106.

12. "Vološinov," "Discourse in Life," p. 106.

13. "Vološinov," "Discourse in Life," p. 100.

14. "Vološinov," "Discourse in Life," p. 103.

15. "Vološinov," "Discourse in Life," p. 106.

16. "Vološinov," "Discourse in Life," p. 106.

17. M. M. Bakhtin, "Discourse in the Novel," *The Dialogic Imagination*, ed. Michael Holquist, trans. Caryl Emerson and Michael Holquist (Austin: University of Texas Press, 1981), pp. 341–353.

18. Bakhtin, *The Dialogic Imagination*, p. 204.

10. MARXISM AND THE PHILOSOPHY OF LANGUAGE

1. "V. N. Vološinov," *Marxism and the Philosophy of Language,* trans. Ladislav Matejka and I. R. Titunik (New York: Seminar Press, 1973), pp. 67–68.

2. "Vološinov," *Marxism,* pp. 85–86.

3. R. Burling, *Man's Many Voices* (New York: Holt, Rinehart, and Winston, 1970); Paul Friedrich, "Structural Implications of Russian Pronominal Usage," in *Sociolinguistics,* ed. W. Bright (The Hague: Mouton, 1966), pp. 214–233; S. M. Erwin-Tripp, *Sociolinguistics,* in *Advances in Experimental Social Psychology,* vol. 4, ed. T. Berkowitz (Berkeley: University of California Press, 1969), pp. 93–107.

4. W. Labov, P. Cohen, C. Robins, and J. Lewis, *A Study of the Non-Standard English of Negro and Puerto Rican Speakers in New York,* vol. 2 of *The Use of Language in the Speech Community* (New York: IDKP, 1968); E. M. Albert, *Sociolinguistics,* ed. J. B. Pride and Janet Holmes (Harmondsworth: Penguin Books, 1972), p. 167.

5. M. M. Baxtin, *Èstetika slovesnogo tvorčestva* (Moscow: Iskusstvo, 1979), p. 79.

6. Baxtin, *Èstetika,* p. 256.

7. Roman Jakobson, with Morris Halle, "Two Aspects of Language," in *Fundamentals of Language* (The Hague: Mouton, 1956), p. 74.

8. "Vološinov," *Marxism,* p. 41.

9. "Vološinov," *Marxism,* p. 86.

10. "Vološinov," *Marxism,* p. 24.

11. "Vološinov," *Marxism,* pp. 72, 74.

12. "Vološinov," *Marxism,* p. 77. But see Geoffrey Sampson, *Schools of Linguistic Thought* (Stanford: Stanford University Press, 1980), pp. 34–56.

13. "Vološinov," *Marxism,* p. 48.

14. "Vološinov," *Marxism,* p. 49.

15. Yurii Lotman and Boris Uspensky, "On the Semiotic Mechanism of Culture," *New Literary History* 9.2 (1978): pp. 211, 213.

16. "Vološinov," *Marxism,* p. 10.

17. "Vološinov," *Marxism,* p. 11.

18. "Vološinov," *Marxism,* p. 12.

19. "Vološinov," *Marxism,* pp. 13–14.

20. "Vološinov," *Marxism,* p. 14.

21. A. R. Luria, *The Making of Mind: A Personal Account of Soviet Psychology,* ed. M. Cole and S. Cole (Cambridge: Harvard University Press, 1979), pp. 69–70.

22. "Vološinov," *Marxism,* p. 14.

23. "Vološinov," *Marxism,* p. 26.

24. "Vološinov," *Marxism*, p. 33.

25. L. S. Vygotsky, *Izbrannye psixologičeskie issledovanija* (Moscow: Izdatel'stvo Akademii Pedagogičeskix Nauk, 1956), pp. 25, 87. Vygotsky and Bakhtin never met. Bakhtin knew Vygotsky's early work, but there is no record that Vygotsky was aware of Bakhtin. Caryl Emerson, "The Outer Word and Inner Speech," *Critical Inquiry* 10.2 (Dec. 1983): 245–264; James Wertsch, "The Role of Semiotic Mediation in Vygotsky's Account of Higher Mental Processes," in *Semiotic Mediation: Psychological and Sociocultural Perspectives*, ed. E. Mertz and R. J. Parmentier, forthcoming.

26. "Vološinov," *Marxism*, p. 39.

27. "Vološinov," *Marxism*, p. 99.

28. "Vološinov," *Marxism*, p. 98.

29. "Vološinov," *Marxism*, p. 100.

30. Dostoevsky does not indicate the precise noun, but he clearly means "mother" (*mat'*), which in Russian, as in Black American English, is a shortened form of "motherfuck." Roger Abrahams, *Talking Black* (Rowley, Mass.: Newbury House, 1976), p. 28.

31. "Vološinov," *Marxism*, pp. 103, 105.

32. "Vološinov," *Marxism*, pp. 105, 102–103.

33. "Vološinov," *Marxism*, p. 106.

34. "Vološinov," *Marxism*, pp. 115, 99.

35. "Vološinov," *Marxism*, p. 115.

36. "Vološinov," *Marxism*, pp. 103, 199.

37. "Vološinov," *Marxism*, p. 120.

38. "Vološinov," *Marxism*, pp. 120, 130.

39. "Vološinov," *Marxism*, p. 131.

40. "Vološinov," *Marxism*, p. 157.

11. DOSTOEVSKY'S POETICS

1. K. Nevel'skaja, ed., "M. M. Baxtin i M. I. Kagan," *Pamjat'*, no. 4 (1981): 263.

2. An obvious extension of the deleted portion from the 1929 text appears in two of Bakhtin's later texts, "From the Prehistory of Novelistic Discourse" and "Forms of Time and the Chronotope in the Novel."

3. Mikhail Bakhtin, *Problems of Dostoevsky's Poetics*, ed. and trans. Caryl Emerson (Minneapolis: University of Minnesota Press, 1984), p. 6. Appendix II of this edition includes Bakhtin's notes "Toward a Reworking of the Dostoevsky Book" (1961). For these notes, see also M. M. Baxtin, *Èstetika slovesnogo tvorčestva* (Moscow: Iskusstvo, 1979), pp. 308–327.

4. Bakhtin, *Problems*, p. 30.

5. Bakhtin, *Problems*, p. 8.

6. Bakhtin, *Problems*, p. 32.
7. Baxtin, *Èstetika*, p. 317.
8. Baxtin, *Èstetika*, p. 324; *Problems*, pp. 298–99.
9. Baxtin, *Èstetika*, p. 310; *Problems*, p. 285.
10. Baxtin, *Èstetika*, p. 310; *Problems*, p. 285.
11. Bakhtin, *Problems*, p. 49; Baxtin, *Èstetika*, p. 324 (*Problems*, p. 298).
12. Baxtin, *Èstetika*, p. 302.
13. Bakhtin, *Problems*, p. 11.
14. Baxtin, *Èstetika*, p. 314; *Problems*, pp. 289–90.
15. Baxtin, *Èstetika*, p. 322; *Problems*, p. 296.
16. Erich Auerbach, *Mimesis: The Representation of Reality in Western Literature*, trans. Willard R. Trask (Princeton: Princeton University Press, 1974), p. 72.

12. KUSTANAI, SARANSK, AND SAVELOVO, 1930–1945

1. *Narodnoe xozjajstvo kazaxskoj SSSR: Statističeskij sbornik* (Alma-Ata: Kazaxskoe gos. izd., 1957), p. 11.
2. I. Mexoncev, *Kustanajskaja oblast': Pamjatka dlja ot"ezžajuščix na celinnye i zaležnye zemli Kustanajskoj oblasti* (Cheliabinsk, 1955).
3. Martha Brill Olcott, "The Collectivization Drive in Kazakhstan," *Russian Review* 40.2 (Apr. 1981): 122–142.
4. M. M. Baxtin, "Opyt izučenija sprosa kolxoznikov," *Sovetskaja torgovlja*, no. 3 (May–June 1934): 107–117.
5. Interview of Nina Arkadievna Voloshinova by Susan Layton, May 6, 1980.
6. Bakhtin to Kanaev, Aug. 7, 1936, "Iz pisem M. I. Kagana k S. I. Kagan," *Pamjat': Istoričeskij sbornik*, no. 4 (Paris: YMCA Press, 1981), p. 268.
7. Jurij Basixin, "O Mixaile Mixajloviče Baxtine," in *Rodyne prostory: Literaturno-xudožestvennyj sbornik* (Saransk: Mordovskoe knižnoe izdatel'stvo, 1978), p. 203.
8. Grigorij Jakovlevič Merkušin, *Istorija kul'tury i nauki Mordovskoj ASSR: Avtoreferat dissertacii na soiskanie učenoj stepeni doktora istoričeskix nauk* (Leningrad: Leningrad State University, 1973), p. 36.
9. I. D. Voronin, "Pervyj vuz v Mordovii," *Očerki i stat'i* (Saransk: Mordovskoe knižnoe izdatel'stvo, 1957), pp. 55–57; G. Ja. Merkušin, *Razvitie nauki v Mordovii* (Saransk: Mordovskoe knižnoe izdatel'stvo, 1967), pp. 56–65.
10. "Iz pisem M. I. Kagana k S. I. Kagan," pp. 269–270.
11. M. I. Kagan, "O poèmax Puškina," in *V mire Puškina: Sbornik statej* (Moscow: Sovetskij pisatel', 1974), pp. 85–119.
12. *Kimrijskij muzej mestnogo kraja: Putevoditel'* (Kimry, 1967), p.

57; Nadezhda Mandelshtam, *Hope Against Hope*, trans. Max Hayward (London: Penguin, 1975), pp. 5, 357.

13. V. Kožinov and S. Konkin, "Mixail Mixajlovič Baxtin: Kratkij očerk žizni i dejatel'nosti," in *Problemy poètiki i istorii literatury* (Saransk, 1973), p. 9. Kožinov wrote the section of this article on Bakhtin's life through 1945. Bakhtin later developed these lectures into a number of articles that were published in the 1960s and 1970s. "The Novel as a Literary Genre" was converted into two articles, "From the Prehistory of Novelistic Discourse" and "Epic and Novel."

14. Sovetskij pisatel' reminded Bakhtin in a letter of December 1937 that he was to hand in the manuscript by December 15. As usual, Bakhtin was having trouble finishing.

15. Published in 1979 with Bakhtin's annotations as "Problema teksta v lingvistike, filologii i drugix gumanitarnyx naukax: Opyt filosofskogo analiza," in *Èstetika slovesnogo tvorčestva*, pp. 281–307.

16. See e.g. *Lenin o Gor'kom: Izvlečenie iz statej i pisem 1901–1921 gg.*, ed. and introd. P. N. Medvedev (Moscow-Leningrad: GIXL, 1932); *Metodičeskaja razrabotka po kursu istorii russkoj literatury èpoxi imperializma i proletarskoj revoljucii* (Leningrad: Leningradskij pedagogičeskij institut imeni Gercena, 1933); P. N. Medvedev, *M. Gor'kij* (Leningrad: izd. Gorkoma pisatelej, 1934).

17. *Aziatskij muzej—Leningradskoe otdelenie Instituta vostokovedenija AN SSSR* (Moscow: Nauka, 1972), pp. 163–165, 227.

18. "Vološinov, Valentin Nikolaevič," in *Nauka i naučnye rabotniki Leningrada*, vol. 6 of *Nauka i naučnye rabotniki SSSR* (Leningrad: Akademija nauk, 1934), p. 18; interview of Nina Arkadievna Voloshinova by Clark, Nov. 19, 1983; Prof. B. M. Zubakin, *Xol'mogorskaja rez'ba po kosti: Istorija i texnika* (Arxangel'sk: Severnoe kraevoe izdatel'stvo, 1931).

19. D. Šostakovič, "I. I Sollertinskij," in I. I. Sollertinskij, *Istoričeskie ètjudy*, 2nd. ed. (Leningrad: Gos. muzykal'noe izdatel'stvo, 1963), p. 4; Sollertinskij, "Istoričeskie tipy simfoničeskoj dramaturgii," in *Istoričeskie ètjudy*, p. 338.

20. "Problema teorii romana," *Literaturnyj kritik*, no. 2 (1935): 214–249; no. 3 (1935): 231–254.

21. Bakhtin had apparently dropped "polyphony" from his vocabulary, which may have had something to do with the fact that authoritative voices in literature in the 1930s habitually invoked Gorky's metaphor for socialist realism as an orchestra in which all the instruments are in harmony. See e.g. A. Fadeev, "Za xorošee kačestvo, za masterstvo," *Literaturnyj kritik*, no. 4 (1934): 45.

22. Bakhtin polemicizes with Vinogradov in "Slovo v romane," *Voprosy literatury i èstetiki* (Moscow: Xudožestvennaja literatura, 1975),

pp. 81, 93, 137. See also Baxtin, "Slovo v romane," pp. 87, 96, 114–122, 126–127, 142, 161, 220, 222, 224–225; Baxtin, "Iz predistorii romannogo slova," *Voprosy literatury i èstetiki,* pp. 410–416, 418.

23. Baxtin, "Slovo v romane," pp. 78, 82, 84–85, 146.

24. Katerina Clark, *The Soviet Novel: History as Ritual* (Chicago: The University of Chicago Press, 1981).

25. Baxtin, "Slovo v romane," p. 140.

26. M. Gor'kij, "O proze," *Literaturnaja učeba,* no. 1 (1933): 125; Gor'kij, "O jazyke," *Literaturnaja učeba,* no. 3 (1934): 3–9; Baxtin, "Slovo v romane," p. 146.

27. M. Gor'kij, "Doklad A. M. Gor'kogo o sovetskoj literature," *Pervyj s"ezd pisatelej: Stenografičeskij otčet* (Moscow: Ogiz, 1934), pp. 6, 10.

28. Bakhtin specifically names "folklore" as the moving force only in his 1940 work "Iz predistorii romannogo slova," *Voprosy literatury i èstetiki,* p. 417; Gor'kij, "Doklad A. M. Gor'kogo o sovetskoj literature," p. 6.

29. In the 1960s Bakhtin's old friend Kanaev wrote two books on Goethe—*Iogann Vol'fgang Gëte: Očerki iz žizni poèta-naturalista* (Leningrad, 1962) and *Gëte kak estestvoispytatel'* (Leningrad, 1970)—each of which moved Bakhtin to write long review-letters. Bakhtin insists that Goethe was a great philosopher, standing out in the modern period as one of the very few figures (Bakhtin is another) who refused to accept the subject/object distinction as the basis for his theory of knowledge. Bakhtin compares him specifically with Heidegger. Baxtin, *Èstetika slovesnogo tvorčestva,* pp. 396–397.

30. Baxtin, "Slovo v romane," pp. 77, 81, 14, 177.

13. THE THEORY OF THE NOVEL

1. For these four essays, see Bakhtin, *The Dialogic Imagination,* ed. Michael Holquist, trans. Caryl Emerson and Michael Holquist (Austin: University of Texas Press, 1981).

2. Bakhtin, *Dialogic Imagination,* pp. 7, 8.

3. See Lawrence Sklar, *Space, Time, and Spacetime* (Berkeley: University of California Press, 1974); German Minkovskij, *Prostranstvo: Vremja* (Petersburg: "Physice," 1911).

4. Bakhtin, *Dialogic Imagination,* p. 85.

5. Bakhtin, *Dialogic Imagination,* p. 252.

6. Bakhtin, *Dialogic Imagination,* pp. 253, 254.

7. Bakhtin, *Dialogic Imagination,* pp. 66–67, 84, 85, 254.

8. Bakhtin, *Dialogic Imagination,* pp. 89–90.

9. Bakhtin, *Dialogic Imagination,* p. 94.

10. Bakhtin, *Dialogic Imagination,* p. 100.

11. Bakhtin, *Dialogic Imagination*, p. 113.

12. Victor Turner, *The Forest of Symbols: Aspects of Ndembu Ritual* (Ithaca: Cornell University Press, 1967), p. 106.

13. Bakhtin, *Dialogic Imagination*, p. 120.

14. Bakhtin, *Dialogic Imagination*, p. 129.

15. Bakhtin, *Dialogic Imagination*, p. 131.

16. Bakhtin, *Dialogic Imagination*, p. 132.

17. Bakhtin, *Dialogic Imagination*, p. 134.

18. Bakhtin, *Dialogic Imagination*, p. 141.

19. Bakhtin, *Dialogic Imagination*, p. 143.

20. Bakhtin, *Dialogic Imagination*, p. 247.

21. Bakhtin, *Dialogic Imagination*, pp. 13, 84.

22. Bakhtin, *Dialogic Imagination*, pp. 15, 17.

23. Bakhtin, *Dialogic Imagination*, p. 20.

24. Bakhtin, *Dialogic Imagination*, p. 61.

25. Bakhtin, *Dialogic Imagination*, p. 65.

26. Bakhtin, *Dialogic Imagination*, p. 59.

27. Bakhtin, *Dialogic Imagination*, p. 60.

28. Bakhtin, *Dialogic Imagination*, pp. 60, 63.

29. Bakhtin, *Dialogic Imagination*, p. 272.

30. Bakhtin, *Dialogic Imagination*, pp. 375–376.

31. Bakhtin, *Dialogic Imagination*, pp. 401–402.

32. Bakhtin, *Dialogic Imagination*, pp. 406, 409.

33. Edward Sapir, *Selected Writings in Language and Culture,* ed. David Mandel (Berkeley: University of California Press, 1949), p. 162.

14. RABELAIS AND HIS WORLD

1. *Rabelais and His World,* trans. Helen Iswolsky (Cambridge: MIT Press, 1965), p. 3. This edition has now gone out of print. A second edition, with the same pagination, will be published by Indiana University Press in late 1984.

2. *Rabelais,* p. 268.

3. *Rabelais,* pp. 188, 421.

4. *Rabelais,* p. 11.

5. *Rabelais,* p. 7.

6. *Rabelais,* p. 7.

7. *Rabelais,* p. 8.

8. *Rabelais,* p. 81, 83.

9. *Rabelais,* p. 276.

10. *Rabelais,* p. 281.

11. *Rabelais,* pp. 281, 283, 284.

12. *Rabelais,* pp. 10, 154, 255.

13. *Rabelais,* pp. 255–256.

14. *Rabelais,* pp. 25–26.

15. *Rabelais,* pp. 317–318.

16. *Rabelais,* p. 32.

17. *Rabelais,* pp. 81, 39–40.

18. *Rabelais,* pp. 296, 297.

19. *Rabelais,* pp. 270–271.

20. See Mircea Eliade, *The Myth of the Eternal Return* (Princeton: Princeton University Press, 1971), pp. 141–150.

21. See Katerina Clark, *The Soviet Novel: History as Ritual* (Chicago: University of Chicago Press, 1981).

22. *Rabelais,* pp. 265, 89, 84, 46, 107, 515, 94.

23. *Rabelais,* p. 88.

24. *Rabelais,* pp. 401–403.

25. *Rabelais,* pp. 380–396.

26. Victor Turner, "Variations on a Theme of Liminality," and Roberto Da Matta, "Constraint and License: A Preliminary Study of Two Brazilian National Rituals," in *Secular Ritual,* ed. Sally F. Moore and Barbara G. Meyerhoof (Assen/Amsterdam: Van Gorcum, 1977), pp. 36–70, 244–264; *Rabelais,* p. 397.

27. M. Gor'kij, "Doklad M. Gor'kogo o sovetskoj literature," *Pervij s"jezd pisatelej: Stenografičeskij otčet* (Moscow: Ogiz, 1934), p. 6; *Rabelais,* pp. 161, 147, 94, 335–336, 487.

28. *Rabelais,* p. 347.

29. Mary Douglas, *Natural Symbols: Explorations in Cosmology* (New York: Pantheon Books, 1970), p. viii; *Rabelais,* pp. 346–347.

30. V. Kirpotin, "Reč'," in *Sovetskaja literatura na novom ètape: Stenogramma 1-ogo plenuma orgkomiteta sojuza sovetskix pisatelej* (Moscow: Ogiz, 1933), p. 24; *Rabelais,* p. 243.

31. Hans Günther, "Michail Bakhtins Konzeption als Alternative zum Soczialistischen Realismus," in *Semiotics and Dialectics,* ed. Peter V. Zima (Amsterdam: John Benjamins B. V., 1981), pp. 137–178.

32. Gor'kij, *Pervyj s"jezd,* p. 10.

33. A. V. Lunačarskij, "O smexe," *Literaturnyj kritik,* no. 4 (1935): 3–9. See also Turner, "Variations on a Theme of Liminality." Another likely source for *Rabelais* is a 1900 essay by Henri Bergson, a thinker who was very influential in Petersburg and Leningrad in the 1910s and 1920s, which distinguishes between all kinds of rigidity, as in thought or mores, and "the inner suppleness of life," and remarks on how often something mechanical is encrusted on some living form of life. Public ceremonial in particular begs to be parodied and unmasked by laughter, as in carnival. Bergson, "Laughter," in *Comedy,* ed. Wylie Sypher (New York: Anchor Books, 1956), p. 89.

34. *Rabelais,* pp. 243, 399, 477; M. M. Baxtin, "Rable i Gogol," in *Voprosy literatury i èstetiki* (Moscow: Xudožestvennaja Literatura, 1975), p. 492.

35. *Rabelais,* pp. 28, 44, 114.

36. *Rabelais,* pp. 292, 491–492.

37. Diary entry of Feb. 18, 1918, in V. I. Orlov, *Gamajun* (Moscow: Sovetskij pisatel', 1978), p. 593. For the second viewpoint on Catholicism, see A. Ždanov, "Reč' sekretarja CK VKP (v) A. A. Ždanov," *Pervyj s"jezd,* pp. 3–4; *Rabelais,* pp. 159, 181, 249, 258–259.

38. *Rabelais,* pp. 111–114, 119.

39. Yevgeny Zamyatin, *A Soviet Heretic: Essays,* trans. Mirra Ginzburg (Chicago: University of Chicago Press, 1975), pp. 107–108.

40. Baxtin, *Èstetika slovesnogo tvorčestva,* p. 373; *Rabelais,* pp. 503–504, 477, 463, 423.

41. Gleb Struve, *Russian Literature under Lenin and Stalin* (Norman: University of Oklahoma Press, 1971), pp. 268–275. Sidney Monas has defined the relation between Rabelais, Joyce, and Bakhtin best by insisting that the link between them all is "folklore—a deep involvement in the most ancient, most basic and universal folkloric traditions. Not, certainly, sentimental *folklorico* in the manner of the Celtic twilight. Really the most fundamental stuff: fertility rituals, assisted by ritual clowns, who, like the Zuni clowns, drink their own urine, the celebration of life-out-of-death, degradation and renewal, debasement and resurrection . . . reaching back beyond Christian times to the Roman Saturnalia and beyond that to the prehistoric." Monas, "Verbal Carnival: Bakhtin, Rabelais, *Finnegans Wake,* and the Growthesk," paper read at International Bakhtin Conference, Queen's University, Kingston, Ontario, Oct. 8, 1983.

42. "V. N. Vološinov," *Marxism and the Philosophy of Language,* trans. Ladislav Matejka and I. R. Titunik (New York: Seminar Press, 1973), p. 471.

43. *Rabelais,* pp. 256, 454.

44. *Rabelais,* pp. 465, 467.

45. *Rabelais,* p. 467.

46. *Rabelais,* p. 420.

47. *Rabelais,* pp. 433, 109, 320.

15. SARANSK TO MOSCOW, 1945–1975

1. I. Voronin, V. Ostroumov, and I. Čemakin, *Saransk, stolica Mordovskoj ASSR: Istoriko-arxitekturnyj očerk* (Saransk: Mordovskoe knižnoe izdatel'stvo, 1960), p. 20.

2. Berta Urickaja, "Vspominaja prošloe," to appear in 2nd. edition of *Marija Veniaminovna Judina.*

3. "Doklad t. Ždanova o žurnalax 'Zvezda' i 'Leningrad,' " *Oktjabr',* no. 9 (1946): 3, 19; Nikolaj Leont'ev, "Zatylok k buduščemu," *Novyj mir,* no. 9 (1948): 248–266.

4. "Rable v istorii realizma," in "Zaščita dissertacij," *Vestnik Akademii nauk SSSR,* no. 9 (1948): 3, 19.

5. A. Najdenova, head of the University Section of the Higher Attestation Committee of the Ministry of Higher Education, to Bakhtin, May 9, 1947.

6. V. Nikolaev, "Preodolet' otstavanie v razrabotke aktual'nyx problem literaturovedenija," *Kul'tura i žizn',* no. 32 (Nov. 20, 1947): 3; N. Janevič, "Institut mirovoj literatury v 1930-e—1970-e gody," *Pamjat': Istoričeskij sbornik,* no. 5 (Paris: YMCA Press, 1982), pp. 98–101.

7. Nikolaj Lepin, "Parafrazy i pamjatovanija," *Sintaksis,* no. 7 (1980): 104.

8. V. Kožinov and S. Konkin, "Mixail Mixajlovič Baxtin: Kratkij očerk žizni i dejatel'nosti," in *Problemy poètiki v istorii literatury: Sbornik statej,* ed. S. S. Konkin *et al.* (Saransk: Mordovia University, 1973), p. 14.

9. Jurij Basixin, "O Mixaile Mixajloviče Baxtine," *Rodnye prostory: Literaturno-xudožestvennyj sbornik* (Saransk: Mordovskoe knižnoe izdatel'stvo, 1978), p. 204.

10. Basixin, "O Mixaile Mixajloviče Baxtine," pp. 206–207.

11. Kožinov and Konkin, "Mixail Mixajlovič Baxtin," pp. 14–15.

12. Baxtin, "Marija Stjuart," *Sovetskaja Mordovija,* no. 245 (Dec. 12, 1954): 2.

13. Urickaja, "Vspominaja prošloe."

14. No. 31 Sovetskaya Street, apt. 30. See Voronin *et al., Saransk,* p. 23.

15. Basixin, "O Mixaile Mixajloviče Baxtine," p. 205. See also Bakhtin's discussion of Pinsky's work in *Rabelais and His World,* trans. Helen Iswolsky (Cambridge: MIT Press, 1968), pp. 32, 130, 140–143.

16. Vladimir Seduro, *Dostoevskovedenie v SSSR* (Munich: Institute for the Study of History and Culture of the U.S.S.R., 1955), pp. 67, 68; V. I. Seduro, "Dostoevskij kak sozdatel' polifoničeskogo romana: Baxtin o forme romana u Dostoevskogo," *Novyj žurnal,* no. 52 (1958): 71–93; V. Šklovskij, *Za i protiv: Zametki o Dostoevskom* (Moscow: Sovetskij pisatel', 1957), pp. 221–223; V. V. Ivanov, "Roman Jakobson: The Future," in *A Tribute to Roman Jakobson, 1896–1982* (Berlin, New York, Amsterdam: Mouton, 1983), p. 51; R. Jakobson, "Za i protiv Viktora Šklovskogo," *International Journal of Slavic Linguistics and Poetics,* no. 1–2 (1959): 305–310.

17. "Literatura i literaturovedenie," *Literatura i žizn',* no. 32 (Mar.

16, 1962). Einaudi to Bakhtin, Mar. 23, 1961; Bakhtin to Einaudi, Apr. 9, 1961; International Book (the former Soviet copyright agency) to Einaudi, Apr. 22, 1961 (authorizing the project); Einaudi to International Book, June 8, 1961 (enclosing the contracts).

18. A. Dymšic, "Ideologija i monopolija," *Literaturnaja gazeta,* July 11, 1964.

19. K. Fedin, V. Vinogradov, and N. Ljubimov, "Kniga nužna ljudjam," *Literaturnaja gazeta,* no. 74 (June 23, 1962). As part of his campaign for the Rabelais book, Kozhinov also published an article in *Destin du roman,* a special issue of *Recherches internationales,* no. 50 (Nov.–Dec. 1965).

20. Joseph Kraft, "Letter from Moscow," *The New Yorker* (Jan. 31, 1983): 105.

21. Seliverstov did the engraving of Bakhtin used on the front cover of M. M. Bakhtine, *Esthetique et théorie du roman,* trans. Darian Olivier (Paris: Gallimard, 1978).

CONCLUSION

1. M. M. Baxtin, "K metodologii gumanitarnyx nauk," *Èstetika slovesnogo tvorčestva* (Moscow: Iskusstvo, 1979), p. 373.

INDEX

Academy of Sciences, 116, 141–142. *See also* Gorky Institute of World Literature; Institute for Eastern Studies
Acmeism, 28
Addressivity, 6, 84, 86, 214, 217
Aesthetics of Verbal Creation, The, 53, 152, 328, 345
Akselrod-Ortodoks (Lyubov I. Akselrod), 154
Albert, E. M., 216
Alibi, 64, 67
Alterity (*drugost'*). *See* Self/other
"Answer to Questions from the Editorial Board of *Novy mir,*" 337
Anticosmopolitanism, 323, 324, 325, 328
American literature, 110
Andreev, Archpriest F. K., 138, 140
Andreev, I. M. (I. M. Andreevsky), 132
Andropov, Y. P., 336, 337
Annensky, Innokenty, 25
Answerability, 7, 8, 75–76, 81, 82
Antsiferov, N. P., 126, 127, 129, 141
Apuleius, 282–284
Architectonics, 8, 64, 68, 72, 83
"Architectonics of Answerability, The," 54–55, 56, 57, 63–94, 365n1; and disputed texts, 156, 157, 158, 161, 164, 165; mentioned, 172, 180, 181, 183, 189, 195, 200, 204, 239, 242, 243, 251, 271
Aristotle, 6, 8, 80, 275, 285
Art (Iskusstvo), 49, 53, 54
"Art and Answerability," 53, 55–57, 59, 150, 279
Asian Museum, Leningrad. *See* Institute for Eastern Studies
Askoldov, S. A. (S. A. Alekseev), 121, 126, 132–133, 135, 159
Athenaeus of Nausatis, 302
Auerbach, Erich, 250
Augustine, Saint, 9, 39, 81, 286
"Author and Protagonist in Aesthetic Activity," 35, 54, 340

Authoring, 54, 79, 83, 87–93; in utterance, 10, 15; and dialogism, 63, 64; in disputed texts, 151, 165, 169–170
Avant-garde art (left art), 35, 38, 44, 46–48, 105
Axiology, 10, 11, 63, 64, 80; axiological desert, 75; axiological reflex, 76

Bakhtin, Mikhail Fedorovich, 16, 17, 38, 55, 99
Bakhtin, Mikhail Mikhailovich: character, 2, 4, 16, 17, 51, 52, 108–109, 149, 151–153, 254, 329, 335–336, 337, 340; periods, 3, 63, 117, 131–132, 266; residences, 16, 21–22, 26, 27, 38, 45, 50–51, 253, 258, 260, 321, 330, 338–340; health, 27, 51, 95–96, 142, 143, 257, 261, 263, 332, 336, 338, 341–342; employment, 38, 44, 49, 97, 98–99, 145, 254, 257, 259, 261, 262, 263, 321, 325, 330, 333, 361–362n6; work habits, 53, 99, 268, 330, 341; writings, 53–54, 99–100, 108–109, 117, 149, 152–153, 262–263, 266, 328, 333, 337, 340, 341, 344–345; arrest, 140–145, 167, 269; death, 343
Bakhtin, Nikolai M., 16–34, 38, 40, 41
Bakhtina (Bakhtin's mother), 16, 17, 99, 261
Bakhtina, Ekaterina M., 16, 17, 38
Bakhtina, Elena Aleksandrovna (née Okolovich), 51–52, 98, 99, 254, 336, 337, 338, 339, 343
Bakhtina, Maria M., 16, 17, 38
Bakhtina, Natalya M., 16, 17, 38
Balzac, Honoré de, 287
Baron Münchhausen's Adventures, 272
Baudelaire, Charles, 23–24
Baudouin de Courtenay, Ivan A., 11
Beethoven, Ludwig van, 114, 266
Belorussia. *See* Vitebsk
Bely, Andrei (Boris Nikolaevich Bugaev), 24, 125, 126

Leningrad (Petrograd, Petersburg); pre-Revolutionary, 27–34; in Civil War, 36–37; Bakhtin in, 95–119, 366n2; religious circles in, 123–142; Bakhtin visits, 257, 260, 262, 329; mentioned, 39–40, 45, 46, 104
Leningrad Conservatory, 41, 45, 46, 105, 107–108, 117, 264, 266
Leningrad University: Bakhtin attends, 27–31, 38, 328; Neo-Kantianism at, 58; Bakhtin circle at, 39–40, 42, 48, 49, 95, 101, 102, 104, 105; and Pumpiansky, 264
Leonardo da Vinci, 24, 42
Leontiev, A. A., 146
Lermontov, Mikhail, 305
Lévi-Strauss, Claude, 6
Levinas, Emmanuel, 8
Life of Art (Leningrad), 53, 54
Linguistics, 7, 10, 11, 13, 20–21. See also Dialogism; Language; Utterance
Lissitzky, Lazar (El), 47
Literature and Marxism, 110, 112
Literary Critic, The, 267
Literary Study, 161, 167, 168, 264
Lithuania, 39, 45. See also Vilnius
Liubimov, Nikolai Mikhailovich, 335
Locke, John, 38, 58
Loeb, Jacques, 163, 164
Lomonosov, Mikhail V., 265
Longus, 281
Loophole, 60, 298, 318, 348
Lorentz, Hendrik A., 70
Lossky, N. O., 126, 130
Lucian of Samosata, 22–23, 250
Lukacs, Georg: The Theory of the Novel, 99, 271; at Communist Academy, 267, 275; on epic and novel, 288
Lunacharsky, Anatoly V., 37, 47, 123, 139, 143, 155, 313
Luria, A. R., 227–228

Macrobius, Ambrosius Theodosius, 302
Malevich, Casimir, 38, 47, 48, 53, 105
Malko, Nikolai, 46
Man and Nature, 102
Mandelshtam, Nadezhda Y., 261
Mandelshtam, Osip E., 18, 28, 106, 254, 261
Marburg school, 54, 57, 59. See also Neo-Kantianism
Marcus Aurelius, Antonius, 286
"Maria Stuart," 328
Mariinsky Theater. See Kirov Theater of Opera and Ballet
Marr, Nikolai Y., 328
Marx, Karl, 23, 70, 156–157, 164, 326
Marxism: Bakhtin and, 38, 43, 50, 96, 260; Bakhtin circle and, 43, 116, 117, 123;

mentioned, 3, 126. See also Bolshevik Party; Communism; Disputed texts; Ideology; Marx; Marxism and the Philosophy of Language
Marxism and the Philosophy of Language, 212–237; as a disputed text, 146, 147, 159, 160, 166, 194; mentioned, 3, 9, 166, 167, 268, 318
Mayakovsky, Vladimir V., 28, 35
Meaning (značenie), 231–232. See also Theme
Medvedev, Pavel N.: in Vitebsk, 49–50; at State Publishing House; in Leningrad, 97, 100, 103, 108–109, 110, 117–118; and Soviet writers, 111–112, 115, 117, 369n35; and religion, 112–114; and Symbolism, 113; and disputed texts, 146–160, 170, 190, 191; in 1930s, 153, 257, 258, 264
Medvedev, Yury P., 148
Medvedeva, Natalya P., 148
Meier, A. A., 30, 126–131, 141, 261
Melikhova, Leontina S., 333, 341
Menippea, 240, 249–250, 277
Merezhkovsky, Dmitry S., 24, 126
Merkushin, 258, 325
"Methodology of Literary Scholarship, The," 340–341
Meyerhold, Vs. E., 97, 125
Mind/world (mind/body), 38, 66–68, 76, 80, 81, 175
Minkowski, Hermann, 278
Mirkina, Miriam M., 51, 98
Mirkina, Rakhil Moiseevna, 50–51, 98, 107, 345
Monas, Sidney, 388n41
Mongolia, 264–265
Monoglossia. See Heteroglossia
Monologue. See Dialogism; Dialogue
Mordovia, 259. See also Saransk
Mordovia Pedagogical Institute (Polezhaev Pedagogical Institute of Mordovia, Ogarev University of Mordovia), 258, 259–260, 321, 325–327, 329–340
Moscow, Bakhtin circle and, 100, 101, 108; Bakhtin visits, in 1930s, 257–258, 260, 262; Bakhtin in, during postwar years, 323–324, 328–329, 330–332, 333–345
Moshin, Prokhor. See Seraphim, Saint
Mycenae, 34
Mystical anarchism, 29

Natorp, Paul, 54
Neo-Kantianism, 57–62, 174; and Moscow, 54, 56, 156; and disputed texts, 165; mentioned, 3, 67, 80, 94, 118, 122, 131, 132, 277
Neologisms, 74, 75, 76, 136, 161

p. 126 - "Voskresenie" - means Resurrection   Founded 1917
108 - Bak = "a sincere christian"
106· circle .. inc, Mandelstams ...
142 - Arrested (1929)
108- B. a sincere christian   —